Ruskin & Architecture

Ruskin & Architecture

Edited by
Rebecca Daniels &
Geoff Brandwood

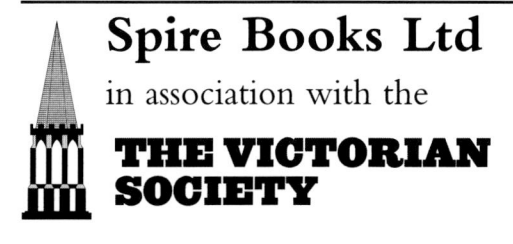

Spire Books Ltd
in association with the
THE VICTORIAN SOCIETY

Published by
Spire Books Ltd
PO Box 2336
Reading RG4 5WJ

Copyright © 2003
Spire Books Ltd, Rebecca Daniels, Geoff Brandwood and the authors
All rights reserved

Publication of this book was assisted by a generous grant from the Victorian Society

CIP data:
A catalogue record for this book is available from the British Library
ISBN 0 9543615 1 2

Designed and produced by John Elliott
Thanks to John Armstrong, Stephen Hone, Graham Longmate & John Sims for their assistance
Text set in Adobe Bembo

Opposite:
Northampton Town Hall, E.W. Godwin (1860-5) (*Mick Slaughter*).

Printed by Alden Group Ltd, Osney Mead, Oxford OX2 0EF

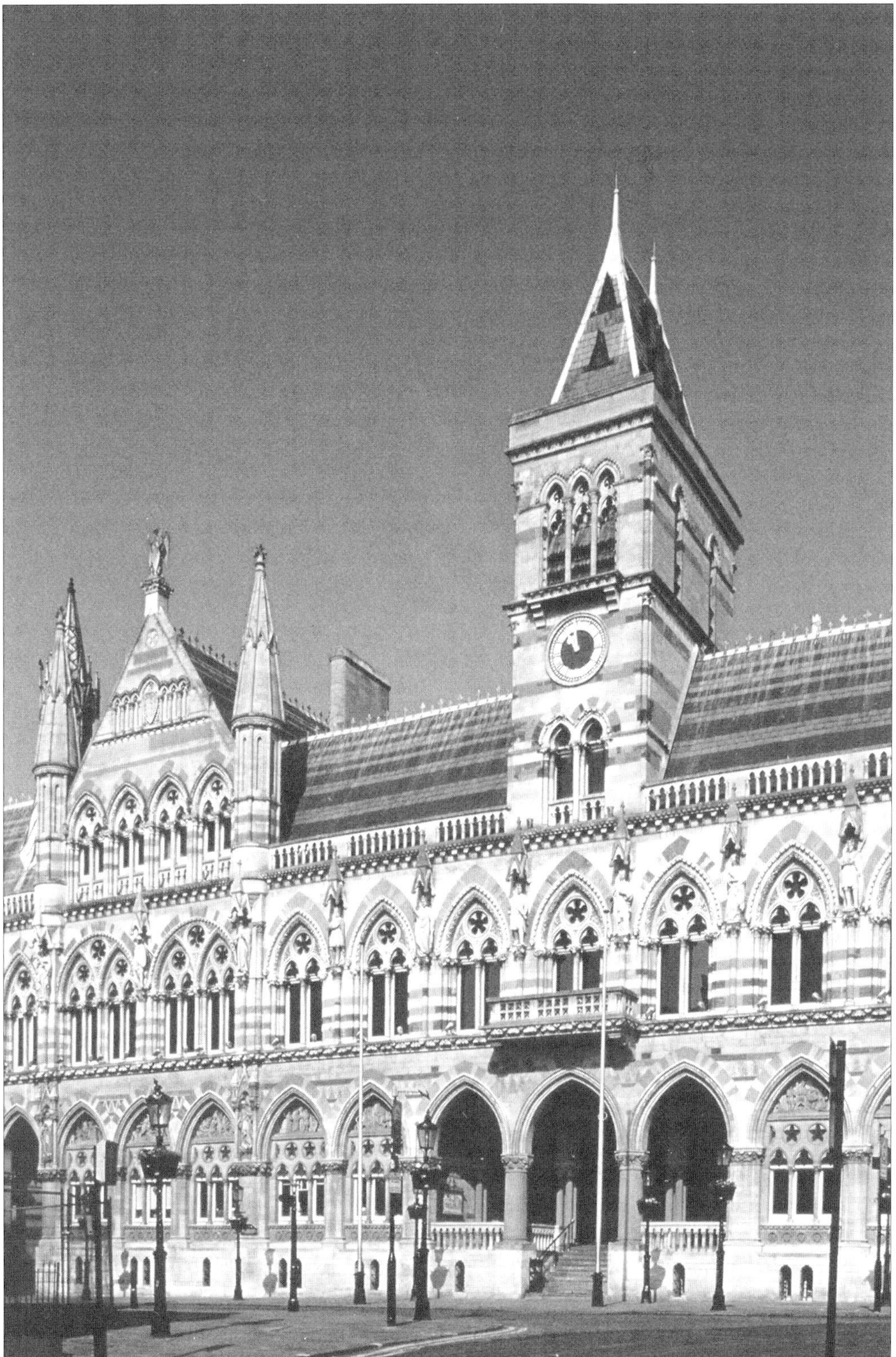

Dedicated to the memory of Chris Brooks,
cultural historian and conservationist,
1949–2002

Contents

	Foreword *David Barrie*	11
	Introduction: Ruskinisms *Michael Brooks*	13
1	Ruskin's Architectural Heritage: *The Seven Lamps of Architecture* – Reception and Legacy *Gill Chitty*	25
2	'As beautiful as anything I know in civil Gothic', or 'a very shabby bit of work of mine': Ruskin and the Oxford University Museum *Peter Howell*	57
3	Ruskin and the English House *Geoffrey Tyack*	89
4	*Labor ipse voluptas*: Scott, Street, Ruskin, and the Value of Work *Brian Hanson*	123
5	Ruskin and the Politics of Gothic *Chris Brooks*	165
6	'Intellectual Lens and Moral Retina': A Reappraisal of Ruskin's Architectural Vision *Malcolm Hardman*	191
7	Ruskin and Pugin *Rosemary Hill*	223
8	G. F. Bodley and the Response to Ruskin in Ecclesiastical Architecture in the 1850s *Michael Hall*	249
9	'Theoria' in Practice: E.W. Godwin, Ruskin and Art-Architecture *Aileen Reid*	279

10 John Dando Sedding and Sculpture in Architecture: 321
    The Fulfilment of a Ruskinian Ideal?
    Paul Snell

11 Ruskin Today: Building the Ruskin Library, Lancaster   357
    Richard MacCormac

    Notes on contributors   367

    Index   373

References to Ruskin's writings

Throughout this book writings by John Ruskin are referenced to his collected works published in 39 volumes by E. T. Cook and A. D. O. Wedderburn as *The Works of John Ruskin* (London, 1903-12). The convention used is 'W*orks*, volume number, page(s).'

Abbreviations
RIBA - Royal Institute of British Architects
V&A - Victoria and Albert Museum

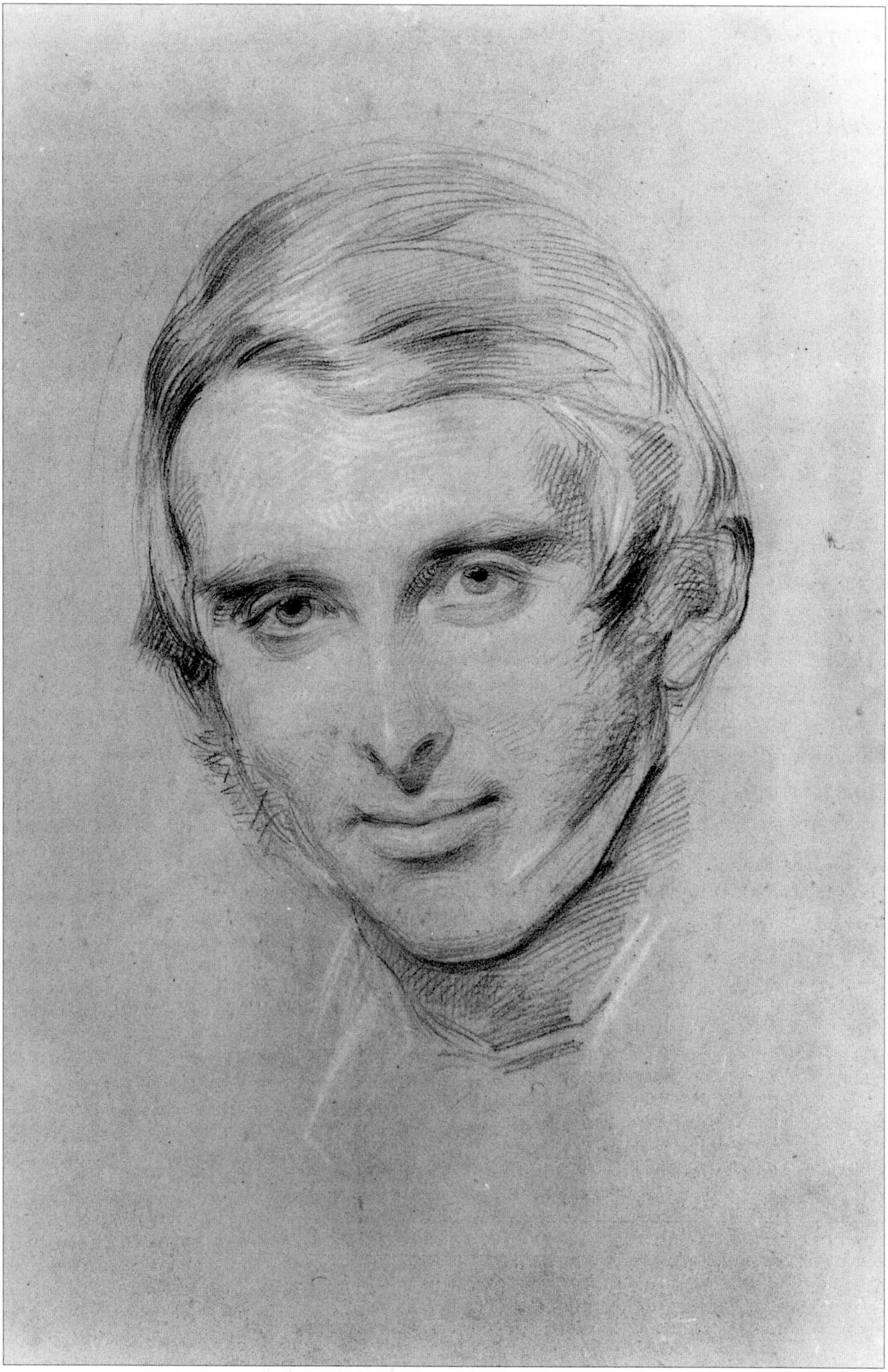

Foreword

David Barrie
Chairman of the *Ruskin To-Day* programme, and Director of the National Art Collections Fund

Ruskin To-Day was the title given to the programme of events that took place in 2000 to celebrate the centenary of John Ruskin's death. 'To-Day' was Ruskin's personal motto – implying, as he himself made clear, the need to use every moment of life that we are given, in the knowledge that 'The night cometh, when no man can work.'[1] To those of us who were involved in organising the centenary the choice of this word – spelt Ruskin's way – was irresistible because we were convinced of the contemporary relevance of so many of the principles for which Ruskin fought.

The Victorian Society's welcome contribution to *Ruskin To-Day* was a one-day conference examining Ruskin and Architecture, organised by Rebecca Daniels, one of the two editors of these essays, under the auspices of the Victorian Society's Activities Committee, chaired by Geoff Brandwood, who is the other. The conference took place in March 2000 at the Linnean Society, under the chairmanship of Professor Andrew Saint.

All too often such events, however stimulating and informative, leave little or no tangible trace. This book makes a very welcome exception to that rule. It evolved from the papers given at the conference, and has been enriched by the addition of several specially-commissioned chapters. It is not intended as a comprehensive study of Ruskin and architecture, but rather explores the interactions between Ruskin and the Victorian architects who were influenced by his writings and teachings, as well as his impact on later generations – right up to the present day. Michael W. Brooks, in his classic study, *Ruskin and Victorian Architecture*, was one of the very first to explore this subject in detail, and I am delighted that he has contributed the Introduction.

As Brooks rightly observes, Ruskin's relationship with the architects and designers of his own day was far from straightforward. In fact, as these essays reveal, it was a complex

John Ruskin (1819–1900) by George Richmond, c.1843. Richmond was a celebrated portrayer of eminent Victorians, a status which Ruskin achieved, while Pugin remained an outsider (*by courtesy of the National Portrait Gallery, London*).

interaction in which Ruskin's own views underwent considerable revision, both by him and by his followers. I am particularly glad that Ruskin's posthumous legacy is also addressed, and that Sir Richard McCormac has contributed an essay about the origins of his remarkable design for the Ruskin Library at Lancaster University.

Another leading contemporary architect, Daniel Libeskind, was interviewed recently on BBC radio, following the announcement that he had won the competition to design the structure that is to replace the 'twin towers' of New York, so brutally destroyed on 11 September 2001. He described himself as 'a medievalist at heart' and expressed the belief that architecture was a communal endeavour embodying spiritual values, in which the freedom and inspiration of the individual workman should find expression. Libeskind did not mention Ruskin by name, but that hardly matters – his ideas will live on.

Note
[1] *Works*, 35, p. 391.

Introduction: Ruskinisms

Michael Brooks

'RUSKINIAN' IS ONE of the commonest terms in the description of architecture but also one of the most complex. In *The Seven Lamps of Architecture* (1849), in *The Stones of Venice* (1851-3), and in subsequent books, essays, and lectures, John Ruskin expressed the most powerful currents of Victorian thought and exerted a wide influence. By 1874, the *British Architect* was able to declare him 'the Foster-father of one half of our younger architects.'[1]

The essays that make up this volume portray the width, the depth, and, above all, the intricacy of architectural Ruskinism. Gill Chitty points out that Ruskin began writing about architecture at a time when educated Victorians were already becoming passionate about the subject and that he powerfully extended their debates with new forms of prose and new styles of architectural illustration. Chris Brooks reveals the ways in which his theories of Gothic negotiate between the contrary impulses of the Victorian mind – its ceaseless drive toward innovation and its desperate need for stability. Malcolm Hardman shows how Ruskin pointed the way beyond the mid-century wars between Classic and Gothic toward an architecture based on local landscape and vernacular tradition. Geoffrey Tyack shows how this emphasis opened new and fruitful directions for domestic architecture.

Other essays explore Ruskin's relations with his architectural contemporaries. Rosemary Hill brings new light to the old question of how much Ruskin derived from A. W. N. Pugin. Brian Hanson explores his interactions with George Gilbert Scott and G. E. Street and shows that he gained as much from them as they did from him.

Still others scrutinise Ruskin's relations with his younger contemporaries. Peter Howell shows that however great Ruskin's impact on Benjamin Woodward's Oxford Museum may be, he cannot be thought of, as he once was, as its sole inspirer. Michael Hall traces the process by which G. F. Bodley deployed Ruskin's rigorously Protestant ideas in the service of a High Church ritual that Ruskin himself distrusted. Aileen Reid helps us understand how E. W. Godwin used ideas from *The Seven Lamps of Architecture* not only in the self-consciously Ruskinian Northampton Town Hall but also in his seemingly unRuskinian houses for aesthetes in Chelsea. Paul Snell shows how J. D. Sedding gave brilliant life to Ruskin's call for architects who were also artists and craftsmen. Finally, Sir Richard MacCormac establishes beyond doubt that Ruskin's influence continues in vibrant and creative ways today.

The greatest factor complicating any simple image of Ruskin as *Master* and architects as *Disciples* is that Ruskin's influence lasted a long time and even an architect who proclaimed discipleship, as many did, was nevertheless likely to develop Ruskin's ideas in ways that the *Master* could not have anticipated and in directions toward which he was cool or even hostile. The movement that Aileen Reid traces, in which Ruskinian ideas persist in the work of an architect who seems to have abandoned his initial allegiance, is not an exception. It is a paradigm.

If Ruskin's ideas were always significantly revised by his disciples, it follows that there can be no one version of Ruskinism. There can only be many Ruskinisms. The task of the cultural historian is not to decide which one is authentic but to trace their lines of descent.

What follows is an effort to map the sequence of Ruskin's influence by tracing the progress of three ideas. The three don't provide even an outline of his theories. They are, however, Ruskinian motifs that are especially likely to be interpreted, reinterpreted, rejected, and revised during the course of a High Victorian Ruskinism, which lasts from 1850 to 1870; an Arts and Crafts Ruskinism, which fades in the early 20th century; an error-prone Ruskinism, which serves as bogeyman for architectural modernism; and a Post-Modern Ruskinism which emerges in the 1970s. In each period there are two questions to answer: which of Ruskin's ideas had most appeal and what quite unRuskinian concerns were present in the minds of his admirers.

Both *The Seven Lamps of Architecture* and *The Stones of Venice* begin with a sharp distinction between building and architecture. 'I suppose no one', Ruskin said in 'The Lamp of Sacrifice', 'would call the laws architectural which determine the height of a breastwork or the position of a bastion. But if to the stone facing of that bastion be added an unnecessary feature, as a cable moulding, *that* is Architecture.'[2] This idea would be anathema in the Modernist period but Ruskin's first admirers were not troubled by it at all.

And why should they have been, since it so powerfully supported the second crucial element of his thought – his insistence on the expressive power of ornament? 'The fact is, there are only two arts possible to the human race,' he declared, 'sculpture and painting.'[3] 'What we call architecture,' he added, 'is only the association of these in noble masses, or the placing them in fit places.' That flamboyant statement demanded the revival of mural painting, stone carving, and architectural sculpture. The classic expression of first generation Ruskinism is the Oxford Museum and Peter Howell shows how Ruskin's work there was primarily focused on its carving. Ruskin hoped that by the profusion and richness of its ornament the Oxford Museum would become, like St Mark's in Venice, 'a vast illuminated missal, bound with alabaster instead of parchment, studded with porphyry pillars instead of jewels, and written within and without in letters of enamel and gold.'[4]

Finally, the High Victorian architects found Ruskin a great aid in the quest for the one appropriate style for the 19th century.[5] The Gothic Revivalists had focused on English until the late 1840s. In 'The Lamp of Obedience' Ruskin endorsed a Gothic Revival based on English Decorated but the larger effect of his books was to draw attention to the glories of Normandy, the Île-de-France, Siena, Pisa, and Venice. It is not entirely cynical to say that a mid-Victorian building's most obviously Ruskinian quality is that it looks as though it should be in Italy.

This phase of Ruskinism came to an end with two changes – one in Ruskin himself, the other in his admirers. In the 1860s the social criticism that had been implicit in Ruskin's writing became overt.[6] The Gothic Revival, he suddenly declared, had started at the wrong end by focusing on individual buildings rather than the society that produced them. 'All lovely architecture', Ruskin told the Royal Institute of British Architects in 1865, 'was designed for cities in cloudless air'.[7] In 19th-century English cities, by contrast, skies were darkened by coal dust, streams were polluted by chemical waste, and meadows, trees, and gardens have been replaced by tunnels, viaducts, and smokestacks.

Ruskin now proposed not great buildings but small reforms. Geoffrey Tyack reminds us that before Ruskin had written on the Cathedral at Amiens or the Ducal Palace, he had published an anonymous series of essays on cottages, villas, and the ways in which they related to their natural landscapes. He never dropped those themes and in the 1870s emphasised them anew as part of his campaign for social reform. He urged better sanitation, legislation against pollution, and, above all, towns that kept private residences in balance with surrounding countryside. If the typical structure of the first Ruskinism had been a museum or a government building, it was now more likely to be a private house or a garden city.

The most influential figures in this second phase of Ruskinism are Philip Webb and William Morris. Since many histories treat Ruskin-Morris as a single person, it is all the most important to stress, first, that Webb was more influential on architects than Morris and, second, that while both men were disciples, they were also revisionists.

They began by rejecting Ruskin's founding distinction between architecture and building. 'J.R.', Webb wrote to a friend, 'once held that a building wasn't architecture without sculpture and painting – to me a fallacy.'[8] 'Build big and solid and with an eye to strict utility,' Morris told a Birmingham audience; 'you will find that will be expressive work enough and will by no means be utilitarian.'[9]

The Arts and Crafts Ruskinians sought craftsmen who were builders rather than ornamental stone carvers. They wanted their buildings to look English and vernacular, not foreign. They gave a new direction to Ruskin's demand for handcrafts by promoting cooperation between builders, craftsmen, and architects – first in Morris & Co. and later in the Art Workers' Guild, Arthur Mackmurdo's Century Guild, and Charles Robert Ashbee's Guild of Handicrafts.[10]

But the Arts and Crafts gave ground steadily in the early 20th century before the growing prestige of mechanisation. In 1901 Frank Lloyd Wright urged advocates of the arts and crafts to see the machine as their salvation in disguise and suggested that 'artists who feel toward Modernity and the Machine now as William Morris and Ruskin were justified in feeling then, had best distinctly wait and work sociologically where great work may still be done by them.'[11]

The social imperatives of Ruskinism remain quite vigorous in the modern period. Frank Lloyd Wright was on target when he suggested that admirers of Ruskin should work sociologically.[12] The writing of Patrick Geddes and the achievements of the Garden City movement in England and the work of Lewis Mumford and the Regional Planning Association in America carry Ruskinian social concerns into the Modernist period.[13]

But the fate of Ruskinism in more narrowly architectural matters can be represented by two historians – Nikolaus Pevsner and Reyner Banham.[14] At least so far as Ruskin is concerned, the former is by far the more complex of the two.

Pevsner excises Ruskin from the development of architectural modernism. The first paragraph of his classic *Pioneers of Modern Design* (1936) cites Ruskin's view that ornament is the principal part of architecture; the second traces the consequence of this heresy in the mid-Victorian battle of the styles; and his third swiftly concludes 'the campaign of William Morris's lifetime was directed against the complete lack of feeling for the essential unity of architecture which made this comedy possible.'[15] Morris thus appears not as the man who reinterpreted Ruskinism and continued it but as the revolutionary who left it behind. Pevsner returned to Ruskin in his Walter Neurath Memorial Lecture on *Ruskin and Viollet-le-Duc* (1969) and in a chapter of *Some Architectural Writers of the Nineteenth Century* (1972) but always with the assumption that while Ruskin was valuable for understanding the Victorians, he had little to offer moderns.

Pevsner's minimising of Ruskin's influence in the development of modern design is even more emphatic in Reyner Banham's *Theory and Design in the First Machine Age* (1960).

Like Pevsner, Banham sees a break in architectural development in which Ruskin is left behind. He locates it, however, not between Ruskin and Morris but between Ruskin and the first High Moderns. 'If there is a test that divides the men from the boys in say, 1912,' Banham declares, 'it is their attitude to Ruskin.'[16] The appropriate attitude for the men was loathing.

Since Banham removed Ruskin not only from the history of early-20th-century architecture but also from its current discussion and practice, it is appropriate that one of the first challenges to Modernist hegemony evoked Ruskin. In 1959 Banham used the *Architectural Review* to attack a group of Italian architects who were displaying an unseemly interest in the forms of Otto Wagner, early Frank Lloyd Wright, and Art Nouveau. Denouncing their Neo-Liberty style as a retreat from Modernism, Banham warned against wearing costumes from earlier cultures: 'To want to put on those old clothes again is to be, in Marinetti's words describing Ruskin, like a man who has attained full physical maturity, yet wants to sleep in his cot again, to be suckled again by his decrepit nurse, in order to regain the nonchalance of his childhood.'[17]

This was a provocation that Ernesto Rogers, a designer of the Velasca Tower in Milan, couldn't resist. He concluded his reply in *Casabella* with a challenge:

> I would like to invite Mr. Banham, who I believe knows English better than Italian, to read directly from *The Poetry of Architecture* by John Ruskin, a great Englishman, without repeating the outdated interpretation of Marinetti, a 'revolutionary' Fascist who died wearing the cap of the Academy: 'We shall consider the architecture of nations as it is influenced by their feelings and manners, as it is connected with the scenery in which it is found, and with the skies under which it was erected.'[18]

That sentence, Rogers said, contained appropriate starting points for the evolution of architecture.

During the following years many architects began citing Ruskinian principles that had once seemed heretical. Robert Venturi, Denise Scott Brown, and Steven Izenour declared in *Learning From Las Vegas* (1972) that it was now time 'to reevaluate the once-horrifying statement of John Ruskin that architecture is the decoration of construction'.[19] In 1976 the *Architectural Review* reasserted Ruskin's distinction between building and architecture. The something added to mere building was no longer, as in *The Seven Lamps*, a mere cable moulding. It was now, as we might expect in the 1970s, semiotic: 'The make-up of a building … is like the make-up on an actor's face. Its aim is to raise the building to the level of a communicating object.'[20]

So where are we today? What kind of Ruskinism do we see? Ruskin certainly figures in recent architectural discussion as an exponent of ornament. He is always relevant to architects who derive their understanding of architecture from the forms of nature. And he remains a powerful advocate for a kind of regional planning that keeps development in a balanced relation to natural setting. But above all, Ruskin emerges in the Post-Modern period as the exponent of historical consciousness in architecture.[21] In 'The Lamp of Memory', Ruskin argued that civil and domestic buildings can become memorial and monumental, first, if they are built to last through time and so represent the past to future ages and, second, if their decorations convey metaphorical or historical meanings. Like other Ruskinian principles, this has found successive interpretations.

In the High Victorian period the historical consciousness manifested itself most obviously in decorative schemes like those for Benjamin Woodward's projected Foreign Office or E. W. Godwin's Northampton Town Hall where sculpture, painting, and stained glass represented national heroes or local history. After 1870 the Arts and Crafts architects were more concerned that their buildings achieve a historical dimension by continuing ancient craft traditions. Modern masterpieces combined pride in the present and optimism about the future with a deliberate amnesia toward the past.

It is in this context that Sir Richard MacCormac's design for the Ruskin Library at Lancaster University takes on such importance. It awakens historical memories through pure forms that are suddenly perceived as challenging architectural metaphors. The siting of the building recalls Venice and its lagoons. The exterior walls, with their contrast of shot-blasted lignacite blocks with bands of polished pre-cast concrete, recall Venetian polychromy. The archive itself, set on an island of green slate amid an Adriatic Sea of glass floor, evokes the treasury in a medieval cathedral. The building is both a homage and an act of liberation. It entirely removes Ruskin from the stylistic wars that preoccupied the Victorians and amused Pevsner.[22] It points toward a future in which Ruskinian imperatives acquire new and unexpected kinds of relevance.

Notes

[1] 'The Mutation and Cultivation of the Popular Taste: Mr. Ruskin; Mr. Gladstone; Mr. Beresford-Hope,' *British Architect*, 2 (1874), p. 241. Ruskin's ideas and his influence are explored in Kristen Ottesen Garrigan's *Ruskin on Architecture* (Madison, 1973), John Unrau's *Looking at Architecture with Ruskin* (Toronto, 1978), and Michael Brooks's *John Ruskin and Victorian Architecture* (New Brunswick, 1987, reprinted London, 1989). J. Mordaunt Crook's 'Ruskinian Gothic' and Edward N. Kaufman's '"The Weight and Vigour of their Masses": Mid-Victorian Country Churches and "The Lamp of Power"' in John Dixon Hunt and Faith M. Holland, (editors), *The Ruskin Polygon* (Manchester, 1982).

[2] *Works*, 8, pp. 28-9.

[3] Ibid., p. 11.

[4] *Works*, 10, p. 112.

[5] The rule of Ruskinian ideas in the search for a 19th-century style is explored in Robert Macleod's *Style and Society: Architectural Ideology in Britain 1835-1914* (London, 1971) and J. Mordaunt Crook's *The Dilemma of Style: Architectural Ideas from the Picturesque to the Post-Modern* (Chicago, 1987).

[6] This phase of Ruskin's career is treated in Tim Hilton, *John Ruskin: The Later Years* (New Haven and London, 2000). See also Jeffrey L. Spear, *Dreams of an English Eden: Ruskin and his Tradition in Social Criticism* (New York, 1984) and Linda Austen, *The Practical Ruskin: Economics and Audience in the Late Work* (Baltimore, 1991).

[7] *Works*, 19, p. 24.

[8] W. R. Lethaby, *Philip Webb and his Work* (Oxford, 1935, reprinted London, 1979), p. 132.

[9] William Morris, 'The Gothic Revival II,' in Eugene LeMire (editor), *The Unpublished Lectures of William Morris* (Detroit, 1969), pp. 82-3.

[10] Ruskin's influence on the nature of architectural work is explored in Mark Swenarton's *Artisans and Architects: The Ruskinian Tradition in Architectural Thought* (New York, 1989).

[11] Frank Lloyd Wright, 'The Art and Craft of the Machine', in Edgar Kaufmann and Ben Raeburn (editors), *Frank Lloyd Wright: Writings and Buildings* (New York, 1960).

12 Mark Swenarton explores Ruskin's influence on Frank Lloyd Wright, Le Corbusier, and Walter Gropius in the last chapter of *Artisans and Architects* [note 10]. Michael T. Saler's *The Avant-Garde in Interwar England: Medieval Modernism and the London Underground* (New York, 1999) reveals the continuing influence of Ruskin and Morris in the work of Frank Pick for the London Underground.

13 Michael H. Lang's *Designing Utopia: John Ruskin's Urban Vision for Britain and America* (Montreal, 1999) traces Ruskin's influence on planning throughout the 20th century.

14 A stimulating account of Pevsner, Banham, and their attitudes toward Ruskin can be found in Nigel Whiteley's *Reyner Banham, Historian of the Immediate Future* (Cambridge, Massachusetts, 2002).

15 Nikolaus Pevsner, *Pioneers of Modern Design* ([3rd edition], Harmondsworth, 1960), p. 20.

16 Reyner Banham, *Theory and Design in the First Machine Age* (New York, 1967), p. 12.

17 Reyner Banham, 'Neo-Liberty: The Italian Retreat from Modern Architecture,' *Architectural Review*, 125 (1959), p. 235.

18 Ernesto Nathan Rogers, 'The Evolution of Architecture: Reply to the Custodian of Frigidaires,' in Joan Ockman (editor with the collaboration of Edward Eigan), *Architecture Culture 1943-1968: A Documentary Anthology* (New York, 1993), p. 307.

19 Robert Venturi, Denise Scott Brown, and Steven Izenour, *Learning from Las Vegas* (Cambridge, Massachusetts, 1972), p. 109. John Unrau writes on 'John Ruskin, Robert Venturi, and Modernism in Architecture' in Toni Cerutti (editor), *Ruskin and the Twentieth Century: The Modernity of Ruskinism*, (Vercelli, 2000), pp. 159-68.

20 'What Does Architecture Do?', *Architectural Review*, 160 (1976), p. 81. Other examples of recent reinterpretations can be found in the special issue of *Assemblage*, 32 (1997) devoted to Ruskin.

21 Both Victorian and modern aspects of this topic are explored in Michael Wheeler and Nigel Whiteley (editors), *The Lamp of Memory: Ruskin, Tradition, and Architecture* (Manchester, 1992).

22 For a modern interpretation that detaches Ruskin's thought from Victorian stylistic wars, see Giovanni Leoni, 'Architecture as Commentary: Ruskin's Pre-modern Architectural Thought and Its Influence on Modern Architecture' in Giovanni Cianci and Peter Nicholls (editors), *Ruskin and Modernism* (London, 2001).

1

Ruskin's Architectural Heritage: The Seven Lamps of Architecture – Reception and Legacy

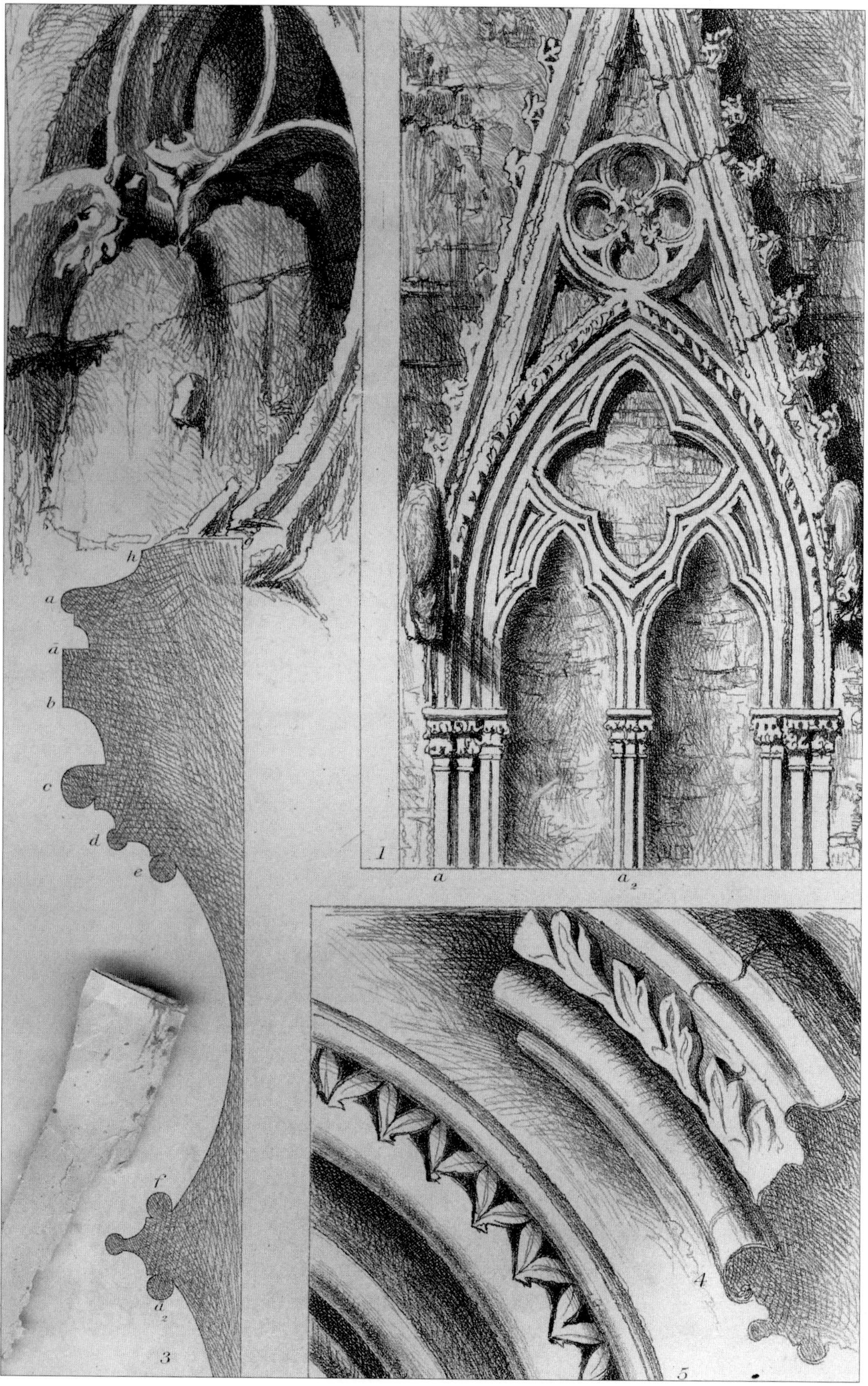
h
a
ā
b
c
d
e
f
a2
3
1
a
a2
4
5

Ruskin's Architectural Heritage: The Seven Lamps of Architecture – Reception and Legacy

Gill Chitty

ON JOHN RUSKIN'S death in 1900, the Royal Institute of British Architects published its tribute to the exceptional contribution that Ruskin had made in 'their own particular art':

> Probably no man in this age had influenced architecture as he had. He was the man who first awakened the English people to a knowledge of what art really meant: art in the life of its people, art in the true sense of the word, as an ennobling faculty which raised men … In that connection no work had more influence and deserved higher commendation, not only to students of architecture, but to all who were striving for culture, than that magnificent book, 'The Seven Lamps of Architecture'.[1]

For his own part Ruskin judged that his first book on architecture, written half a century earlier, was of all his works 'the most useless I ever wrote; the buildings it describes with so much delight being now either knocked down, or scraped and patched up into smugness and smoothness more tragic than uttermost ruin'.[2] His refusal of the Royal Institute of British Architects' Gold Medal in 1874 was a mark of the extent to which he had failed in his attempts to change attitudes among those responsible for the care of the architectural heritage. He declined the award with vehemence on the grounds that the architectural profession had colluded for its own financial benefit in the exploitation and neglect of England's and Europe's historic architecture, believing that he had made 'fatal mistakes' in his efforts to halt this.[3] It is not clear what he felt those mistakes had been but there was no doubt of his own sense of failure. One wonders how he would have viewed his obituary for the Society

'Traceries and mouldings from Rouen and Salisbury', plate X, *The Seven Lamps of Architecture* (1849), soft ground etching by Ruskin from drawings of 1848.

for the Protection of Ancient Buildings which declared that in *The Seven Lamps* he had 'set down for all time the principles which should govern the treatment of ancient buildings'.[4] By 1900 his few words of 1849 had achieved iconic status, taken out of their time and place and isolated from the body of thought from which they had sprung.

The dislocation of Ruskin's texts and cultural readings of his work is an interesting aspect of Ruskin studies. As Brian Maidment has remarked: 'Reading books about Ruskin always makes me wonder if anyone ever reads, or ever read, Ruskin's own books. His cultural presence has always been something more than that of a producer of texts.'[5] It was rediscovering Maidment's insights into Ruskin's evanescent cultural presence that provided the impulse for the present exploration of Ruskin's readership and the reception of his ideas among a wider audience. Perhaps it is there that we can look for the cultural legacy that might be characterised as his architectural heritage. If we regard 'Ruskin' as existing largely as a set of cultural responses among his readers rather than as a coherent body of intellectual thought embodied in his texts, as Maidment proposed, then how does his method of literary production in architecture move his work into this different form of social discourse? Certainly what distinguished Ruskin's work was the scale of intuitive response among a very broad readership and the reception of 'Ruskinian' precepts almost independently of his texts through their absorption and transformation in the writing and the work of others. In architectural circles, for example, one thinks of George Gilbert Scott, George Edmund Street, and William Morris. What is striking, too, is that the process seems to have begun almost immediately. 'We know a literary lady who cannot tell a Doric shaft from a flying buttress, who is nevertheless profound in the "Seven Lamps",' wrote Coventry Patmore in 1850 in a review of *The Seven Lamps of Architecture*.[6] 'This kind of popularity', he added with a tone of disapproval shared by many of Ruskin's contemporaries, 'ought to be *avoided* by a man of science like Mr Ruskin'.

The purpose of this chapter, then, is not an art historical study of Ruskinian influence in the work of particular architects, nor is it a reassessment of his own achievement in architectural design, which was extremely modest. The intention is to map the territory that Ruskin made his own in the discourse of architectural heritage and to explore what his legacy has been. What do we know of Ruskin's Victorian readership and how did they receive his architectural writing? How far has the reception of his work – his texts, his lectures and his practical enterprises – and his far-reaching influence among contemporaries preconditioned modern views of historic architecture, for better or worse? For Ruskin's cultural presence exists in a pervasive and open context, rewritten by successive generations and taken variously to confirm, extend, or confound received ideas. His has been the voice of heterodox social viewpoints, the radical and the establishment. One is as likely to find him quoted now in a New Labour policy statement on regeneration as one was in a Conservative white paper on the historic environment in the 1990s. However, to look in detail at reception and response across the range of Ruskin's architectural and related writing would be an unrealistic goal. Here, on a limited scale, the focus will be on the work of the younger writer: his earliest architectural writing; the *Modern Painters* project which overarched the period of his most influential architectural work; and particularly the far-reaching impact of his first architectural book, *The Seven Lamps of Architecture*.

The polemical tone of much of Ruskin's writing and the sermonic style of the early works can be uncongenial for the modern reader. This may be one prosaic reason why his ideas have continued to be far more popular than his texts. He teaches, as George Eliot remarked, with the enthusiasm of a young Hebrew prophet.[7] The authorial voice is dominant, sentences are of epic proportions, the syntax is elaborate and formal; it all suggests that he *has* a mission and is pursuing a coherent programme to promote his particular point of view. Certainly Ruskin's diverse literary output is unified by an intense personal vision: 'The greatest thing a human soul ever does in this world is to see something, and to tell what it saw in a plain way. ...To see clearly is poetry, philosophy and religion – all in one'.[8] But there is no simple linear progression in his work and his vision is continuously modified.

Characteristically Ruskin wrote in response to specific sights, incidents and occasions that could, at different times, draw him in apparently opposite directions. He wrote about architecture not as an expert but as an observer, but also as one whose acuity of vision could offer new insights to his readership. A habit of careful observation and a scientific mode of inquiry, established in his youth, were barely modified by three years at Oxford and an acquaintance with academic scholarship. The history of his architectural writing reflects the heterodox means that he chose to promulgate his ideas to very different readerships and audiences. It was also a reflex of particular occasions for authorship: incidents, experiences and events that gave his work an immediate currency for contemporary readers.

The Poetry of Architecture, Ruskin's first sustained architectural writing, was a series of fourteen essays drawing on the Ruskin family's summer tours of the Continent and of northern England, particularly the Lake District. They were written while he was an undergraduate at Oxford in the late 1830s and are as much a study of landscape character as of architecture. Modern readers who know these essays will encounter them as a single volume, but they were not published in book form until over fifty years later in 1893. Originally they appeared under a pseudonym, 'Kata Phusin', as articles in a monthly periodical, the *Architectural Magazine*. The magazine was conducted by John Claudius Loudon, landscape gardener and a prolific compiler of books and encyclopaedias, and it was an influential periodical, the first devoted entirely to architectural matters.[9] Loudon was a populariser and his illustrated magazine, with its emphasis on technical and practical matters, aimed to introduce architecture as a matter of everyday taste to a general readership:

> by improving the public taste in architecture generally, by rendering it a more intellectual profession, by recommending it as a fit study for ladies, and by inducing young architects to read, write and think as well as to see and draw.[10]

This then was the readership for Ruskin's first

architectural enterprise, to reclaim architecture as 'a science of feeling more than of rule, a ministry to the mind, more than to the eye'. He made it clear that his subject was not 'the attainment of architectural data, but the formation of taste' and it is revealing that he chose to make his first serious foray into publication in an illustrated magazine designed to introduce architectural discrimination in popular opinion. Written at the age of eighteen and illustrated with woodcuts from his own drawings, *The Poetry of Architecture* uncannily prefigures the cultural context in which the mature author would develop his literary projects.

Modern Painters was Ruskin's first major work as an author, one that would ultimately take eighteen years and five volumes to complete. Impossible to categorise (indeed most of Ruskin's work is difficult to assign to a genre), his celebration of Turner's art was part art criticism and art history, part philosophy and aesthetic treatise. The first volume of *Modern Painters* (1843) had a popular reception among a

'Coniston Old Hall' from 'A Chapter on Chimneys', *The Poetry of Architecture* (1893 edition), engraving based on an original woodcut in the *Architectural Magazine*.

'Chimneys' from 'A Chapter on Chimneys', *The Poetry of Architecture* (1893 edition), engraving based on an original woodcut in the *Architectural Magazine*.

distinguished and influential literary readership: Wordsworth recommended it to visitors, Tennyson sought it out, Charlotte Brontë and Mrs Gaskell read it together, George Eliot applauded it.[11] The critics gave it generally kind notice and the young Ruskin became a minor celebrity in literary and artistic circles, his serious career as an author had begun and he had established a broad and influential audience. The readership he sought was not the connoisseur and the wealthy collector (nor, yet, the working man) but people like his parents: visitors to galleries and exhibitions, the first generation of a new middle class, uncertain how to judge and to value art, eager for an education of the eye in a visual aesthetic for their times. Again, as in the *Architectural Magazine*, Ruskin explicitly presented the work as a corrective to public taste, 'plunging deeper and deeper into degradation', and to counterbalance 'the shallow and false criticisms of the periodicals of the day'.[12]

The active period of Ruskin's most influential architectural writing spans the mid-century, from 1849 to 1854. It has sometimes been viewed as an interruption in his *Modern Painters* project, with the publication of *The Seven Lamps of Architecture* and *The Stones of Venice* falling between the second and third volumes of the larger work. To look at the architectural writing in this way, as though it were some kind of interlude, is really to miss the point. It diminishes an understanding of it as part of his greater enterprise and our understanding of how it was received by his contemporaries. His Victorian readership by and large read Ruskin 'whole' as a cultural critic and not as an architectural commentator. It is true that his ideas about the sources of social and spiritual value in architecture did not find a place in the early volumes of *Modern Painters*, but they clearly evolved through a natural progression of thought and form part of a coherent whole.[13] *The Seven Lamps*, as an inclusive investigation of the true character of architecture and its moral purpose, is ingrained with the thinking of *Modern Painters*. Moreover, during the five-year gestation period of *Modern Painters* 1 and 2, Ruskin's correspondence and diaries reveal an increasing preoccupation with the study and appreciation of historic buildings and a passionate concern with the impact of change in Europe's historic cultural centres – Paris, Rouen, Florence, Pisa, Rome and, above all, Venice.

Visiting Venice again in the mid-1840s, Ruskin found the impact of modernisation worse than he could have anticipated. 'Of all the fearful changes I ever saw wrought in a given time, that on Venice since I was last here beats', he wrote disjointedly, 'it amounts to destruction – all that can be done of picture now is in the way of restoration'.[14] He gave a dramatic account in his daily letters of the struggle to make records of 'a few of the more precious details before they are lost forever'. The alteration he saw in Venice was experienced in most large cities in Europe in the course of the 19th century – the introduction of railways and gas lighting, the development of ports and harbours, warehousing and suburbs, the renewal and rebuilding of long-neglected historic quarters, and in Europe the effects of revolution, war and occupation. These 'fearful changes', to which we will return later, were central to the formation of his architectural project.

By the end of 1846 Ruskin had already gathered much of the material that he would need for an architectural study to complement his theoretical work on art in *Modern Painters* 2. It is important to recognise that, like his writing on art, Ruskin's interpretation of architecture was an intensely

Sketches of columns in the Cathedral of Ferrara, Italy, in Ruskin's 1846 notebook (*collection of the Ruskin Museum, Coniston, CONRM 1990.381*).

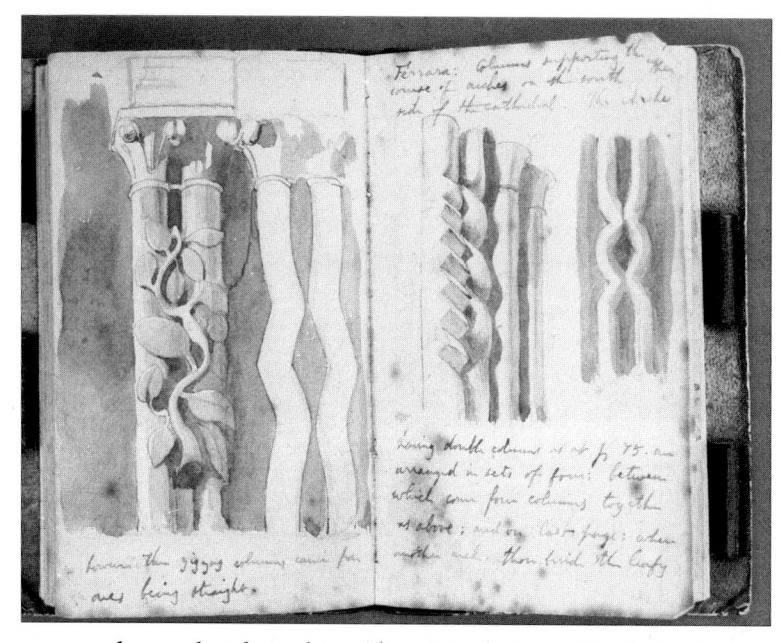

personal one developed in relative isolation. *The Seven Lamps of Architecture*, published in 1849, would be as unlike most contemporary architectural studies as *Modern Painters* had been unlike early-Victorian critiques of art. Ruskin seems to have shunned participation in the network of historical and architectural scholarship that could have been available to him, for example through his active membership of the Oxford Society for the Promotion and Study of Gothic Architecture.[15] Sensitive to the times in which he lived, and acutely aware of the visual quality of his environment, it seems that he worked instinctively and eccentrically outside the scholarly circles of the historian and ecclesiologist and the professional realm of the architect.

There was no shortage of competition in architectural publication in the years around 1850 which were exceptionally prolific. Works by Edward A. Freeman, John Henry Parker and James Fergusson appeared in the same year as *The Seven Lamps of Architecture* and many more in the years immediately before and after it.[16] The 1840s had seen a flood of architectural guides and illustrated works on architectural history from the Oxford Society and the Cambridge Camden (later Ecclesiological) Society, from A. W. N. Pugin and other architects of the Gothic Revival. Parker's *Glossary of Architecture* was in its fifth edition by 1850; F. A. Paley's *A*

Manual of Gothic Mouldings appeared in 1845, followed a year later by his *Manual of Gothic Architecture*; Thomas Rickman's *An Attempt to Discriminate the Styles of Architecture in England* had just been republished. As one of Ruskin's reviewers remarked:

> Were an indefatigable and thoroughly conscientious collection and publication of details all that is wanted for the revival of Gothic architecture in England, little would be left to be done after the labours of such men as Pugin, Rickman, Willis, Brandon, Bloxham [*sic*] and Paley.17

Unlike his contemporaries, however, Ruskin's concern was with more than the indefatigable collection of details. He had, it is true, adopted a new method of making meticulously observed notes, with measurements, profiles and sections, but there was the world of difference between the representation of architecture with which Ruskin was experimenting and the average architectural book. Architectural plates often showed diagrammatic elevations, thin and mechanical, lacking any representation of modelling or finish. Even the engravings which illustrated architectural guides like John Britton's *Architectural Antiquities* or the Oxford Society's own

'Portions of an Arcade on the South Side of the Cathedral of Ferrara', plate XIII, *The Seven Lamps of Architecture*. The prints are mirror images of the original drawings. Ruskin 'did not think it necessary to risk losing some of their accuracy by reversing them on the steel - and they are therefore reversed in the impression'.

'Intersectional mouldings', plate IV, *The Seven Lamps of Architecture*.

Guide to the Architectural Antiquities in the Neighbourhood of Oxford (1846) were evocative but generalised. The lines and measures of architectural convention were not a natural medium for Ruskin and he struggled to find a method of making an expressive and truthful record of the qualities which he observed and valued in historic places. It was not just the texture and weathering of surface and finish which formed such an important part of a building's character for him, he also sought a means of accurate representation which would capture other expressive qualities conveyed by design and form.

Ruskin put his ideas about truthful representation in architectural illustration into practice with the plates for *The Seven Lamps*. In his Preface, he wrote a disclaimer about the quality of the plates (a tactical error since it drew the unkind attention of his reviewers immediately) but he sincerely believed his drawings to be 'by far the most sternly faithful records of the portions of architecture they represent which have ever been published'. 'Few persons have any idea of the inaccuracy of architectural works generally', he complained to George Smith, his publisher: 'The reader will therefore, perhaps, think my ugly black plate of somewhat more value upon the whole, in its rough veracity, than the other in its delicate fiction'.[18] Ruskin completed the plates for his book in haste as he travelled in France in 1849: his etchings were not only 'every line of them by my own hand, but bitten also (the last of them in a washhand basin at "La Cloche" in Dijon) by myself, with savage carelessness.'[19] To the modern eye, these unconventional and expressive etchings have an enormous appeal and are unique in Ruskin's long and prolific output of printmaking. They were strikingly innovative for his Victorian audience.[20]

While Ruskin sought an expressive new form of illustration to educate the reader's eye, he also proposed an alternative to the systematisation of architectural analysis which dominated 19th-century architectural literature and to articulate a new theoretical framework for valuing 'the distinctively political art of Architecture'.[21] 'The book I called *The Seven Lamps*', Ruskin wrote many years later, 'was to show that certain right states of temper and moral feeling were the magic powers by which all good architecture had been produced'.[22] As always with Ruskin, it is worth asking what the context was for this new thinking. What had stimulated these ideas and whom did he aim to influence in publicising them? The background requires some brief biographical explanation.

As Chris Brooks shows in a later chapter, *The Seven Lamps*

'Ornament from Rouen, St Lo and Venice', plate I, *The Seven Lamps of Architecture*.

of Architecture was written against the background of the Chartist movement in England and the revolutionary upheavals of 1848 in Europe. Ruskin, who married in April of that year, had planned a wedding tour to Switzerland but this had to be deferred when news of serious disturbances in Europe began to reach Britain. Street riots and unrest spread from Milan and Venice to other Italian cities and martial law was imposed in Lombardy and the Veneto as the Austrian army fought to re-establish imperial control. In France, appalling social conditions in the towns, unemployment and political tensions had also erupted into violent disorder. In England, where economic recession was also biting, the Chartists were inspired by the Republican victory in France to protest against the same social inequalities and lack of political representation. The marches and violence in London, Ruskin's father claimed, had prevented the family from attending their son's wedding in Scotland. Everywhere there was an acute fear of the changes and potential violence that might be in waiting. Ruskin, touring with his wife in the Lake District, was profoundly disturbed by what he heard of events in Europe:

> I should be very, very happy just now but for these wild storm-clouds bursting on my dear Italy and my fair France ... I begin to feel that all the work I have been doing, and all the loves I have been cherishing are ineffective and frivolous – that these are not times for watching clouds or dreaming over quiet waters, that more serious work is to be done.[23]

The serious work to be done, in Ruskin's case, was *The Seven Lamps of Architecture*. For a man of his temperament and background, this 'wretched rant of a book', as he later called it, was the only form of direct action he could take. It was an expression as the mid-century approached of his anxieties about the future of culture and society. He began to develop the 'Lamps' as an informal structure, albeit a carefully composed one, within which he could share his visual observations and his personal and political response to the changes taking place.

By August 1848 the situation in France was more settled and the Ruskins began a three-month tour of Normandy ending in a visit to Paris. It was designed specifically to gather more material to illustrate Ruskin's study of architecture as part of the next volume of *Modern Painters*. What he found there overturned his plans and he brought forward a separate publication with urgency. He claimed that his whole time 'had been lately occupied in taking drawings from one side of the buildings, of which masons were knocking down the other'. The material for *The Seven Lamps* had been 'thrown together' under the necessity of 'obtaining as many memoranda as possible of medieval buildings in Italy and Normandy, now in process of destruction, before that destruction should be consummated by the Restorer, or Revolutionist'.[24]

Ruskin had returned from France in 1848 freshly reminded of the street violence of the June Days in Paris, the aftermath of the disastrous national workshops experiment, and 'all the open evidences of increasing – universal – and hopeless suffering'.[25] It is clear that alongside his investigation of architecture, *The Seven Lamps of Architecture* was also a polemical work written for a particular moment in time and reflecting its author's concern with immediate social and economic issues. He was careful to keep the immediate context of current affairs in the forefront of his reader's mind. 'A period like the present', we are reminded, 'is no time for the idleness of metaphysics, or the entertainment of the arts'.[26] Poverty, poor living conditions and educational disadvantage were not explicitly named until the final pages of *The Seven Lamps* but the closure of the 'Lamp of Obedience' was no less than an address on the evils of unemployment and an advocacy for the revival of architecture in England as 'useful in the sense of a National employment'.[27] Ruskin spoke to his readers about architecture not in terms of historical details and styles but in terms of its social value as the fullest expression of human art and labour, 'uniting the technical and imaginative elements as essentially as humanity does soul and body'. His writing now openly, if naively, displayed the direction in which his political economy would lead him:

> It is not enough to find men absolute subsistence; we should think of the manner of life which our demands necessitate; and endeavour, as far as may be, to make all our needs such as may, in the supply of them, raise, as well as feed, the poor.[28]

There was, then, a radical social and economic imperative openly expressed in Ruskin's writing for the first time. 'The Lamp of Sacrifice' calls for recognition of those signs of creative human work in the built environment which are above and beyond its common use: 'the signs that enough has been devoted to the great purposes of human stewardship'.²⁹

The theme of a common heritage and its stewardship can be traced through Ruskin's earlier writing. Between 1838 and 1849, his ideas on this subject had matured into a belief in a duty to safeguard an inalienable heritage, 'the great entail', whose resources were held in trust for future generations. His ideas were characterised by two orthodoxies: a grounding in Protestant religious conviction and a Burkean notion of natural order by which the succession of constitutional liberties was secured (one wonders whether, on his return from Paris in the aftermath of the 1848 revolution, Ruskin had turned to re-read Edmund Burke's *Reflections on the Revolution in France*).³⁰ In the Introductory to *The Seven Lamps*, Ruskin worked his way across the problematic terrain of the relation of architecture to the scheme of moral perception constructed around his theory of instinctive beauty. He wrote in an evenly phrased, non-sectarian prose consciously chosen, like *Modern Painters* 2, to be 'extremely palatable to everybody, and especially to the amiable Protestant'.³¹ Ruskin was quite deliberately occupying a new territory, not only different from the academic scholarship of the architectural writers of Oxford and Cambridge, but different also from the dangerous, moral high ground of the ecclesiologists and Tractarians (and Pugin specifically), which had formed the context for much of the new writing on architecture in the 1840s. Charles Eastlake, writing his history of the Gothic Revival of 1872, was the first to claim for Ruskin that:

> He wrote rather as a moral philosopher than as a churchman, and though his theological views found here and there decided expression they could hardly be identified with any particular sect. His book, therefore, found favour with a large class of readers who had turned from Pugin's arguments with impatience, and to whom even the 'Ecclesiologist' had preached in vain.³²

The evangelical tone and unambiguous Protestant orthodoxy found a large new readership.

A large part of the impact which *The Seven Lamps* had on

Victorian audiences also lay in the conviction with which Ruskin was able to write in such a complex area as the causes of mental impressions from nature and art, confident in his powers as an interpreter of the visual imagination. That confidence rested partly in the knowledge that he had systematically investigated the reasoning which underpinned his interpretation over many years; and partly in the fact that he was the successful author of two works of art criticism with a popular, discerning, readership. Ruskin's own name appeared for the first time on the title page in *The Seven Lamps* but he was still the 'Author of "Modern Painters"'. His assured self-belief spoke directly to his readership through passages where he disarmingly sought their trust in the eloquence of his argument:

> There are ... cases in which men feel too keenly to be silent, and perhaps too strongly to be wrong; I have been forced into this impertinence; and have suffered too much from the destruction or neglect of the architecture I best loved, and from the erection of that which I cannot love, to reason cautiously.[33]

Arguing that the 'distinctively political art of architecture' is analogous to human polity, he encouraged the reader-viewer to have confidence to see and judge for themselves, sharing his own highly developed faculties – 'the imagination penetrative' – for such perception with his audience.

Ruskin had, then, provided his audience with a reading of architecture for its moral and symbolical value, a reading notable in the architectural scene of the 1840s for its Protestant orthodoxy. He had placed architecture in a socially meaningful context against a safely familiar background of established Burkean principle. He had developed a theoretical framework for appreciating beauty and human creative achievement in the built environment; and in his concluding chapter he looked forward to a revival of architecture grounded in the principles he had expounded. This was a rich blend calculated to persuade. But above all in 'The Lamp of Memory', he spoke to what would become a universal theme in the Victorian age, from Carlyle onwards: a preoccupation with changing times and a self-conscious regard of the discontinuity of past and present. 'Now, when the place both of the past and future is too much usurped in our minds by the restless and discontented present. The very quietness of nature is gradually withdrawn from us'.[34] Ruskin had begun to articulate what urban living in the 20th century has made only too plain: the visual quality of the built environment and a sense of belonging in the places where people live is essential to balance the loss of natural beauty and harmony in our surroundings. This was not, however, an aspect of *The Seven Lamps of Architecture* which his readers at mid-century could have recognised and to understand something of the impact which it made we need to look further ahead.

Intuitively or not, Ruskin had chosen to publicise his own ideas on architecture at a moment when the market was near to saturation with architectural literature. There was a rapidly growing middle-class readership and at a time when every new manual of Gothic architecture sold like a novel, as one reviewer put it, there was evidently no lack of interest in the subject. Ruskin's reviewers received the new book enthusiastically as one of the most significant pieces of criticism in the field for many years. If they also found some grounds for adverse comment, even the most hostile allowed the brilliance of Ruskin's theorising, and most commented on the exceptional powers of imagination and language which he exercised in the treatment of his subject. It was the virtuosity of Ruskin's language, and his imaginative as well as his moral insights which were truly innovative; and reflexes of this soon began to appear in the work of other Victorian architectural writers.[35] The *Ecclesiologist* and others welcomed it 'as a book for amateurs' but some of Ruskin's critics were disturbed, nonetheless, by the possible consequences of a work written with such persuasive style and potential popular appeal on a subject – architectural aesthetics – which was regarded in the matter of taste as the special province of a small number of knowledgeable critics and practitioners. Not only did Ruskin's approach transcend the exclusive doctrinal, academic or professional limits of other studies, it also opened up these preserves to the lay public. If the professional critic of architectural aesthetics, like Coventry Patmore, did not welcome popularisation of his domain with 'literary ladies', neither did the professional architect nor architectural historian. The book's reception in professional and scholarly circles was largely hostile and contemptuous. According to the *Ecclesiologist,* an eminent architect characterised the book as 'almost mad'.[36] New College, Oxford, refused to have it in the library. George Gilbert Scott equivocated characteristically about the book's value and piously demurred: 'It is not for me to give an opinion, as its praises are in everyone's mouth (it were well if its spirit were in everyone's heart)'.[37] But as the *Athenaeum*'s critic acutely remarked: 'by merely stirring up the subject, and courting an investigation into true and rightful elementary principles, Mr. Ruskin's work, were it three times as full of eccentricities as it is, must do good, and we hope lasting, service'.[38]

One of its noted eccentricities, and an issue that had seldom been stirred up in public before, was the treatment of ancient buildings. Ruskin believed not only that such historic places were part of a common inheritance but also that the public had a real interest in what was happening to them. He admonished his readers with 'a few words ... especially necessary in modern times', asserting that neither they nor the professionals and public servants responsible for safeguarding the built heritage (and this included the Church) understood what restoration really meant and how destructive it had been. For the first time this placed the subject squarely and controversially in the public arena. The timing was appropriate. It was largely Ruskin's experience on the Continent, as we have seen, that fired his rhetoric in *The Seven Lamps* but the movement there was paralleled by an equally rapid growth in the restoration of medieval buildings in England. How closely Ruskin was aware of this trend in his own country is uncertain, but the real boom in the rebuilding of medieval churches and cathedrals began in the 1840s, reaching its peak through the 1860s and 1870s.[39]

To the modern scholar it can appear that discussion of principles bearing on the treatment of historic buildings was well-publicised in the 1840s and 1850s. It remains perfectly accessible to us now through the numerous journals and learned society proceedings of the time. But these kinds of questions were only aired in restricted academic and ecclesiastical circles, from which large sectors of society were excluded on grounds of gender or religious belief. It was only later in the 1860s and 1870s, by which time more popular periodicals and newspapers began to feature articles on such topics, that it gained any currency in public affairs. With *The Seven Lamps*, however, restoration entered the public domain controversially in a book with popular appeal designed to equip interested middle-class people to judge the value of their architectural inheritance and to take a view on what was happening to historic buildings as well as the design of new ones.

The architectural debate of mid-century was a formative one. Ruskin opened the way for the formulation of an ethical approach to the treatment of the built environment and its recognition as a matter of public interest. Superficially it appears that his ideas on restoration were not immediately appealing, and he advanced no practical measures for conservation as an alternative to restoration. But, as Patmore remarked, 'as is often the case with greatly useful books, Mr Ruskin's "Seven Lamps of Architecture" bears, at first glance, an unpractical character'.[40] His polemical stand on architectural restoration entered the controversy very rapidly and one can scarcely find any discussion of the subject, after the publication of *The Seven Lamps of Architecture*, that does not make some reference to him, or the substance of his argument, however dismissively. Thus what Freeman described as Ruskin's 'extreme and chimerical' contribution had a polarising effect on the debate.[41] The sheer authority of Ruskin's writing, his reputation and the popularity his work achieved with a broad readership were powerful factors. The fact that Ruskin's views were considered seriously enough to be challenged immediately in academic and professional papers, written by respected figures like Scott and Freeman, began the process of loosening the hold of formalist art historical thinking over early Victorian architectural practice.

One consequence of his controversial contribution to this debate was that Ruskin's position on the restoration question preoccupied the attention of his contemporaries, as it has of most recent writers on the history of the conservation movement, at the expense of his wider thought in this area.

Undoubtedly 'The Lamp of Memory' was, as William Morris said of 'The Nature of Gothic', 'one of the very few necessary and inevitable utterances of the century'.[42] But there has been a tendency to reduce the significance of Ruskin's thinking for the conservation of the historic environment to those few passages in *The Seven Lamps* and to the acknowledged influence of his teaching on Morris. In other words, one tends to find that Ruskin's writing from the 1840s and 1850s has been interpreted as relevant only in so far as it provided some moral authority for action by others in the 1870s. It can be shown that the adoption of a modified form of Ruskinism through the 1860s, with the endorsement of Scott through the Royal Institute of British Architects, and of other influential architectural writers such as Street, began to bring about a significant change in the climate of opinion and gradual reform of restoration practice.[43] Morris was keen to appropriate Ruskin's work for his own enterprise and in 1877 when he founded the Society for the Protection of Ancient Buildings, its manifesto self-consciously proclaimed its debt to Ruskin. He was a valuable figurehead for their movement. As Slade Professor of Fine Art at Oxford he held a position in the establishment but was also known by this time as an outspoken social critic with a reputation for challenging the values of his time.

Ruskin's actual role in the setting up of the Society for the Protection of Ancient Buildings appears to have been negligible in real terms. His own attempt to promote the formation of a campaigning society like the SPAB, two decades earlier, had been proposed in a pamphlet, *The Opening of the Crystal Palace*. The idea received wide circulation through the Society of Antiquaries and in November 1854 Ruskin approached the Executive Committee of the Society with a proposal that they should sponsor his scheme to form an Association and establish a Conservation Fund. It never attracted either the finances or the energetic support needed to make the enterprise successful and lacked the inspired leadership that Morris would later bring to the SPAB.[44]

In the years between the writing of *The Seven Lamps of Architecture* and *The Opening of the Crystal Palace,* Ruskin had been engaged in his greatest architectural work, *The Stones of*

Venice (1851-3), followed by a period of active public speaking published as *Lectures on Architecture and Painting* (1854). The project which he had envisioned to 'restore Venice' in the imagination 'to some resemblance of what she must have been before her fall' was realised in his voluminous work on the architecture of Venice. He had begun the detailed architectural study for *The Stones* in 1849, before *The Seven Lamps of Architecture* was published, and it was in the second chapter of the first volume, 'The Virtues of Architecture', that Ruskin set out, apparently uncontentiously, the two primary duties of architecture: to be practical and pleasing. The practical duty was divided into two aspects:

> Acting and talking: - acting, as to defend us from weather or violence; talking, as the duty of monuments or tombs, to record facts and express feelings; or of churches, temples and public edifices, treated as books of history, to tell such history clearly and forcibly.[45]

Ruskin quite explicitly included the expressive qualities of architecture as a part of its practical function. Challenging the prevalent tendency of his age to privilege utilitarianism – the 'usefulness' of architecture – Ruskin interpreted an inclusive utility in which the symbolic value of a building, as expressive of history or feeling, ranked with its practical function of keeping the rain out. We can recall that this is familiar territory from *Modern Painters* 2 and Ruskin's redefinition of the aesthetic, as the 'Theoretic' faculty: 'the entire system of useful and contemplative knowledge is one'.[46] It lies at the heart of his argument on the impossibility of restoration and uniquely characterises his work. For Ruskin's understanding of usefulness was profoundly different from the conventional Victorian 'uses' of material heritage. What he contemplated in the historic environment was a moral legacy; and morality, for Ruskin, was expressed in the whole ethos of a creative individual and the culture to which he or she belonged. Theoria, the 'authoritative and right instinct of mankind', equipped Ruskin's readers to contemplate that moral legacy in the built heritage.

In his Edinburgh lectures in 1853, Ruskin entered into a new form of dialogue with his audience in his first sustained programme of public speaking, a medium for which he found he had a particular talent. The tone of these lectures, although they present little that is new in terms of his architectural thinking, is significantly different in its discourse, encouraging a critical sight of the Edinburgh townscape and inviting his audience to feel empowered to influence the quality of buildings that form the character of their neighbourhood.

> If you feel that your present school of architecture is unattractive to you, I say there is something wrong, either in the architecture or in you; and I trust you will not think I mean to flatter you, when I tell you that the wrong is *not* in you, but in the architecture. ... You would like all the best things if only you saw them. What is wrong is your temper, not your taste; your patient and trustful temper, which lives in houses whose architecture it takes for granted, and subscribes to public edifices from which it derives no enjoyment. ... Architecture is an art for all men to learn because all men are concerned with it.[47]

While the lectures in Edinburgh were a public success, the doubtful reception of *The Opening of the Crystal Palace* and the quiet failure of his Conservation Fund proposal were discouraging. Some years later, in 1861, Ruskin said publicly that it was what he had seen in France in 1854 that had brought about the end of his architectural project. He had intended to write, he said, an architectural history of the 13th century 'but found that all his documents were then in fact destroyed by the operation of the system of restoration which was adopted. So he gave up the undertaking'.[48] There are hints that he might have turned his attention to writing a political economy for the architectural heritage. In one of his *Lectures on Architecture and Painting* of 1854 he set out the beginnings of a clear argument for what we would now think of as cultural sustainability:

> Nothing appears to me much more wonderful, than the remorseless way in which the educated ignorance, even of the present day, will sweep away an ancient monument, if its preservation be not absolutely consistent with

immediate convenience or economy. Putting aside all antiquarian considerations, and all artistical ones, I wish that people would only consider the steps and the weight of the following very simple argument. You allow it wrong to waste time, that is, your own time; but then it must be still more wrong to waste other people's; for you have some right to your own time, but none to theirs. Well, then, if it is thus wrong to waste the time of the living, it must be still more wrong to waste the time of the dead; for the living can redeem their time, the dead cannot. But you waste the best of the time of the dead when you destroy the works they have left you; for to those works they gave the best of their time, intending them for immortality.[49]

Ruskin had an acute sense of visual beauty which he discovered and renewed lifelong in the natural landscape. While he was appalled by many aspects of urban life – 'the modern aggregate of bad building, and ill-living held in check by constables which we call a town'[50] – he loved the old towns and cities of Europe. He could only account for the sense of intense pleasure which he experienced in such places, and which he recognised was analogous to the contemplation of natural beauty in the living world, by integrating this experience in his ideas about impressions of beauty in nature. *The Seven Lamps* and *The Stones of Venice* were the work of an interlocutor between humanity and the built and natural environments: 'We are forced for the sake of accumulating our power and knowledge, to live in cities: but such advantage as we have in association with each other is in great part counterbalanced by our loss of fellowship with Nature'. In the streets and buildings of the urban scene, he found those qualities and expressions of human history that could stand for the deeply-felt responses evoked in the natural world.

> If in the square of the city, you can find delight, finite indeed, but pure and intense, like that which you have in a valley among the hills, then its art and architecture are right; but if, after fair trial, you can find no delight in them, nor any instruction like that of nature, I call on you fearlessly to condemn them.[51]

'Vercelli 1846' in
The Poetry of Architecture
(1893 edition).

It is because Ruskin did not, indeed could not, distinguish between his responses to beauty in the natural and the built environment that his writing fits so well with current ideas about sustainability and the historic environment. The animation of the built environment by historical and metaphorical meaning was, in his view, as crucial for the viability of human spiritual life as the natural environment is for humanity's physical survival.

The concept of an 'environment' – as an alternative to the

orthodoxies of landscape appreciation – gained currency during the second half of the 19th century. Landscape, defined by selective vision and interpreted in the terms of well-established pictorial tradition, was an exclusive and culturally determined subject. 'Environment' with its modern usage emerged slowly as an all-embracing concept, to mean the physical world that surrounds and sustains us and the places where we live and work. Ruskin conceived of environment in inclusive but specific terms. It was in Italy in the early 1840s that he began the careful examination of historic urban character and to discover that 'if studied closely and well ... there was not a single corner of a street which would not be beautiful'.52 What applied to a street corner in Italy was just as true for one in Croydon. His studies of architectural details display his concern, both with the particular and with what contextual detail can express about individual localities. 'Talkative truths', Ruskin wrote in *Modern Painters* 1, 'are always more interesting and more important than silent ones' and those truths are 'most

'End of Market Street, Croydon' in *The Poetry of Architecture* (1893 edition).

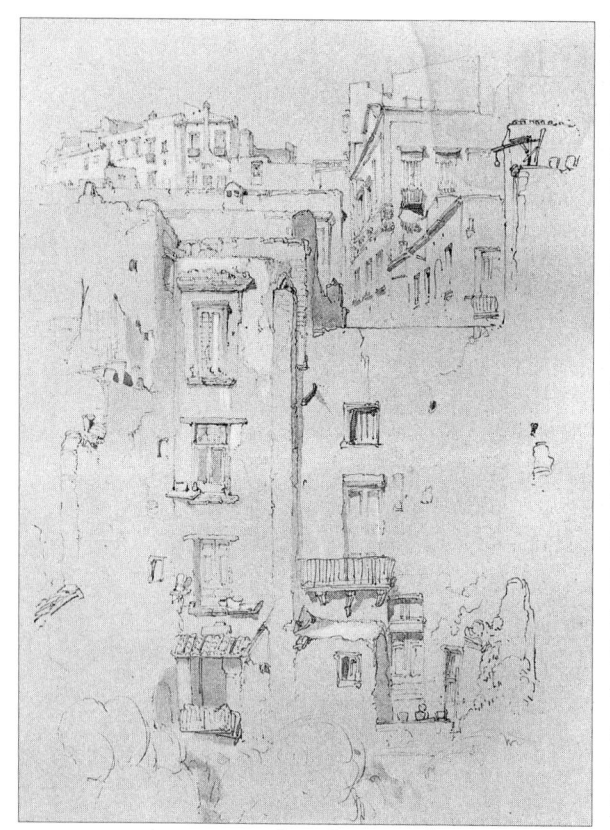

valuable which are most historical; that is which tell us most about the past and future states of the object to which they belong'.[53]

One of Ruskin's important innovations in 19th-century thinking was his contemplation of the historic built environment as sustaining humanity by moral — that is by imaginative and spiritual insights — in the same way that the natural environment sustains by physical means. He prized two qualities in the architectural heritage: firstly, its imaginative and symbolic meaning in which the practical function of design included the expression of individual spirit and of social identity. Secondly (and his drawings and painting show this as eloquently as his words) he valued the particular: the fine grain of distinctive character which is displayed in every historic place and which marks its difference and uniqueness.

'Windows at Naples' in *The Poetry of Architecture* (1893 edition).

One is struck by the way that these attributes have now emerged as key qualities in approaches to recognising what is valued in the modern scene, particularly in the context of planning for sustainable change. Public perception studies chart the emergence of new cultural networks that display fresh patterns of citizenship and environmental awareness focused around preoccupations such as 'sense of place', family history, community heritage, biodiversity, alternative therapies, reliance on intuitive rather than rational judgement: forms of personal, spiritual, even self-regarding, activity, but ones which engage moral energies that may be very relevant to sustainable life-styles and lend cohesion to the pluralism of post-modern societies such as our own.

Such patterns of personal vision are characteristic of Ruskin's world view. If his work had a unified purpose, it was above all to enable individuals to see and to value the quality of their environment, especially those aspects which enrich and strengthen inner life. His concern with the distinctive historical truths that comprise the unique character of buildings and places, and with their moral rather than their economic value, provides a healthy counter-balance to modern preoccupation with commercial and entrepreneurial potential, now as it did then. The most characteristic aspects of his vision – an inclusivity of associative and historical meaning, the distinctive imprint of 'the individual acting with hand and mind', and a common responsibility to safeguard this social legacy - remain key elements in today's thinking about environmental conservation.

If Ruskin appears to anticipate modern notions of environmental stewardship, it is not to suggest that his ideas necessarily provide a meaningful index for contemporary movements of thought. However, there are some aspects of his work which prefigure modern ideas about the care of the historic environment so closely that they should not pass without remark. Their proximity is not coincidental and owes much to a common lineage in a distinctive and continuing British tradition of historical consciousness about the environment.[54] It draws, as Ruskin did, on a plurality of cultural sources and a deep-rooted sense of specific place. In the context of his times, his work can be understood as the outcome of a defining period when that distinctive historical sensibility – rooted in Romantic literary, pictorial and antiquarian traditions – merged with a new social and environmental awareness. As an individual achievement, it was also the exceptional outcome of a cultural project to move architecture into a new form of social discourse on the built environment, equipping the reader-viewer to see and make their own critical judgements on the changes taking place in their historic cities and surroundings, to consider 'the idea of self-denial for the sake of posterity, of practising present economy for the sake of debtors yet unborn, of planting forests that our descendants may live under their shade, or of raising cities for future nations to inhabit'.[55]

It is arguable that even today Ruskin's pervasive texts, and their transmission through the response of his extensive and influential 19th-century audience, temper our valuation of the historic environment and its architectural heritage. In one sense he may have been rightly claimed for the preservation movement as one who 'set down for all time the principles which should govern the treatment of ancient buildings'[56] but at the end of his life he reflected astutely that the world cared more for his books than he did himself. What Ruskin required in his readers was that they contemplate and act to respect their surroundings in a radically new way: to see clearly and to value what they saw. This had little to do with a desire to preserve the past and everything to do with cultural viability for the future.

Acknowledgements:
I would like to express my gratitude to members of the Ruskin Seminar at Lancaster University, and to the dozens of Ruskin scholars who have given papers there, with whom I have had the pleasure and stimulation of sharing research on this and many other subjects over the last ten years. My special thanks are due to Alan Davis, Ray Haslam and Claire Wildsmith and to the Directors of the Ruskin Programme, past and present, Michael Wheeler and Keith Hanley.

Notes

1 *Works,* 8, p. xlii quoting the *Journal of the Royal Institute of British Architects,* 3rd series, 7 (1900), p. 116.

2 *Works,* 8, p. 15.

3 *Works,* 34, pp. 513-16; John Harris, 'The Ruskin Gold Medal Controversy', *Journal of the Royal Institute of British Architects,* 70 (1963), pp. 165-7; 'After Twenty-Five Years, John Ruskin and the Royal Institute of British Architects: Three hitherto suppressed Ruskin Letters', *Ruskin Union Journal,* 1 (1900), pp. 25-8.

4 Society for the Protection of Ancient Buildings, 'John Ruskin, 1819-1900', *23rd Annual Report of the Committee* (1900), p. 5.

5 Brian Maidment, 'Reading Ruskin and Ruskin Readers', *PN Review,* 14 (1988), pp. 50-3.

6 Coventry Patmore, 'Ruskin's "Seven Lamps of Architecture"', *North British Review,* 12 (February 1850), pp. 349-50.

7 J. W. Cross, *The Life of George Eliot,* vol. 2, (London, 1885), p. 7.

8 *Works,* 5, p. 333.

9 See Frank Jenkins, 'Nineteenth Century Architectural Periodicals' in John Summerson (editor), *Concerning Architecture: Essays on Architectural Writers and Writing Presented to Nikolaus Pevsner,* (London, 1968), pp. 154-8.

10 'Preface', *Architectural Magazine,* 1 (1834), unpaginated.

11 Tim Hilton, *John Ruskin: The Early Years*, (London, 1985).
12 *Works*, 3, p. 3.
13 Gill Chitty, 'John Ruskin and the Historic Environment' (unpublished PhD thesis, Lancaster University, 1998).
14 H. Shapiro (editor), *Ruskin in Italy: Letters to his Parents 1845* (Oxford, 1972), p. 199.
15 Gill Chitty, 'John Ruskin, Oxford and the Architectural Society, 1837 to 1840', *Oxoniensia*, 65 (2000), pp. 111-31. He acknowledged Robert Willis, as 'having taught me all my grammar of central Gothic' (*Works*, 8, p. 87), and William Whewell, the two Cambridge authorities on architectural history whom he knew through his Oxford Society connections; and only one other source, Thomas Hope's *An Historical Essay on Architecture* (London, 1835).
16 Edward A. Freeman, *A History of Architecture* (London, 1849); George Ayliffe Poole, *The History of Ecclesiastical Architecture in England* (London, 1848); Raphael and J. Arthur Brandon, *An Analysis of Gothick Architecture*, 2 vol (London, 1847); John Henry Parker, *An Introduction to the Study of Gothic Architecture* (Oxford, 1849) and James Fergusson, *An Historical Inquiry into the True Principles of Beauty in Art, more especially with Reference to Architecture* (London, 1849).
17 Coventry Patmore, 'The Aesthetics of Gothic Architecture', *British Quarterly Review*, 10 (1849), p. 50.
18 *Works*, 9, p. 431.
19 *Works*, 8, p. 15.
20 Alan Davis, *'A Pen of Iron' Ruskin and Printmaking*, exhibition catalogue, Ruskin Library, Lancaster University (Lancaster, 2003), pp. 21-3.
21 *Works*, 8, p. 20.
22 *Works*, 18, p. 443.
23 *Works*, 36, p. 86.
24 *Works*, 8, p. 3.
25 Ibid., p. xxxii.
26 Ibid., p. 25.
27 Ibid., p. 26.
28 Ibid., p. 264.
29 Ibid., p. 37.
30 Gill Chitty, 'A Great Entail' in Michael Wheeler (editor), *Ruskin and Environment* (Manchester, 1995), p. 105n.
31 *Works*, 4, p. 217n.
32 Charles Eastlake, *A History of the Gothic Revival* (London, 1872), p. 266.
33 *Works*, 8, p. 3-4.
34 Ibid., p. 246.
35 Michael Brooks, 'Describing Buildings: John Ruskin and Nineteenth-Century Architectural Prose', *Prose Studies: History, Theory, Criticism*, 3 (3) (December 1980), pp. 241-53; *John Ruskin and Victorian Architecture* (London, 1989), p. 72.
36 Benjamin Webb, 'Mr Ruskin's Seven Lamps of Architecture', *Ecclesiologist*, 10 (1849), p. 119.

37 George Gilbert Scott, *A Plea for the Faithful Restoration of Our Ancient Churches* ... (London, 1850), p. 7.

38 *Athenaeum*, 1 September 1849, quoted in *Works,* 8, p. xxxix.

39 Chris Miele, '"Their Interest and Habit": Professionalism and the Restoration of Medieval Churches, 1837-77' in Chris Brooks and Andrew Saint (editors), *The Victorian Church: Architecture and Society* (Manchester, 1995), pp. 151-72. 'Between 1840 and 1875 more than 7,000 medieval parish churches were restored, rebuilt or enlarged. This represented nearly 80 per cent of all old parish churches in England and Wales, and is more than double the number of new churches built over the same period' (pp.159-60).

40 Patmore [note 6], p. 349.

41 Edward A. Freeman, *The Preservation and Restoration of Ancient Monuments: A Paper read before the Archaeological Institute at Bristol July 29, 1851* (Oxford, 1852).

42 J. W. Mackail, *The Life of William Morris* (London, 1899), vol. 2, p. 275.

43 Michael Brooks [note 35]; Chris Miele, 'The Gothic Revival and Gothic Architecture: The Restoration of Medieval Churches in Victorian Britain' (unpublished PhD thesis, Institute of Fine Arts, University of New York, 1992).

44 Joan Evans, *History of the Society of Antiquaries* (Oxford, 1956), pp. 309-12.

45 *Works,* 9, p. 60.

46 *Works,* 4, p. 35: ('Of the Theoretic Faculty', which is 'concerned with the moral perception and appreciation of ideas of beauty.').

47 *Works,* 12, p. 20.

48 'Twenty-second Anniversary Meeting', *Ecclesiologist,* 22 (1861), p. 254.

49 *Works,* 12, pp. 98-9n.

50 *Works,* 33, p. 123.

51 *Works,* 9, p. 411.

52 J. Evans and J. H. Whitehouse (editors), *The Diaries of John Ruskin* (Oxford, 1956-9), vol. 1, p. 118.

53 *Works,* 3, p. 163.

54 Jonathan Bate, *Romantic Ecology: Wordsworth and the Environmental Tradition* (London, 1991), pp. 60-1.

55 *Works,* 8, p. 233.

56 Society for the Protection of Ancient Buildings [note 4].

2

'As beautiful as anything I know in civil Gothic', or 'a very shabby bit of work of mine': Ruskin and the Oxford University Museum

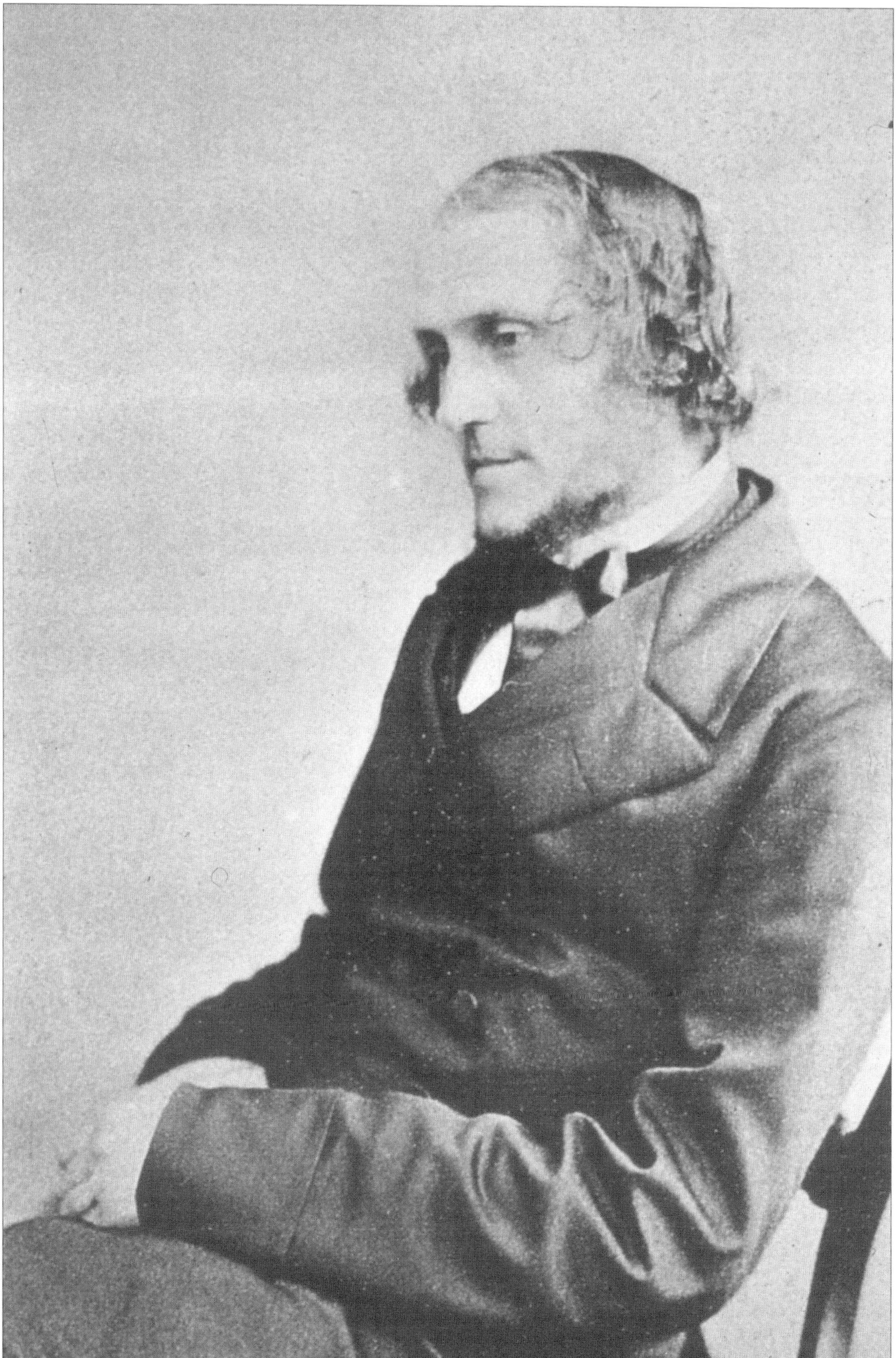

'As beautiful as anything I know in civil Gothic', or 'a very shabby bit of work of mine': Ruskin and the Oxford University Museum

Peter Howell

IN JUNE 1861 Dante Gabriel Rossetti wrote to his friend, the writer Alexander Gilchrist:

> I am sure that no-one would be readier than Ruskin to contradict the absurd reports which have gone abroad – and indeed I think he has done so publicly – as to *his* being the real author of Woodward's chief designs. The calumny – founded on the friendship and sympathy of the two men – deserves no mention, but it has been so zealously repeated in some quarters as to require a word of denial which cannot be made too absolute.[1]

In 1877 John Ruskin, lecturing at the Oxford Museum, spoke as follows:

> Now ... here is a very shabby bit of work of mine – this museum, namely – for the existence of which in such form, or at least in such manner, I am virtually answerable, and will answer, so far as either my old friend and scholar, Mr Woodward, or I myself, had our way with it, or were permitted by fate to follow our way through.[2]

Given the apparent inconsistency of these two statements, it is not surprising that confusion has existed over the extent of Ruskin's role in the design and construction of the Oxford University Museum. The publication in 1997 of Frederick O'Dwyer's massive book *The Architecture of Deane and Woodward* (Cork University Press) makes it possible at least to get closer to a true answer.

Benjamin Woodward, born in 1816, was the son of an

Opposite:
Benjamin Woodward, taken by an unknown photographer. Rossetti called him 'the stillest creature out of an oyster-shell' (*Oxford University Museum Archives*).

army officer from Co. Meath. He was articled to the civil engineer William Stokes, whose family was acquainted with his own. After his articles, he became assistant to Stokes, who was engaged in surveying and engineering works on the River Shannon, as well as doing works for county grand juries which were responsible for roads and bridges. There is no evidence that Stokes carried out architectural works.

In 1842 Henry Wentworth Acland, a medical doctor, of a Devon family and a year older than Woodward, was touring Ireland. His father was an old friend of the architect Sir Thomas Deane, whom he had visited in Cork in 1837. Acland wrote to his mother that he had hoped to meet Woodward on the Shannon. However, whether he knew about Woodward from Deane is unclear, as it is uncertain when they met. Nor is it known when Woodward set himself up as an architect. His earliest known work (a lodge at Drumbarrow) dates from *c.*1838. In 1844 he signs himself 'architect' on his measured drawings of Holy Cross Abbey, Co. Tipperary. It may have been these which led Deane to employ him in 1846.

Sir Thomas Deane (1792-1871) was both a builder and an architect. He had been knighted as High Sheriff of Cork in

Museum Building, Trinity College, Dublin. Ruskin described it as 'quite the noblest thing ever done from my teaching' (*Jeanne Sheehy*).

1830. His younger brother, Kearns (born 1804), was probably responsible for the firm's best work, until his early death in 1847. It was probably his illness that caused Sir Thomas to look for another assistant. The first important work with which Woodward was involved was Queen's College, Cork, built in 1847-9. This was one of three new colleges set up by Act of Parliament in 1845. Woodward seems to have been involved in the design from the start, and it was he who wrote to Hardman to order metalwork. The college's design was of a traditional form, based on Oxford, but the stone-carving was noteworthy.[3]

In 1851 Sir Thomas Deane, then aged sixty, formed a partnership with his son Thomas Newenham Deane and Woodward, under the title 'Sir Thomas Deane, Knt., Son, and Woodward, Architects'. T. N. Deane was born in 1828, and thought of becoming an artist. He was a shy man, with a speech impediment. In the year the partnership was formed, the firm entered a competition for a new town hall for Cork. They did not win, but the design was interesting. Said by the *Builder* to be 'founded on the Belgic Town-halls', it also recalls the 'Hôtel de Ville' illustrated by Pugin in *Contrasts*.[4] With its tall, flat façade and central tower, it was an important precedent for the Oxford Museum.

In 1852 the firm was invited to compete for a new 'Museum Building' for Trinity College, Dublin, and won the commission in the next year. In 1854 the contract was signed, for £23,400 and the partners opened an office in Dublin. The building, which was completed in 1857, was to house a museum and lecture-rooms.[5] The style was something of a hybrid. At the time it was variously described as Venetian Lombardic, Romanesque, and Renaissance. It is much indebted to Sir Charles Barry's Travellers' Club of 1828-32. One thing which is quite obvious is that careful study had been made of Ruskin's *Seven Lamps of Architecture* (1849) and *The Stones of Venice* (1851-3). A number of details came directly from Venice. The marble disks were based on those of the Palazzo Dario, illustrated in *The Stones,* as well as in the *Builder* in 1851.[6] The entrance recalls the Casa Visetti, also illustrated in the *Builder* (which claimed that Woodward acknowledged the debt).[7] The corner chimneystacks, and the

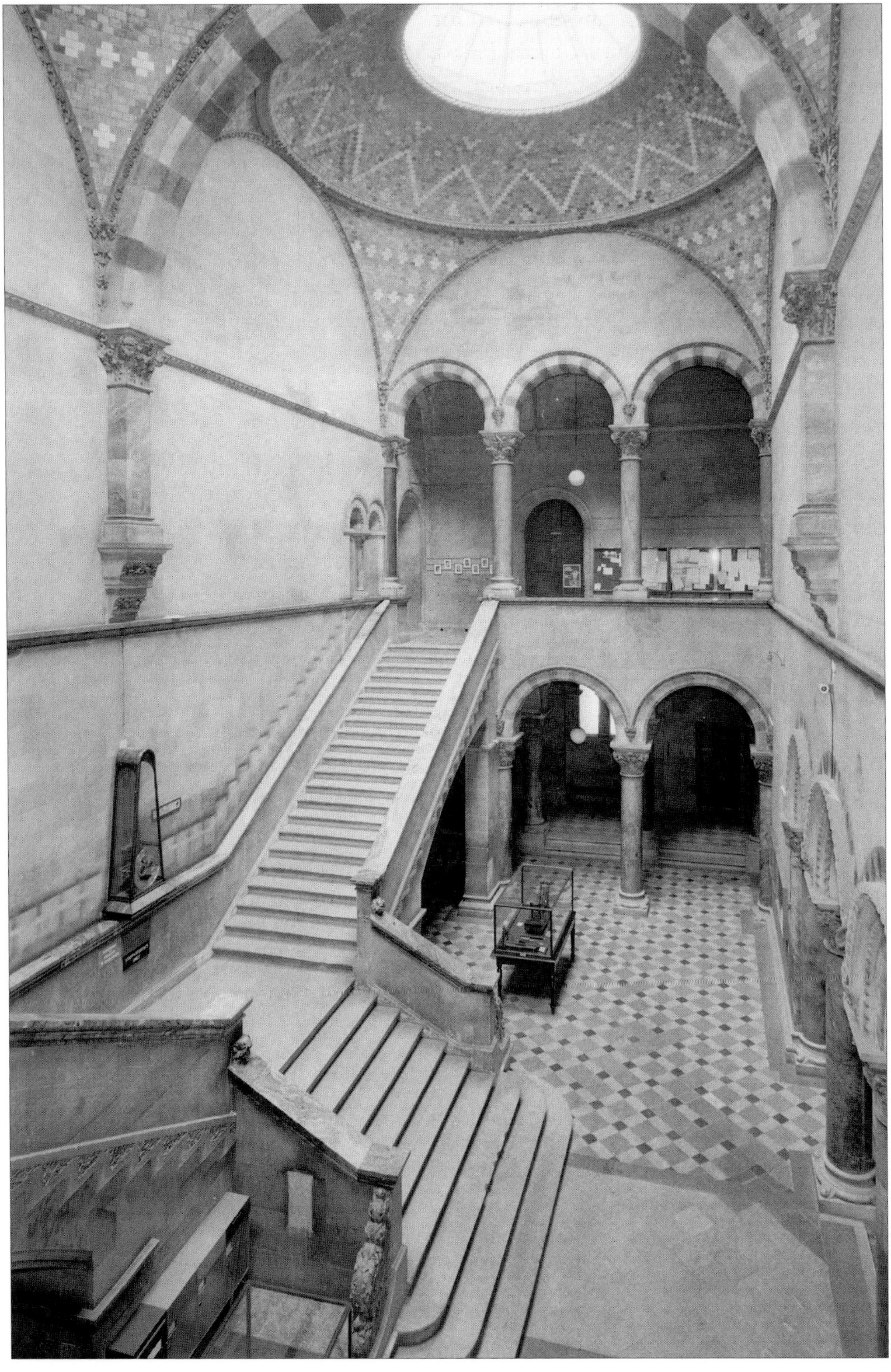

twisted rope-mouldings on the corners, also come from Venice. Ruskin had described the Palazzo Dario and Casa Visetti as belonging to the Venetian Byzantine revival of c.1480–1520.[8]

The polychromy of the staircase hall, whose domes look Byzantine, is also Ruskinian. Enamelled bricks are used, and the mostly Irish marbles have a didactic aim. The carving is naturalistic, especially on the 108 capitals. The *Builder* reported that their design was left to the workmen, of whom the most notable were James and John O'Shea, under the direction of Mr Roe of Lambeth.[9]

It has sometimes been suggested that Ruskin may have been directly involved in the design of the Dublin Museum. However, between May and October 1854 he was travelling on the Continent, after his wife Effie left him. He probably only heard about the Museum on his return, by which time building was under way. In May 1855 the Irish poet William Allingham wrote to Rossetti, telling him that he had visited the Museum, which was 'after Ruskin's heart. Ruskin has written to the architect ... expressing his high approval of the plans; so by and by all your cognoscenti will be rushing over to examine the stones of Dublin'.[10] Rossetti replied, 'the building you saw in Dublin is *the* one'.[11] While Allingham was in Dublin, Rossetti had met Woodward in Oxford, and thought him 'a particularly nice fellow'. He continued: 'Miss S[iddal] made several lovely designs for him, but Ruskin thought them too good for his workmen at Dublin to carve'.[12]

In a letter of April 1856, Woodward said that he wanted Ruskin to see the Museum.[13] However, he did not visit Ireland until August 1861 (invited by the La Touches), by which time Woodward was dead. He did not like Dublin – 'it joins the filth of Manchester to the gloom of Modena'.[14] But he wrote to his father that the Museum was 'quite the noblest thing ever done from my teaching'.[15] There is then no evidence for any direct involvement in its conception on the part of Ruskin.[16]

The crucial figure in the building of the Oxford University Museum was H.W. Acland, who has already been mentioned.[17] It has recently been suggested that his role has

Opposite:
Museum Building, Trinity College, Dublin: staircase hall (Country Life *Picture Library*).

been overestimated, but it is undeniable that he was the most important person in establishing its architectural form. He and various others submitted a memorandum in 1847 which urged the erection of a building to house the scientific teaching and collections of the University, followed in 1849 by a memorial to Convocation (the University's governing body). Since 1845 Acland had been Reader in Medicine, and in 1851 he became Professor of Clinical Medicine, and also the Radcliffe Librarian (who was responsible for the University's scientific books). In 1857 he was appointed as Regius Professor of Medicine, and in 1884 he was knighted. He was one of the earliest members of the Oxford Architectural Society, the champions of Gothic. He was also an amateur painter.

Professor Ruskin and Sir Henry Acland, Bart.: a photograph taken at Brantwood in 1893 by Acland's daughter, Sarah (*H. W. Acland and J. Ruskin, The Oxford Museum, 5th Edition, 1893*).

As a result of the 1849 memorial, a delegacy was appointed. In 1850 the local architect H. J. Underwood estimated that the proposed building would cost £50,000. In 1853-4 a site in the Parks was bought. Meanwhile suggestions were being made about the design. A pamphlet by J. H. Parker recommended the 'Old English' style, while in 1853 G. E. Street published one with the title *An Urgent Plea for the Revival of True Principles of Architecture in the Public Buildings of the University of Oxford* which included a sketch of a building in 14th-century English Gothic. Street shared the opinion of Pugin and others that the choice of a Classical style for the University's most recent important building, the Taylorian and Randolph Building (now the Ashmolean Museum), was a mistake.

In April 1854 a delegacy was appointed to choose a design: it included Acland and John Phillips, Deputy Reader in Geology and Keeper of the Ashmolean Museum. A competition was set up. The cost must not (despite Underwood's estimate) exceed £30,000. The building was to be 'of two storeys in height, in the form of three sides of a quadrangle, and the area covered in by a glass roof; the fourth side being so adapted as to admit of extension of the building at some future period'. The rules also provided a detailed schedule, to include a library, and detached curator's house, chemical laboratory, and dissecting rooms. This suggested an irregular scheme, but nothing was laid down about style. The idea of the glass roof came from Philip Pusey, brother of the Rev. E. B. Pusey, who is said to have been inspired by railway stations such as Euston. It will be noted that the use of iron was not specified, but the railway parallel suggests that it was in people's minds.

How far was Ruskin involved? He and Acland had become friends as undergraduates at Christ Church. He intended to lecture at Oxford 'On the uses of Gothic' in June 1853, presumably to support Acland's preference for Gothic, but he was too tired. In May 1854 he left England (as mentioned above). His marriage was annulled in July. At the end of September he returned, and intended to go to Oxford 'about Acland's Museum' on 14 October. This was the date set for submission of drawings: presumably Acland wanted him to see them.

On 19 October Ruskin wrote to Mrs Acland: 'As for the plans, it is no use troubling myself about them, because they certainly won't build a Gothic Museum, and if they would I haven't the workmen to do it yet, and I mean to give my whole strength, which is not more than I want, to teaching the workmen'.[18] Nevertheless, he did spend several days in Oxford at the time of the preliminary judging: 33 designs were put on display in November, and a shortlist of six was made by the Delegacy. Philip Hardwick (1792-1870), a distinguished architect who in the same year was awarded the Gold Medal of the RIBA, was appointed adjudicator. Of the

Opposite: design by Edward Middleton Barry ('*Fiat Justitia*') for the Oxford University Museum (*RIBA Library Drawings Collection*).

six designs, four were by architects who have not been identified, and do not appear to survive. Their styles were described as Italian, Jacobean, Roman and Belgian Gothic. The remaining two were the 'Rhenish Gothic' of '*Nisi Dominus*' (Deane and Woodward), and the 'Palladian' of '*Fiat Justitia*' (Edward Middleton Barry). Hardwick (who acted in association with his son Philip Charles) thought that none could be built for £30,000, though '*Fiat Justitia*' came closest.

Convocation was due to meet on 12 December. On the previous day Acland circulated a pamphlet under the pseudonym '*ergates*', arguing for Gothic. On the same day, Ruskin wrote to him. He told him that a few days before, when about to lecture at the Architectural Museum, he had happened to see Hardwick, and quizzed him. He asked whether he had taken into account the cost of the sculpture groups in 'F.J.'. Hardwick said he had not. Ruskin pointed out that the stonework of 'F.J.' must be more costly than that of 'N.D.'. While they were talking, G. G. Scott ('the architect of Camberwell and other good Gothic churches') came up, and also quizzed Hardwick about the point. Hardwick had to admit that they were right, but claimed that 'F.J.' saved money by using three storeys – which, said Ruskin, was against the competition rules.[19]

He asked Acland to point this out to the Delegates (though it may have been too late for them to take note of it), and to tell them that 'though I do not like Italian designs in general, I have had more opportunities of studying those at Venice by the greatest masters – Sanmicheli, Sansovino, and Palladio, than many architects have, and that F.J. is one of the most commonplace and contemptible imitations of those masters I have ever seen'.[20] He added a postcript: 'I ought to add that I think N.D., though by no means a first rate design, yet quite as good as is likely to be got in these days and on the whole good'.[21]

On 12 December, Convocation voted for 'N.D.'. Ruskin wrote to Acland the same evening: 'I have just received your telegraphic message from Woodward, and am going to thank God for it and lie down to sleep. It means much, I think, both to you and to me.'[22] It is not known for certain when

·TRANSVERSE SECTION·

Ruskin first met Woodward, but it was presumably about this time. Rossetti wrote in 1861 that he first met him 'at dinner at Ruskin's ... about the end of 1854'.[23] In an undated letter to Acland, Ruskin wrote: 'The great good of this matter is that Mr Woodward is evidently a person who will allow of suggestion and is glad of help – though better able himself to do without either than most'.[24] What remains to be discovered is what form this 'help' took. A clue is given in a letter Ruskin wrote one month after the result was announced to Lady Trevelyan: 'The main thing is – Acland has got his museum – Gothic – the architect is a friend of mine – I can do whatever I like with it – and if we don't have capitals & archivolts! – & expect the architect here to day – I shall get all the pre-Raphaelites to design one – each an archivolt and some capitals – & we will have all the plants in England and all the monsters in the museum'.[25]

On 18 December Sir Thomas Deane wrote to Acland's father in effusive style (not for nothing was he known as 'Blatherum'): 'Your high-minded, energetic and talented son Dr Acland of course knew not who were the architects of *Nisi Dominus*. I am thus doubly proud that he was one of its anxious supporters, merit alone leading him in his opinion ...

I know I shall have a continuance of your affection and countenance, and that in England (and particularly in Oxford) you will say that hitherto I have had your confidence and support' (the last word is crossed out and replaced with 'friendship').[26] Was this true? There is no real evidence, and opinions differ. O'Dwyer thinks that Deane and Woodward were 'personally briefed' by Acland.[27] Certainly it is true that Acland produced a letter from 'the author of N.D.' for the Delegates on 4 December, but this is hardly conclusive.

Unfortunately the competition drawings for the Museum do not survive, although some tracings exist in Toronto which seem to be earlier than the other known drawings.[28] There are differences in the plan, and there are extra dormers in the conical towers and on the south roof, but the main elevation is as on the contract drawings of February 1855, which do survive.[29] The contract was placed in May 1855. The design had already been 'improved' by February 1855, as well as having changes made to the planning, as requested. For example, the east elevation was simplified, and buttresses

Contract drawing for the west elevation of the Museum, dated 21 February 1855. The position of the stair-turret on the tower is shown as changed. The buttresses were later omitted (*Oxford University Archives, UM/P/3/5*: by permission of the Keeper of Archives, University of Oxford).

were added. Ruskin may possibly have been consulted by Woodward about these. We know that Woodward often visited him in 1855, because Dr F. J. Furnivall says that he frequently met him there.[30] However, the only letter of Ruskin's surviving from the period (28 March, to Lady Trevelyan) does not give much help: 'It is not *certain* yet that Woodward has it – depends still on confirmation by convocation till it is sure – I do not trouble my head much about the matter – as soon as it is secure to Woodward I will set to work upon various monstrosities to his advantage'.[31] Clearly Ruskin is thinking mostly of decoration, but another letter, probably written about the middle of 1855, to Mrs Carlyle, is certainly puzzling: 'I have also designed and drawn a window for the Museum at Oxford; and have every now and then had to look over a parcel of five or six new designs for fronts and backs to the said Museum'.[32] 'Fronts and backs' sound like elevations. O'Dwyer argues that the competition design did not show much advance from the Cork Town Hall design, but that the revisions introduced more specifically Italian Gothic features.[33]

At the February meeting, Deane (who was there with Woodward) volunteered various alterations, including the elimination of the stair-towers (one wonders how the upper floors would have been reached), and a masonry structure for the court like the 'mosque of Cordova' . He was perhaps thinking of the roof of the staircase hall at the Dublin Museum. It was a strange suggestion to make when the Delegates had just been admiring Woodward's design for the iron roof. O'Dwyer thinks that Ruskin might have suggested the change, as a way of avoiding the use of iron, but it seems much more likely that it was mere 'blathering' by Deane.

In January 1855 Lucas Brothers had offered to carry out the works for £30,000. Tenders were received in April: theirs was for £29,041, and was approved. The foundation stone was laid on 20 June. Further alterations were made to the designs in 1856: drawings in Woodward's sketch-books (at the National Gallery of Ireland) relate to these. For example, the detached Chemistry Laboratory was made less like its model, the Abbot's Kitchen at Glastonbury. It will be best to take the various elements of the building separately.

Porch

The first design showed double doors below tracery, with a seated figure within a quatrefoil, and another figure over the arch within a crocketed gable. Woodward's estimate of March 1856 included 'preparing jambs for ... statues'. Acland said that the design was based on Chartres, but in April the Delegacy asked for something less ecclesiastical.[34] The new design is shown on the engraved views: big pinnacles flank the gable; there are no statues; and the porch projects further than on the contract drawing.[35] In March 1857 Rossetti

Design for decoration of entrance porch, *c.*1860. Adam and Eve are depicted at the base of the arch (one on each side). At the top is an angel bearing the open book of nature in one hand, and three living cells in the other (*Oxford University Museum*).

Engraving by J. H. Le Keux, c.1858, showing the Museum as built, apart from the porch, for which this is the second design (*Oxford University Archives*).

wrote that he had promised to design sculpture for the 'arched doorway to the street'.[36] However, in May 1858 Convocation rejected the projecting porch. Later John Hungerford Pollen was asked to design decoration for the doorway, with Thomas Woolner as sculptor and designer of the figurative sculpture. In September 1858 Woolner wrote to Woodward suggesting 'the Tree of Knowledge as exhibited in the Temptation and Expulsion'.[37] Pollen's design survives in the Museum.[38] Ruskin wrote to Woodward that 'nice pretty Eve always makes a good bas-relief', and suggested, for example, the inclusion of the Four Evangelists and figures of Life and Death – suggestions not likely to have been welcomed.[39] In his diary for 1861 William Michael Rossetti wrote that Woolner told him that 'Ruskin had compelled a carver he had sent down to discontinue carving a figure by Pollen ... on the ground of its being sensual'.[40] It is interesting that in his 'Second Letter' to Acland (January 1859), Ruskin still emphasised the importance of the porch, and the inclusion of portrait sculpture.[41]

Polychromy

The contract drawings give no indication of polychromy. All the same, it began to appear, in the form of coloured stonework. The first examples, dating to March 1856, are some red voussoirs in the court arcade. In October Woodward proposed to introduce bands of coloured stone on the façade. The Curator's House was redesigned at this point, although it was not begun until March 1857. It has polychromy on the ground floor, which causes O'Dwyer to wonder whether, had the Museum façade not already reached above this height, it too might have had polychromy there as well as on the upper floors. In August and September Woodward had visited Venice, in connection with the Government Offices competition, and that might have influenced him. It is noteworthy too that Gilbert Scott's design

Design for a balcony at the Museum by John Ruskin (Works, 16, plate xii). The drawing (one of ten) then belonged to Sarah Acland: she bequeathed them to the Ashmolean Museum, Oxford.

for the Hamburg Rathaus, which seems to have been contemporary with the Museum design, had polychrome voussoirs: it was illustrated in the *Builder* in February 1856.[42] Furthermore, William Butterfield's new chapel for Balliol College, with its bands of red and cream stone, was begun in the same year.

Decoration

The 1855 contract made no provision for carving or decoration, and so a Special Fund was set up in June 1855. This was exclusively for stonework, of three types – column shafts representing British rocks; capitals illustrating flora; and statues of scientists. The letter which Ruskin sent to Lady Trevelyan just after the competition result was announced has already been quoted. In 1855 he wrote to Acland that he hoped

> to be able to get Millais and Rossetti to design flower and beast borders – crocodiles and various vermin – such as you are particularly fond of ... and we will carve them and inlay them with serpentine all about your windows. I will pay for a good deal myself, and I doubt not to find funds. *Such* capitals as we will have![43]

Similar carvings from Rouen Cathedral had been illustrated in *The Seven Lamps*.[44] One can also compare the design for a window made at Glenfinlas in 1853 by Millais and Ruskin.[45]

In January 1854 Ruskin told Rossetti that there would be 'interior decoration'.[46] In July 1855 Woodward asked him and Lizzie Siddal to make some designs for carving, but they did nothing.[47] Clearly Rossetti was thinking of painted decoration. He was asked to do a mural of 'Newton gathering pebbles on the shore of the Ocean of Truth', but this did not suit him.[48] However, he did get to do a mural for Woodward at his Union Society Debating Hall the next year. The only murals carried out at the Museum were by the Rev. Richard St John Tyrwhitt, the Vicar of St Mary Magdalen, Oxford, and an admirer of Ruskin (who wrote a preface to his *Christian Art and Symbolism*, published in 1872).[49]

In a letter to Acland (undated, but possibly of mid-1855),

Ruskin wrote that he thought it better to decorate the outside, rather than the inside: 'my main principle being simple life, and richly bestowed public joy'. In any case, the interior of a museum did not need decoration. He offered £300 towards the cost, but wanted to set aside £30 'for a particular fancy of my own ... £30 worth of traceried balcony put before a couple of those upper windows'. Some of his designs survive.[50] This may well have been one of those suggestions by Ruskin which, the Rev. W. Tuckwell tells us, Woodward 'smilingly put by'.[51]

In the same letter, Ruskin says that his father will give £70 for a statue of Bacon by Alexander Munro, to go in the porch. Later he heard that the Queen had promised Bacon, and said that his father would give Hippocrates instead, but only if he were to go with the other 'ancients' 'in the Gothic porch, under niches, so as to help the architecture'.[52] This refers to the proposal in the 1855 Special Fund prospectus for six 'ancients' in the porch and eleven 'moderns' in the court. The porch was dropped in 1858 (see above), but Ruskin's father gave Hippocrates all the same, and by 1859 it was placed in the court. Ruskin approved of the 'series of noble statues'.[53]

Statue of Hippocrates by Alexander Munro, in the Museum court. It was a gift of John Ruskin senior (*Peter Howell*).

In October 1855 Ruskin wrote to the Secretary of the Delegates: 'If Mr Woodward will undertake that the capitals in the inside shall be decorated with floral sculpture, I wish all my contribution to be spent in decorating the external windows of the façade – or porch of the same as Mr Woodward thinks best'.[54] The interior carving will be dealt with first.

Interior carving

Woodward wanted to use the O'Sheas, but Ruskin feared that they would not be up to the job. Photographs of their work were sent to convince him.[55] The scheme for botanical specimens was devised by John Phillips. The O'Sheas did not like to copy drawings, which meant that Ruskin's notion of Pre-Raphaelite designs would not have suited them.[56] Instead they went every day to the Botanic Garden to collect plants. This was after Ruskin's heart. In January 1858, in giving one of the O'Sheas a prize in a sculptural competition at the Architectural Museum, he described him as 'a most skilful carver, [who] had executed many lovely cornices' (a curious term).[57] By June 1858, six capitals and twelve corbels on the lower west side had been done. Carving continued until 1861, and some of the carvers can be identified.

Capital representing 'British Ferns', carved by James O'Shea, and engraved by J. H. Le Keux from a photograph (*frontispiece to* The Oxford Museum).

In his 'Second Letter' of January 1859, Ruskin wrote about the fern capital (an engraving of which appeared as the frontispiece to Acland's book on the Museum): 'Your museum at Oxford is literally the first building raised in England since the close of the 15th century which has fearlessly put to new trial the old faith in nature, and in the genius of the unassisted workman, who gathered out of nature the materials he needed. I am entirely glad, therefore, that you have decided on engraving for publication one of O'Shea's capitals; it will be a complete type of the whole work, in its inner meaning, and far better to show one of them in its completeness, than to give any reduced sketch of the building. Nevertheless, beautiful as that capital is, and as

Window on the ground floor of the west elevation of the Museum, carved in November 1859 after a design by John Ruskin (*Architect*, 7 (1872), p. 226).

all the rest of O'Shea's work is likely to be, it is not yet perfect Gothic sculpture; and it might give rise to dangerous error, if the admiration given to these carvings were unqualified'.[58] With regard to this criticism, it is worth reading the perceptive analysis by John Unrau in his *Looking at Architecture with Ruskin*.[59] He compares an Oxford capital with capitals at St Mark's, Venice, arguing that the Oxford one is not properly integrated into an organic whole.

Exterior carving

When Lucas Brothers' contract was terminated in October 1858, little had been done. This included the windows of the stair-towers: obviously the higher parts had to be done first. Their carving was praised by Ruskin in a letter to Acland of May 1858: 'as beautiful in effect as anything I know in civil Gothic,' he wrote.[60] In March 1856 Woodward was thinking of using Ruskin's donation (see above) for carving the lower windows, with some for the entrance doorway, but in the end it was mainly used to introduce shafts and to substitute cusped arches for solid tympana in the lower windows: little was left for carving, and nothing for the doorway.

As well as the designs for balconies which have already been mentioned, Ruskin made several designs for the carving of the lower windows. One of these was actually carved to his design, but not until November 1859. It was the second window to the right of the main entrance, and was illustrated in the *Architect* for 1872.[61] Ruskin probably supervised the carving of this window at least. Woodward's health was

The 'cat window' on the first floor of the west elevation of the Museum, carved by James O'Shea in 1859 (*Architect*, 7 (1872), p. 226).

breaking down. Tuberculosis ran in his family. Already in 1854, said Rossetti, he looked as if he had been 'snatched … from the very brink of the grave'.[62] In the spring of 1858 he had to go abroad, and in November Woolner told Mrs Tennyson that 'his life looks as weak as a little candle in the open air'.[63] He had to spend the winter of 1859-60 abroad, and Ruskin wrote in January: 'Mr Woodward is ill, and had to go to Madeira for the winter, and I was obliged to take the conduct of the decoration while he was away'.[64] O'Dwyer thinks this refers only to his own window, but it may refer to more. In the event, only two of the double windows on the ground floor were carved, together with the jambs of one lancet.

The carving of the upper windows did not begin until 1859. It seems that the 'cat window', above the Ruskin window, was the first to be done, suggesting that Woodward wanted a vertical sequence. The famous story about O'Shea being obliged to convert his monkeys into cats first appeared in the fifth (1893) edition of Acland's book on the Museum. The window was illustrated in the *Building News* in September 1860.[65] In 1862 James Fergusson criticised the 'strangely pre-historic attitudes' of these 'long-backed specimens'.[66] This probably explains why Ruskin spoke in a lecture at Oxford in 1870 of 'offence … taken at the unnecessary introduction of cats'.[67]

In all, five of the upper windows received carving by November 1860, though only three had their jambs carved. Ruskin wrote in November 1859 that the 'Oxford workmen work for love and their bread and cheese. Two pounds a week, and five weeks to do a window just nicely'.[68]

Roof

In February 1855 the Delegates were told that Francis Skidmore of Coventry would contract for the iron roof. Acland knew Skidmore through the Oxford Architectural Society, which the latter had joined in 1852 and to which he had read two papers.[69] There is no evidence that Skidmore had ever done any structural ironwork before. This was the meeting at which Deane suggested as an alternative a roof like the 'mosque of Cordova', as mentioned above. In July

1854 Ruskin had sent Acland his pamphlet on the Crystal Palace, writing 'You don't want your museum of glass – do you? If you do, I will have nothing to do with it'.[70] This was an odd thing to write, when the competition rules had specified glass: perhaps Ruskin (who was abroad at the time) did not know this.

O'Dwyer quotes a newly-discovered contract of 8 May 1855.[71] This allows £3,000 for the ironwork of the roof, and £1,000 for glass, to include the stone corbels and bases to the iron columns. It adds that 'should the Delegacy ... decide on having the roof executed in timber supported by stone columns and brick arches', such work should be measured and valued. O'Dwyer thinks that this refers to the 'mosque of Cordova' idea, but that has domical vaults, which do not seem to be implied here.[72] Skidmore costed Deane and Woodward's design at £5,216, but offered to build it in wrought, rather than cast, iron for only £3,100.[73] He had a passionate belief in the superiority of wrought iron, whose lightness and malleability he emphasised as particularly suited to the Gothic style. Unfortunately there is scanty evidence for the appearance of his first roof, but it had thin clusters of tubes as 'columns', tubular arches, and tubular lattice girders above.[74] In February 1858 the incomplete roof partly collapsed. In April William Fairbairn (author of *On the Application of Cast and Wrought Iron to Building Purposes* (1854), produced a report, in which he recommended the use of cast-iron for the supports, and a mixture of plate and angle iron above. Skidmore agreed to carry out the design first proposed by Woodward for the amount of the original estimate. In the second (1860) edition of *The Oxford Museum*, Acland wrote, 'some persons will probably regret that, when the new roof was erected, it was hopeless for the architects to propose, as they would have wished, the substitution of stone

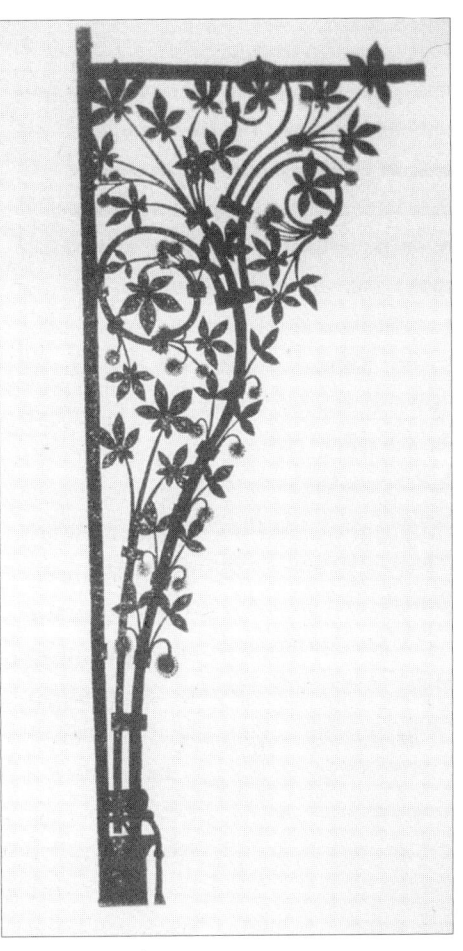

Design for a spandrel in the roof of the Museum, representing horse-chestnuts, illustrated by John Ruskin in *The Oxford Museum* (1893 edition, p. 89).

shafts, fewer in number, to support the roof'.[75] This is a puzzling remark.

What did Ruskin think about the roof? In his 'Second Letter' of 1859, he published a design for one of the spandrels. He wrote that the horse-chestnut leaf and nut 'are not ill-arranged, and produce a more agreeable effect than convolutions of the iron could have given, unhelped by reference to natural objects'. But it was not 'an absolutely good design' – it should be more conventional in treatment, and stronger in 'constructive arrangement'.[76] Cook and Wedderburn say that Ruskin made six or eight designs for 'brackets', which were photographed by Bedford Lemere, but neither the drawings nor the photographs survive.[77] It is not known whether Skidmore used them. In 1859 Acland told the Oxford Architectural Society that one piece of foliage was made of twenty-five pieces of iron, welded in different ways. Ruskin must surely have been impressed by this.[78]

The colouring of the ironwork was a complicated business. It seems that experiments were made with rich colours (e.g. green, chocolate and maroon for the ironwork, with green, purple, pink and red for the woodwork). Skidmore was very anxious about the matter, and would have agreed with Ruskin that 'all the ironwork I have ever seen look beautiful was rusty, and rusty iron will not answer modern purposes'.[79] The scheme eventually carried out must be the one criticised by the *Building News* in 1860, which said that a column 'looked very much as if it had been drawn through a river of bread-sauce, or as if some foul animal with an unwholesome tongue had licked it'.[80] Ruskin wrote to his father in January 1859: 'I've been over the Museum carefully. All the practical part excellent. All the decorative colour, vile. It is the best error to make of the two'.[81]

Brick-laying

It is often said that Ruskin tried his hand at brick-laying at the Museum. In fact, on 3 July 1857, when he was lodging in Cowley, he wrote: 'I write ... till half past twelve every day; then walk into Oxford to dine with my friend Dr Acland, and after dinner take a lesson in brick-laying. He is building a study, and I built a great bit yesterday, which the bricklayer my tutor in a most provoking manner pulled all down again. But this bit I have done today is to stand'.[82] The 'study' was a library designed by Woodward, the first extension built by Acland to his house at 40 Broad Street.[83]

The Oxford Museum was opened in June 1860 for the meeting of the British Association for the Advancement of Science, when the famous debate on evolution took place in the unfinished library. Woodward was in Oxford in December, and Mrs Acland wrote to Lady Trevelyan: 'Mr Woodward ... looks oh so ill. It is most touching to see him so gentle and uncomplaining and so changed from what he was'.[84] That winter he spent a few months on the Iles d'Hyères, setting out in May to return. Acland was preparing rooms so that he could be looked after, but he died in a hotel at Lyons on 15 May 1861.

Rossetti wrote that he had been the last person in England who saw him, when he called on his way to the station: 'It is too sad to speak or think of – such a lonely deathbed of such a man who so loved what he must leave, but he was the very soul of gentleness and doubtless of cheerful patience to the last'.[85] Four years earlier, in 1857, he had described Woodward to William Bell Scott as 'well worth knowing, but ... the stillest creature out of an oyster-shell'.[86] His personal magnetism had got him numerous jobs, in Oxford and elsewhere, within a very short time. Rossetti emphasised Woodward's dissatisfaction with many aspects of the Museum, and the antagonism he had to face, largely due to 'the presumptuous interference

Benjamin Woodward: marble portrait tondo, in Connemara marble frame, by Alexander Munro, presented to the Museum by the Memorial Committee (*Jeanne Sheehy*).

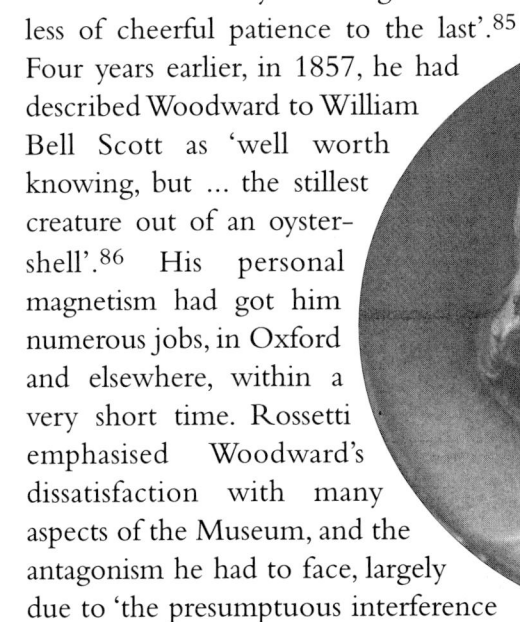

of Oxford dons'.[87] He praised his 'influence in creating artistic comprehension among his workmen', and especially the 'works of real beauty' produced by O'Shea, and claimed that he was unsurpassed by any other architect for 'poetic beauty'. Rossetti's high opinion of the man is particularly significant when one considers the close links between Ruskin and Rossetti.

Woodward's friends decided that he deserved a memorial, and a committee was formed, including Acland, Pollen, Bodley, Street, Munro, Woolner and others. Alexander Gilchrist was commissioned to write a memoir, and Ruskin – whose absence from the committee is puzzling – wrote, 'I wonder who will write a memoir of me,' suggesting W. M. Rossetti as author.[88] He continued, 'There is nothing whatever to criticise in the Oxford Museum or in this other thing [the Oxford Union]. Nothing bad and nothing good.' Unfortunately the memoir (later entrusted to F. T. Palgrave) never appeared, because of the refusal of cooperation on the part of the jealous Deanes. In the event the committee commissioned a marble tondo portrait from Alexander Munro.

After Woodward's death, Ruskin finally visited Trinity College, Dublin. In 1868 he returned to Dublin to give a lecture on 'The Mystery of Life and its Arts'. In it he said:

> Among several personal reasons which caused me to desire that I might give this, my closing lecture on the subject of art, here in Ireland, one of the chief was, that in reading it I should stand near the beautiful building – the engineers' school of your college – which was the first realisation I had the joy to see, of the principles I had, until then, been endeavouring to teach, but which, alas, is now to me no more than the richly canopied monument of one of the most earnest souls that ever gave itself to the arts, one of my truest and most loving friends, Benjamin Woodward.[89]

However, he was less enthusiastic about the Oxford Museum. In the 'Second Letter' to Acland, he complained of its 'discouraging aspect of parsimony', because it was unfinished.[90] In his first draft, he wrote that 'the Future's verdict' will be that the University 'chose the design of her Museum by chance, thwarted its development by her distrust, and carved on its facade the image of her Parsimony'. He again emphasised the importance of the exterior decoration.[91] Shortly after writing this, he told his father, 'the real fact was, I couldn't make up my mind what was the fault in the Museum'.[92]

However, his severest criticism came in 1877. His Slade Lecture has already been quoted at the beginning of this chapter. He also criticised O'Shea's work. He called him 'a man of truest genius and of the kindest nature', but said that he needed 'many years of honest learning, and he too easily thought in the pleasure of his first essays, that he had nothing to learn … I hoped he would find his way in time, but hoped, as so often, in vain'. He explained that the building was an 'experiment', and outlined the principles he and Woodward had tried to work on, but commented: 'In declaring that the material should be honestly shown, I never meant that a handsome building could be built of common brickbats, if only you showed the bricks inside as well as out [clearly a reference to the walls of the court]. And in saying that ornament should be founded on natural form, I no more meant that a mason could carve a capital by merely looking at a leaf, than that a painter could paint a Madonna by merely looking at a young lady. And when I said that the workman should be left free to design his work as he went on, I never meant that you could secure a great natural monument of art by letting loose the first lively Irishman you could get hold of to do what he liked in it.'[93]

Obviously this is grossly unfair. In the same year he wrote to the Rev. Richard St John Tyrwhitt, 'For the Museum, of course it is I – not Acland – who am answerable for it. Woodward was my pupil. I knew from the moment he allowed ironwork, it was all over with the building; nor did I ever approve the design – but it was a first effort in [the] right direction'.[94] O'Dwyer explains this by reference to the contract, with its allowance for an alternative roof of timber, stone and brick, but this does not really fit the situation: it was not up to Woodward to 'allow' an iron roof.

It is important to bear in mind that the year 1877 was only two years after the death of Rose La Touche, and

Ruskin's mental health was already shaky. He was well aware that popular opinion regarded the Museum as very much his responsibility. After so many years he could see its defects only too clearly, and his self-tormenting nature led him to apportion a larger share of blame to himself than would seem to have been justified by the actual history of the design and execution of the building.

Notes.
This chapter draws extensively on Frederick O'Dwyer, *The Architecture of Deane and Woodward* (Cork, 1997) and it seems unnecessary to provide constant references to it.

[1] O. Doughty and J. R. Wahl (editors), *Letters of Dante Gabriel Rossetti* (Oxford, 1965-7), vol. 2, p. 408.

[2] *Works*, 22, p. 523.

[3] There is no evidence that the O'Sheas, the local carvers who later worked at the Oxford Museum, were responsible.

[4] *Builder*, 10 (1852), p. 483. Deane and Woodward's design is illustrated by O'Dwyer on pp. 122, 125-6.

[5] A separate museum was built later, and the building now houses only lecture-rooms.

[6] *Works*, 9, p. 33; *Builder*, 9 (1851), p. 202.

[7] *Builder*, 19 (1861), p. 436: see also 9 (1851), p. 331, 11 (1853), p. 420.

[8] *Works*, 11, p. 20.

[9] *Builder*, 12 (1854), p. 425.

[10] G. B. Hill (editor), *Letters of Dante Gabriel Rossetti to William Allingham* (London, 1897), p. 146.

[11] Doughty and Wahl [note 1], vol. 1, p. 257.

[12] Ibid. He said that nevertheless one design was used – 'an angel with some children', 'near' one designed by Millais showing mice eating corn. Neither can be identified, though one capital shows squirrels eating corn.

[13] Oxford University Museum Archives (at the Museum), HBM 1/3.

[14] *Works*, 36, p. 383.

[15] Van Akin Burd, *John Ruskin and Rose La Touche* (Oxford, 1979), p. 62.

[16] O'Dwyer (p. 143) guesses that he may have been concerned with a proposal for painted decoration of the domes, but there is no evidence.

[17] On the Museum, see Robert Fox in *History of the University of Oxford*, 6 (Oxford, 1997), pp. 641-91; Peter Howell, ibid., 7 (2000), pp. 739-41; Carla Yanni, *Nature and Museums* (London, 1999).

[18] Bodleian Library, Ms Acland d.72, fol. 39.

[19] Ibid., fols. 44-5. O'Dwyer makes surprisingly little of this letter. Ruskin is referring to the cellars as the 'third storey'.

[20] It is interesting that he mentions Sanmicheli first. Compare his letter to Lady Trevelyan of September 1854: 'I want to have a black hole …

filled with Claudes, and Sir Charles Barry's architecture' (V. Surtees, *Reflections of a Friendship* (London, 1979), p. 88).
21 The caution is typically Ruskinian.
22 Ms Acland d.72, fol. 41.
23 Doughty and Wahl [note 1], vol. 2, p. 405.
24 Ms Acland d.72, fols. 43-4.
25 Surtees [note 20], pp. 94-5.
26 Ms Acland d.71, fols. 7-8.
27 O'Dwyer, p. 173.
28 Archives of Ontario, Horwood Collection, 1655 (1-5).
29 University of Oxford Archives, UM/P/3/1-7. The elevation of the principal front is illustrated in the Tate exhibition catalogue, *Ruskin, Turner and the Pre-Raphaelites* (London, 2000), p. 108.
30 *Works* 16, p. xlvi.
31 Surtees [note 20], p. 98.
32 *Works* 5, pp. xlix-l.
33 O'Dwyer, p. 178.
34 Ms Acland d.95, fol. 4.
35 For example, an engraving by J. H. Le Keux, illustrated by O'Dwyer on p. 189.
36 Doughty and Wahl [note 1], vol. 1, p. 322.
37 Bodleian Library Ms Acland d.95, fol. 62.
38 Illustrated in the Tate catalogue [note 29], p. 112.
39 Ms English Letters c.33, fols. 157-8.
40 W. M. Rossetti, *Ruskin: Rossetti: Pre-Raphaelitism* (London, 1899), p. 283.
41 H. W. Acland and J. Ruskin, *The Oxford Museum* (London, 1893), pp. 78-81.
42 *Builder*, 14 (1856), p. 63.
43 Ms Acland d.72, fol. 43.
44 *Works*, 8, p. 216.
45 Mary Lutyens, *Millais and the Ruskins* (London, 1967), p. 147; T. Hilton, *The Pre-Raphaelites* (London, 1970), p. 75.
46 Letter in the John Rylands Library, Manchester, Rylands English Ms 1254/16.
47 W. M. Rossetti [note 40], pp. 47-8.
48 R. Glynn Grylls, *Portrait of Rossetti* (London, 1964), p. 64.
49 *Builder*, 17 (1859), p. 401.
50 Ms Acland d.72, fols. 75-6. Ten drawings which Ruskin gave to Acland's daughter are in the Ashmolean Museum.
51 W. Tuckwell, *Reminiscences of Oxford* (London, 1900), p. 49.
52 Ms Acland d.72, fol. 85.
53 Acland and Ruskin [note 41], p. 77.
54 Ms Acland d.72, fol. 66.
55 Now in the University Museum Archives.
56 W. Minto (editor), *Autobiographical Notes of the Life of William Bell Scott*

(London, 1892), vol. 2, p. 38.

[57] *Building News,* 4 (1858), p. 93: *Works,* 16, p. lix.

[58] Acland and Ruskin [note 41], pp. 83-4.

[59] J. Unrau, *Looking at Architecture with Ruskin* (London, 1978), p. 130.

[60] Ms Acland d.72, fol. 83.

[61] *Architect,* 7 (1872), p. 226. Ruskin's watercolour design (in Birmingham Art Gallery) is illustrated in the Tate catalogue [note 29], p. 110.

[62] Doughty and Wahl [note 1], vol. 2, p. 405.

[63] Amy Woolner, *Thomas Woolner, R.A.* (London, 1917), p. 156.

[64] V. Surtees, *Sublime and Instructive* (London 1972), p. 223.

[65] Pp. 107-8; *Building News,* 6 (1860), p. 715. See also C. L. Eastlake, *A History of the Gothic Revival* (London, 1872), p. 284; *Architect,* 7 (1872), p. 226.

[66] J. Fergusson, *History of the Modern Styles of Architecture* (London, 1862), p. 328. See also Acland and Ruskin, [note 41], pp. 105-6.

[67] *Works,* 20, p. 292.

[68] V. Surtees [note 64], p. 222.

[69] Election on 16 June 1852: *Oxford Architectural Society Reports of Meetings from January 1851 to July 1853,* p. 73. He read a paper on metalwork on 22 February 1854, and one on warming churches on 22 March 1854 (*OAS Reports of Meetings from July 1853 to May 31 1856,* pp. 34-5, 37-9). On Skidmore see Peter Howell, 'Francis Skidmore and the Metalwork', in Chris Brooks (editor), *The Albert Memorial* (London, 2000), p. 252-85.

[70] Ms Acland d.72, fol. 37c.

[71] Oxford University Museum Archives, HBM 1/2.

[72] O'Dwyer, pp. 258-60.

[73] Oxford University Museum Archives, HBM 1/3.

[74] See: (1) the lithograph accompanying the Special Fund prospectus of June 1855, illustrated by O'Dwyer on p. 215; (2) the engraving in the *Builder,* 13 (1855), p. 318 (O'Dwyer, p. 259); (3) also (possibly) the watercolour design for murals, at the Museum (O'Dwyer, p. 217).

[75] H. W. Acland and J. Ruskin, *The Oxford Museum* (2nd edition, 1860), p. 16.

[76] Acland and Ruskin [note 41], p. 88.

[77] *Works,* 16, p. xlvi.

[78] *Oxford Architectural Society Reports of Meetings* (1856-9), p. 55. Eastlake, however, disapproved of fixing applied wrought-iron decoration to cast-iron capitals (*Gothic Revival* [note 65], pp. 285-6).

[79] *Works,* 16, p. 423.

[80] *Building News,* 6 (1860), p. 273: see also *Builder,* 17 (1859), p. 401.

[81] *Works,* 16, p. lii.

[82] Quoted in E. T. Cook, *The Life of John Ruskin* (London, 1911), vol.1, p. 447.

[83] On it see O'Dwyer, pp. 507-11. The house was demolished in the 1930s to make way for the New Bodleian Library.

[84] University of Newcastle upon Tyne, Trevelyan Papers, WCT 70.

85 Doughty and Wahl [note 1], vol. 2, p. 407.
86 Ibid., vol. 1, p. 322.
87 Ibid., vol. 2, p. 408. Rossetti made a drawing of 'Sir Galahad and the Angel', apparently in 1857, which was also known as 'Alma Mater and Mr Woodward'. It is supposed to be a satire on the University's treatment of Woodward, whose head the knight bears (illustrated by O'Dwyer, p. 308; also in V. Surtees, *The Paintings and Drawings of D. G. Rossetti* (Oxford, 1971), plate 128, with p. 55).
88 Ms Acland d.72, fol. 93.
89 *Works,* 18, pp. 149-50.
90 Acland and Ruskin [note 41], p. 74.
91 *Works,* 16, p. 227 note 1.
92 Ibid., p. lxii.
93 Ibid., 22, pp. 524-5.
94 Quoted by M. W. Brooks, *Ruskin and Victorian Architecture* (London, 1989), pp. 127-8, from J. W. Claiborne, 'Two Secretaries: The Letters of John Ruskin to Charles Augustus Howell and the Revd Richard St John Tyrwhitt' (unpublished PhD thesis, University of Texas at Austin, 1969), pp. 345-6.

3
Ruskin and the English House

Fisher Street through to English Street, Carlisle by John Ruskin. © Brantwood Trust

Ruskin and the English House

Geoffrey Tyack

RUSKIN'S INFLUENCE on English domestic architecture has been widely acknowleged ever since the 1850s. Suburban villas in south London, north Oxford and elsewhere have often been described as 'Ruskinian', and many writers have seen Ruskin's shadow lurking behind the houses of Philip Webb and the Arts and Crafts architects who followed him, not to mention the first Garden Cities and, by extension, the whole English tradition of 20th-century suburban planning. The precise nature of Ruskin's influence on these very diverse phenomena will always be a matter for debate. His scattered and sporadic writings on the English house are an expression of the extraordinary diversity of his interests and the strangely obsessive, quixotic nature of his personality. But, when taken together, they constitute a radical critique of the domestic architecture of his time, and it is this which both inspired his contemporaries and disciples, and challenges modern readers over a century after his death.

Ruskin's attitude to domestic architecture was deeply influenced by his own upbringing in London. He was born in a plain brick house, 54 Hunter Street, on the Skinners' Company estate to the north of Brunswick Square, Bloomsbury, developed after 1809 by James Burton, and typical of countless terraced houses built for the commercial and professional classes from which Ruskin's parents came.[1] In 1823 the family joined the growing middle-class exodus to the suburbs and settled at 27 Herne Hill, four miles south of the river. This was a hilly area, still semi-rural but experiencing ribbon development alongside the roads leading to the City and West End via the recently constructed bridges over the Thames. Judging from a view of *c.*1830 the houses on Herne Hill represented a chaotic mixture of fashionable styles.[2] But the Ruskins' house, which has since been demolished, was a plain semi-detached brick villa of a kind which can still be seen on the fringes of most English towns. For the young Ruskin, the charm lay not so much in the architecture

House in Fisher Street, looking towards English Street, Carlisle, drawing by Ruskin 1837. This accomplished drawing of a late-medieval timber-framed merchant's house shows the influence of Samuel Prout on the young Ruskin. Ruskin later singled out features such as the detailing around the doorway and on the upper floors in *The Seven Lamps of Architecture* as exemplars for modern urban shops and houses (*Ruskin Foundation, Ruskin Library, University of Lancaster*).

27 Herne Hill, drawing by Arthur Severn: Ruskin lived here from the age of four to 23 (*Ruskin Foundation, Ruskin Library, University of Lancaster*).

as in the proximity of unspoilt but domesticated countryside. The house, 'three-storied, with garrets above, commanded ... a very notable view from its garret windows ... It had front and back garden in sufficient proportion to its size; the front, richly set with old evergreens, and well-grown lilac and laburnum; the back, seventy yards long by twenty wide, renowned over all the hill for its pears and apples ... and possessing also a strong old mulberry tree, a tall white-heart cherry tree, a black Kentish one, and an almost unbroken hedge, all round'.[3] In 1842 the family moved to a larger, detached classical villa in Denmark Hill, a short distance to the north, and in this three-storied brick box, with its large garden – now a public park – Ruskin spent most of the next 30 years.[4]

Some of Ruskin's later architectural preoccupations grew out of his early memories of London's semi-rural suburban fringe. Among the places which 'formed [his] instincts' as a child was Croydon, then a small market town ten miles south

The Ruskins' house in Denmark Hill, drawing by Arthur Severn. This was John Ruskin's home from 1842 until 1871, when he moved to Brantwood. Its site can be identified in the present Ruskin Park (Ruskin Foundation, Ruskin Library, University of Lancaster).

of London, where his aunt lived, and in an unpublished part of his autobiography, *Praeterita,* he recalled 'Market Street … and its lovely rough wooden pump with rude stones round it and tiled cottage roofs. Thence all my steady love of cottages, lattices, littlenesses, roughnesses, humilities – to this day – so that I am never at ease in a fine house, nor happy among anything proud or polished'.[5] But his first concrete memory was of seeing Derwentwater from Friar's Crag in the Lake District at the age of five in 1824, and in 1830, when he was eleven, he spent three weeks in the Lakes with his parents. Other summer trips took him to Scotland, Wales and the Peak District: all of them parts of a well-trodden tourist itinerary which can be traced back to the second half of the 18th century. In these highland districts, with their pastoral economy, he could observe a world in which men and women lived in harmony with nature, a harmony echoed in the stone-built houses which seemed to grow organically out of the hills themselves. His parents also introduced him to ruined abbeys and castles, and he returned to draw some of them in later years, though he subsequently wrote that 'it was probably much happier to live in a small house, and have

House in Market Street, Croydon, Surrey, drawing by Ruskin. Croydon was swallowed up into the southern suburbs of London during Ruskin's lifetime, and this house has long since vanished. (*Birmingham Museums and Art Gallery: reproduced as the frontispiece to Ruskin's* Works, 1, *by permission of the Bodleian Library, Oxford*).

Warwick Castle to be astonished at, than to live in Warwick Castle and have nothing to be astonished at'.[6]

It was the relationship between domestic architecture and its human and natural environment which Ruskin sought to bring out in *The Poetry of Architecture*, a series of essays published while he was an undergraduate at Oxford. The publisher was the energetic Scotsman John Claudius Loudon, who had in many respects taken on the landscape-gardening mantle of Humphry Repton, adapting his insights to the smaller gardens of the prosperous middle classes and publishing them in a series of prolix works of which the most celebrated is the *Encyclopedia of Cottage, Farm and Villa Architecture* (1833).[7] Ruskin was introduced to Loudon by his father, and Loudon published the first piece of Ruskin's prose in his

Magazine of Natural History in 1834. *The Poetry of Architecture* came out as a a series of essays in Loudon's short-lived *Architectural Magazine* from 1837 until it ceased publication in 1839. Ruskin's essays were not published separately until 1873, and then only in the U.S.A. The first British edition did not appear until 1893, when the author was in his dotage. The interest of the essays lies therefore not in their immediate influence, which was negligible, but on the light they throw on the development of Ruskin's ideas on architecture.

The subtitle of *The Poetry of Architecture* was 'The Architecture of the Nations of Europe considered in its

The hall of Haddon Hall, Derbyshire, drawing by Ruskin dated 29 August 1838 (*Works*, 2, facing p. 284). Built by the Vernon family, 'kings of the Peak', in the 14th and 15th centuries, and subsequently extended by the Earls of Rutland, Haddon was and is one of the best-preserved medieval houses in England. The roof shown in Ruskin's drawing is not the original, and was replaced by a more substantial roof designed by Harold Breakspear in 1923-5. Ruskin visited Haddon on at least three occasions in the 1830s and wrote a poem about it on his first visit (*Bodleian Library, Oxford*).

association with Natural Scenery and National Character'. Here Ruskin alluded to two of the chief preoccupations of his age: the influence of landscape on human emotions, and the importance of nationality, and national history, on social habits and individual identity. These influences, Ruskin argued, had shaped the architecture of the past, but the breakdown of accustomed social ties and the spread of rampant individualism had made enlightened patronage difficult, if not impossible: the

> power [of patronage] is generally diffused. Every citizen may box himself up in as barbarous a tenement as suits his taste or inclination; the architect is his vassal, and must permit him, not only to criticise, but to perpetrate. The palace or the nobleman's seat may be raised in good taste, and become the admiration of a nation; but the influence of the owner is terminated by the boundary of his estate: he has no command over the adjacent scenery, and the possessor of every thirty acres around him has him at his mercy. The streets of our cities are examples of the effects of this clashing of different tastes; and they are either remarkable for the utter absence of all attempt at embellishment, or disgraced by every variety of abomination.[8]

The result was stylistic chaos, with 'Swiss cottages falsely and calumniously so entitled, dropped in the brick-fields round the metropolis; and we have staring, square-windowed flat-roofed gentlemen's seats, of the lath and plaster, mock-magnificent, Regent's Park description, rising on the woody promontaries of Derwent Water'.[9] Ruskin's tone here recalls that of Pugin, whose *Contrasts* had appeared a year before in 1836. But at this stage he did not share Pugin's interest in the minutiae of medieval architecture, still less his Roman Catholicism. His aim was to examine the main categories of domestic building, starting with the cottage and the villa; plans for essays on 'street architecture' and larger houses were set aside when the magazine closed. Churches and public buildings were only referred to in passing, and Gothic architecture, though clearly admired, was not yet seen as a universal panacea.

Ruskin often referred to his love of cottages. A drawing by

Samuel Prout of a cottage near Perth in Scotland hung in the dining-room of his parents' house and 'had a most fateful and continued power over [his] childhood mind'.[10] And he told readers of *The Seven Lamps of Architecture* (1849): 'I know what it is to live in a cottage with a deal floor and roof, and a hearth of mica slate; and I know it to be in many respects healthier and happier than living between a Turkey carpet and gilded ceiling, beside a steel grate and polished fender'.[11] For him, as for Gainsborough, Morland and their many imitators, English cottages and farmhouses, like those of the mountainous districts of France and Switzerland, represented an ideal of picturesque yet unpretentious beauty allied to a somewhat sentimental idea of a simple, untroubled rural life which captivated him throughout his life.[12] But the *cottages ornés* and 'Swiss cottages' of Regency England had perverted this ideal with their

> neat little bow windows, supported on neat little mahogany brackets, full of neat little squares of red and yellow glass ... the whole being surrounded by a garden full of flints, burnt bricks, and cinders ... and a fountain in the middle of it, which won't play; accompanied by some goldfish, which won't swim; and by two or three ducks, which will splash'.[13]

Cottage at Malham, Yorkshire, drawing by Ruskin, 1876. The stone-built house, allegedly the highest in England, stood on the Pennines and demonstrated the qualities which Ruskin admired in the vernacular architecture of the north of England: unpretentious simplicity, fitness to function, and the use of local materials. The drawing was chosen by W. G. Collingwood to illustrate the section on mountain cottages from *The Poetry of Architecture* in Ruskin's *Works* 1, p. 51 (*Ruskin Foundation, Ruskin Library, University of Lancaster*).

Cottage architecture in its truest sense was to be found in mountainous places like the Jura or the Lake District, which had preserved a 'gentle, pure and pastoral' traditional way of life, eschewing the 'foppery' of fashion and manufactured materials.[14] This centred around small, independent peasant farms of the kind celebrated by William Wordsworth in his *Guide to the Lakes* (1810).[15] Ruskin followed Wordsworth's lead in explaining the design of the local farmhouses and cottages in terms of the local climate and geology, and of the satisfaction of functional needs in the most straightforward possible way:

> The uncultivated mountaineer of Cumberland has no taste, and no idea of what architecture means; he never thinks of what is right, or what is beautiful, but he builds what is most adapted to his purposes, and most easily erected: by suiting the building to the uses of his own life, he gives it humility; and, by raising it with the nearest material, adapts it to its situation. That is all that is required.[16]

The simple beauties of such houses were, he implied, preferable to the meretricious glamour of the *cottage orné*. Ruskin was never very interested in the practical aspects of architecture, and he did not probe deeply into the planning or construction of these attractive buildings.[17] But echoes of his advocacy of plain, unaffected vernacular building can be seen in the writings of William Morris, in the smaller houses of Arts and Crafts architects such as Ernest Gimson and Raymond Unwin, and in the conservation work of the National Trust both in the Lake District and elsewhere.[18]

In contrast to his feelings about cottages, Ruskin's ideas on villa architecture were deeply ambivalent. He was brought up in a suburban villa, and Brantwood, his final Lake District home, qualifies as a villa if we follow his own definition of the villa as a 'ruralised domicile of a gentleman'.[19] He admired the villas he saw alongside Lake Como in Italy during his first Italian journey with his parents. But he was appalled by the architectural quality of the villas which were 'crowded together, and form gingerbread rows in the environs of the capital',[20] and he poured scorn on 'cubic erections' thrown up for 'ruralising cheesemongers':[21] a description which could have been applied to some of the houses on Herne Hill and Denmark Hill. He also bemoaned the infiltration of middle-class villas into places like the Lake District, just as architecturally sensitive visitors to the west coast of Ireland today often deplore the rash of recently-built bungalows there. For the young Ruskin, a stockbroker who built a fashionable house among the Lakeland fells was as absurd as the 'polished courtier' who aped 'the Arcadian rustic in Devonshire'.[22] Gentlemen seeking rest and leisure on relatively small plots of land in the suburbs or in attractive rural scenery like that of the Lakes were less likely to exhibit 'national' – by which Ruskin means locally-rooted – feelings than peasants who rarely left their local communities, or landlords whose families had lived there for many generations. Their houses would therefore often 'offend us by perpetual discords with scene and climate'.[23] He emphasised this point by highlighting six houses erected alongside Lake Windermere, among them John Plaw's extraordinary Belle Isle of 1774-5, a domed oval-shaped building with a Classical portico.[24] For the builders of such houses the villa was essentially a plaything, expressing 'the peculiar independence of the Englishman's disposition'[25] rather than 'the deep feeling of the mind'.[26] And to satisfy the patron's love of display the architect was often forced into an absurdly pretentious historicism or a wild and chaotic eclecticism.[27]

In discussing the best style for villa-building, Ruskin touched on a perennial problem in 19th-century architecture. He pointed out the absurdities of recent 'cottage villas', where 'the architect considers himself licensed to try all sorts of experiments, and jumbles together pieces of imitation, taken at random from his note-book, as carelessly as a bad chemist mixing elements'.[28] And it was a distaste for what he called 'imitation' which explained his disappointment with Sir Walter Scott's recently-erected house at Abbotsford in the Scottish Borders, which he visited in 1838.[29] Following Humphry Repton, whose writings on landscape and architecture had recently been collected and republished by

Loudon, Ruskin believed that different kinds of landscape were conducive to different styles of domestic architecture; irregular Italianate villas, for instance, looked best in scenery which induced a sense of 'felicitous repose' approximating to that of Italy.[30] But if 'national feeling' were to be properly evoked the Elizabethan style offered the best way forward. This had already been singled out by Loudon, who had published a design for a *beau ideal* villa in the Elizabethan style:[31] for Ruskin it was 'a style fantastic in its details, and capable of being subjected to no rule, but ... well adapted for the scenery in which it arose' and even though it was often 'utterly barbarous' as architecture at least it was not 'false' in taste.[32] Elizabethan houses were often 'playful' and 'lifelike', in contrast to Italian villas which were 'dreamy and drowsy in effect'.[33] Yet for Elizabethan-revival houses to be successful in modern times they needed to be 'either quite chaste, or excessively rich in decoration', while their architects 'should endeavour to be grotesque rather than graceful', exhibiting 'wit and humour in every feature, fun and frolic in every attitude'.[34] Different landscapes also demanded different building materials, in contrast to the ubiquitous stucco which Ruskin, like many of his contemporaries, deplored; thus brick was appropriate in cultivated country but not in hilly areas where abundant building stone existed.[35] These were sentiments which would be shared by George Devey and Norman Shaw, and the idea of Elizabethan houses being in some way quintessentially 'English' was one which was to have an enormous effect on the domestic architecture of the later 19th century, and on popular architectural taste down to our own times.

Ruskin's intention of writing about domestic architecture in towns was thwarted when the *Architectural Magazine* ceased publication, but he returned to the subject in his best-known architectural works, *The Seven Lamps* and *The Stones of Venice*, and in a lecture on architecture given in Edinburgh in 1853 and published the following year. By the late 1840s his enthusiasm for certain aspects of English domestic architecture had become muted:

> How small, how cramped, how poor, how miserable in its petty neatness is our best [domestic architecture]! ... What a strange sense of formalised deformity, of shrivelled precision, of starved accuracy, or minute misanthropy have we, as we leave even the rude streets of Picardy for the market towns of Kent! Until that street architecture of ours is bettered, until we give it some size and boldness, until we give our windows recess, and our walls thickness, I know not how we can blame our architects for their feebleness in more important work ... An architect should live as little in cities as a painter. Send him to our hills, and let him study there what nature understands by a buttress, and what by a dome'.[36]

The Seven Lamps was published in 1849, at a time when economic distress and political turmoil had brought the 'Condition of England Question' – as Thomas Carlyle, one of Ruskin's chief mentors, called it – to the forefront of public discourse. Public concern was focused on the shocking conditions of the poor in the rapidly expanding cities, and although Ruskin did not address this issue directly, a social concern is implicit in much of what he wrote at the time, and is made powerfully explicit in the famous 'Nature of Gothic' chapter in *The Stones of Venice* 2, which came out in 1853. Even in *The Seven Lamps* his aesthetic disgust at the results of rapid and unplanned suburbanisation modulated into a critique of the middle-class civilisation in which he himself was nurtured. The 'pitiful concretions of lime and clay which spring up, in mildewed forwardness, out of the kneaded fields about our capital' were for him 'the signs of a great and spreading spirit of popular discontent'.[37] By contrast:

> Our God is a household God, as well as a heavenly one; He has an altar in every man's dwelling ... It is no question of intellectual pride, or of cultivated and critical fancy, how, and with what aspect of durability and of completeness, the domestic buildings of a nation shall be raised. It is one of those moral duties ... to build our dwellings with care, and patience, and fondness, and diligent completion, and with a view to their duration at least for such a period as ... might be supposed likely to

Opposite: window in Oakham Castle, Rutland, drawing by Ruskin illustrating his Edinburgh lectures on architecture of 1853 (*Works*, 12, facing p. 19). Ruskin contrasted this window from the late-12th-century aisled hall of Oakham Castle with the monotonous windows of the houses in Edinburgh's New Town, telling his listeners that 'you would all like the best things best, if you only saw them. What is wrong in you is your temper, not your taste; your patient and trustful temper, which lives in houses whose architecture it takes for granted, and subscribes to public edifices from which it derives no enjoyment.' (*Works*, p. 19) (Bodleian Library, Oxford).

extend to the entire alteration of the direction of local interests. ... And when houses are thus built, we may have that true domestic architecture ... which does not disdain to treat with respect and thoughtfulness the small habitation as well as the large, and which invests with the dignity of contented manhood the narrowness of worldly circumstance.[38]

As for the architectural style which might be employed in urban domestic architecture, Ruskin was characteristically vague, preferring, as so often, prophecy to practicality: it will be said that much of the best wooden decoration of the middle ages was in shop fronts. No; it was in *house* fronts, of which the shop was a part and received its natural and consistent portion of the ornament. In those days men lived, and intended to live *by* their shops, and over them, all their days. They were contented with them, and happy in them: they were their palaces and castle ... The upper stories were always the richest, and the shop was decorated chiefly about the door, which belonged more to the house than to it. And when our tradesmen settle to their shops in the same way, and form no plans respecting future villa architecture, let their whole houses be decorated, and their shops too, but with a national and domestic decoration.[39]

In *The Stones of Venice* he made a more explicit plea for the introduction of Gothic architecture into English towns. One of the main themes of the book is that Gothic was not purely, or even primarily, an ecclesiastical style in the Middle Ages, and that church architecture was 'merely the perfect development of the common dwelling-house architecture of the period'.[40] So, as he urged in the peroration to the whole work: 'In this architecture let us henceforward build the church, the palace, and the cottage; but chiefly let us use it for our civil and domestic buildings'[41] in order that 'the London of the nineteenth century may yet become as Venice without her despotism, and as Florence without her dispeace'.[42] Gothic was not only more beautiful than other forms of architecture; it was also 'the only form of faithful, strong, enduring, and honourable building, in such materials as come daily into our hands. By increase of scale and cost, it is possible to build, in any style, what will last for ages; but only in the Gothic is it possible to give security and dignity to work wrought with imperfect means and materials'. This might be Butterfield or Street speaking. And Ruskin countered a common criticism of modern Gothic by claiming that it was easily adaptable to modern needs:

> There is not the smallest necessity, because the arch is pointed, that the aperture should be so. The work of the arch is to sustain the building above; when this is once done securely, the pointed head of it may be filled in any way we choose … Give the groups of associated lights bold gabled canopies; charge the gables with sculpture and colour; and instead of the base and almost useless Greek portico, letting the rain and wind enter it at will, build the steeply vaulted and completely sheltered Gothic porch; and on all these fields for rich decoration let the common workman carve what he pleases, to the best of his power, and we may have a school of domestic architecture of the nineteenth century, which will make our children grateful to us, and proud of us, to the thirtieth.[43]

Ruskin's scattered aperçus in *The Seven Lamps* and *The Stones of Venice* were developed in a more concentrated and coherent form in his lectures delivered to the Edinburgh Philosophical Institution at the end of 1853, just after the disastrous holiday at Glenfinlas when his wife Effie fell in love with the painter John Everett Millais. Ruskin's parents came from Edinburgh, and he flattered his audience by admitting that there were no streets which 'in simplicity and manliness of style, or general breadth or brightness of effect, equal those

Fig. 2

of the New Town of Edinburgh'.[44] But, for all its spacious grandeur, the New Town was 'a wilderness of square-cut stone for ever and for ever; so that your houses look like prisons, and truly are so; for the worst feature of Greek architecture is, indeed, not its costliness but its tyranny'.[45] Far preferable was the domestic architecture of medieval Europe, with its profusion of steeply gabled roofs and pointed windows:

> You surely must all of you feel and admit the delightfulness of a bow window; I can hardly fancy a room can be perfect without one. Now you have nothing to do but resolve that every one of your principal rooms shall have a bow window ... Sustain the projection of it on a bracket, crown it above with a little peaked roof, and give a massy piece of stone sculpture to the pointed arch in each of its casements, and you will have as inexhaustible a source of quaint richness in your street architecture, as of additional comfort and delight in the interiors of your rooms'.[46]

In his second Edinburgh lecture he went on to say:

> Do not be afraid of incongruities – do not think of unity of effect. Introduce your Gothic line by line and stone by stone ... [Your] existing houses will be little the worse for having little bits of better work fitted to them ... Remember that it is the glory of Gothic architecture that it can do *anything*.'[47]

This sounds like a recipe for aesthetic anarchy. But Ruskin believed that, if the principles of Gothic architecture were adopted, as they had been in towns he admired like Verona, Strasbourg and Abbeville:

> your architecture would be as if you all sang together in one mighty choir ... [The] great concerted music of the streets of the city, when turret rises over turret, and casement frowns beyond casement, and tower succeeds to tower along the farthest ridges of the inhabited hills – this is a sublimity of which you can at present form no conception.[48]

If this desirable outcome were to be achievable, the initiative had to come from the public and not just from architects, whom Ruskin dismissed as a lost cause. Good architecture could not be had merely by paying for it.[49] It was, rather, 'an art for all to learn ... For less trouble than is necessary to learn how to play chess, or whist, or golf, tolerably ... would acquaint you with all the main principles of the construction of a Gothic cathedral':[50] find

> out what will make you comfortable, build that in the strongest and boldest way, and then set your fancy free in the decoration of it ... Do what is convenient, and if the form be a new one so much the better; then set your mason's wits to work to find out some new way of treating it ... [If] you cannot get the best Gothic, at least, you will have no Greek; and, in a few year's time ... the whole art of your native country will be reanimated.[51]

But there was a major drawback to the education of taste which Ruskin regarded as a *sine qua non* of good architecture. In his poem *The Scholar Gipsy*, Matthew Arnold spoke of 'the infection of our mental strife/ Which, though it gives no bliss, yet spoils for rest'. Ruskin believed that this restlessness, endemic in modern commercial and industrial society, led people to treat their homes as mere commodities:

> I believe that the wandering habits which have now become almost necessary to our existence, lie more at the root of our bad architecture than any other character of modern times. We always look upon our homes as mere temporary lodgings. We are always hoping to get larger and finer ones, or are forced ... to live where we would not choose, and in continual expectation of changing our place of abode ... [It] surely is a subject for serious thought, whether it might not be better for many of us if, on attaining a certain position in life, we determined ... to choose a home in which to live and die.[52]

This echoes a passage in the 'Lamp of Memory' from *The Seven Lamps*:

> I cannot but think it an evil sign of a people when their

The porch of Highbury, King's Heath, Birmingham. Highbury was built in 1879-80 for Joseph Chamberlain, former mayor of Birmingham and future Colonial Secretary, to the designs of his namesake J. H. Chamberlain, an admirer of Ruskin and one of the best provincial architects of the late 19th century. It is a large suburban redbrick villa built in a style which has sometimes been dubbed 'Ruskinian Gothic'. Ruskin, however, himself showed little enthusiasm for the attempts of contemporary architects and builders to incorporate elements of the continental Gothic he had praised in his published works into their houses (*Geoffrey Tyack*).

houses are built to last for one generation only ... [If] men lived like men indeed, their houses would be temples ... and there must be a strange dissolution of natural affection ... when each man would fain build to himself, and build for the little revolution of his own life only.[53]

This insight formed part of a wider critique of modern society which preoccupied Ruskin for the rest of his life.

The most tangible immediate effect of Ruskin's writings on domestic architecture in the 1850s was to encourage the adoption of 'constructional polychromy' and some of the stylistic mannerisms of Continental, especially Venetian, Gothic. Charles Locke Eastlake, writing in 1872, recalled how, after the completion of *The Stones of Venice* in 1853, students, 'who but a year or so previously had been content to regard Pugin as their leader ... found a new field open to them, and hastened to occupy it', designing 'mansions which borrowed their parapets from the Calle del Bagatin, and windows from the Ca' d'Oro'. The fashion spread to suburban architecture, and discs 'of marble, billet-mouldings, and other details of Italian Gothic, crept into many a London street-front. Then bands of coloured brick (chiefly red and yellow) were introduced, and the voussoirs of arches were treated after the same fashion'.[54] Ruskin was not the only writer to praise Italian Gothic in the 1850s, but, as one of England's foremost art critics, he was probably the most influential. The Birmingham architect J. H. Chamberlain, to name just one of the young architects of the 1850s, collected his books, and he eventually became a trustee of the Guild of St George; Italian Gothic motifs permeate the houses he designed for Birmingham's *haute bourgeoisie* in the 1860s and 1870s.[55] By this time, however, Ruskin had disclaimed responsibility for the results of his advocacy of Italian Gothic. As he wrote in a much-quoted letter to the *Pall Mall Gazette*, published on 16 March 1872:

> I have had an indirect influence on nearly every cheap villa-builder between [Denmark Hill] and Bromley; and there is scarcely a public house near the Crystal Palace but sells its gin and bitters under pseudo-Venetian capitals copied from the Church of the Madonna of Health or of Miracles. And one of my principal notions for leaving my present house [on Denmark Hill] is that it is surrounded everywhere by the accursed Frankenstein monsters of, *in*directly, my own making.[56]

And, in a subsequent letter to the same journal, he insisted: 'For Venetian architecture developed out of British moral consciousness I decline to be answerable'.[57]

Ruskin was right to feel that his readers had missed the main point of his books with regard to domestic architecture.

This was not about style *per se* but about owners' responsibility for the design of their houses, and the need to employ craftsmen directly, liberating the innate creativity of the workmen in the process. That message was articulated most forcefully at the beginning of 'The Nature of Gothic' chapter of *The Stones of Venice*:

> And now, reader, look round this English room of yours, about which you have been proud so often, because the work of it was so good and strong, and the ornaments of it so finished. Examine again all those accurate mouldings, and perfect polishings, and unerring adjustments of the seasoned wood and termpered steel ... Alas! if read rightly, these perfectnesses are signs of a slavery in England a thousand times more bitter and more degrading than that of the scourged African, or helot Greek ... And, on the other hand, go forth to gaze upon the old cathedral front, where you have smiled so often at the fantastic ignorance of the old sculptors ... [Do] not mock at them, for they are signs of the life and liberty of every workman who struck the stone ... which it must be the first aim of all Europe at this day to regain for her children.[58]

Not only should the manual worker become an artist; the architect should also, in effect, become a craftsman, working 'in the mason's yard with his men'.[59] Ruskin later told J. D. Sedding that modern 'so-called architects are merely the employers of workmen on commission and if you would be a real architect, you must always have either pencil or chisel in your own hand'.[60] This was not something which any architect of the 1850s or 1860s was prepared or even, perhaps, able to do, however sympathetic he might be to the general tenor of Ruskin's writings. Philip Webb met Ruskin in the late 1850s, and took much of what he said to heart, haunting workshops and masons' yards and preferring the company of craftsmen to that of other architects.[61] But, like Street, in whose office he trained, he retained control over the whole of the building process, leaving little to the initiative of the builders. Ruskin later said that the only person who 'went straight to the accurate point of the craftsman's question' was William Morris,[62] and even he can hardly be said to have liberated the craftsmen into creativity in his most famous house, Red House at Bexleyheath (1859), designed down to the smallest detail by Webb.

The 'craftsman's question' led Ruskin into a radical rethinking of the position of work in modern society, above all in *Unto this Last* (1862). He did not return to the subject of English domestic architecture until the 1870s, by which time it had become linked in his mind with a growing awareness of the horrors of rapid and unplanned suburbanisation: something which had proceeded apace in the middle years of the century.[63] Like many people of his romantic conservative disposition, Ruskin had always believed that aesthetic and moral virtue was to be found in small towns and rural communities which had kept change at bay rather than in the giant modern metropolis. And, in his fourth Slade Lecture at Oxford in 1870, on 'the relation of art to use', he quoted his former Oxford tutor Osborne Gordon, who had told him that he could not enter London except with closed eyes, 'lest the sight of the blocks of houses which the railroad intersected should unfit him, by the horror of it, for his day's work'.[64] He went on to tell his audience:

> [it] is not possible to have any right morality, happiness, or art, in any country where the cities are thus built, or thus, let me say rather, clotted and coagulated, spots of dreadful mildew, spreading by patches and blotches over the country they consume. You must have lovely cities, crystallised, not coagulated, into form; limited in size, and not casting out the sum and surf of them into an encircling corruption of shame, but girded each with its sacred pomoerium, and with garlands of gardens full of blossoming trees and softly guided streams'.[65]

This later became a rallying-cry for the pioneers of the Garden City movement. As for the forms urban houses might take, Ruskin now dropped any references to English or Continental Gothic and urged his audience to consider the basic requirements of shelter. The architectural arts 'begin with the shaping of the cup and platter, and they end in the glorified roof'. Men should 'desire to have a house, which they do not wish to quit any more ... built as strongly as possible, and furnished daintily'. And since aesthetic *laissez-faire* had clearly failed, city-dwellers 'must have so much civic fellowship as to subject their architecture to a common law, and so much civic pride as to desire that the whole gathered group of buildings should be a lovely thing, not a frightful one on the face of the earth'.[66] Here he returned to a theme which surfaced in several of his writings, including *The Stones of Venice*, where he asserted that the 'outsides of our houses belong not so much to us as to the passer-by'.[67] He thus anticipated the later involvement of public authorities in planning and urban conservation.

In his second set of Oxford lectures, in 1872, Ruskin returned to the theme of the cottage which had preoccupied him since his youth:

> The first 'wisdom of calm' is to plan, and resolve to labour for, the comfort and beauty of a home such as, if we could obtain it, we would quit no more. Not a compartment of a model lodging-house, not the number so-and-so of Paradise Row; but a cottage all of our own, with its little garden, its pleasant view, its surrounding fields, its neighbouring stream, its healthy air, and clean kitchen, parlours, and bedrooms. Less than this, no man should be content with for his nest; more than this few should seek: but if it seem to you impossible ... that such houses should ever be obtained for the greater part of the English people ... the obstacles which are in the way of our obtaining them are the things which it must be the main object now of all science, true art, and true literature to overcome.[68]

This seductive vision of a semi-rural arcadia entranced many of the architects and Garden City pioneers who came to their maturity in the last third of the 19th century, but it is questionable whether Ruskin would have approved of the dirigiste methods some of them advocated to achieve their goal. His future utopia was not so much a bureaucratic state of the kind which eventually emerged in this country as an imagined community of independent craftsmen and small proprietors with an aristocracy at its apex. He believed that no landlord has any business with building cottages for his people. Every peasant should be able to build his own cottage - to build it in his mind; and to have a mind to build it to ... [If] cottages are ever to be wisely built again, the peasant must enjoy his cottage and be himself an artist, as a bird is. Shall ... your English yeoman be fitted by his landlord with four dead walls and a drainpipe? This is the result of your spending £30,000 a year at Kensington on science and art, then?[69]

The 20th-century council estate would probably have horrified Ruskin as much as the slums and suburbs of Victorian London.

It was the inexorable spread of those suburbs which contributed to Ruskin's decision to buy a house in the Lake District. In one of the *Fors Clavigera* letters of 1873, he wrote:

What a pestilence of [houses], and unseemly plague of builder's work ... has fallen on the suburbs of loathsome London? The road from the village of Shirley, near Addington, where my father and mother are buried, to the house they lived in when I was four years old [Herne Hill], lay, at that time, through a quite secluded district of field and wood, traversed here and there by winding lanes, and by one or two smooth mail-coach roads, besides which, at intervals of a mile or two, stood some gentleman's house, with its lawn, gardens, offices, and attached fields, indicating a country life of long continuance and quiet respectability. Except such an one here and there, one saw no dwellings above the size of cottages and small farmsteads ... There were no signs of distress, or effort, or of change; many of enjoyment, and not a few of wealth beyond the daily needs of life. That same district is now covered by, literally, many thousands of houses built within the last ten years, of rotten brick, with various iron devices to hold it together. They, every one, have a drawing room and dining-room, transparent, from back to front, so that from the road one sees the people's heads inside, clear against the light. They have a second story [*sic*] of bedrooms, and an underground one of kitchen. They are fastened in a Siamese-twin manner together by their sides, and each couple has a Greek or Gothic portico shared between them, with magnificent

Opposite: 58-60 Woodstock Road, Oxford. This pair of semi-detached brick houses, dating from 1872, was designed by Frederick Codd, one of the architects employed by St John's College in the speculative development of its north Oxford estate. Built when Ruskin was Slade Professor at Oxford, they exemplify many of the features he singled out in his diatribe on middle-class suburban housing of the south London suburbs in his 29th *Fors Clavigera* letter written in the following year, from the general layout to the highly ornamented Gothic capitals around the doorways (*Geoffrey Tyack*).

steps, and highly ornamented capitals. Attached to every double block are exactly similar parallelograms of garden, laid out in new gravel and scanty turf ... The gardens in front are fenced from the road with an immense weight of cast iron, and entered between two square gate-posts, with projecting stucco cornices, bearing the information that the eligible residence within is Mortimer House or Montague Villa.[70]

The occupants of such houses were for the most part not

> possessed of one common manly or womanly skill, knowledge, or means of happiness ... They know nothing of painting, sculpture, or architecture ... They never think of taking a walk ... The women and girls have no pleasures but in calling on each other in false hair, cheap dresses of gaudy stuffs, machine made, and high-heeled boots, of which the pattern was set to them by Parisian prostitutes of the lowest order: the men have no faculty beyond that of cheating in business; no pleasures but in smoking or eating; and no ideas ... of anything that has yet been done of great, or seen of good, in this world. This is the typical condition of five-sixths, at least, of the "rising" middle classes about London - the lodgers in those damp shells of brick, which one cannot say they inhabit, nor call their 'houses' ... but packing-cases in which they are temporarily stored, for bad use'.[71]

This bitter and unfair critique of English middle-class suburbia was to find many echoes in the future, most of them from people who, like Ruskin, themselves came from the suburban middle classes.

As for the working man, Ruskin now urged him to build his own house, and in another of the *Fors Clavigera* letters he anticipated some of the possible objections:

> 'But I mean to make money, and have a better and better house, every ten years.' Yes, I know you do. If you intend you to keep that notion, I have no word more to say to ... But if you have sense, and feeling, determine what sort of house will be fit for you; determine to work for it – to get it – and to die in it, if the Lord will you ... I mean, [a house] that you can entirely enjoy and

manage; but which you will not be proud of, except as you make it charming in its modesty ... You don't know, you answer, how to make a brick, a tile, or a pot; or how to build a dyke, or drive a stake that will stand. No more do I. Our education has to begin; – mine as much as yours. ... But you don't want to make your bricks yourself; you want to have them made for you by the United Grand Junction Limited Liability Brick-without-Straw Company, paying twenty-five per cent. to its idle shareholders? Well, what will you do, yourself, then? Nothing? ... Build, my man, – build, or dig, ... and then eat your honestly-earned meat, thankfully, and let other people alone, if you can't help them.[72]

This quasi-anarchist injunction resonated through the century after Ruskin's death, in the inter-war flight of working people from London to 'plotlands' in the marshes of Essex, where they lived in self-built houses and converted railway carriages. And echoes of it can even be seen in the activities of do-it-yourself enthusiasts nowadays, though Ruskin would doubtless have had little good to say about D-I-Y superstores which profit from supplying them.[73]

In 1871 Ruskin bought Brantwood, a cottage on the east-

ern shore of Lake Coniston, from a radical writer and artist, William Linton, and over the next few years he remodelled and extended it in the manner recommended in his 1853 Edinburgh lecture: piecemeal, and without the help of an

architect.[74] The result is idiosyncratic but, from a purely aesthetic point of view, incoherent. The plain and straightforward lines of the original house, built towards the end of the 18th century, were obscured by sundry additions: a first-floor turret to command the view of the lake; a new lodge; a single-storied dining-room with Venetian-inspired Gothic windows, added in about 1878; and much larger extensions in the 1890s, when Ruskin was being looked after by Joan and Arthur Severn, which continued after his death in 1900. Ruskin does not seem to have been worried by the resulting incongruity: it was, he had reminded readers of *The Stones of Venice* 'one of the chief virtues of the Gothic builders, that they never suffered ideas of outside symmetries and consistencies to interfere with the real use and value of what they did. If they wanted a window, they opened one; a room, they added one; a buttress, they built one'.[75] As one recent commentator has written: 'This is a house to be looked from, not a house to be looked at. It is a machine for seeing in'.[76]

Brantwood is in a sense a 'cottage villa' of the type which Ruskin had discussed in *The Poetry of Architecture*: a rural house on a small estate built so as to harmonise with its surroundings. That same ideal was shared by many other Englishmen from similar social milieux in the second half of the 19th century, and in the twenty years before the outbreak of the First World War a generation of talented architects inspired by the writings of Ruskin and William Morris supplied for them some of the finest examples of English domestic architecture of any period. The rediscovery of Ruskin by younger architects in the 1880s was tied up with the Arts and Crafts movement, and his influence was admitted in varying degrees by, *inter alios*, Sedding, Mackmurdo, Lethaby and Ashbee.[77] The young Arthur Mackmurdo accompanied Ruskin to Italy in 1874, and it was Ruskin who discovered the Architectural Association student Detmar Blow sketching in St Wulfran's church, Abbeville, in 1888, and directed him towards Sedding, Webb and Morris.[78] Blow later spent a year learning to be a stonemason, and became foreman under Sedding's pupil Ernest Gimson in the building of the famous cottages at Ulverscroft on the edge of Charnwood Forest, near Leicester (1897-1908): among the most 'Ruskinian' of

Opposite top: Brantwood, Cumbria, in 1871, watercolour by Ruskin. When purchased by Ruskin in 1871, Brantwood was an unpretentious example of the 'mountain cottages' whose architecture he had praised in *The Poetry of Architecture* over 30 years before. Stone-built and whitewashed in the normal Lake District manner, it perches on a hill slope on the east side of Lake Coniston. Ruskin's drawing captures the ruggedness of the setting, a ruggedness that still survives today thanks to the careful conservation of the surroundings – something of which Ruskin would surely have approved (*Ruskin Foundation, Ruskin Library, University of Lancaster*).

Opposite bottom: Brantwood today. The original cottage is on the left, with the upstairs turret and ground-floor dining room of the 1870s in front. On the right are the extensions carried out by the Severns during the 1890s and after Ruskin's death, at Brantwood, in 1900. The house is now administered by the Ruskin Foundation, and is regularly open to the public (*Geoffrey Tyack*).

Stoneywell Cottage, Ulverscroft, Leicestershire, drawing by F. L. Griggs from *Ernest Gimson and his Work* (Stratford and London, 1924). Stoneywell (1897-9) is one of a group of houses in Charnwood Forest built to the designs of the Leicester-born Ernest Gimson, using the local granite, and dispensing with the services of a contractor. The client was Sydney Gimson and the foreman in charge of the construction was Ruskin's protégé, Detmar Blow. The thatched roof shown in Griggs's drawing was replaced with slate after a fire in 1938.

all Arts and Crafts houses.[79] The example of Ruskin can be seen in both the writings and the houses of C. F. A. Voysey, who may have been introduced to his works by his father, a heterodox Anglican clergyman who, with Ruskin's support, founded a new 'theistic' church in London after being ejected from his living.[80] Another leading Arts and Crafts architect, Baillie Scott, quoted Ruskin's 1870 Oxford lecture in his article 'On the Choice of Simple Furniture' in the *Studio* in April 1897, and later, in 1917, he spoke of the 'uncompromising Ruskinism' which ran through his own work.[81] And Raymond Unwin, one of the apostles of the Garden City movement, attended at least one of Ruskin's lectures as a youth in Oxford and subsequently read his works – especially the 'Nature of Gothic', *Unto this Last* and the *Fors Clavigera* letters – 'avidly', quoting the 1870 Oxford lecture in his *Cottage Plans and Common Sense*, published by the Fabian Society in 1902.[82] Some architects even took Ruskin's views to their logical extent by dispensing with a clerk of works and literally building houses themselves. They included Harold Falkner of Farnham – home of William Cobbett and George Sturt – whose extraordinary timber-framed houses at Dippenhall, just outside the town, were built between the Wars with the help of just two labourers.[83]

By the time the Arts and Crafts house had reached its apogee, in the 1890s, Ruskin had lapsed into silence; his last published architectural statement was made in the *Fors Clavigera* letter of 1874, quoted above, and *Praeterita*, his last published work, came out in 1885-9. But the spirit of late Ruskin pervades the smaller houses of architects such as Voysey and Baillie Scott, Gimson and Unwin, and at places such as New Earswick and Letchworth Garden City. It is inescapable: the integration of house and landscape, the love of domestic simplicity, the presence of large, sweeping roofs, the concern for materials, the craftsmanlike interiors. Hermann Muthesius began his magisterial survey of English domestic architecture with Ruskin, to whom he believed England owed 'measureless gratitude in matters of art ... [He] was the first to champion the ideals that later became the principles of the Arts and Crafts movement: simplicity and naturalness in art, honesty in tectonic design ... emphasis on the workmanlike, the characteristic, the indigenous, a synthesis of artistic creation and observation of nature'.[84] These were the very qualities singled out by the Italian Futurist Filippo Marinetti when he urged the English in

Waterlow Court, Hampstead Garden Suburb, London. Waterlow Court is a quadrangle of self-contained flats built in 1907-9 to house 51 working women. The architect, Mackay Hugh Baillie Scott, was one of the Arts and Crafts architects who explicitly acknowledged Ruskin's influence, and the overall simplicity of Waterlow Court, its roughcast walls, its cloister and its bold roofline all reflect ideas articulated by Ruskin in his later lectures and writings (*Geoffrey Tyack*).

Ruskin and the English House

1912 to 'disencumber yourselves of the lymphatic ideology of your deplorable Ruskin ... [with] his sick dream of primitive pastoral life' and to embrace the exciting technologically-driven Brave New World of the 20th century.[85] But for many English people Ruskin's comments on the house and home, its design and its place in modern society, continued, and still continue, to strike a chord long after his death, and that is why they are relevant today.

Notes

[1] Tim Hilton, *John Ruskin: the Early Years* (New Haven and London 1985), pp. 8-9; Bridget Cherry & Nikolaus Pevsner, *The Buildings of England: London 4* (Harmondsworth, 1998), pp. 329-30.

[2] Mark Girouard, *Cities & People* (New Haven and London, 1985), p. 275; original in the Guildhall Library, London.

[3] *Works*, 35, pp. 35-6.

[4] Hilton [note 1], pp. 70-1. The house has been demolished, but its foundations can still be seen in Ruskin Park, to the north of King's College Hospital.

[5] *Works*, 35, p. 609.

[6] Ibid., p. 16.

[7] John Gloag, *Mr Loudon's England* (Newcastle upon Tyne, 1970), *passim*.

[8] *Works*, 1, p. 7.

[9] Ibid., p. 6.

10 J. S. Dearden, *Ruskin, Bembridge and Brantwood* (Keele, 1994), p. 185, quoting Ruskin's catalogue to his exhibition of Prout and W. H. Hunt in 1880.
11 *Works*, 8, p. 39.
12 He was deeply influenced by the pervasive aesthetic philosophy of the picturesque: see G. L. Hersey, *High Victorian Gothic: A Study in Associationism* (Baltimore and London, 1972), p. 24.
13 *Works* 1, p. 32.
14 Ibid., pp. 37, 43-4, 48.
15 See especially 5th edition, 1835 (London, 1906), pp. 58-64, 79-80. The young Ruskin and his parents had sat behind Wordsworth in church on their visit to the Lakes in 1830.
16 *Works*, 1, p. 52. Ruskin returned to the subject in a *Fors Clavigera* letter of September 1872, written just after buying Brantwood: *Works*, 27, p. 361.
17 For this, see R. W. Brunskill, *Vernacular Architecture of the Lake Counties* (London, 1974).
18 See, for instance, H. D. Rawnsley, *Ruskin and the English Lakes* (Glasgow, 1901), p. 15. Townend, near Troutbeck, in one of Ruskin's favourite valleys, acquired by the National Trust in 1947, is an example of the kind of Lakeland farmhouse which Ruskin admired.
19 *Works*, 1, p. 74.
20 Ibid., pp. 102-3.
21 Ibid., p. 103.
22 Ibid., p. 134. The courtier in question was presumably the Duke of Bedford, who had employed Jeffrey Wyatville to build him a large *cottage orné* by the banks of the River Tamar at Endsleigh in 1810.
23 Ibid., p. 75.
24 Ibid., p. 77. The villas are identified in J. M. Crook, *The Rise of the Nouveaux Riches* (London, 1999), p. 83 and notes.
25 *Works*, 1, p. 118.
26i Ibid., p. 128.
27 Ibid., pp. 129-30.
28 Ibid., pp. 167-8. He approved, however, like Pugin, of the accurate copying of approved styles.
29 Ibid., p. 163 and note; *Works*, 36, pp. 16-17 (letter to Loudon, September 1838). Abbotsford was built between 1813 and 1825, incorporating the structure of an older farmhouse: Clive Wainwright, 'Abbotsford House', *Country Life*, 8 June 1989, pp. 262-7. On the first page of *Praeterita*, Ruskin said that Scott was, along with Homer, one of his 'own two masters', and he returned to Scott and Abbotsford in one of his last *Fors Clavigera* letters: *Works*, 29, pp. 449-50 (26 September 1883).
30 Such houses had become fashionable in England following John Nash's Cronkhill, Shropshire, of c.1802, and designs of Italian prototypes were given in pattern-books such as Parker's *Villa Rustica* (London, 1832).
31 *Encyclopedia of Cottage, Farm and Villa Architecture* (London 1833), pp. 790-3.

Opposite: New Earswick, York. The 'garden village' of New Earswick was begun in 1903 by the Joseph Rowntree Village Trust on a site close to the Rowntrees' chocolate factory. The layout was the responsibility of Raymond Unwin, and most of the houses and public buildings were designed by him and by his partner Barry Parker, who became sole architect after 1919. The influence of Ruskin's later writings is clearly seen both in the architecture – especially the Folk Hall of 1905-7, with its massive roof – and in the landscaping, shown in this picture, where cottages are grouped informally around a grassy tree-studded open space. This concept goes back to John Nash's Blaise Hamlet, near Bristol, of 1810-11, and was revived by Ruskin in his fourth Slade Lecture of 1870. Unwin went on to design Letchworth, the first true Garden City, and to become the principal architect and planner of Hampstead Garden Suburb (*Geoffrey Tyack*).

32 *Works* 1, pp. 121-2.
33 Ibid., pp. 124-5.
34 Ibid., pp. 153-4.
35 Ibid., pp. 142-3, 151-3, 162-3.
36 *Works*, 8, p. 136.
37 Ibid., p. 226.
38 Ibid. pp. 227-8.
39 Ibid., p. 158.
40 *Works*, 10, p. 120.
41 *Works*, 11, p. 228.
42 Ibid., p. 230.
43i *Works*, 10, pp. 314-15.
44 *Works*, 12, p. 14. His father lived in St James's Square, now demolished.
45 Ibid., p. 62.
46 Ibid., p. 50.
47 Ibid., p. 78.
48 Ibid., p. 71.
49 Ibid., p. 16.
50 Ibid., pp. 19-20.
51 Ibid., p. 79.
52 Ibid., p. 72.
53 *Works*, 8, pp. 225-6.
54 C. L. Eastlake, *A History of the Gothic Revival* (London, 1872), pp. 278-9. See also M. W. Brooks, *John Ruskin and Victorian Architecture* (London, 1989), chapter 8.
55 For example, Highbury, built for the politician and former mayor, Joseph Chamberlain, in 1879-80. For J. H. Chamberlain, see Brooks [note 54], pp. 234-53.
56 *Works*, 10, p. 459.
57 Ibid., p. 460, letter of 21 March 1872. See J. M. Crook, *The Dilemma of Style* (London, 1987), pp. 93-4 and notes.
58 *Works*, 10, p. 193.
59 Ibid., p. 201.
60 *Works* 37, p. 199, 27 May 1876.
61 W. R. Lethaby, *Philip Webb and his Work* (Oxford, 1935), pp. 19, 28-9. Webb later called Ruskin 'that invaluable madman of Coniston': ibid., p. 228.
62 W. Mackail, *Life of William Morris*, vol. 2 (London, 1911), p. 201.
63 See, for instance, D. Olson, *The Growth of Victorian London* (First published London, 1976), chapter 5; F. M. L. Thompson (editor), *The Rise of Suburbia* (Leicester, 1982), esp. pp. 2-23.
64 *Works*, 20, pp. 112-13.
65 Ibid., p. 113.
66 Ibid., pp. 96, 112.
67 *Works*, 11, p. 226.

68 *Works*, 22, p. 263.

69 Ibid., p. 260. The reference here is to the Government-funded schools of design based in South Kensington

70 *Works*, 27, pp. 528-9.

71 Ibid., p. 530.

72 Ibid., pp. 190-200.

73 For do-it-yourself, see Raphael Samuel, *Theatres of Memory* (London, 1994); for the plotlands, D. Hardy, *Arcadia for All* (London, 1984).

74 Tim Hilton, *John Ruskin: the Later Years* (New Haven and London, 2000), pp. 212-3, 255-9; Brian Hanson, *Brantwood; John Ruskin's Home* (Brantwood Trust, n.d.), pp. 22-7; J. S. Dearden, *Facets of Ruskin* (London, 1970), pp. 23-32. The builders were superintended in Ruskin's frequent absences by Thomas Richmond, brother of the painter George Richmond, who lived near Lake Windermere.

75 *Works*, 10, p. 212.

76 Crook [note 24], p. 98.

77 Brooks [note 54], pp. 307-317; Alan Crawford, *C. R. Ashbee* (New Haven and London 1985); Godfrey Rubens, *William Richard Lethaby* (London, 1986), pp. 73-4. In later life, however, Lethaby apparently read Ruskin with 'amused contempt'.

78 Michael Drury, 'The Wandering Architects', in Chris Miele (editor), *Morris and Architecture* (Sheffield, 1996), pp. 84-6; M. Drury, *Wandering Architects* (Stamford, 2000), pp. 5-18.

79 [F. L. Griggs], *Ernest Gimson, his Life and Work* (Stratford and London, 1924), pp. 8-10; Roderick Gradidge, *Dream Houses: The Edwardian Ideal* (London, 1980), pp. 165-6. The cottages were built for members of Gimson's family.

80 Wendy Hitchmough, *C. F. A. Voysey* (London, 1995), p. 16.

81 *Studio*, 10 (1897), pp. 156-7, quoted in J. Kornwulf, *M. H. Baillie Scott and the Arts and Crafts Movement* (Baltimore and London, 1972), pp. 14, 403.

82 F. Jackson, *Sir Raymond Unwin: Architect, Planner and Visionary* (London, 1985), p. 13. Unwin spent some of his formative years as a child in Oxford, where, according to 'family legend', Ruskin 'corrected' some his drawings: W. L. Creese, *The Search for Environment* (New Haven, 1966), p. 159.

83 N. Taylor, 'The Private World of Dippenhall', *Architectural Review*, 143 (1968), pp. 158-60. Falkner is discussed, together with other architects of a similar bent such as Herbert North and Geoffrey Lupton, a close associate of Ernest Gimson, in Drury [note 78], pp. 169-94.

84 H. Muthesius, *Das Englische Haus*, 3 vols (Berlin, 1908-11; ed. D. Sharp, trans. J, Seligman, Oxford 1979).

85 Quoted in R. Banham, *Theory and Design in the First Machine Age* (London, 1960), p. 123. Ruskin, said Marinetti, resembled 'a man who in his full maturity wants to sleep in his cot again and drink at the breasts of a nurse who has grown old, in order to regain the carefree state of infancy'.

4

Labor ipse voluptas:
Scott, Street, Ruskin, and the
Value of Work

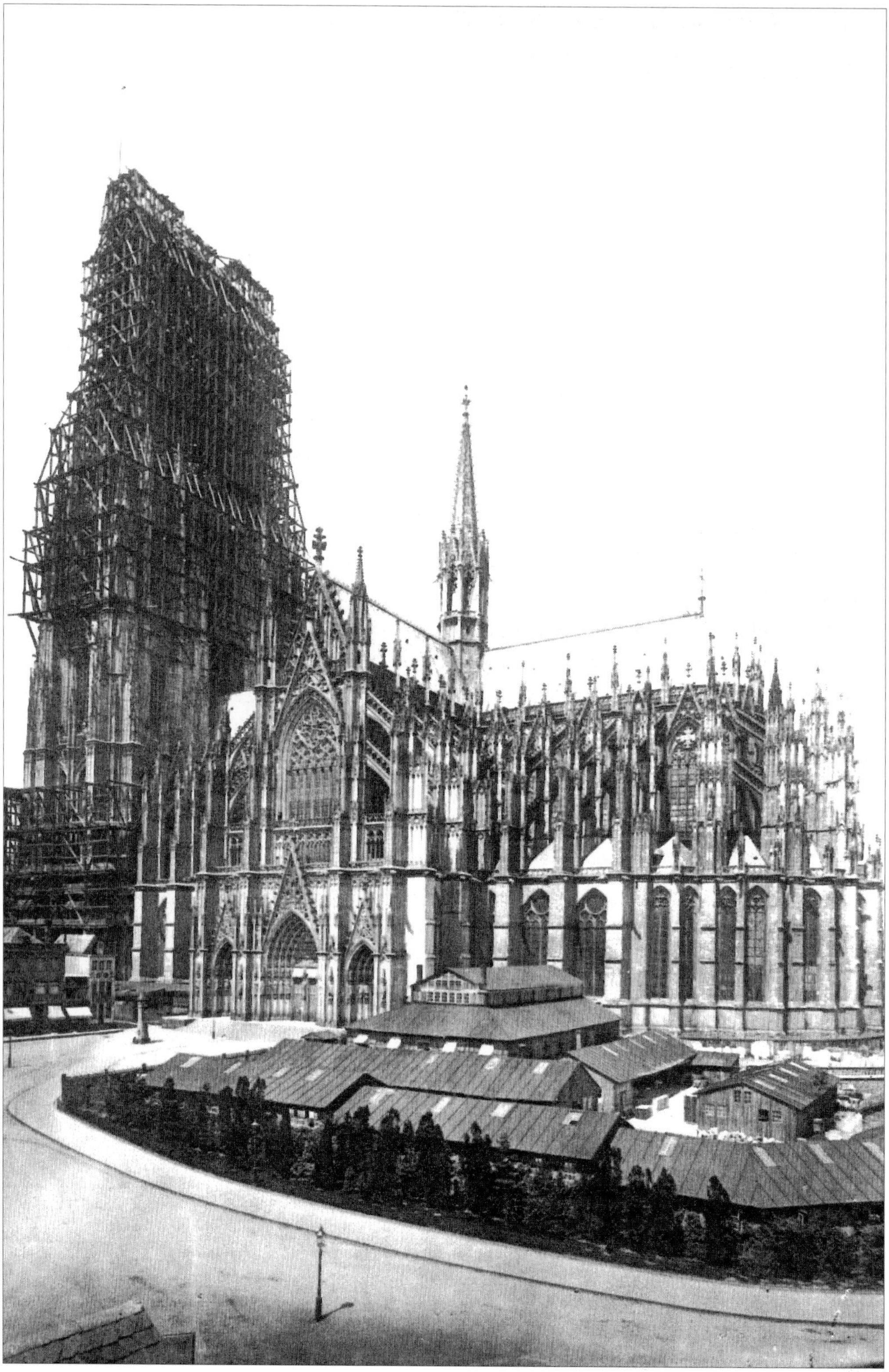

Labor ipse voluptas: Scott, Street, Ruskin, and the Value of Work

Brian Hanson

It is unfortunate that Ruskin's best-remembered comment about the building artisan was also one of his earliest, and least representative. It appeared in his very first book on architecture, *The Seven Lamps of Architecture* of 1849, in the form of a question Ruskin asked of all ornament: 'Was it done with enjoyment – was the carver happy while he was about it?'[1] Still a little unsure at this stage about the craftsman's skills, and not yet confident enough to query the business of the architect, Ruskin asked for no more than a small niche of contentment in which the life and spirit of a building might be nurtured. If the 'severity' of architectural law could thereby be relieved by the 'accidental carelessnesses' of an artisan left free to enjoy himself, then all would be well.[2]

It has always been too easy to dismiss that 'happy carver' as a myth of Merrie England, and to fail to recognise the depths Ruskin saw contained in that image: depths which would only be revealed in the years that followed. Fifteen years later – long after he had published his *last* book on architecture – he gave a lecture on architectural education at the Royal Institute of British Architects. To an audience which viewed him with a mixture of feigned indifference and real hostility, he defined his central aim as having been 'to set forth the life of the individual human spirit as modifying the application of the formal laws of architecture, no less than of all other arts'.[3] Such a statement, as much political as artistic, puts the 'happy carver' in perspective, and reveals him to be an integral part of the constitution of building: the life-giver, complementing the architect's role as lawgiver. The implication was that if architectural laws had to adapt to the 'individual human spirit', then the architect would have to yield up some control over building to the artisan.

It was in the second edition of *The Seven Lamps*, in 1855, that Ruskin's best-remembered comment about the *architect*

Cologne Cathedral under construction, c.1870, showing the *Bauhütte* in the foreground (*Rheinisches Bildarchiv, Cologne*).

'Aspen, Unidealized', drawn by Ruskin and engraved by J. C. Armytage, plate 28 of *Modern Painters* 4 (1865). The plate follows on from one showing 'The Aspen, under Idealization' in the works of Giotto, Constable, Harding etc. (including a 'Purist' example), and is emblematic of the view of nature Ruskin claimed to have obtained in the forest of Fontainebleau in 1842 (*Works*, 35, pp. 314-15).

28. ASPEN, UNIDEALIZED

appeared. If his early thoughts about ornament were to tempt later commentators to trivialise them, this was to open him up to the accusation that he did not understand architecture at all: 'the architect who was not a sculptor or painter', he claimed, 'was nothing better than a frame-maker on a large scale ... the idea of an independent architectural profession was a mere modern fallacy'.[4] Pevsner, for one, chose to interpret this narrowly, as meaning that building without decoration could not be architecture, but it was not this particular distinction which Ruskin had in mind here.[5] He intended it, rather, to be a plea for architects to see nature in the same way that Pre-Raphaelite sculptors and painters could. That is, he was urging architects to abandon their mania for idealising and abstracting nature, and to focus instead on the complexity of nature's outward aspects. In 1853 he had spent some weeks holidaying with John Everett Millais in Scotland, and had been hugely impressed with the painter's abilities as an architect, or, as Millais remembered it, 'Master Mason'.[6] After this Ruskin began to find it difficult to regard professional architects, and their abstractions, as anything other than irrelevant. This marked a significant departure from his earlier view of the architect. In 'The Lamp of Beauty' (1849) he had been content to picture the architect lying on a bank of grass, before nature, and employing his 'intellectual exertion' to 'watch and penetrate the intertwining of it'.[7] Now it seemed to him that in wishing to penetrate to the supposed *essence* of nature one was apt to overlook what was most valuable. The architect's and artisan's common understanding of the world, which had underpinned architecture in the finest age, was therefore at risk.

By seeing nature as Millais saw it architects would be able to discover laws of a finer sort than those based on abstraction. Ruskin had been able to recognise the operation of such laws in nature only after liberating himself from his drawing masters – whose formal conventions for rendering nature were not dissimilar to the approach to it the architect took in his search for formal principles. In his autobiography of 1886-9 he recounted a stroll he took in the forest of Fontainebleau in the 1840s, while he was recuperating from an illness. He found himself 'lying on the bank of a cart-road', facing an aspen tree, from where

> Languidly, but not idly, I began to draw it; and as I drew ... the beautiful lines insisted on being traced ... More and more beautiful they became, as each rose out of the rest, and took its place in the air. With wonder increasing every instant, I saw that they 'composed' themselves, by finer laws than any known of men.[8]

The position on the bank Ruskin described here was the very same as that of the architect in 'The Lamp of Beauty', but what we are shown now are the wonders visible to those prepared to leave artistic conventions behind. He plays with the fact that the aspen, with its 'light and quivering leafage', expressive of 'fragility, faintness, and inconstancy', was the very type of the 'disembodied spirit', and yet – like any other tree – was subject to the laws of nature.[9] It was an archetype, then, of that interaction between spirit and law which informed Ruskin's view of painting, architecture, and politics – not to mention science. As Peter Fuller suggested, Ruskin, by virtue of his intense concentration on nature, anticipated many of the concerns of the natural sciences of the present day: sciences reaching out beyond reductionism in order to grapple with the complex whole; which value 'emergent' qualities arising, unpremeditated, from apparent disorder; and which point to a critical balance between rule and contingency as the possible origin of living systems.[10]

His rapid abandonment, between 1849 and 1855, of the idea that architecture's 'Imitation of Nature' had to involve some Platonic truth, in favour of the idea that – like painting and sculpture – it should be concerned more with nature's superficial aspects, brought Ruskin into line with a venerable British tradition. According to this tradition, not all useful knowledge of nature was prelapsarian: some of it involved toil – a point of view on which British and German theorists wholeheartedly agreed, placing both at odds with their old enemy the French. The French rationalist position had been formalised ten years before Ruskin's Fontainebleau walk, in the *Historical Dictionary of Architecture* (1832) of A. C. Quatremère de Quincy. Quatremère had defended the Platonic idea of 'Imitation', and concluded that while the hand of the 'artificer' could offer little more than a 'resemblance' of nature, the architect's intellectual understanding of its principles enabled him to recognise in it the *types* more useful for his art.[11] Such ideas were being popularised in England through the efforts of Joseph Gwilt and A. W. N. Pugin, both of whom displayed an overt preference for French over British thinking on this subject. The political implications of all this had been laid out some years before by Edmund Burke, who had observed that the British Constitution, was drafted *after* nature, while the French one was artificial, requiring it to be imposed *on* human nature.[12]

The social unrest of the 1830s and 1840s was enough to convince Ruskin, and others, that – even in the arts – the French way of governing carried the greater risk. And it was Burke's earlier claim that 'The idea of bodily pain, in all the modes and degrees of labour, pain, anguish, torment, is productive of the sublime' – suggesting that even the most elevated aesthetic sensations were accessible simply through the work of the hand – that presaged Ruskin's practical response to this.[13] He came to believe that the artisan's more intimate and direct connection with nature afforded him an alternative, yet equally valid, revelation of nature's truth. This implied that a common understanding of nature was possible for all mankind: one that would not drive a wedge between the thinking and working components of society. He was helped in coming to this conclusion by Thomas Carlyle, who looked for inspiration to Germany rather than France, and who wrote in his *Past and Present* (1843) that there was

> perennial nobleness, and even sacredness, in Work ... Work, never so Mammonish, mean, *is* in communication with Nature; the real desire to get Work done will itself lead one more and more to truth, to Nature's appointments and regulations, which are truth.[14]

Ruskin's generation proved fertile soil for such arguments. For example, Henry Acland, instigator of the Oxford Museum, confessed to being taught as a youth, by the carpenter on his father's estate, to value 'the principle of martyrdom for truth's sake'.[15] For different reasons, Burke, Carlyle, Acland, and Ruskin came to believe that theory was only of use when it was translated into practice by means of a shared aesthetic, a process which they saw as mirroring that by which laws became effectively embodied in the *polis*. Ruskin's first, somewhat naïve, contribution to this tradition came in the concluding chapter of his *Seven Lamps* – where 'Obedience' was glossed as the adoption of an agreed national style of architecture, within which architects and artisans alike could work together – but he would continue to develop it in 'The Nature of Gothic' (1853) and in the writings and lectures of his later years.[16]

So Ruskin's view of the relationship between architect and building artisan – designing mind and executive hand – was not as sentimental as talk of happy artisans and painter-architects might imply. It is true that in large English cities such as London, Birmingham and Manchester, the possibility of the building artisan playing the kind of role Ruskin envisaged was fast diminishing – through a combination of architectural professionalisation and the rise of competitive practices in building, including general contracting.[17] Yet on the fringes of industrialisation a relatively large measure of give and take persisted between architects and artisans, and would continue to do so for some time. And it was mainly through working practices on the fringes that Ruskin's cause would be advanced.[18] For example, the team of architects and artisans that came closest to embodying his architectural ambitions, in the Oxford Museum, came from the south of Ireland; and between *The Seven Lamps* of 1849 and the RIBA lecture of 1865 he would draw inspiration from German attitudes to work. It was also Germany that helped shape the divergent attitudes to the workforce of the two metropolitan architects closest to Ruskin – George Gilbert Scott and George Edmund Street. In the 1840s, when George Gilbert Scott first visited the country[19] – seeking inspiration for his competition entry for a new church in Hamburg – it still retained features of what Karl Polanyi called an 'embedded' economy: traditional concepts of social obligation determining economic relations to a larger extent than they did in a more modern economy like Britain's.[20] What this meant was that German building processes constituted a social microcosm, of a sort highly compatible with Ruskin's particular amalgam of the artistic and the political. In addition, in one of the chief German cities a building was taking shape, intended to celebrate the superiority of the national character over that of the French who had occupied the country just a generation before.

Shortly after Napoleon's celebrated defeat at Leipzig in 1813, the demands began for a German National Monument which could celebrate both the intellectual and the practical aspects of German identity, as well as embody the cherished values of participation and consent.[21] K. F. Schinkel had been one of the first to call for 'a living monument for the nation; in other words, a monument whose method of construction would implant in the nation something that would bear fruit ... [recalling] The old craftsmanship ethic of our forefathers, in which love, humility and a just sense of pride combined ... a living and regenerative monument'.[22] He knew already, as he wrote these words, that to achieve this the monument would have to be Gothic, and it was only a decade later that the serious restoration of Cologne Cathedral began.[23] It was here — in a project which began as a restoration, and ended as a building brought to completion from its original drawings — that many of the values Schinkel outlined would come to be expressed.

Scott's friend, the politician August Reichensperger — who did more than anyone to bring the building to completion — observed in 1850 that 'It could well be that the whole future of art [*die höhere Kunstübung*] ... depend[s] on whether it can forge new links with craftsmanship [*Handwerk*] ... Art must once again speak to the people of the people, it must become flesh of their flesh, life of their life'.[24] Failing this, he thought art and craftsmanship would be driven apart: the one becoming 'etherial' and the other like 'factory work'.[25] That a Protestant Classicist and a Catholic Goth should, at thirty-five years distance, agree so completely — not only on the style of the monument, but also on its aims — shows how widespread and persistent was the desire to root aesthetics in the common life and practices of the German people: to bring together high and low through art.[26] Before 1850, Ruskin had thought it a particularly German vice to value words above things,[27] but the influence first of Thomas Carlyle's idiosyncratic reading of Goethe, and then of Scott's experience of German building practice, helped him appreciate the Germans' growing sense that the Gothic style could be a bridge between words and things, thoughts and actions.

One of the main tools for bringing this about at Cologne was the building lodge, or *Bauhütte*, which stood adjacent to the Cathedral.[28] Serving as both ecclesiastical workshop and school for artisans, it was not a phenomenon unique to Germany, but there was greater fascination with it there than

Cologne Cathedral under construction, 1844. The low sheds of the *Bauhütte* can be seen to the right of the medieval choir, with new bases for the shafts of the south porch in the foreground, replacing some earlier modern work. The drawing was made in the year that G. G. Scott first visited the cathedral, where he met the director of new construction, E. F. Zwirner, who would shortly be decisive in his obtaining the Hamburg Nikolaikirche commission (*drawing by J. A. Ramboux, Rheinisches Bildarchiv, Cologne*).

elsewhere. Only there would it usher in a whole new age of design: the Bauhaus at Weimar being consciously based on the *Bauhütte*; its first 'logo' being Lyonel Feininger's gleaming 'Cathedral of Socialism'.[29] Pugin's pattern book on *Floriated Ornament* (1849) was inspired by a lodge he visited at Antwerp Cathedral, where he had seen artisans working from a combination of casts (some of them of natural foliage) and medieval specimens.[30] Scott visited Antwerp himself en route to Germany in the summer of 1844, and was as impressed as Pugin by the way these workshops resorted to nature, albeit through casts, which offered a welcome alternative to the 'artificial' methods employed in Government education programmes in England at the time.[31] It was a pupil of Schinkel, Ernst Friedrich Zwirner, who, in the 1830s, established the first modern lodge in connection with the restoration of the Cathedral. But it was not until 1840, with the decision to complete that structure, that it took on new significance, becoming more evangelistic in its outlook.[32] It would not be long before accomplished architects would emerge from the ranks of the artisans there: men such as Vincenz Statz, the first German architect since the Middle Ages to build a new Cathedral, at Linz, Austria (begun 1857); or Friedrich F. von Schmidt, who was responsible for the imposing secular Gothic of Vienna Town Hall (designed 1868). Purely in formal terms, these buildings seem conservative in comparison to contemporary British works, like William Burges's St Finn Bar Cathedral in Cork (begun 1863), or Alfred Waterhouse's Manchester Town Hall (1868-77), but they stand as powerful testament to the German belief in the sublime heights to which building craft was capable of raising itself.

It was the fact that the '*deutscher Baukunst*'[33] represented more than a mere intellectual ideal that enabled German enthusiasm for the Gothic to be sustained even after it was established, in 1841, that the style was of French origin.[34] In

Drawing of the interior of the Cologne *Bauhütte* by Vincenz Statz, 1846. The view is to the southeast, towards the medieval tower of Gross St Martin. Statz proved the worth of the *Bauhütte* system by rising from the ranks of building artisan to become a celebrated architect. He was the first German architect of modern times to build a new Cathedral - at Linz, Austria (*Rheinisches Bildarchiv, Cologne*).

its success in uniting diverse religious and political factions behind a national symbol, the part played by Gothic form in post-Napoleonic Germany resembles that which Terry Eagleton has recently suggested the English verbal form played in late 19th-century Ireland. The latter was, according to Eagleton, able to raise the sights of the native Irish to the '*Gesellschaft*' of monarchy and society, while at the same time encouraging the Anglo-Irish to descend to an appreciation of the '*Gemeinschaft*' of country and folk – a reciprocity, note, that even now needs German words to describe it. It would have been inconceivable, in a society such as Germany's, for workers to be asked to enlarge their horizons if those above them were unwilling to stoop to lend them aid. Goethe continually urged upon his countrymen the value and necessity of condescension, for making possible a greater engagement with the world. In his view there was no greater misfortune than for a man to let an 'idea' distract or withdraw him from 'active life'.[35] Germany may not have given birth to the Gothic *ideal*, then, but it stood a better chance than other nations – France in particular – to give practical *reality* to a 19th-century Gothic. Scott was no doubt introduced to some of these undercurrents by Zwirner when they met at Cologne in 1844, because he cleverly played on such hopes in the report he wrote to accompany his entry for the Hamburg Nikolaikirche competition – which he submitted under the apt motto *labor ipse voluptas* (work is a pleasure in itself): questions about the origins and the inventors of the style, he wrote, had now 'given place to the more important inquiry of how it can most successfully be revived and re-established'.[36]

Zwirner was to prove of further use to Scott when he was called upon to arbitrate over the results of the competition, and ensured that Scott's third-placed design was given victory. Scott subsequently set up an office in the city, headed by John Burlison, spent some time there making preparations for the start of work, and went on to make near-annual progress visits.[37] In London, he retained George Edmund Street (then aged twenty) as a draughtsman for the project. Given that it was not only his own church, but the entire centre of Hamburg, which was being rebuilt after the 'Great Fire' of 1842,[38] Scott had an enviable opportunity, over the twenty years it took to complete the main volume of the Nikolaikirche, to see a wide range of native working

Scott's Nikolaikirche in Hamburg's Hopfenmarkt, (*Hamburg: 36 Ansichten nach Künstlerischen Aufnahmen, c.*1912).

Spire of Nikolaikirche from the west, behind a typical group of mercantile buildings overlooking the canal.

practices being deployed about the city.[39] And we can be sure these would have interested him: from childhood, he had shown himself unusually attentive to the idiosyncracies of custom.[40] And, indeed, the effects on him of German practice began to be seen at once, and over the next decade would set him apart in various ways from his English architect-peers. It was in the late 1840s, for example, that he developed the particular way of working, which infuriated many of his younger staff (including Street), whereby he would give only general directions to artisans, allowing them to 'kick over the traces' in their interpretation of his designs.[41] By 1847 he was showing an unfashionable interest in something called the 'Freemasons of the Church', an ambitious organisation begun five years before by the second editor of the *Builder*, Alfred Bartholmew, who shared a belief with the Germans that in the finest ages of architecture 'the most delicate refinement of theory, and the most exact practical skill went hand in hand, and were interchangeably the result of each other, so that it is impossible to separate their theory from their practice.'[42]

Then, in June 1852, just a few months after one of his German visits, Scott recommended to his peers the methods of the Cologne *Bauhütte*, writing a letter for publication to Benjamin Webb, Secretary of the Ecclesiological Society: 'I have lately been much gratified at Cologne Cathedral by the way in which they compose their ornamental foliage by joint reference to casts from ancient carving and casts from natu-

The (plaster) riches of the Architectural Museum, crowded cock-loft in the slums of Westminster (Builder, *12 (1854), p. 335)*. It was in November 1854 that Ruskin attended the Museum on three Saturday afternoons to deliver his addresses on 'Decorative Colour' to a sizeable audience. Over the weeks he drew increasing numbers of artisans (*Works*, 12, p. lxvi). It was here he also made what may have been a decisive intervention on behalf of Deane and Woodward's design for the Oxford Museum.

ral leaves ... really one of the most cheering things I have witnessed.'[43] In the same letter he announced he was throwing open in Westminster what he intended to be, in effect, the first modern English version of the *Bauhütte* – the Architectural Museum.

Though Scott regularly used the Ecclesiological Society as a sounding board in this way, he could seldom rely on its unequivocal support for his efforts on behalf of the workman. In the very first issue of the Society's journal, the *Ecclesiologist*, it was observed that 'the workman's part in the great work of church-building is to follow rather than to lead, and his labour should be directed accordingly'.[44] Benjamin Webb was a long-standing friend of Scott's,[45] but the Society's powerful Chairman of Committees, A. J. B. Hope, was never less than cautious about encouraging artisans to play a larger part in the work of building, and was positively dismissive of Ruskin.[46] No wonder Scott became anxious about what the Society might say about some of the specimens he wished to include in the Architectural Museum.[47] The *Ecclesiologist* had also taken some of the shine off Scott's Hamburg success: accusing him of casting pearls before swine by lavishing ecclesiological principles on a Lutheran church.[48] So it was no surprise when, just six months after Scott's Nikolaikirche victory was confirmed, the journal carried a contribution, 'From a Correspondent', on the subject of 'Ecclesiastical Architects'. Its author regretted that the modern architect had become a 'man of the world too much occupied designing ... workhouses' (Scott's previous staple), and 'sectarian places of assembly', to give more than 'general directions ... work for the architectural draughtsman ... one of those unhappy creatures of modern times and modern customs', when what was required instead was 'a single pious and laborious artist alone, pondering deeply over his duty to do his utmost for the service of God's holy religion, and obtaining by devout exercise of mind a semi-inspiration for his holy taste ... a worthy successor of those glorious Freemasons of old.'[49]

An artist-architect of this kind – who would need a 'conventual or collegiate ... [and] at the same time, religious' programme of education – would not contemplate the design of a church without 'rigid abstinence and humble prostration of mind', and without making 'drawings of every portion of his work with his own hands … apart from the noise and bustle of a crowded city'. This sounds like the *cri-du-coeur* of a young idealist, condemned to working in a venal manner he deplored. As such, it could very well have been the work of Scott's young assistant, his 'architectural draughtsman' on the Nikolaikirche, George Edmund Street, who joined the Society that year. Street's first signed contribution to the journal would not appear until three years later – when he was finally ready to set up an office on his own account – but the anonymous contribution on 'Ecclesiastical Architects' bears many of his hallmarks. We know, for instance, that when he was about to leave Scott he toyed with the idea of establishing a monastic community of architects, which would have fleshed out the distinctly pious programme for the education of the artist-architect set out in the letter to the *Ecclesiologist*.[50] He was also ever-critical of Scott's penchant for guiding artisans more by influence than direct instruction, seeing it as an abdication of responsibility for the progress of architecture, and an enticement to builders to begin to reassert their traditional, conservative, values. In the revealing marginal notes and underlinings made over thirty years later in his copy of Scott's *Recollections*, Street never fails to highlight instances where his old employer's faith in the intelligence of artisans seemed to go too far, or to lead him into error.[51] He also – with heavy irony – placed two firm pencil strokes by Scott's comment that 'No real art can stand against a constant high-pressure and working against time'.[52]

The 'glorious' freemasonry to which both Street and the anonymous 'Correspondent' were attracted was the speculative kind, and Street was never happy with the German experiments in operative freemasonry. He visited Hamburg and Cologne in the summer of 1851, commenting afterwards that 'I cannot think that the new works at the cathedral are so satisfying as they are generally said to be … there was a degree of poverty in the execution which was not felt in the old work; it looks thin, "liney" and attenuated'.[53] In a paper he delivered six years later to the Oxford Architectural Society he extended such critical comments even to some of the country's 'old work', which he felt was 'in most respects … entirely inferior to the developement [sic] of the same style in France and England … the result of the sudden conversion of a slow and sluggish people to the beauties of foreign work … an architecture of fits and starts and conceits, not of growth'.[54] For architecture to grow it was essential that the contract between architect and artisan did not inhibit the architect's freedom to innovate. There was a lack of variety in ornamental mouldings in German work, according to Street, because 'the science of mouldings was never worked out thoroughly by the early German school'.[55] But it is the tracery of the later school that attracted his most withering invective:

> Whilst one admires and wonders at the ingenuity which has devised so many combinations of spherical triangles and circles, one is tempted to think that the men who excelled in this sort of work would have been admirably fitted for designing children's toys and puzzles, but had much better have been kept away from church windows.[56]

Before the Adam brothers developed their efficient production-line classicism in the late 18th century, it had generally been assumed that mouldings could safely be left to builders and their 'rules-of-thumb'.[57] But the growth of a 'science of mouldings', given a boost after 1810 by Sir John Soane's lectures at the Royal Academy, would later become one of the measures by which the architect's increasing control over the building process could be traced.[58] Their stylistic preferences may have been radically opposed, but in their desire to secure as much control over the building process as possible, Soane and Street were at one. As the above quote implies, Street would have liked nothing better than to relegate artisanal independence to the playroom, where it could be indulged in relative safety. He could certainly never bring himself to offer it the same support as Scott did. The two men stood from the first, therefore, at twin poles in their attitude to the German Goths' experiments in artisanal education and practice: and this disagreement exposes a significant fault line within the English Gothic Revival of the 1840s and 1850s, to which Ruskin – no less than others – was obliged to respond.[59]

In 1849 Ruskin had prided himself on the disinterestedness with which he was able to survey modern society. He described his position in an early draft of *The Seven Lamps* as that of 'the fisherman contending with the waves and currents, [who] leaves his comrade on the cliff to mark for him the movement of the shoals, and the soldier descending into conflict to another the direction of his energy and disposal of his life'.[60] But not long after he wrote this Thomas Carlyle began to convince him that to be merely a 'comrade on the cliff', divorced from action, was futile, and that, if one were to be of any use at all, one had to descend oneself 'into conflict'. Carlyle had been led to this conclusion himself in the early 1820s – as he was approaching the age of thirty – while translating Goethe's *Wilhelm Meister*, the celebrated *Bildungsroman* which offered him the means of escape from the narrow Calvinism of his youth.[61] Ruskin was also thirty when he fell under Carlyle's spell, discovering through him aspects of German thought which pointed beyond the callow Protestantism of *The Seven Lamps of Architecture*. We can even trace the means by which a characteristic image from Goethe came to be applied first to politics by Carlyle, and then to the arts by Ruskin.[62] Book 6 of *Wilhelm Meister* includes an account by the 'Fair Saint' of how she gained her freedom from her lover. Carlyle's portentous tone comes through clearly in his translation of it:

> at last, when after many thousand struggles … I began to cast a steady eye upon the bond which had held me to him, I discovered that it was but weak, that it might be torn asunder. I at once perceived it to be as a glass bell, which shut me up in the exhausted airless space: One bold stroke to break the bell in pieces, and thou art delivered![63]

He later adapted this striking image for use in his own analysis of the 'Condition of England'. It adds drama to the challenge he threw down, in *Past and Present*, to the 'Unworking Aristocracy', who had 'only a thin fence of window-glass' – their own equivalent of the glass bell – standing between them and the world they so proudly surveyed:

> this that thou seest with those sick eyes is no firm Eldorado, and Corn-Law Paradise of Donothings, but a dream of thy own fevered brain. It is a glass-window, I tell thee, so many stories from the street; where are iron spikes and the law of gravitation!
>
> What is the meaning of nobleness, if this be 'noble?'
>
> ... Descend, O Donothing Pomp; quit thy down-cushions; expose thyself to learn what wretches feel, and how to cure it!64

Ruskin could have read these words when the book was published in 1843, but the heavy scoring of this passage in pencil in his own copy of the book was probably done about seven years later, by which time there were clear signs that he had decided to follow Carlyle's prompting.65 One way he did this was by going against the judgement of his father by issuing, in 1851, his first pamphlet, on the subject of Pre-Raphaelitism. In so doing, the 'Oxford Graduate', and author of *Modern Painters*, stooped for the first time to address an issue of current moment, in a form less elevated than the bound book. Moreover, the pamphlet contained its own Carlylean plea for true 'nobleness' to reveal itself through a willingness to 'descend': 'I do not believe that any greater good could be achieved for the country', Ruskin claimed, 'than ... by a few benevolent men, undeniably in the class of 'gentleman', who would, on principle, enter into some of our commonest trades, and make them honourable'.66

There are traces in this also of the theology of Incarnation, which – through the influential teachings of men like F. D. Maurice – was just beginning to mould the views that many of Ruskin's generation held of their responsibilities to society.67 Ruskin was determined to remain in the vanguard. As soon as the final volumes of *The Stones of Venice* were off his hands, he turned to the unfamiliar medium of lectures, delivering his first series (which included one on Pre-Raphaelitism) to the people of Edinburgh, and so coming face to face with his reading public for the first time. He fled England in the summer of 1854, after the annulment of his marriage, but on his return in the autumn he entered into his most intensive phase yet of practical engagement. At Maurice's Working Men's College (which had also been inspired to some extent by Carlyle's writings on the 'Condition of England')[68] he taught alongside his new Pre-Raphaelite friends, to train up artists from among the artisan classes;[69] at Scott's Architectural Museum he hoped to educate workmen ready to accept direction from such artists (ideally without the intermediary of an architect); and the Oxford Museum provided a practical building programme to which these combined efforts could be applied. Through this interlocking programme of work, Ruskin was emulating some aspects of the German model as it had come to him from Carlyle and Scott. Just after he received the news that a Gothic design had been accepted by the University of Oxford for the new Museum, Ruskin wrote a letter of mutual congratulation to Henry Acland: a letter which has regularly been misconstrued, even by that fastidious biographer of the Museum's architects, Frederick O'Dwyer. What Ruskin wrote was that 'I had no sooner formed certain plans for helping the workmen than Maurice set the college as proof ... there seems to be something quite providential in the way my work is being laid out for me at present here in this college with you and Woodward both ready to do anything - possible with money'.[70] Writers have been tempted to insert '*sic*' after 'here in this college', implying that Ruskin had meant to write 'museum' – that is, the Oxford Museum.[71] What he was doing here, however, was pointing out to Acland how symbiotic he believed his activities to be at Maurice's College and the Oxford Museum. He might easily have added his hopes that a similar connection might develop between the Oxford work and Scott's Architectural Museum in London.

It is highly likely that it was a meeting in Venice with Ruskin in October 1851 that finally convinced Scott to set up his Architectural Museum. If his encounter with German methods had prepared the ground for this enterprise, the seed was planted by an architect called C. Bruce Allen, who suggested to Scott just before he left for the Continent that year, that he might lend his support to a new scheme of artisan education.[72] A short while before this, an effort by the painter Thomas Seddon to set up classes for artisans in Camden Town (inspired by a visit *he* had made to the forest of Fontainebleau)[73] had proven unexpectedly successful, foundering only as a result of Seddon's ill-health. Scott's journey to Venice in 1851 took him through Cologne, and, as we know from his letter to Benjamin Webb just a few months later, he was more impressed than ever by what he saw there. In October, he visited Ruskin, who wrote to his father shortly afterwards: 'Who should arrive – in time to be asked to tea – but Scott the architect – whom you must remember at Denmark Hill – So we had a great architectural séance – and I enjoyed it.'[74]

We can be fairly certain that one topic of conversation at this séance (in addition to the basilica of St Mark's, which Scott had just been sketching)[75] was the approach to artisan education being undertaken at Cologne, and Scott's thoughts about doing something similar in London. On his return to England shortly afterwards, Scott would take part in a series of discussions on the subject, with Allen and others, before taking charge of the enterprise. An initial prospectus had already been drafted (presumably by Allen) which shared a number of features with the Government education schemes of the 1840s, deplored by reformers such as Seddon.[76] The student would attend daily classes, copying 'some well known and approved model' in stone, and only when sufficiently advanced in copying would he be given some insight into the principles which had guided the original artist. Except for simple, repetitive ornaments like dog-tooth moulding, he would be entirely dependent on an artist to supply a design. Should the student have the temerity to think himself an artist he would be encouraged to leave for an art school. The ambition of this prospectus was to produce a class of artisans better equipped to be an *instrument* for the elevated artist/designer. Scott, having observed at the Cologne *Bauhütte* the much less hierarchical relationship between the intellectual and operative parts of the common effort, believed the workforce better able to educate itself than this initial outline implied. In his revised prospectus, he expressed the hope that, by contrast, the school attached to the Museum would set about '*Educating* [original emphasis] a superior class of men at the same time both Artists and Workmen – Artists able to Design – and Workmen able to carry out themselves such Designs.'[77]

It was particularly important to Scott that these men should be able to fulfil the dual functions of artists and workmen, because he was far less sanguine than Ruskin then was about the possibility of getting fine artists – such as Millais and Dante Gabriel Rossetti – to engage directly in building work.[78] In the students' instruction preeminence was now to be given to drawing, which led on to modelling and carving from an approved piece. And the carver's independent field of activity would no longer be limited to conventional, repetitive ornament, but also include 'the Figure, Animals, Leaves, Flowers, Fruit'. Even more importantly, there was to be a 'Class of Pupils' who

> will … instead of wandering about in search of a drawing to copy, be independent of such a precarious mode of obtaining a living, but will always be ready to offer an able and willing hand in converting the raw materials of nature into Works of Art – not on paper – but in some actual material, and for which there always is, and always must be, a steadily increasing demand, and thus adding to National *wealth* – and *money* – which is not the CAUSE but the RESULT of it.

This was close to the form of education promoted by the *Bauhütte*, in which design and operative functions were brought together in a form of 'orthodox practice'. And it is linked to a view of political economy – in which it is not 'money' that creates 'wealth', but *vice versa* – which is patently 'Ruskinian', even though Ruskin had not yet expressed it in print.[79] But Scott did far more than re-draft the prospectus. By June 1852, only eight months after he met Ruskin in Venice, he had found premises for the Museum and its school (a 'cock-loft' in the 'slums of Westminster').[80] He enlisted a Visiting Committee, which included the leading architect of the day (Charles Barry) and the leading editor (George Godwin, who had also been on the Board of Seddon's school), had secured a senior episcopal patron in the form of the Bishop of London, gained the support of John Ruskin, and received gifts of architectural casts from him and others. Scott himself was also able to promise a steady supply of casts from Germany. He later remembered with affection the days which ensued, 'of the greatest and most earnest vitality of the institution', when the 'lectures were crowded [and] the conversaziones overflowed with earnest visitors'.[81] If there was one shadow cast over this scene, it was when he approached his old assistant Street for support, only to be turned down: he said he feared it would encourage 'copyism'.[82]

Scott had clearly been galvanised by his meeting with Ruskin in Venice, but did Ruskin get anything from it, beyond simple enjoyment? At the time he met Scott he was at a turning point. The introductory volume of his Venetian trilogy had just been published, and it was only in the previous month that he had begun his draft of the second volume, in which he would grapple with the difficult question of where the origins lay of the architectural qualities which so fascinated him. The crucial chapter for this second volume was to be on 'The Nature of Gothic', and in it Ruskin would explain the style as a consequence of certain characteristics of its builders. As he was turning his attention to these things, Scott arrived to have tea – bearing more practical knowledge of the role of building artisans in Gothic architecture than Ruskin would ever have. Ruskin had got to know precious few architects in the 1840s.[83] After *The Seven Lamps*, he had been accused of operating 'in the way of solitary reflection, rather than in contest with other minds of equal calibre with his own',[84] and so had determined on securing what allies he could in the field. The Appendices of the first volume of *The Stones of Venice* contain attempts to engage with two such potential allies – James Fergusson and E. L. Garbett – but, suggestive and helpful though these two writers were to him at that time, they disappointed him on the question of the right relationship between the intellectual and practical parts of architecture.[85] The relationship with Scott, therefore, was the first one that Ruskin had established within the architectural community which promised to give him insight into the actual potential for modern practice of the intelligent artisan, and he seems to have been encouraged by what he heard.

In *The Seven Lamps* of 1849 he had appeared cautious about the prospects of reviving the power of the craftsman. A few of them, he conceded, had shown themselves skilful enough to be ranked with Academicians, but 'from the mass of available handicraftsmen the power is gone – how recoverable I know not ... the only manner of rich ornament that is open to us is the geometrical colour-mosaic'.[86] But, beginning with 'The Nature of Gothic', he began to reassess the chances of recovering that power. The audience at one of his Edinburgh lectures in 1853 was treated to a picture of some medieval carving from Lyons, and was promised by the lecturer that

> the very men who could do sculpture like that ... for you are here! still here in your despised workmen: the race has not degenerated, it is you who have bound them down, and buried them beneath your Greek stones. There would be a resurrection of them, as of renewed souls, if you would only lift the weight of these weary walls from off their hearts.[87]

It was at this point, then, that Ruskin began to articulate the opinion that the future of architecture would be fought out between the two opposing tendencies he would return to at the RIBA: on the one hand, its 'formal *laws*' – embodied here in the 'Greek stones' of Edinburgh – and, on the other, the '*life* of the individual human spirit', struggling to be free. And one cannot miss the new note of optimism in this lecture, as, newly inspired by Carlyle, he readied himself to take a leap from his window-ledge to engage with the world of men. The great change which took place between 1849 and 1853 in Ruskin's attitude to the building artisan owed a good deal, therefore, to what Carlyle and Scott passed on to him respectively of German thought and German practice.

Furthermore, following his séance with Scott – who had been so impressed with the way casts were being used at

Cologne – architectural casts overtook daguerreotypes in Ruskin's estimation, as the most useful medium of record for a world disappearing under demolition and 'restoration'.[88] Two and a half months after the meeting he had twenty-one sizeable casts taken from the Ducal Palace, which, to the dismay of his father, he then shipped home.[89] Forty-five separate smaller casts were then taken from these, and presented to the Architectural Museum. In 1854 further gifts to the Museum followed, of casts and drawings, and at the end of that year Ruskin delivered three addresses to Scott's artisan-students, offering to provide additional private tuition to those who required it.[90] At this point Scott's Museum had effectively assumed in Ruskin's mind (in tandem with the Working Men's College) the form of a *Bauhütte* serving the Oxford Museum.[91] Despite his ambition, though, we know of only two instances where his efforts with artisans in London directly supported the great architectural work in Oxford: once when, at the Architectural Museum, Ruskin and Scott cornered Philip Hardwick – a member of Scott's Visiting Committee, who also happened to be an assessor for the Oxford Museum – to secure an admission from him about the two designs on the final shortlist, which may well have been decisive in enabling Henry Acland to sway the vote of the University Convocation in favour of the Gothic design;[92] and then later, when J. J. Laing, a pupil at the Working Men's College, was sent by Ruskin to work on the Museum under the direction of the architect Benjamin Woodward.[93] In July 1855, in the preface to the second edition of *The Seven Lamps*, Ruskin urged his readers to follow his lead in donating casts to the Architectural Museum as he had done but this was part of a doomed, last-ditch attempt to preserve the Museum in its original form.[94] Even as the words appeared in print, the enterprise was encountering financial difficulties, which meant, as Scott remembered later, that a 'time of trial' was 'at hand'.[95]

Because of this, Scott was forced to go, cap-in-hand, to the Prince Consort, to seek his help in keeping the Museum open.[96] The Prince handed him over to Henry Cole at South Kensington – whose Department of Practical Art represented the very antithesis of what Ruskin and Scott had had in mind for their Museum.[97] In the opinion of Cole – whom Scott remembered bitterly as the 'great Ingulphus' – the artisan was the mere instrument of the designer, who was beholden to the manufacturer, himself the servant of the public.[98] Within this strictly commercial hierarchy, it was little wonder that the spirit which had animated Scott's Museum was soon lost. Whilst remaining as Treasurer, its founder remained at arm's length as long as it remained at South Kensington.[99] Nevertheless, Ruskin agreed to re-inaugurate the Museum there on 13 January 1858, though the theme he chose for his lecture, of 'The Deteriorative Power of Conventional Art over Nations', was surely a thinly-veiled attack on the methods of the South Kensington school, which he felt paid too little attention to natural form. But then, by giving the chair on this occasion to the eminent classical architect, C. R. Cockerell, the Museum's new management was able to return the gesture in kind. After the Museum had been surrendered to South Kensington, however, G. E. Street realised its threat to architectural progress was probably over. His pupil, Philip Webb, attended Ruskin's lecture, and Street himself consented, for the first time, to lecture to the artisans there later in the year. George Godwin continued to be involved, but he had never had any great attachment to the 'Ruskinian' view of the building artisan. The Museum's new President was A. J. B. Beresford-Hope - the powerful Chairman of Committees of the Ecclesiological Society - and he gradually grew bold enough to be openly scornful of his predecessors, whose thoughts had, as he described it, been 'pervaded by a kind of floating idea that you merely have to set an oak branch, or an ivy bunch, or a dead woodcock, before a man, with or without education, and that if he does carve on accordingly then the result must come out graceful and beautiful.'[100]

When the Museum was once again looking for financial support in the 1870s – having been obliged to return to Westminster from South Kensington[101] – Ruskin was once again approached for help, but was astute enough to recognise that the Museum's main interest had now shifted from the artisan to the *architect*: 'I am very sorry', he wrote in reply, 'that any appeal needs to be made for the Architectural Museum outside of the Profession ... I have always maintained', he continued, quite without foundation, 'that Painters should be educated by Painters and Architects by Architects'.[102] His suspicions were confirmed posthumously when the Museum's collection – first gathered together for the edification of building artisans – ended up as the property of the Architectural Association, which, in 1902, was granted use of the Museum's building on condition the collection remained open to the public 'for ever'.[103]

This shift of emphasis, away from the 'building world' which had so inspired Scott and the Germans, towards the single creative individual, was part of a much broader shift – recently outlined by the labour historian Richard Price – by which a largely paternalistic society was giving way to one more industrialised and class-based.[104] Street's lectures – at the Architectural Museum and later at the Royal Academy – exemplify this change. In them, and in his various writings, he sought to unravel the concept, promoted by Ruskin, of architecture as the 'distinctively political art',[105] arguing instead that

> The men in the thirteenth and nineteenth centuries work on the same principle, which is that of obedience to one controlling authority, so as to leave no room whatsoever for the exercise of any of the personal fancies or tastes of individual workmen ...
>
> [The mere workman of the 13th century] confined himself to doing what he was told, implicitly following the directions of the master ... [such men] had no more pleasure in their work, no more originality in their way of doing it, than our workmen have at the present time, all the pretty fables to the contrary notwithstanding.[106]

He also insisted that the architect – the 'controlling authority' to which workmen must defer – should not seek inspiration in the *physical remains* of medieval buildings (which had contributed, in his view, to the Ruskinian preoccupation with building *process*), so much as in what remained of the literature and the art of the period. Naturally, this required a type and a level of education then beyond the reach of most artisans. E. W. Godwin was a follower of both Ruskin and Street, but, when he took one of his carvers to Chartres in the early 1860s, it was Street's advice he chose to follow, being careful not to become too distracted by the physical presence of the building, and coming away with only 'a drawing of a bit of shadow ... the shadow of the ornament cast on the string course.'[107] The more one reads Street's words to artisans, with their appeals to literature and culture, the more one is reminded of Tacitus's tart comment that the Romans' main aim in 'civilising' the Ancient Britons was to teach them 'the outlines of slavery'.[108]

During the 1850s Ruskin's practical efforts had been sustained in part by a dream of Cologne. At the height of his 'earthly ministry', in the preface to the second edition of *The Seven Lamps* (1855), he wrote that 'The name by which the architect of Cologne Cathedral is designated in the contracts for the work, is '*magister lapicida*', the 'master stone-cutter''. An architect cutting stone was a hero of the kind that Carlyle had taught Ruskin to admire. In the third volume of *Modern Painters* (1856), he mused that the most heroic depiction of Homer's Achilles would include his 'cutting pork chops for Ulysses'.[109] It was only when he re-visited the *real* Cologne at the end of the decade that Ruskin's dream finally collapsed. By that time he had also become deeply disillusioned by the Oxford Museum, and was taking stock of his life – as he was wont to do at the end of every decade (he had just reached forty). He found the Cathedral 'good for nothing – old or new, it is all bad' ... 'a miserable humbug'.[110] Nevertheless, his admiration for Goethe – or at least for the second book of *Faust* – lived on, as he confessed to his father three years later: 'My opinions will never more change - they are now one with Bacon's and Goethe's - and I shall not live long enough to be wiser than either of these men.'[111]

Arguably, [Francis] Bacon's 'Order or Society, which we call *Salomon's House*; the noblest foundation ... that ever was upon the earth; and the lanthorn of this kingdom', offered Ruskin one model for his St George's Guild.[112] The image from Goethe which Ruskin kept returning to appeared at the close of the second book of *Faust*, in which a band of

G. E. Street's Law Courts in The Strand, London (in the early 20th century). Ruskin praised Street's 'purity' as an architect, and compared these buildings favourably with the gin palace and cod-Venetian villa, but nevertheless believed that the architect fell short of the very highest quality in art, which was Naturalism (*Rebecca Daniels' collection*).

angels offend Mephistopheles by strewing rose petals on the ground – an image in which, Ruskin stated, 'the whole science of aesthetics is … expressed',[113] and which must also have evoked memories of his beloved Rose La Touche.[114] And he never forgot that Faust had been spared damnation, in Goethe's account, through turning his thoughts to action, by draining marshland for the common good. When, in the late 1860s, Ruskin was himself involved in a project to provide water for Swiss villagers, by cutting drainage channels in the slopes to catch and conserve what melted off the peaks, he wrote to a friend that 'if I die, I will die digging like Faust'.[115] What increasingly angered him was the fact that architects seemed *un*prepared to 'die … like Faust'. On the contrary, they thought that, like God Himself, they could 'create without toil', and exert their authority through abstractions alone.[116] The result was – as he told them in 1865, in his lecture on architectural education – that even their best efforts were good only for 'cities in cloudless air', and were ill-equipped for the 'black air' of their own day.[117] In Ruskin's famous classification of artists into Sensualists,

Purists and Naturalists, modern architects conformed to the middle category: they may not have been the worst of men, but nor were they the best.

The Purist was one who 'does not mend nature, but receives from nature and from God that which is good for him'. Though preferable to the Sensualist, who 'fills himself with the husks that the swine did eat', he was greatly inferior to the Naturalist. The Naturalist would 'take all home', and by doing so be in a position to forge a higher unity out of both the good and the evil in the world.[118] G. G. Scott agreed with Ruskin on the preeminence of Naturalism, observing in the late 1850s, to the young Thomas Graham Jackson, that the architecture of their day was in need of Pre-Raphaelites.[119] Street, on the other hand, came to epitomise for Ruskin the shortcomings of the 'Purist' modern architect. Along with the vast majority of the Pre-Raphaelite painters themselves – who preferred to decorate the upper walls of the Oxford Union with the *Morte d'Arthur*, rather than provide more down-to-earth models for the carvers at the Oxford Museum[120] – he rejected Ruskin's Carlylean call to 'descend' to the level of building artisans, and chose to remain in the more elevated, 'poetic', world of legend and literature.[121] So, when, in 1859, Ruskin called Street's buildings 'pure beyond anything he had ever seen in modern architecture',[122] he was being a little indulgent: it was not his highest praise. And when, later, he compared Street's designs for the new Law Courts favourably with the cod-Venetian of the 'cheap villa' and the gin palace (the sight of which, he claimed, had driven him out of London to the Lake District), he was merely expressing his customary preference for Purism over Sensualism – 'the Purists, in their sanctity' being more enlightened

Drawing of an angel, taken from an 8th-century psalter at St John's College, Cambridge, and used by Ruskin to illustrate his lecture of January 1858 on 'The Deteriorative Power of Conventional Art over Nations' (*Works*, 16, p. 275). William Morris's architect, Philip Webb, was in the audience and strongly disagreed with Ruskin's judgement on this angel in a way that revealed important divisions between Ruskin and the subsequent Arts and Crafts sensibility.

than 'the Sensualists in their foulness'.[123] William Morris left Street's office because he felt his master's way of working prevented him engaging with the crafts at 'first hand'.[124] Yet Philip Webb – who was to inspire so many subsequent Arts and Crafts architects – had no such difficulties with Street's views and methods. When, in the middle of his 1858 lecture on 'Conventional Art', Ruskin produced his *pièce de résistance* to illustrate the pernicious effects of abstraction – a superficially crude drawing of an angel taken from an 8th century psalter at St John's College, Cambridge – the young Webb found himself violently at odds with the lecturer, believing that he was too apt to dismiss the figure's greatest asset: namely the quality or 'breadth' which made it such a perfect model for architecture.[125]

In many ways, then, it was this lecture of 1858 that marked a parting of the ways between Ruskin and an architectural profession growing ever more confident in its powers. At the core of the mature Ruskinian view of architecture, as it had taken shape over the previous decade, was a desire to temper the abstract laws beloved of architects with the life characteristic of the artisan, so as to infuse the man-made world with something akin to the rich order of nature.[126] Philip Webb's defence of 'breadth' was just one small sign that this would not be an easy task. In coming to his mature view, Ruskin had found aspects of Goethe's thought (mediated through Carlyle), and German building practice (mediated through Scott) extremely useful. By the end of the 1850s, though, all his practical strategies had failed: his hopes for the Architectural Museum had been frustrated, along with those for the Oxford Museum. At the same time G. E. Street and his followers had begun to move the profession safely beyond his assaults, to establish a relationship between intellectual and practical concerns – far more favourable to the *architect* – which would come to predominate during the last quarter of the 19th century, and for the whole of the 20th. However, the ends to which Ruskin aspired did not change, and he began after 1860 to search only for different means of achieving them, and it was this which was to lead him to the studies of myth and political economy which became such such a significant feature of his later output.[127]

Notes

1 *Works*, 8, p. 218. Nearly thirty years later – in the 78th of his *Fors Clavigera* letters – Ruskin would summarise his early architectural work as having revealed 'the dependence of all human work or edifice, for its beauty, on the happy life of the workman (*Works*, 29, p. 137). These letters were, however, directed at workmen.

2 *Works*, 8, p. 200.

3 *Works*, 19, p. 20.

4 *Works*, 8, p. 15.

5 Nikolaus Pevsner, *Ruskin and Viollet-le-Duc: Englishness and Frenchness in the Appreciation of Gothic Architecture* (London, 1969), p. 22.

6 *Works*, 12, p. xxviii. Millais' exquisite 'angel' window from this time is illustrated and discussed in John G. Millais, *The Life and Letters of Sir John Everett Millais*, 2 vols (London, 1899), pp. 204-9.

7 *Works*, 8, p. 155.

8 *Works*, 35, p. 314. It is generally accepted that, like a good deal else Ruskin wrote about his life, he constructed this account for dramatic effect from a number of separate such episodes. The fact that he places this experience in 1842, and seven years later had still not modified his view of the architect, suggests that its lesson was slower to take effect than his autobiography suggests.

9 *Works*, 5, p. 237.

10 Peter Fuller, *Theoria: Art, and the Absence of Grace* (London, 1988). A recent discussion of the new sciences of complexity, and their relationship to architecture, appears in Lucien Steil (editor), 'New Science, New Architecture, New Urbanism', *Katarxis*, 3 (2003), www.katarxis-publications.com/katarxis3

11 Samir Younés, *The True, the Fictive and the Real: The Historical Dictionary of Architecture of Quatremère de Quincy* (London, 1999).

12 *Reflections on the French Revolution* (1790), para. 56.

13 *The Works and Correspondence of … Edmund Burke*, 8 vols (1852), vol. 2, p. 652 (*Sublime & Beautiful*, part 4, section 6, 1756). Terry Eagleton examines Burke's attitude to labour in *The Ideology of the Aesthetic* (Oxford, 1990). Another strand of the English alternative to idealism is discussed in Patricia M. Ball, *The Science of Aspects: The Changing Role of Fact in the Work of Coleridge, Ruskin and Hopkins* (London, 1971).

14 *Past and Present* (1845 edition), pp. 264-9: Chapter 11: 'Labour'.

15 H. W. D. Acland, 'Health, Work and Play' (Oxford, 1856), p. 14. Teufelsdröckh, the fictional hero of Carlyle's *Sartor Resartus* (1831), had supplemented his poor schooling at the Hinterschlag Gymnasium by 'learning many things' from the craftsmen's workshops in the town – book 2, chapter 3, para. 7.

16 *Works*, 8, p. 248ff.

17 Brian Hanson, *Architects and the 'Building World' from Chambers to Ruskin: Constructing Authority* (Cambridge, 2003).

18 It is hard to find evidence for the claim made by Mark Swenarton, in his *Artisans and Architects: The Ruskinian Tradition in Architectural Thought*

(Basingstoke, 1989) that 'Ruskinism' was mainly a phenomenon of the prosperous south-east of England. Other 'fringes' of significance to Ruskin included: his 'Scottish Heritage'; his links with Venice and Switzerland; and his relationship with the 'georgic' traditions persisting in the West Country, where Henry Acland's family seat was located. For further discussion of these fringe influences, see Hanson [note 17], p. 17 and chapter 6.

[19] It was, in fact, his first trip beyond Calais – G. G. Scott Jr (editor), *Personal and Professional Recollections* (London, 1879), pp. 113ff.

[20] Polanyi in fact located pre-market 'embedded' economies in the Middle Ages – see *Origins of Our Time: The Great Transformation* (London 1945). I am applying it to 19th-century Germany in the spirit of Lars Edgren ('Crafts in Transition?: Masters, Journeymen and Apprentices in a Swedish Town, 1800-1850, *Continuity and Change*, 1, part 3 (December, 1986), pp. 363-83) who identifies certain 'embedded' characteristics in the working practices of early 19th-century Sweden, where craft structures were based on the German model. Table 3.6 of T. C. W. Blanning (editor), *The Nineteenth Century* (The Short Oxford History of Europe) (Oxford, 2000) shows that Germany's share of world manufacturing output increased by 1.4% between 1800 and 1860, compared with the UK's increase of 15.6%.

[21] The conclusive 'Battle of the Nations' at Leipzig had witnessed an unprecedented rising up of the German people in response to an impassioned appeal to them by King Friedrich Wilhelm III of Prussia.

[22] Georg A. Germann, *Gothic Revival in Europe and Britain: Sources, Influences and Ideas* (London, 1972), p. 92.

[23] By contrast, a National Monument was begun in Scotland in the same period, which was modelled on the Parthenon.

[24] Germann [note 22], p.161.

[25] Ibid.

[26] That Scott shared this desire is clear from his lecture on 'The Future of the Gothic Revival' in *Associated Architectural Societies' Reports and Papers*, 4 (1857), p. 70.

[27] 'the base sciences of grammar, logic, and rhetoric; studies utterly unworthy of the serious labour of men' – *Works*, 11, p. 127. Even after he had gained respect for Goethe's arguments for uniting thought with action, Ruskin still associated Germans in general with this school of thought.

[28] In the angle between the south transept and choir.

[29] Germann [note 22], p. 177. See also Chris Brooks's chapter in this volume.

[30] At the time the Geerts brothers were carving choir stalls under the direction of the architect Durlèt. The casts they worked from were of natural foliage and the great Gothic masters, and their medieval specimens came from the Belgian city of Leuven. We get only part of the story from Pugin, the gaps being filled by Matthew Digby Wyatt's account of the Geerts in *The Industrial Arts of the Nineteenth Century* (London, 1851-3),

text to plate IX.

31 Pugin was one of a number – which included the painter G. R. Lewis (see Hanson [note 17], pp. 67-70), and Thomas Seddon – who opposed the Government Schools in the mid-1840s. Paradoxically the Schools had taken their lead from earlier, pioneering, educational programmes in Germany – see Quentin Bell, *The Schools of Design* (London, 1963), pp. 59, 84.

32 The Nuremberg architect, Carl Alexander Heideloff (whose buildings Reichensperger thought poor - Michael J. Lewis, *The Politics of the German Gothic Revival: August Reichensperger* (Cambridge, Massachusetts, 1993), p. 72)) published his translation of Mathias Roriczer's 1486 work on building geometry in 1844 as *Die Bauhütte des Mittelalters in Deutschland*. In 1845 Reichensperger wrote the foreword to an alternative translation of Roriczer's book.

33 Goethe used this term, in his famous essay of 1770 on Strasbourg Minster.

34 It was Franz Mertens who established the style's French origins – see W. D. Robson Scott, *The Literary Background of the Gothic Revival in Germany: A Chapter in the History of Taste* (Oxford, 1965), p. 299.

35 *Wilhelm Meister*, book 5, chapter 16, in Carlyle's translation.

36 Scott [note 19], p. 123.

37 Lewis [note 32], p. 185. The foundation stone was laid on 24 September 1846. An engraving of the ceremony is included in Julius Faulwasser, *Die St. Nikolai-Kirche* (1926).

38 Faulwasser wrote an account of *Der grosse Brand* in 1892.

39 The 'topping out' of the Nikolaikirche, accompanied by a *Richtfeier* (see Faulwasser [note 37]), took place in 1859, the roof being completed four years later. The tower was finished only in 1874.

40 The early parts of his *Recollections* constitute what Gavin Stamp called a 'folk history' of Gawcott in Buckinghamshire ('Sir Gilbert Scott's *Recollections*', *Architectural History*, 19 (1976), p. 53. Scott's account of the quaint inhabitants of Gawcott was published in full in Ian Toplis, George Clarke, Ian Beckett and Hugh Hanley (editors), *Recollections of Nineteenth-Century Buckinghamshire*, Buckinghamshire Record Society, 31 (1998), pp. 1-63.

41 Scott [note 19], pp. 215-16. T. G. Jackson and Street both reacted to Scott's *laissez faire* way with artisans by ensuring that they delegated nothing in their own work – see Basil H. Jackson (editor), *The Recollections of Thomas Graham Jackson, 1835-1924* (London, 1950), pp. 59-60.

42 Bartholomew's words as recalled by his successor as Honorary Secretary to the Freemasons of the Church, W. P. Griffith, in an address attached to the *Proceedings of the Architectural College*, 1845. Scott raised the matter of the Freemasons of the Church following a session of the Ecclesiological Society – reported in the *Ecclesiologist*, 7 (1847), pp. 239-40. By that time, though, Bartholemew was dead, and the organisation was unravelling. See Hanson [note 17], pp. 110-16, 120-1.

43 The letter was read out at the 13th Annual Meeting of the

Ecclesiological Society, on 9 June 1852, and later reprinted in the *Ecclesiologist*, 13 (1852), pp. 280-2.

44 *Ecclesiologist*, 1 (1842), pp. 149-50. For a fuller development of the Ecclesiologists' attitude to artisanal labour, and its political subtext, see Hanson [note 17], pp. 86-90. Chris Brooks, in Christopher Webster and John Elliott (editors), '*A Church as it Should be*': *The Cambridge Camden Society and its Influence* (Stamford, 2000), p. 130, also considers the wider political ramifications of ecclesiological activity.

45 It was Pugin and Webb who introduced Scott to ecclesiological principles (Scott [note 19], p. 87).

46 'I have often faced with awe the outside of his "Modern Painters" and once or twice opened it, but somehow I have always funked him' – quoted in Henry William Law and Irene Law, *The Book of the Beresford Hopes* (London, 1925), p. 225.

47 Scott [note 19], p. 203. Scott gave a lecture at the Museum 'On the Selection of Objects for Study' on 24 March 1858, which was published in the *Builder*, 16 (1858), pp. 202-4, 226-8.

48 Scott [note 19], pp. 134, 135ff for Scott's response.

49 *Ecclesiologist*, 4 (1845), pp. 277-9.

50 Arthur Edmund Street (editor), *Memoir of G. E. Street R.A., 1824-1881. By His Son Arthur Edmund Street* (London, 1888), p. 56. Such monastic attitudes were being encouraged at this time by J. H. Newman's conversion to Roman Catholicism, which was concluded on 9 October 1845, just as this letter was being written. See Frank M. Turner, *John Henry Newman: The Challenge to Evangelical Religion* (New Haven and London, 2002), chapters 9, 12.

51 For example (Street's emphasis), when Scott praises Francis Skidmore (p. 265): 'who has worked out [for the Albert Memorial] every species of ornament in the true spirit of the ancient model'; when he writes about the decoration of the choir-aisle vaulting in Worcester Cathedral (p. 344), which 'I unluckily left to Mr. Hardman, who made it too monotonous'; and of the side chapels in Exeter Cathedral (p. 348): 'Mr. Clayton weakly departed from the old design, so far as to add some foolish patterns to the mouldings'. Street's annotated copy of Scott's *Recollections* is in the British Architectural Library.

52 Ibid., p. 222.

53 G. G. King, *George Edmund Street: Unpublished Notes and Reprinted Papers* (New York, 1916), p. 308.

54 *Ecclesiologist*, 18 (1857), pp. 162, 163, 164.

55 Ibid., p. 168.

56 Ibid., pp. 169-70.

57 Hanson [note 17], pp. 44-5. A few earlier attempts had been made, notably in the late 17th century by Inigo Jones's pupil, John Webb, to dictate the shape of mouldings to artisans – see Frank Jenkins, *Architect and Patron* (London, 1961), p. 138.

58 For Soane's view of mouldings, see Lecture 2 in David Watkin (editor), *Sir John Soane: The Royal Academy Lectures* (Cambridge, 2000), p. 30. For

Gothic revivalists, the science of mouldings began with F. A. Paley's celebrated *Manual of Gothic Mouldings* (London, 1845).

59 The 1850s debate over conventionalisation in ornament – discussed in Priscilla Metcalfe, *James Knowles: Victorian Editor and Architect* (Oxford, 1980) – was part of this. Street became a strong supporter of the conventional decoration characteristic of French Gothic, 'the very thing we were striving to avoid' in setting up the Museum, according to Scott [note 19], p. 210.

60 *Works*, 8, p. 282.

61 Goethe's novel, the first part of which was published in 1795-6, is the classic example of a *Bildungsroman*, concerned with tracing an individual's personal growth and development. Carlyle continued to refer to it as a crucial influence on his life, still expounding its educational programme as late as the 1860s, when he assumed the Rectorship of Edinburgh University. See also Gerhart Hoffmeister, 'Reception in Germany and abroad', in Lesley Sharpe (editor), *The Cambridge Companion to Goethe* (Cambridge, 2002), pp. 232-55.

62 It needed Ruskin to see the artistic implications of the image, as Carlyle had little sympathy with the visual arts – see G. A. Cate, 'Ruskin's Discipleship to Carlyle: a revaluation', in John Clubbe (editor), *Carlyle and his Contemporaries* (Durham, North Carolina, 1976), pp. 227ff.

63 'Confessions of a Fair Saint', in book 6 of *Wilhelm Meister*.

64 Carlyle, *Past and Present* (1845 edition), pp. 242-3.

65 Ruskin's 1845 edition of *Past and Present* is now in the British Library. Arguments for the date of the markings in it are given in Hanson [note 17] pp. 165-7, where the relevant pages (figure 16), showing Ruskin's markings, are also illustrated.

66 *Works*, 12, p. 343.

67 See Michael Wheeler, *Ruskin's God* (Cambridge, 1999).

68 Olive J. Brose, *Frederick Denison Maurice: Rebellious Conformist* (Athens, Ohio, 1971), p. 165, says that 'during the 30's and 40's, national education, Chartism, and the disturbing presence of Thomas Carlyle were all interwoven in Maurice's life and thought. But it was Carlyle … who acted both as catalyst for his social thought and as a disturbing influence in his personal life.' Maurice's figure appears alongside that of Carlyle in Ford Madox Brown's famous painting, *Work* (1852-63).

69 Ray Haslam, 'Seeing, drawing and learning with John Ruskin at the Working Men's College', *Journal of Art and Design Education*, 7, no. 1 (1988), pp. 65ff.

70 Bodleian Library, Ms Acland Ac d.72, fol. 43 ().

71 See, for example, Frederick O'Dwyer, *The Architecture of Deane and Woodward* (Cork, 1997), p. 175; and Eve Blau, *Ruskinian Gothic: The Architecture of Deane and Woodward, 1845-1861* (Princeton, 1982), p. 66 – who mistranscribes it as 'here is this college'.

72 Scott [note 19], p. 165. The sale of L. N. Cottingham's extensive collection of casts in 1851 was also a factor (ibid., pp. 165-6). This collection had already prompted a bid in the 1840s to get a cast collection attached

to the British Museum.

73 J. P. Seddon, *Memoir and Letters of the Late Thomas Seddon, Artist, by his Brother* (London and Edinburgh, 1863), pp. 9-10.

74 J. L. Bradley, *Ruskin's Letters from Venice* (Westport, Connecticut, 1955), letter 40 – John Ruskin to John James Ruskin, 21 October 1851.

75 He had also sketched the Ducal Palace. Together these sketches fill sixteen pages of a book, now in the RIBA Drawings Collection. Scott [note 19, pp. 158-9] remembered: 'At Venice, all was enchantment! ... here met Ruskin, whom I knew before, and we [he and Benjamin Ferrey] spent a most delightful evening with him.' Of St Mark's he says: 'The most impressive interior I have ever seen. The Venetian Gothic, excepting the ducal palace, disappointed me at first, but by degrees it grew upon me greatly.'

76 *Proposals for Establishing in the Metropolis a School for Artist-Workmen together with a Museum of Medieval Sculpture. Under the Patronage of Gentlemen eminent in the Fine Arts* (n.d., c.1851).

77 *School of Art for Art-Artizans & Museum of Architectural Art, Cannon Row, Westminster. Patron. The Right Rev. The Lord Bishop of London* (n.d., c.1852).

78 'It is vain to hope that sculptors of the highest class will again (at least in our day) go hand in hand with architects' – *Builder*, 12 (1854), p. 358.

79 'Money ... is not wealth' is the phrase Ruskin uses in *Munera Pulveris*, which appeared in 1862-3 – *Works*, 17, p. 157.

80 G. G. Scott, *A Guide to the Royal Architectural Museum*, pamphlet (London, 1876), p. 3.

81 Ibid., and Scott [note 19], pp. 166-7.

82 Ibid., p.166.

83 As both Ruskin's letter to his father, and Scott's recollection, indicate, the two had met before – in the early 1840s when Scott had redesigned the Ruskins' local church of St Giles, Camberwell. Ruskin had become involved at that time with a schoolfriend, Edmund Oldfield, in the design of the glass for the early Decorated Gothic East window. Yet despite the fact that this church represented an important turning point for Scott – being his first designed according to ecclesiological principles, with real stone instead of plaster (Scott [note 19], p. 92) – Ruskin was too preoccupied with the glass to pay any attention to the church or its architect, and in the end he left even that to his friend to finish off (*Works*, 12, pp. lxiv ff.).

84 Review of *The Seven Lamps* in the *Rambler*, September 1849. A review of *The Stones of Venice* 2, in the *Ecclesiologist*, continued this line of attack, accusing him of taking 'no notice of the efforts and successes of other architectural writers and thinkers in the same field' – but by this the ecclesiologists would have been referring to themselves.

85 The works Ruskin discussed were Fergusson's *An Historical Inquiry into the True Principles of Beauty in Art, more Especially with Reference to Architecture* (London, 1849); and Garbett's *Rudimentary Treatise on the Principles of Design in Architecture as deducible from Nature and Exemplified in the Works of the Greek and Gothic Architects* (London, 1850). See Hanson

[note 17], pp. 168-80; and Peter Kohane, *Architecture, Labor and the Human Body: Fergusson, Cockerell and Ruskin* (unpublished PhD thesis, University of Pennsylvania, 1993).

86 *Works*, 8, pp. 218-19.

87 *Works*, 12, p. 62.

88 Brian Hanson, 'Carrying off the Grand Canal', *Architectural Review*, 169 (1981), pp. 104-9.

89 *Works*, 10, p. 466. According to a *Fors Clavigera* letter of May 1874 (*Works*, 28, p. 83) these were 8ft high and 12ft wide.

90 *Works*, 12, p. lxxi.

91 Acland built another in Oxford, near to the Museum: it was described as 'an institute, with reading-rooms and other conveniences', for the workmen's use (*Works*, 16, p. xlix).

92 This story is referred to more fully in Peter Howell's chapter in this volume, and in Hanson [note 17], p. 208.

93 *Works*, 36, p. 266.

94 *Works*, 8, pp. 13-14.

95 As note 80.

96 He took with him Henry Clutton, a member of his Visiting Committee, and the Earl de Grey, President of the RIBA.

97 For Prince Albert's, largely vain, desire to 'centralise' activities at South Kensington, see Asa Briggs, 'Prince Albert and the Arts and Sciences', in John A. S. Phillips (editor), *Prince Albert and the Victorian Age* (Cambridge, 1981), p. 73. Cole's treachery in his dealings with the Museum is dealt with at greater length in Scott [note 19], p. 170.

98 Henry Cole, *An Introductory Lecture on the Facilities Afforded by the Department of Practical Art ... 24th of November 1852* (London, 1853), pp. 11-12.

99 He agreed to lecture on his 'Selection of Objects' shortly after the Museum reopened at South Kensington (see note 47 above), but this led to a dispute with Street in the *Builder*, 16 (1858), pp. 228-9. He returned to a fuller involvement – writing a catalogue and guide to the Museum's collections – only after the Museum returned to Westminster, to occupy a specially-designed building in Tufton Street.

100 *The Art Workman's Position. A Lecture Delivered in Behalf of the Architectural Museum at the South Kensington Museum* (London, 1864), p. 8.

101 South Kensington having been been overwhelmed by the increasing numbers of general visitors.

102 Clarke Papers (British Architectural Library) Ac/JC/11.

103 M. B. Adams recalls the transfer, which he helped arrange, in *Journal of the Royal Institute of British Architects*, 3rd series 19 (1912), p. 606.

104 Richard Price, *British Society 1630-1880: Dynamism, Containment and Change* (Cambridge, 1999), p. 296. Earlier, however, Goethe had consistently interpreted the Gothic – particularly that of Strasbourg Minster – as the product of a single great mind (Robson Scott [note 34], pp. 76ff).

105 *Works*, 8, p. 20.

[106] Street [note 50], p. 117. He made the remarks about the work of the original builders of Christ Church Cathedral, Dublin.

[107] As described in a talk to the Architectural Photographic Association, *Building News*, 14 (1867), p. 148.

[108] In fact, Scott accused Street of as much in his 1858 lecture at the Museum (see notes 47 and 99), Street responding by saying 'he should have known better than to attempt to raise a cheer at my expense' (*Builder*, 16 (1858), p. 228).

[109] *Works*, 5, p. 113. The episode comes from the *Iliad*. It was mutton and goat, as well as pork, which Achilles chopped and sliced, cooked over the fire, salted, and then served with bread to Ulysses and Ajax.

[110] *Works*, 36, pp. 306, 309 – letters from Germany to Mrs John Simon, and George Richmond.

[111] Ibid., p. 415.

[112] Francis Bacon, *New Atlantis* (New York, 1909-14), para. 30. Michael Wheeler [note 67] traces a number of interesting parallels between Ruskin and Solomon but does not include this one.

[113] *Works*, 20, p. 208.

[114] Tim Hilton, who in his *John Ruskin: the Later Years*, (New Haven and London, 2000) examines the La Touche connection in some detail, neglects the rose petal symbolism of this episode from *Faust*.

[115] *Works*, 36, p. 567. The much-ridiculed digging expeditions with Oxford students on the Hinksey Road (1874) were clearly yet another example of Ruskin's continuing Faustian obsession.

[116] *Works*, 9, p. 452.

[117] The phrase come from Tennyson's *In Memoriam* (1850), verse 94:
> The memory, like a cloudless air,
> The conscience, like a sea at rest.

[118] *Works*, 10, p. 225. The differences between Naturalism, Purism and Sensualism were first set out in 'The Nature of Gothic' in *The Stones of Venice* 2 (1853), and then expanded for *Modern Painters* 3 (1856). The Purists, when reaping wheat, would select only 'the fine flour'; the Sensualists 'the chaff and straw'; the Naturalists, taking all home, would 'make their cake of the one, and their couch of the other.'

[119] Jackson [note 41], p. 51. 'Pre-Raffaelitism', Scott told Jackson in 1858, was 'exactly what architecture is most in need of at the present time', but conceded that its exponents 'painted like a school of madmen let loose'.

[120] For a fuller account of the Pre-Raphaelite 'rebellion' against Ruskin's expectations over the Museum, see Hanson [note 17], pp. 220-6.

[121] Apart from Millais, who was coached by Ruskin at Glenfinlas in 1853 (and who could be of no further use to him after he had married Effie Ruskin), Thomas Seddon came closest to fulfilling Ruskin's distinctive vision of Pre-Raphaelitism, but he died in 1856. Ruskin's 1857 words in memory of Seddon (*Works*, 14, p. 464) make it clear that it was the 'prosaic' quality in Seddon he chiefly valued.

[122] *Works*, 16, p. 462.

[123] *Works*, 10, p. 224.

[124] W. R. Lethaby, *Philip Webb and His Work* (London, 1935), p. 122.

[125] Ibid, p. 133.

[126] Few present day architects come closer to this 'Ruskinian' ideal than the California-based architect and theorist, Christopher Alexander, whose four-volume work on *The Nature of Order*, has now begun publication with Book One, 'The Phenomenon of Life' (Berkeley, 2002).

[127] See, for example, Dinah Birch, *Ruskin's Myths* (Oxford, 1988).

5
Ruskin and the Politics of Gothic

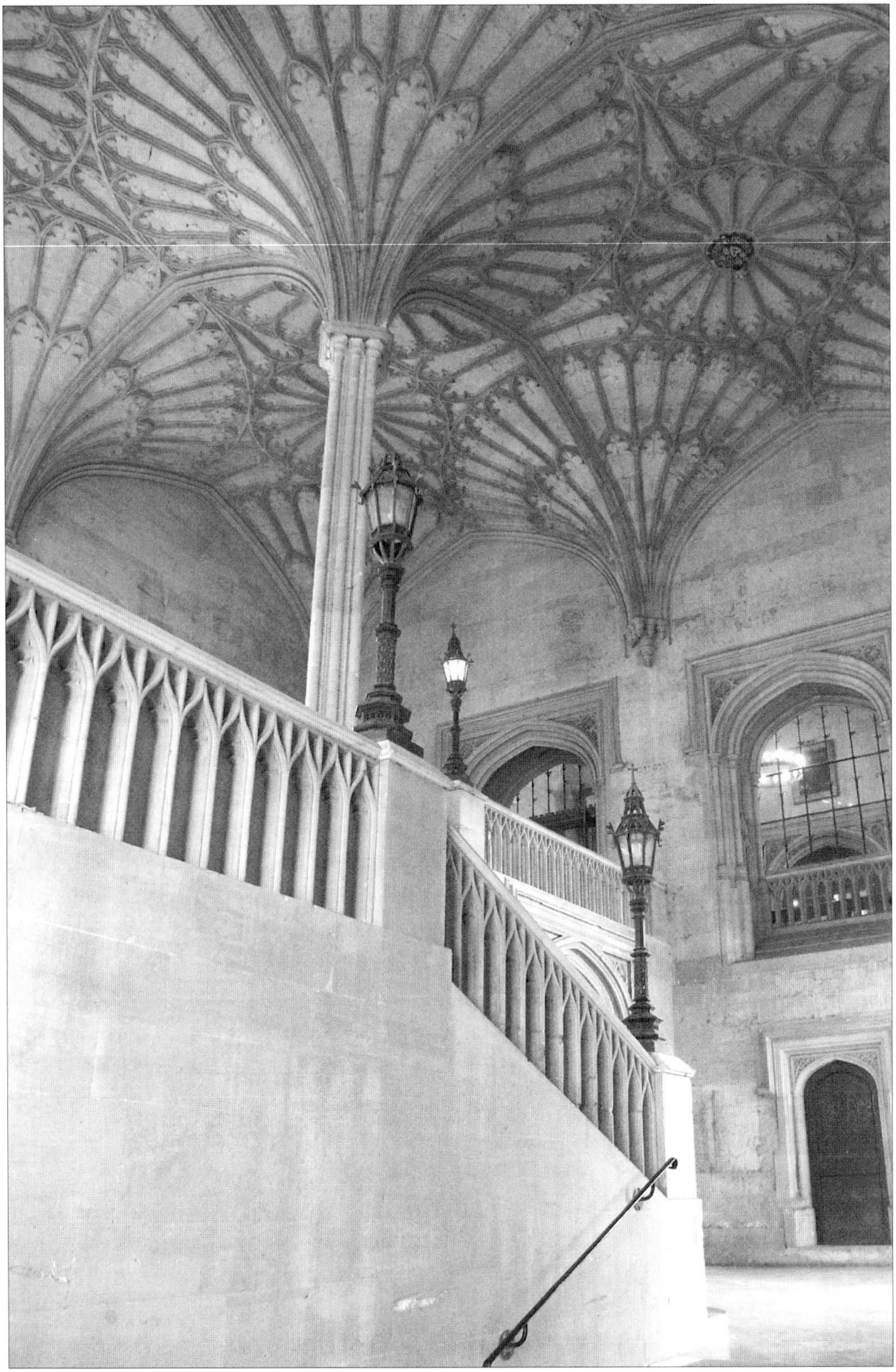

Ruskin and the Politics of Gothic[1]

Chris Brooks

> The aspect of the years that approach us is as solemn as it is full of mystery; and the weight of evil against which we have to contend, is increasing like the letting out of water. It is no time for the idleness of metaphysics, or the entertainment of the arts. The blasphemies of the earth are sounding louder, and its miseries heaped heavier every day'.[2]

SO SAYS JOHN RUSKIN, waxing apocalyptic, in the brief 'Introductory' section to *The Seven Lamps of Architecture*. It is the kind of passage – and it continues for another 140 words or so, all the same sentence – that modern readers, and even learned commentators, are apt to skip, putting it down to a kind of rhetorical lather - sudsy but diffuse. However, as Cook and Wedderburn suggest in a footnote to this passage, both the occasion and the object of this particular apocalyptic outburst were specific, and would have been recognised as such by Ruskin's contemporaries, reading his book in the year of its publication, 1849. The second paragraph of the introduction had already informed them that architecture is 'a distinctively political art', its principles analogous to those that apply to 'human polity' generally.[3] And even before that, the attentive reader would have picked up the political moment of the book's conception: in a lengthy footnote to the preface Ruskin informs us that his researches in France and Italy had been spurred by the need to obtain 'as many memoranda as possible' of buildings 'now in process of destruction, before that destruction should be consummated by the Restorer, or Revolutionist'.[4] Leaving the 'Restorer' to one side for the moment, it is the 'Revolutionist' who points us to the historical genesis of *The Seven Lamps* and to the book's specifically political anxieties. The 'mystery' of the future, the 'weight of evil', the 'blasphemies of the earth', and the 'miseries', all spring from the year Ruskin was writing *The Seven Lamps*, 1848, the European 'Year of Revolutions'.

The insurrections began in France with the overthrow of

Opposite: Christ Church, Oxford. Gothic was revived extensively at Oxford and, to a lesser extent, at Cambridge in the 17th century. It denoted cultural and religious continuity, validating the present through a glorious past (*Stephen Hone*).

THE NEW CONTINENTAL COACH "REVOLUTION."

'The New Continental coach "Revolution"' carries off the crowned heads of Europe (*Punch,* 14 (1848), p. 162). Is it about to call in on John Bull?

Louis-Philippe, then spread across Europe, toppling monarchical governments in Austria and the Hapsburg Empire, in Prussia and the German kingdoms and principalities, in the states that made up Italy, including Rome itself. There were major disturbances in Spain and Belgium, a brief rising in famine-ravished Ireland, and civil disturbances in England and Scotland. Within a year or so all the brave new revolutionary governments of Europe had collapsed or been overthrown, their repression often producing regimes more autocratic than before. Nevertheless, the political status quo that had prevailed since the Congress of Vienna was shattered, and the political shape of the continent transformed. This was the disordered context in which Ruskin had looked at the medieval buildings of France and Italy, the context in which he came to conceive of architecture as 'a distinctively political art' whose principles were to be established by the light that fell from the lamps of Sacrifice, Truth, Power, Beauty, Life, Memory, and Obedience. Principles formerly realised, and – for Ruskin - only capable of being realised in the future, through Gothic.

Pervading the text of *The Seven Lamps,* inherited by Ruskin's architectural discourse though largely unacknowledged, is a complex of cultural relationships in which the concept of Gothic is closely enmeshed with revolutionary politics – both by way of endorsement and by way of antithesis. As this set of relationships has been all but ignored by architectural historians, it is necessary to spend a little time sketching in its origins and development.

We must begin as far back as the early 16th century, in the Swedish University of Uppsala. Here, conscious of the

The great Chartist meeting at Kennington Common [above] (Illustrated London News, *15 April 1848, p. 242*) and conflict at the Place Maubert, Paris, 1848 [left] (Illustrated London News, *1 July 1848, p. 436*). Like so many of his contemporaries, Ruskin was fearful that the English scene might turn into the French one.

Opposite: the Gothic Temple, Shotover, Oxfordshire, 1716-17. The first Gothic Revival garden building in Europe, it was built for James Tyrrell, a propagandist of the Gothic constitution (*Geoff Brandwood*).

growing power and military ambition of Sweden, scholars sought to counter the dominant – and still familiar – cultural history being eagerly promoted by writers of the Italian Renaissance, according to which the destruction of the ancient Roman Empire by the Gothic hordes of northern Europe was a catastrophe for civilisation that ushered in a millennium of darkness. The historical geographers of Uppsala established an alternative Gothic history. This drew extensively on a mid-6th-century work by Jordanes, *De Origine Actibusque Getarum* (The Origin and Deeds of the Getes), usually known as the *Getica*. According to Jordanes the Gothic tribes originated in Scandza, which Uppsala's scholars identified as Sweden and the region round the Baltic. The *Getica* tells how the tribes, growing ever more populous, spread south and east from the 3rd century, increasingly came into conflict with the forces of imperial Rome, eventually defeated them, and established supremacy in Italy itself. Jordanes represents the Goths not as barbarians, but as a young and vigorous people opposing an Empire moribund and corrupt. Rough as it was, Gothic energy had rightly swept aside Roman decadence. Writers outside Sweden expanded the story on the basis of the 1st century work *Germania*, by the Roman historian Tacitus. Like the Goths in the *Getica*, Tacitus's Germans were a warrior race. But they were also distinguished by an intense love of liberty, preferring death to enslavement, living in open countryside on their own land, choosing their own kings, and making major decisions through tribal assemblies. A stalwart folk, continent in their sexual conduct, the Germans were also generous and open-hearted, incapable of the dissimulation which, Tacitus implies, the Romans had learned only too well.

With this compound history in place, ancient cause and effect looked very different. Imperial Rome had not been toppled by mere barbarian muscle, but by the Goths' love of personal and political liberty, their scorn of servitude, their purity – by all the noble simplicity of a people fiercely free. Their triumph brought the establishment across Europe of free Gothic polities, whose origin could be traced back across the reaches of Germania to the distant homeland of Scandza, 'the womb of nations' from whence the whole continent, liberated from Roman oppression, was renewed and replenished.

Once set going, the alternative Gothic history proved to have an extraordinary power. It afforded a compelling analogy and precedent for protagonists of the German

Hampden House, Buckinghamshire, remodelled from c.1738. It had been home to John Hampden who died a martyr for the Parliamentary cause in 1643. The choice of style was surely a celebration in architecture of Gothic liberty (*Geoff Brandwood*).

Reformation: just as the liberty-loving Goths had thrown off the tyranny of imperial Rome, so their descendants, the German Protestants, battled against the dominion of papal Rome. In France in 1573, a work called *Franco-Gallia*, by the Huguenot François Hotman, traced Gauls and Franks - the two historical French peoples - back to Germanic roots. A similar job for the English was done in 1605 by Richard Verstegen's *Restitution of Decayed Intelligence,* according to which the Germanic tribes who settled England after the Roman withdrawal brought with them not only an innate love of liberty but also the specific features of a free Gothic polity.

It was in England that all this had the most dramatic consequences. In their great struggle with the Crown, English Parliamentarians seized on Gothic history to prove that parliaments had a lineage that stretched back before the Norman Conquest, to the representative councils of the Saxons, and ultimately to the tribal assemblies of ancient

Germania. Such parliaments, they claimed, were the inalienable birthright of the English and were ultimately sovereign, retaining the right to elect the king. When the dispute became open revolution in the Civil War of the 1640s, Gothic history and theory were part of the ideological armoury of the Roundheads. In 1647, the parliamentarian Nathaniel Bacon wrote triumphantly, 'Nor can any nation upon Earth shew so much of the ancient Gothique law as this Island hath'. Two years later, under this same 'ancient Gothique law', a sovereign Court of Parliament sent King Charles I to the executioner's block. Forty years later, when the constitutional struggle was re-enacted and James II deposed in the so-called Glorious Revolution, revolt was again justified by an appeal to the Gothic legacy, by now deftly manoeuvred to include the rights of landed property.

It was Gothic's specifically political meaning that first determined its adoption as an architectural style for garden buildings. From the Gothic Temple at Shotover, Oxfordshire, erected in 1716-17 for the Gothic theorist and propagandist James Tyrrell, Gothic structures - temples, towers, ruins - connoting by their style the history of Gothic liberty were

The Temple of Liberty, Stowe, Buckinghamshire, c.1741–2, designed by James Gibbs for the grounds of the house of Richard Temple, Viscount Cobham. It shares its hilltop with the seven deities of Saxon England. Cobham led a section of the Whigs in opposition to the Prime Minister, Sir Robert Walpole. They considered his closeness to the Court a threat to the very freedom of Parliament. So the 'Temple' is, of course, both the building and Cobham himself (*John Elliott*).

Opposite: the Stone Council Chamber of the Provincial Council Buildings, Canterbury, New Zealand, 1864-5. Here, on the other side of the world, north European Gothic was used by the English emigré architect, Benjamin Mountfort (1825-98) to powerful effect (*Duncan Shaw-Brown*).

built in landscape gardens throughout the 18th century. This political semantic also contributed to the emergence of domestic Gothic: thus, Hampden House in Buckinghamshire, Gothicised as early as the 1730s, was the family home of John Hampden, parliamentarian hero and martyr of the Civil War. Ultimately, the political identification of Gothic with constitutional liberty found its fullest expression in Barry and Pugin's new Palace of Westminster, the British Houses of Parliament - still being built, of course, when Ruskin was writing *The Seven Lamps*. And from Westminster, the idea of the free Gothic polity was carried stylistically across the world: to Fuller and Jones' Canadian Parliament Buildings in Ottawa, to Benjamin Mountfort's Council Chamber in Canterbury, New Zealand, to Imre Steindl's Hungarian Parliament Buildings in Budapest - not finished until 1904.

Despite its absorption into political orthodoxy, Gothic never quite lost its original revolutionary associations. Thus, in the 1780s, Charles Howard, later 11th Duke of Norfolk - a thoroughly unlikely radical - expressed his support for the American Revolution by building two Gothic farmhouses on his Lake District estates and naming them Fort Putnam and Bunker Hill, thus recruiting the American struggle for independence into the long history of Gothic liberty. In the 1790s, taking the form of another cultural product, the phenomenal efflorescence of the Gothic novel was linked by

The Palace of Westminster seen in the early 20th century. Gothic, with all its meanings and associations, was the style consciously chosen for the Mother of Parliaments (*Rebecca Daniels' collection*).

contemporary commentators to the violent upheavals of the French Revolution. Even the Palace of Westminster, in the cumulative iconography of its statuary and paintings, is surprisingly frank about Britain's Gothic inheritance of revolutionary disruption.

The whole cluster of political meanings I have been describing came down to Ruskin and his generation as integral to the very idea of Gothic. So too did another, countervailing semantic set, which identified Gothic with traditions of authority in Church and State derived from the Middle Ages. Such meanings also emerged in the early 17th century with the conscious adoption of medieval architectural style – not yet labelled 'Gothic' in England – for new buildings in Oxford and Cambridge Universities, where it connoted the legitimacy of contemporary power by virtue of its continuity with the medieval past. Such meanings also fed into the revived Gothic of the 18th century, and became dominant during the period of the Napoleonic Wars, when Romantic castles spoke of inherited authority, patriotic resistance to enemies abroad, stern defiance in the face of sedition at home – their evocation of chivalric values glamorously supported by Walter Scott's medievalist novels. A kindred ideological significance attends the Manor House or Old English style so widely adopted for the houses of the squirearchy and lesser gentry. And, as with the semantics of Gothic liberty, revolutions and all, Gothic's conservative meanings – monarchical, aristocratic, chivalric – form a major part of the elaborate iconography of the Palace of Westminster.

This brings us back at last to the 1840s and John Ruskin. Ruskin's response to the Year of Revolutions was more than a rather panicky sense that everything was descending into chaos. Because he thought architectural true principles were cognate with the principles that should govern human polities generally; because he regarded architecture as 'a distinctively political art'; and because the understanding of Gothic he inherited was instinct with the complex but contradictory political meanings I have described, the insurrections across Europe confronted him with a crisis in architectural semantics. Neither a revolutionary not a reactionary – or, more accurately perhaps, a revolutionary in some things and a reactionary in others – what could Ruskin find in Gothic that would speak to the distemper of the present? What now was its political agency? Here Ruskin, like other architectural reformers whose aesthetic concerns are meshed with larger social issues, faced a dilemma. In common with so many of his contemporaries, he understood buildings semiotically, convinced that a society's dominant beliefs about the order of things shaped it at every level, continuously repeated, re-enacted, down to the most menial task of the lowliest citizen, so that architecture becomes 'in some sort the embodiment of the Polity, Life, History, and Religious Faith of nations'.[5] But did this mean that a better state of things architecturally had to wait upon the proper constitution of society as a whole? And what hope was there when nations were as profoundly disordered as they appeared to Ruskin in 1848?

Deftly, if not wholly logically, Ruskin worked the conundrum the other way. Because of the continuities and homologies he perceived between architectural polity and social polity, by discovering the principles that make for great architecture he would also be revealing the right principles for running society. In its general discussion, and even more in its accounts of individual buildings, *The Seven Lamps* is focused on the outstanding works of the European Middle Ages, particularly cathedrals. Post-medieval architecture gets hardly a look-in, and the actual products of the Gothic Revival are barely mentioned. Ruskin thus, apparently, vaults over two and a half centuries of Gothic's accumulated meanings and returns to source. Not really, of course, for those meanings were unavoidable, shaping the whole way in which he, and indeed his readers, approached Gothic. The resulting principles, the seven lamps themselves, are prescriptive and strong on the necessity for order – of obvious significance in the context of 1848. There are hierarchies of ornament, hierarchies of detail and of finish. Architectural proportion depends upon subordination and supremacy, and - to quote 'The Lamp of Beauty' – a 'rule of supremacy applies to the smallest as well as to leading features' of Gothic buildings.[6] Sculptural decoration should be obedient to the forms of the natural world because here 'God has stamped those characters of beauty which He has made it man's nature to love'.[7] Indeed, the very act of architectural design replicates a divine hierarchy, for it embodies 'an understanding of the dominion … vested in man' over 'the works of God upon earth'.[8]

All these, it should be stressed, are not just the physical or visual attributes of architecture: they are simultaneously, co-extensively components of a semantic. When we read Gothic buildings through Ruskin's eyes – in 1849 at least – we are reading exemplifications of hierarchy, the law of supremacy, an order ordained by God. As understood by the Victorians, the principle vehicle of architectural semantics was style. Ruskin saves his stylistic programme for the last lamp of all, 'The Lamp of Obedience'. There is no need to labour the contemporary political significance of that: in Ruskin's own words, obedience is the principle 'to which Polity owes its stability, Life its happiness, Faith its acceptance, Creation its continuance'.[9] As dictatorial as Pugin or the young zealots of the Cambridge Camden Society, Ruskin asserts the need for a uniform national architecture. Away with eclectic muddle and with debates about whether the 19th century had its own style.

> We want no new style of architecture ... But we want *some* style. It is of marvellously little importance, if we have a code of laws and they be good laws, whether they be new or old, foreign or native ... But it is of considerable importance that we should have a code of laws of one kind or another, and that code accepted and enforced from one side of the island to another'.[10]

Acceptance he might hope for; but what kind of bizarre authoritarian dream led Ruskin to imagine that stylistic obedience could be 'enforced'? By what mechanism? Act of Parliament? Style-police? Self-appointed vigilantes, perhaps, pouncing on architects who like to indulge in a few Corinthian details in the privacy of their own homes? Rather shamefacedly – I hope – Ruskin back-tracks. 'It may be said that this is impossible. It may be so – I fear it is so'.[11] Yet the rhetoric is not as vapid as it seems, for it has a displaced object, apparent in the chapter's first pages: 'how false is the conception, how frantic the pursuit, of that treacherous phantom which men call Liberty: most treacherous indeed of all phantoms'.[12] The 'phantom', of course, had shaken the whole of Europe in the Year of Revolutions. Strikingly, though doubtless coincidentally, Ruskin's imagery echoes a more famous version of the ghosts of 1848: 'A spectre is haunting Europe – the spectre of Communism', in the words with which Marx and Engels open the *Communist Manifesto*, written in the first weeks of that momentous year. In *The Seven Lamps* Ruskin appears to equate freedom with anarchy, a violation of the principle of law which orders the universe, which should govern both politics and architecture, and which Ruskin found exemplified in medieval Gothic. Hence the insistence upon stylistic conformity, the nonsense about enforcement a measure of just how desperate Ruskin was. In his spectre-haunted state, he converts Gothic's conservative political identity into a binding authoritarianism that seems wholly to repudiate the style's radical semantic – indeed, that divorces Gothic from the very idea of freedom.

But not quite. When Ruskin comes to prescription, to saying what style everybody should adopt – should be obliged to adopt – the spirit of liberty seems less to have scared him than seduced him.

> The choice would lie I think between four styles: – 1. The Pisan Romanesque; 2. The early Gothic of the Western Italian Republics ... 3. The Venetian Gothic in its purest development; 4. The English earliest decorated ... perhaps enriched by some mingling of decorative elements from the exquisite decorated Gothic of France'.[13]

Italian, French, English; Romanesque, Early Gothic, Decorated; no classical styles, it is true, but hardly a recipe for conformity, and far less categorical than - for example - the kind of Gothic purity that Viollet-le-Duc and Jean-Baptiste Lassus were extolling in France at much the same time. The relative lack of dogmatism in Ruskin's prescription is much closer, I think, to his actual experience of architecture than the authoritarianism that precedes it, and is true to the European perspective of *The Seven Lamps*. It suggests a reaction to the events of 1848 far more positive than law and order aesthetics, as impossible to deliver as they are unsavoury. What Ruskin was really seeking, after the disruption of the whole continent, was a species of European unity symbolised through a new international Gothic.

The very open-endedness of Ruskin's stylistic

prescription allows liberty back into the Gothic semantic – by default as it were. But it is granted a more positive architectural presence in 'The Lamp of Life', which celebrates – albeit tentatively – the free creative vitality Ruskin found in medieval buildings, particularly their sculpture. Though carefully hedged by the disciplinary order upon which *The Seven Lamps* insists, the individuality of craftsmanship carves out – literally and metaphorically – a space for the expression of the free self. 'To those who love Architecture', Ruskin writes, 'the life and accent of the hand are everything'.[14] Which is why, in 'The Lamp of Memory', he pitches so violently into architectural restoration: 'the most total destruction which a building can suffer', he declares with grinding irony, 'a destruction out of which no remnants can be gathered: a destruction accompanied with false description of the thing destroyed'.[15] Restoration erases a building's uniqueness: not merely its original design, which can be copied, but the stamp of individuality allowed by the freedom of the decoration, and the wear and tear that witness to the cumulative life of centuries. Every feature of an ancient structure is irreplaceable because it signifies a development through time that is uniquely its own. By a deft intellectual manoeuvre, those twin bogeys from the opening pages of *The Seven Lamps*, the revolutionist and the restorer, become complementary, despite their apparently antithetical purposes. The revolutionary destroys the political order of the past in pursuit of a chimerical liberty; the restorer destroys the creative liberty of the past in pursuit of an illusory order.

It was Ruskin's passionate commitment to 'the life and accent of the hand' that became the basis of his political understanding of architecture. In it he found a historical paradigm for the relationship between cultural production and material production, and he began to read a history of human labour in every mark that the blow of adze or chisel had left on the stone. As Ruskin's thinking developed, he increasingly concentrated upon the material conditions, the economic, social and physical circumstances, in which, and out of which, people make the things of their culture – from cartwheels to cathedrals. That complex of issues was every day compelling greater and greater attention, for there lay the primary shaping force of the 19th century, and indeed the modern world: the colossal, unprecedented expansion in human productive potential brought about by industrialisation and driven by the entrepreneurial dynamic of capitalism. Behind the alarms and disasters of 1848 Marx and Engels – rightly or wrongly – had seen the first attempt of the European proletariat to overthrow the bourgeoisie who commanded the capitalist economy. In Britain, the first nation to industrialise and urbanise, industrial capitalism replaced agrarian capitalism as the dominant mode of production as the century passed its mid-point. The census of 1851 showed that, for the first time, more than half the British population lived in towns and cities. In the same year, of course, came the Great Exhibition, that extraordinary celebration of British and international manufacturing profusion, of the modern world's ability to make more things than humankind had ever dreamed of. At the core of the Exhibition's concerns was the relationship between all this material production and the stuff of culture – the realm of what became known as art manufactures. A principal occupant of that realm was the Gothic Revival, its cultural identity premised on a prodigious output generated from, enabled by, industrial processes and labour structures, mechanised transport, and capitalist enterprise. Witness the fact that a star attraction of the Great Exhibition was the Medieval Court, supervised by none other than Augustus Pugin.

Also in 1851, Ruskin brought out the first volume of *The Stones of Venice*, volumes 2 and 3 following two years later. In its theoretical concerns, *The Stones of Venice* shows an advance upon the panicky authoritarianism of *The Seven Lamps*. It explicitly addresses the relationship between material production and cultural production, and, implicitly, engages the ideological issues raised by the Great Exhibition. And, in the process of its argument, *The Stones of Venice* finds a new place for, and offers a new account of, the age-old politics of Gothic liberty. The crucial chapter opens Ruskin's account of Venice's 'Second, or Gothic Period' in volume 2, and is entitled 'The Nature of Gothic'. Ruskin defines Gothic in terms both of its necessary 'external forms', most importantly the pointed arch and the gable, and its 'internal elements', which he calls 'moral' as well as 'internal': Savageness, Changefulness, Naturalism, Grotesqueness, Rigidity, Redundance. These 'elements' express a matching set of 'mental tendencies' in Gothic's original medieval builders: Savageness or Rudeness, Love of Change, Love of Nature, Disturbed Imagination, Obstinacy, Generosity. It seems striking just how closely these 'mental tendencies' parallel the qualities Tacitus found in the Germanic tribes, and that the historians of the 16th and 17th centuries assigned to the Goths. Rudeness is directly analogous to the anti-sophistication that Tacitus admired in the Germanic folk and that he saw as a concomitant of their fierce independence. Love of Change, and its aesthetic equivalent, Disturbed Imagination, both stem from a refusal to be trammelled, the mental passion for liberty that was the basis of the free Gothic polities. Love of Nature relates to Tacitus's assertion that the German peoples detested cities, and always chose to live on their own farmsteads in the countryside. Obstinacy in Tacitus takes the form of the tribes' refusal to accept conquest, their stalwart preference for death in defence of their freedom, rather than capitulation. There is even Generosity in the original account, for Tacitus pays tribute to the open-heartedness of the Germanic folk.

What Ruskin was responding to was not – by his day – a literal account of Gothic's origins, but a mythological history. About this he is explicit: at the beginning of his discussion of Savageness he sees this first and most important of Gothic's 'internal elements' as being 'like a perpetual reflection of the contrast between the Goth and the Roman in their first encounter'.[16] The history, outlined earlier, was matched with a mythological geography, and this too re-emerges in *The Stones of Venice*. Ruskin's account of Savageness continues with the famously imagined flight northward over Europe, a journey from the Mediterranean's 'great peacefulness of light' to an assignation with the sublime that is at once a destiny, a point of destination, and a place of origin:

farther north still, to see the earth heave into mighty

masses of leaden rock and heathy moor, bordering with a great waste of gloomy purple that belt of field and wood, and splintering into irregular and grisly islands amidst the northern seas, beaten by storm, and chilled by ice-drift, and tormented by furious pulses of contending tide, until the roots of the last forest fail from among the hill ravines, and the hunger of the north wind bites their peaks into barrenness; and, at last, the wall of ice, durable as iron, sets, deathlike, its white teeth against us out of the polar twilight.[18]

The flight's final landscape, I would suggest, is that of Scandza, the womb of nations and the mythic home of the Gothic folk. The flight's direction follows that of the passage's imaginative impetus. So too Ruskin's sweep through Europe's architecture, that asks us to 'reverence' the southerner who 'smoothes with soft sculpture the jasper pillars, that are to reflect a ceaseless sunshine', but finally places us at the shoulder of the northern builder:

let us stand by him, when, with rough strength and hurried stroke, he smites an uncouth animation out of the rocks which he has torn from among the moss of the moorland, and heaves into the darkened air the pile of iron buttress and rugged wall, instinct with a work of an imagination as wild and wayward as the northern sea; creations of ungainly shape and rigid limb, but full of wolfish life; fierce as the winds that beat, and changeful as the clouds that shade them.[18]

Here is the Savageness Ruskin seeks, and for him it is the heart of Gothic's political semantic – as perhaps it always has been. Ruskin finds Savageness in medieval Gothic's untrammelled energy, particularly in the individual vigour of the carving, which speaks of a rude creative liberty in its makers. By contrast, he invites you, the bourgeois reader, to 'look round this English room of yours', with its ornaments 'so finished', its 'accurate mouldings, and perfect polishings, and unerring adjustments of the seasoned wood and tempered steel'.[19] No Savageness here: but also no energy, no vigour, no individuality, because the modern room, modern smartness and convenience, are not products of creative freedom but 'signs of a slavery in our England a thousand times more bitter and more degrading than that of the scourged African, or helot Greek'.[20] They are the end results of a process by which 'flesh and skin' is turned into 'leathern thongs to yoke machinery with', by which the very life-force of England's people is 'given daily to be wasted into the fineness of a web, or racked into the exactness of a line'. They are the consumer products of industrial capitalism. Not just of industry, it should be stressed, but of industry in its capitalist form, dependent upon the principle of the division of labour and upon treating labour as a commodity. Indeed, in Ruskin's dramatic version, the work-force has become nothing more than expendable raw material, 'sent like fuel to feed the factory smoke'. Ruskin then turns back to medieval Gothic and presents it to us afresh, with a new way of understanding what its past tells our present:

> go forth again to gaze upon the old cathedral front, where you have smiled so often at the fantastic ignorance of the old sculptors: examine once more those ugly goblins, and formless monsters, and stern statues, anatomiless and rigid; but do not mock at them, for they are signs of the life and liberty of every workman who struck the stone; a freedom of thought, and rank in scale of being, such as no laws, no charters, no charities can secure; but which it must be the first aim of all Europe at this day to regain for her children.[21]

With the Year of Revolutions and its aftermath in mind, but with a perspective quite different from that of *The Seven Lamps*, Ruskin sees modern economic process, 'the degradation of the operative into a machine', as an intolerable slavery driving 'the mass of the nations everywhere into vain, incoherent, destructive struggling for ... freedom'.[22] The radical logic of Ruskin's position is clear: he demands the abolition of the prevailing conditions of production, and does so in the full knowledge that they are the inevitable concomitants of industrial capitalism. Only by a revolution in the conditions determining how people labour and produce can 'the life and liberty of every workman' be regained, and bringing this about 'must be the

The dignity of human labour and the freedom for the craftsman to express himself is exemplified in the Animal Wall (1887-8) around William Burges's Cardiff Castle. Inspired by the 13th-century drawings of Villard de Honnecourt the carvings were by Thomas Nicholls (*John Elliott*).

Below: capital within the Oxford University Museum probably carved by James O'Shea. The O'Shea brothers, who carried out much of the work in the Museum, epitomised the Ruskinian model of the craftsman (*Jeanne Sheehy*).

first aim of all Europe at this day'. Suddenly, though he would have been appalled at keeping such company, John Ruskin stands very close to Karl Marx: like Marx, he sees an economic origin to the insurrections of 1848; like Marx, he bases his interpretation of economic conditions on the relations of production; like Marx, he sees dehumanisation – 'alienation' in Marxist terminology – as an inherent part of industrial capitalism; and like Marx, he seeks a solution that by its nature is Materialist, in the philosophical sense of the word, not Idealist. Most unlike Marx, however, Ruskin came to such a view by studying medieval architecture. In *The Stones of Venice*, particularly in 'The Nature of Gothic', the old radicalism of Gothic history and political theory is taken over and rewritten, to re-emerge in a new alliance between

Gothic and liberty that opposes economic tyranny in the cause of individual creative freedom. Hierarchically-minded, Ruskin could not stay with the revolutionary position he had arrived at; though he could never quite abandon it either, as witnessed by later works like *Unto This Last* (1860), *The Crown of Wild Olive* (1866), and the extraordinary series of 'Letters to the Workmen and Labourers of Great Britain' that go under the title *Fors Clavigera* and were published between 1871 and 1884. Increasingly, he withdrew support for the Gothic Revival, angry that medieval buildings continued to be restored, bitter that architecture adopted his stylistic proposals while ignoring the arguments that, to his mind, justified them. In an acerbic preface to the 1880 edition of *The Seven Lamps*, he dismissed the book as 'the most useless I ever wrote', adding, in a subsequent footnote, the 'only living art now left in England is Bill-sticking'.

Despite Ruskin's disillusion, his remaking of Gothic's political identity had profound resonances for the Gothic Revival – both its practices and its ideological purposes. The toughness, expressive vigour, and individualism of High Victorian Gothic takes much of its conceptual justification from the characteristics Ruskin described in 'The Nature of Gothic'. His insistence on the liberty of the craftsman not only produced the decorative experimentation of the Oxford University Museum but also encouraged those integrated programmes of craft and architecture of which George Gilbert Scott made such a success, most famously in the creation of the Albert Memorial, and of which William Burges was the most extraordinary exponent. More radically, the workshops and utopian collectives of the Arts and Crafts Movement drew their ideals from Ruskin's account of medieval Gothic production – even when their output was no longer Gothic stylistically. Nor was Ruskin's influence limited to Britain. In the *post bellum* United States the adoption of the characteristic manner of High Victorian Gothic from Britain was underpinned by the high-minded moral and social imperatives of Ruskin's architectural gospel – so much so that American historians refer to the style as 'Ruskinian Gothic'. It was used principally for cultural and educational buildings in northern states intent on exemplary construction – social as well as architectural – during and after the Civil War. In Philadelphia, the brilliant Frank Furness developed Ruskinian Gothic not only in the cause of an extreme and idiosyncratic expressiveness, but also in the service of an explicit political programme. Building for a circle of reformers campaigning against Philadelphia's notoriously corrupt bosses, Furness exploited Gothic qualities of strenuousness, structural honesty, toughness, even Savageness – to use Ruskin's term – to exemplify integrity in a city sapped by political graft and moral dereliction. Although Ruskin's impact was less direct in Continental Europe, his stylistic and ideological influence is clearly evident in the national Gothic Revivals of Germany, Holland – especially the work of Petrus Cuypers - and Belgium. Intriguing too, especially in terms of the wider politics of Gothic, are the parallels and analogies to Ruskinian doctrine. Most notably in the German Revival under the leadership of Auguste Reichensperger, who based his vision of Gothic on the re-establishment of cathedral *Bauhütten* where architects, designers, and craftsmen were joined in collective creative endeavour. For Reichensperger, the *Bauhütten* had an expressly political function as well, for he saw them as centres of reinvigorated regional culture that would act as a counter to the centralising power of Prussia in a unified Germany. This was too much to hope, but the whole idea, like Gothic politics in general, proved to have considerable staying power. In the early 20th century, the Ruskinian ideals of the British Arts and Crafts Movement, mediated through the anti-academy artists of the Vienna Secession, were grafted back onto the German *Bauhütten* tradition to produce that founding institution of architectural modernism, the Weimar Bauhaus.

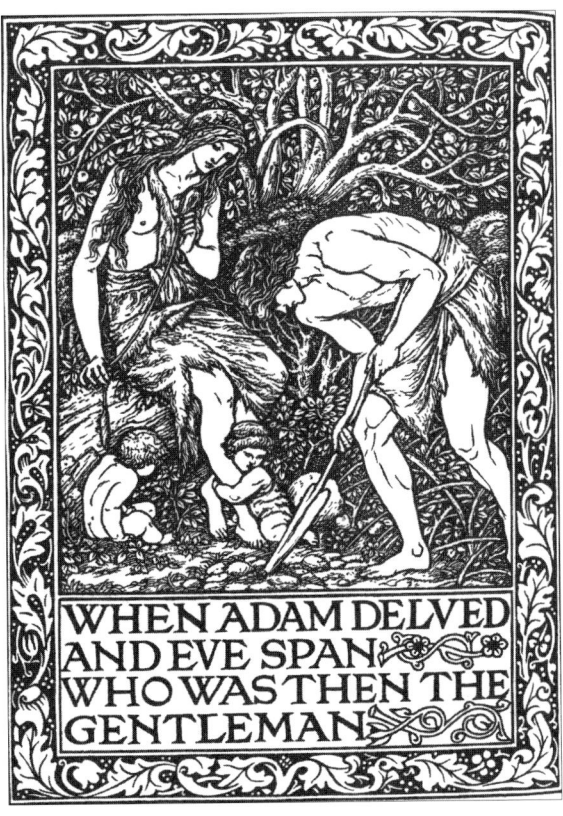

The world before capitalism: *Adam and Eve* by Edward Burne-Jones used by William Morris as the frontispiece to *A Dream of John Ball, and A King's Lesson, Reprinted from* The Commonweal (London, 1888).

The Arts and Crafts Movement was largely shaped, of course, by William Morris and it was Morris, who felt that 'The Nature of Gothic' would become 'one of the very few necessary and inevitable utterances of the [19th] century',[23] who was to become Ruskin's most radical political heir. He made the move that Ruskin could not, linking the campaign for a transformation in material and thus cultural production to an overt revolutionary politic. From the 1870s Morris was a committed Marxist, not only writing and propagandising for the cause but also actively involved in working-class political organisation. In his 'Utopian Romance' of 1890, *News from Nowhere*, he imagined England after the overthrow of capitalism as a loose federation of collectives, industry abolished and money redundant, with a population of craftsmen and craftswomen working for the pleasure of work's creativity and making buildings, clothes and artefacts independent of historical style but closest in spirit to the products of the fourteenth century. It is Marx filtered through Ruskin, or Ruskin read through Marx. But it is also an expression of a radical tradition that predates either of them, the old politics of Gothic liberty, the old story of the ancient Gothic folk fighting the imperialism of their oppressors. And Morris was conscious of the fact. As he put it in an article in *Commonweal*, written the same year as *News from Nowhere*, 'we shall be our own Goths, and at whatever cost break up again the new tyrannous Empire of Capitalism'.[24]

Notes

[1] Chris Brooks gave this paper at a symposium entitled 'Ruskin – Past/Present/Future' held in January 2000 at the Yale Center for British Art in New Haven, Connecticut. After publication in the U.S.A. fell through, he agreed to place it in the present volume but his death, in February 2002, meant he had no opportunity to revise it. He is known to have taken justifiable pride in it and we reproduce it with only a few editorial amendments to take account of the written, rather than the spoken word, and the addition of references and a selection of illustrations of which we hope he would have approved (GB).

[2] *Works*, 8, p. 25.
[3] Ibid., p. 20.
[4] Ibid., p. 3.
[5] Ibid., p. 248.

6 Ibid., p. 165.
7 Ibid., p. 142.
8 Ibid., p. 102.
9 Ibid., p. 248.
10 Ibid., p. 252.
11 Ibid., p. 255.
12 Ibid., p. 248.
13 Ibid., pp. 258-9.
14 Ibid., p. 214.
15 Ibid., p. 242.
16 Ibid., 10, p. 185.
17 Ibid., p. 186-7.
18 Ibid., p. 187.
19 Ibid., p. 193.
20 Ibid.
21 Ibid., pp. 193-4.
22 Ibid., p. 194.
23 Preface to chapter 4 of 'The Nature of Gothic' quoted in *Works*, 10, p. 460.
24 This is the concluding sentence of 'The Development of Modern Society', *The Commonweal*, 16 August 1890, p. 261.

6

'Intellectual Lens and Moral Retina': A Reappraisal of Ruskin's Architectural Vision

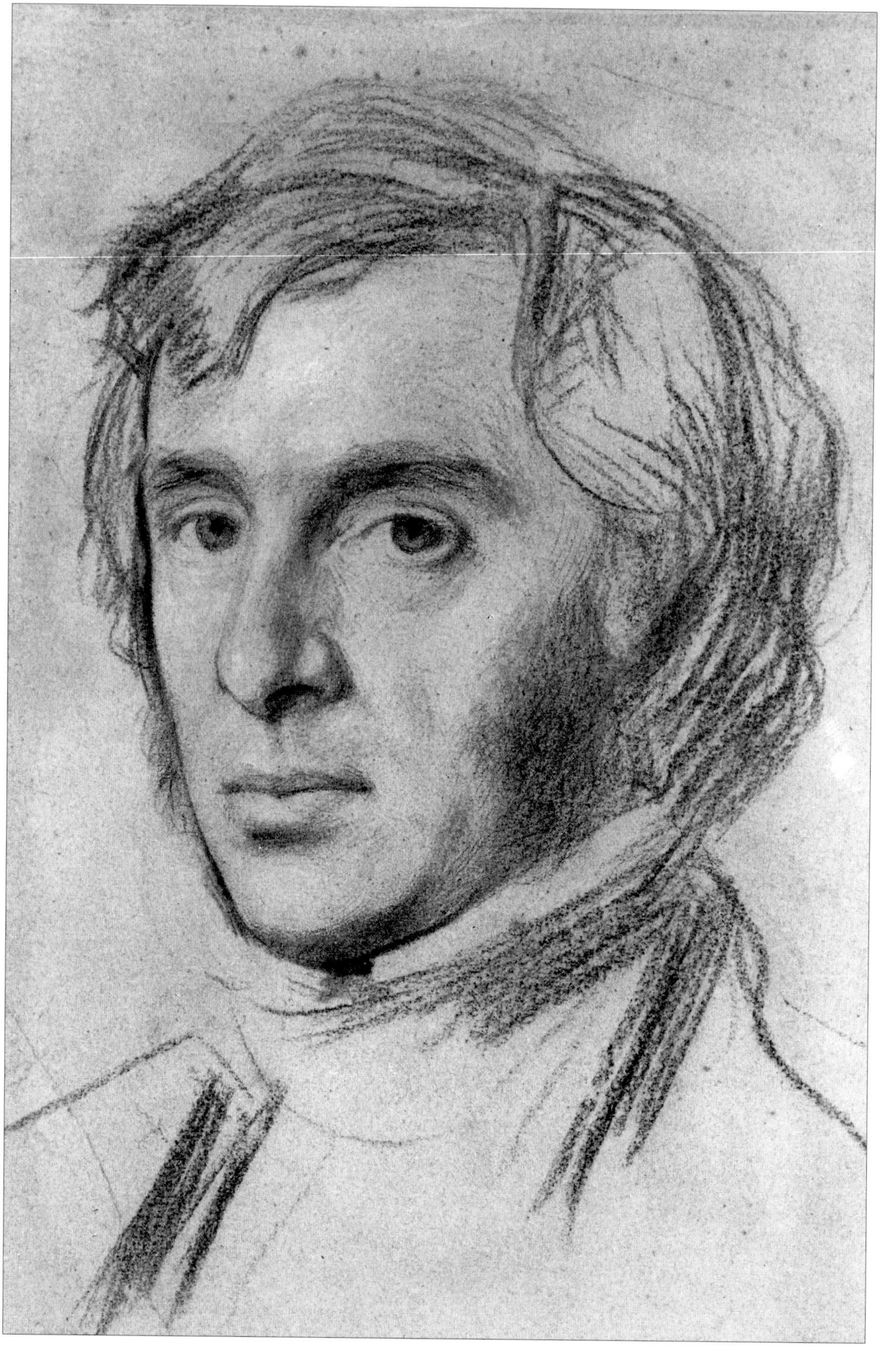

'Intellectual Lens and Moral Retina': A Reappraisal of Ruskin's Architectural Vision

Malcolm Hardman

WE HAVE MANY contemporary references to Ruskin's 'wonderful eyes' – they were of a piercing, almost Alpine, blue. The Samuel Laurence portrait of 1864 shows us the depth and coolness, thoughtfulness and grave compassion animating Ruskin at this time. He was continuing his self-education, the study of Greek authors (begun in the late 1850s) and urgently seeking a viable alternative to the medieval Christian humanism, most perfectly expressed in Dante's response to Aristotle, that he had taught himself to appreciate. Yet he knew this would be inadequate for the harsher world of Darwinism and aggressive imperialism that was coming. Unlike Nietzsche, he did not celebrate a 'recurrence' of aggressively pursued individual and racial interests, but, drawing on a phrase he had first coined in the second volume of *Modern Painters* in 1846, he advocated a realignment of each 'intellectual lens and moral retina' for the reconstruction of a viable working creed of helpfulness and delight. Never a pacifist, he anticipated by a generation governmental thinking of the early 20th century to the effect that the empowerment of individual moral and intellectual energies was the best way to avoid war, or to meet it if it came. One may fairly use the term 'Classical' to define this thinking, since it owed much to Greek philosophy and to the best traditions of the Roman empire. What follows is an attempt to explore his architectural vision within this context of concern.

If one were to make a division between two kinds of architecture with reference to Ruskin's architectural vision, it would not be simply between 'Gothic' and 'Classic'. One recalls that he subvented an edition of Stuart and Revett's *Antiquities of Athens*; that the 'Curve of the Capitals of the Parthenon', as well as the 'small north door' of Notre Dame,

Opposite:
John Ruskin: portrait by Samuel Laurence, 1864, pencil, chalk and white, 40 cm x 30 cm (*The Ruskin Library, University of Lancaster*).

Thomas Cole, *The Architect's Dream*, 1840, 134.6 cm x 213.5 cm, oil on canvas (*Toledo Museum of Art, Ohio*).

featured in his 'Educational Series' as Slade Professor; and that when in Venice with cultivated friends like Sir Walter Trevelyan, it was always the Classical buildings on which he lavished his extempore, but syntactically flawless, appreciations.[1] If his concerted effort was towards Gothic, his cadences, his cadenzas, were classical. The real division seems to be between what might be called 'secondary' and 'primary' architecture. Secondary architecture – and here one might cite the Anglo-American Thomas Cole's *The Architect's Dream* of 1840 – is imported and propagandistic. Superimposed by imperial requirements, it recalls what might be called 'Napoleonic boulevard' architecture, or (with an eye to Milton's Hell, or the inane prolongations of sub-Classical façades beloved of totalitarian dictators during the 20th century) 'Pandemonian' architecture.[2] Pseudo-transcendentalist rather than truly mythical or realist, it is best conceived with one's eyes shut: it is a merely imaginary aesthesis (sense impression) that exists *in vacuo* – the architect's drawings express what mere building can only fail to become, for instance – and if we are permitted to enter its depiction, it is only as an imaginary bird fluttering over it. Its hypothesised population, undifferentiated or stereotyped, is required only to dress it: its existence is subordinated to the festivals that must be invented to excuse it: not a Sabbath made for man, but humanity conceived for the purposes of an alien Sabbath. Like the demonic also-rans permitted to enter Satan's gargantuan Pandemonium, humanity, in this context, is reduced to the level of insect life.

Primary architecture is quite different. It is rooted in landscape and vernacular traditions. It exists in perpetuity in the strict sense; being built to last a thousand years, but in sight of Him for whom a thousand years are but as yesterday. Unlike the 'sublime' of *Modern Painters* 1, it is reconciled to the accidents of its own material, not offering to 'defy' the fallen nature of the world and its inhabitants, but content to accommodate and serve it, according to that 'affectionate watching of what is least' that is the 'sublime' of *Modern Painters* 5. As Plato put it, with Ruskin's approval, man's life is a kind of intensely serious play before the gods: building as though for ever, in the ironic certainty that human perpetuity is only for a moment: a moment, however, made significant because it gestures towards that which it cannot yet encompass (rather than straining to reproduce, in the degraded posture of 'good taste', what could only ever be an insulting parody of the past). As in van Eyck's drawing *Saint Barbara* the best efforts of differentiated human beings are required for this architecture if it is to be – in the defining final word of Ruskin's 'Nature of Gothic' chapter from *The Stones of Venice* – 'entertaining'.[3]

To employ Ruskin's classically-derived terms from *Modern Painters* 2, such an architecture is not merely 'aesthesis': that is, it is not merely dependent on, and celebratory of, the animal senses. Material, it evokes more than 'materialism' in its flattest sense. It deploys material as perceived by the human heart and intelligence. Conserving an intensely-realised and adventurous materiality, such builders achieve, through individuation, a particularity undetectable by preemptive aesthetics, aware, as Ruskin put it, that 'the eye is perpetually influenced ... by what it detects least.'[4] By definition a preemptive aesthetic is disabled by always expecting the derivative satisfaction of a shopworn 'good taste' (a degrading term in Ruskin's view). Primary architecture, on the contrary, enables

Jan van Eyck, *St Barbara*, 1437, brush drawing on panel, 32.2 cm x 18.6 cm (*Antwerp Royal Museum*).

with the shock of the new: it is surprising, and in the deepest sense, 'entertaining'. Borrowing terms from the French Surrealists whom he partly anticipates, one might say Ruskin wants a street architecture that is 'convulsive', never merely 'decor': one that meets, in short, all human requirements, rather than constraining humanity into roles that subserve the architecture.

To revert to van Eyck's drawing, we do not enter it at all (for it has always been the signifier of an irrecoverable moment, and can never be repeated), but rather stand back from it and commit it to memory. Unlike the Cole image, it is not a fantasy substitute for great building, but social and ideological information about great building. 'Memory' is Mnemosyne, mother of the Muses: who, as Ruskin says, 'has power only over things that are passing'.[5] From a drawing like *Saint Barbara*, we receive intellection about the spiritually-perceived universe for which the picture stands as emblem, not substitute. Here is not merely aesthesis, but primarily theoria: Ruskin's term of 1846 for the 'contemplation', or reading, of the universe, as contrasted with the mere knee-jerk reaction implied by aesthesis.

As in the case of *St Barbara*, what we read is also an autobiography that places essential imperfection in the light of 'martyrdom', literally of a 'witnessing' to the shared failure and renewal of Art and Nature alike. 'All Great Art is Praise', Ruskin believed, only because the 'glory' of good art 'is in its shame'. Eschewing those 'spuriously classic' mannerisms of which the later Renaissance was a little too fond, good art is made 'delightful' by its tacit acknowledgement (in the manner of wise science) of those 'numberless souls' alongside whom it finds its 'place ... in the various pavement' of all foundational work.[6] As theoria, architecture of this kind (whatever its materials) is not, like secondary architecture, blasphemously inattentive to the limits a divine wisdom has imposed on the material world: our 'play' is to discover, not 'defy', those limits. All towers, as the name of 'Barbara', their patron, reminds us, approach to a degree the Tower of Babel: hence lowliness is the criterion for building high; the higher, the lowlier. Without that sensible recognition, we are merely confirmed barbarians, gathering for a fall.

We may glean sympathy for Ruskin's penchant for Gothic in this context by turning to a poem exactly contemporary with his *Seven Lamps of Architecture* of 1849. Alfred de Musset dwells delectably on the nuanced form and colour of 'Three

Steps of Rose Marble' by the Orangerie at Versailles, and on the grace and beauty of the marble urn that guards them. Nothing here, he adds, is 'Gothic', since Gothic supposes a Fall. Here, it would follow, is Eden: alas, however, as in Eden, the horizon is bounded by ennui.[7] It is into this, somewhat extensive, context of 19th-century European ennui, that one would wish to introduce Ruskin's Apolline serpent: the concept of architecture as 'entertaining', from *entretenir*. Primary architecture is an 'entertainment' that holds us, for a lifelong moment, among supernal delights. Beyond even the Gothic, the orientalised Greek traditions of Byzantine building seem dearer to Ruskin than he always admits. An 'entertaining' architecture such as that is truly a theatre of myth: a St Mark's basilica that foreshadows something beyond itself. The following speech from *Tamburlaine the Great* contains echoes, perhaps, of Venice; for a subject of Queen Victoria (who held India by dint of treaties with the heirs of Tamburlaine), it seems to beckon to even more exotic entertainments:

> Now walk the angels on the walls of heaven,
> As sentinels to warn th'immortal souls
> To entertain divine Zenocrate:
> Apollo, Cynthia, and the ceaseless lamps
> That gently look'd upon this loathsome earth,
> Shine downwards now no more, but deck the heavens
> To entertain divine Zenocrate:
> The crystal springs, whose taste illuminates
> Refinèd eyes with an eternal sight,
> Like trièd silver run through Paradise
> To entertain divine Zenocrate...
> Then let some holy trance convey my thoughts
> Up to the palace of th'empyreal heaven,
> That this my life may be as short to me
> As are the days of sweet Zenocrate ... [8]

Marlowe's ravishing lines harbour a medieval concept already going out of date as he wrote, yet one Ruskin clung to: the 'empyreal heaven' is a technical term for the 'burning heaven' or 'heaven of fire', the celestial forge in which God the demiurge, or divine 'craftsman', creates the forms which (for Dante as for Plato) the human artist aspires to reimagine.

No ennui in such an Eden, in which the most exotic and refined forms of the visible achieve their form only as emblems of the invisible, not as replicants of the material glory that was Greece, or grandeur that was Rome. As for the swagger that was Venice, arrogantly annexing, rather than anxiously emulating, its Byzantine antecedents, its very foundations were built on risk, spiritual and material, which is the palpable form of 'courage', the foundational virtue – 'presence of mind' – that for Ruskin upheld the ambiguous prosperity of the Serenissima.[9]

Venice, Piazza San Marco, watercolour by Ruskin, 16.3 cm x 12.6 cm (*British Museum*).

One of his rapid sketches of the Piazza San Marco, in his individualised 'Turnerian' manner, provides a momentary impression of the perpetual process of architecture, from the geological sources of the building onwards into its life, renewal, decay; and collapse.[10] Here we have architecture both rooted and kinetic. One sees Ruskin's expressionistic enforcement of sea-roots in the buildings on the right. So tactile and autographic a vision is this that Ruskin's palm-print has become impressed on the weave of the sky, just to the left of the campanile. The scribble of the domes of St Mark's expresses their jouissance, their cynicism, their bewildered ambition to inscribe meaning. The black figure moving towards us seems able not only to write a magic shadow on the campanile (a more conventional shadow, in the words of the Psalmist, *adhaesit pavimento*) but actually to draw down the tower itself with a miraculous thread. We recall the collapse of this tower on 14 July 1902, and its rebuilding with English and American money to the tune of Ruskin's name. There is something that goes well beyond the definable in Ruskin's vision.

As an undergraduate, he had announced in *The Poetry of Architecture* (1837) that 'no man can be an architect, who is not a metaphysician.'[11] His source was the teleology of Aristotle's *Ethics*, constructed on the premise that ethics exist within politics, and taking 'architecture' as exemplifying and enabling that arrangement of subordinate skills which goes towards the building up of the good life in individual and society.

In detail, however, Ruskin at first set out to know better than Aristotle: a perhaps necessary effrontery (an undergraduate must make his name somehow) for which he later apologised. Art, says Aristotle, is something whose making is inexplicable as merely derived from Nature or merely subservient to Necessity: its real origins and motivation are to be sought within the human being who does the making – making being *poiein*, from which we derive 'poetry'. Anxious to be original, Ruskin's *The Poetry of Architecture* defiantly annexes Aristotle's phrase *kata phusin* (derived from Nature) as its *nom de guerre* and manifesto.[12] Later – for example at a meeting of the RIBA in 1865 attended by G. E. Street among others – Ruskin would announce that he had seceded from his old 'poetic' study of architecture as one of the orders of Nature and had turned towards that other Aristotelian cause – Necessity – devoting himself to seeking 'the best modes of getting bread and water' for the city's besieged multitudes rather than to hymning the organic propriety of the 'arrangement' of its towers. *Polis* is, of course, Greek for 'city', and for Ruskin as for Aristotle, the built environment is the 'political' environment by definition.[13] In what follows I propose to take Aristotle at his word, taking up the hint that, in the case of the author of *The Poetry of Architecture*, the origin of what is made lies not so much in Nature or Necessity in the abstract, but within the actual nature and necessity shaping him who makes – the 'poet' who authored that treatise. Ruskin, as J. S. Mill admiringly noted, always wrote from 'a source within'.[14]

Contradiction (without which, according to the Greek law of paradox, there can be no diction) is immediately to be met. Thus, so far from having finished with architectural 'arrangement', the Ruskin of 1865 is about to advise G. E. Street on the arrangement – in the interests of an entertaining variety – of the towers in his new Law Courts in the Strand. Rather than being always on the side of what I have called 'primary' architecture, Ruskin demurs, at this same RIBA meeting of 1865, from G. E. Street's tasteful preference for the intimate alleys of Genoa over the imperialist boulevards of Napoleon III. Conceding himself delighted with Genoa, the bewildering Gothicist expresses almost equal pleasure over the long vistas of Haussmann's Paris: both kinds of architecture have their place, Ruskin insists.[15]

Such contradictions are not marginal, but central. What Ruskin fears and hates is not classicism, but a Roman tradition of imposition: the brutish conviction that the only conviction is 'brute force' ('brute force', incidentally, is the meaning of RÔMÊ which doubles as the Greek transliteration of 'ROMA', or 'ROME'). Savouring certain products of Renaissance Venice, or Augustan Rome, Ruskin notes that both cut off the people from affairs of state, and dislikes them accordingly.[16] 'Rome', that is, 'brute force', merely conquers: it settles arguments without resort to argument. It does not rise to the level of that Greek preference, among mortals at any rate, for dialogue. Not merely for our entertainment, but for our political survival, we cannot avoid trying to have it both ways. Once we recognise that failure is inevitable but incidental, we have little to fear; our 'battle' (in Platonic phrase celebrated by Ruskin) being 'for peace, not a victory', and therefore 'immortal'.[17] Roman military perceptions, nevertheless, are a robust necessity of this battle for Ruskin. In particular, the words 'moral' and 'intellectual' are Roman, not Greek; and imply a less scholastic and more engaged relation to the material world than anything in Aristotle's

Philip Milner, West front of San Matteo, Genoa, 2002. Diagrammatic sketch by the radar pioneer in pen and ink and pencil (*Malcolm Hardman*).

Academy. Ruskin is a Hellenist, and a Goth, but not a Zealot in either camp.

Nevertheless, the little façade of S. Matteo, Genoa (1125, restored 1278) exemplifies a Catholic intellection about architecture, part of the medieval response to Aristotle, that comes closer to Ruskin's vision than anything in Napoleon III's Paris or the Rome of the Caesars. When Ruskin claimed that all great art was Catholic, it seems to have been with reference to this intellection (for him revealed supremely at Amiens): what gives his vision such intensity and bewilderment would seem to be his recognition that this intellection is no longer tenable; and that, on the other hand, neither he nor the rest of humanity has discovered its fit successor.

Reading the west front of S. Matteo as a diagram, we see a medieval, spiritual, version of man's eternal quest for guidance from the air about him. The façade exemplifies the christianised Minerva or Athena (Ruskin's 'queen of the air'), whose essence, as goddess of weaving, is alternation of dark and light, in counterpoint with the Apolline principle of the circle: the pattern exemplifies contradiction, rising towards resolution in circularity, a device as old as Homer's depiction of the shield of Achilles. Christianised, the pattern centres on Christ as *'il buon' Apollo'* (as Dante calls him), and on Sta Lucia, the Christian Minerva, and erstwhile guardian saint of Venice, the blinded saint of hope and inner vision, through all the contradictions of the world. The key to the pattern is the idea of the intelligibility of God. Drawing on Aristotle, the 12th-century scholastic Alain de Lille, a great influence on Dante, defines God as 'the intelligible sphere'. All art is a straining after those icons (*ychones*) of supra-mathematical perfection which are built into the 'empyreal palace' of God's heaven: the miraculous workshop where God makes the forms that form the world. Sometimes the figure of meditation is a triangle, sacred to the Trinity, often shown in Gothic art as a dove with spread wings hovering above a pair of seated male beings on either side of the kneeling Virgin, whom they unite in crowning: for she is not only the heart of the triangle, but in a mystical sense the secret place or enclosed garden in which the Trinity itself is ensphered. Through the pursuit of intellectuality, the human mind, too, writes Alain, is brought to birth, and becomes God (*'fit anima humana Deus'*); but only (like van Eyck's *Saint Barbara*) by becoming fit to read the supreme Author *'in rebus caducis'*: in his cadenzas — those simulacrums of ultimate reality that trickle from the fingers of God into His fallen world.[18] To build as an assertion of human prestige, as though the building in itself matters, rather than its function in promoting the Good (and soul-good is the highest good), is simply to repeat the Babel blasphemy: to be deaf to the music that builds the heavens, and to offer a vicious human cadenza, no icon of Christ descending in redemptive love, but an exacerbation of the original Fall displaying its own guilty pride: not a support and shelter for Necessity, built in reverence for Nature, but the imitation of an imitation, built out of envy and invincible ignorance.

In light of this Greco-Christian theory, it is no longer surprising that Ruskin informed the RIBA in 1865 that he shared Dante's conviction that the true function of architecture was to 'purify the purposes' of the soul. For Ruskin, as for Dante and Aristotle, architecture is an ethical matter within the political commonwealth. Inevitably Victorian, moreover, and sharing J. S. Mill's approval for the Platonic idea of dialogue as a means of recovering first principles beneficial to the polity, Ruskin comes right outside the cathedral, and the academy: 'in architecture, all must in some way commit themselves', runs the preface of 1851 to *The Stones of Venice*: 'it is assuredly intended that all of us should have knowledge, and act upon our knowledge, in matters with which we are daily concerned, and not be left to the caprice of architects, or mercy of contractors.' In scholastic terms of divine election and original sin ('commit ourselves ... intended') Ruskin unveils a code of democratic modernism, rooted in Bacon's conviction as to the human right to go forward only in knowledge.[19]

And yet he was never happy for long away from theological convictions of intellection, such as can be read in the S. Matteo façade. Like the front of S. Miniato, this is suspended like a ticket from the finger of God, yet unlike the Florentine building, it is welded by a side buttress to the household that adjoins it, and paid for it. Like a pair of doleful acolytes, the hump-backed lower lights illustrate the twin tables of Mosaic law: the entrance doorway, however, aspires like a sword in its scabbard (and Dante would not be afraid of such military and amorous connotations) to penetrate the great circle of light above it, that sits conformable to the square that holds it, in childish entertainment achieving that squaring of the circle that is the last image with which Dante attempts to describe his vision of God: that God who, in the argument of Anselm, is to be understood as that than which nothing greater can be imagined: the intelligible sphere of Grossteste of Lincoln, or Alain de Lille. Where Matthew and *ratio* end – the calculating, reckoning serviceability of the tax gatherer or the quantity surveyor – *intellectus*, St Matthew, and architecture begin. From outside, the fenestration appears like wounds, or cavities, darker than the excluding wall; only from inside does it enter our space as light.[20]

Defining the 'sphere' of 'Ideas of Beauty' in *Modern Painters* 2 (1846), Ruskin requires the application of, 'The intellectual lens, and moral retina, by which our informing thoughts are concentrated and represented.'[21] It seems that by 'intellectual' he implies something like Alain de Lille's God as the intelligible sphere, but that by 'moral' he refers literally to mores or modes, the old Roman project of managing an empire. Military and citizen morale begins with feeding, to quote once more from Ruskin's RIBA paper of 1865: with 'modes ... of getting bread and water' to those who need it.[22] In eclectic Victorian manner, Ruskin wants to combine medieval scholasticism minus its hair-splitting with Roman efficiency minus its brutal pride. For him, as for Aristotle, architecture exemplifies and sustains the ethical within the political, and its teleology is to aim for the supreme good, which is happiness: a happiness which for both (and this is the source of Ruskin's agony in an increasingly faithless world) depends ultimately on the contemplation of the divine.

One should not read 'intellectual lens and moral retina' in too 'Victorian' a sense. Ruskin is a Hellenist, but with enough sense of Latin to know that 'intelligence' primarily means 'military intelligence'. We are not here in the world of 19th-century self-regard, but in the world of application: the Roman world of realism, applying the Greek ideas. A Victorian encyclopaedia defines the lens of the eye as 'refractive', and capable of focusing impressions. Therefore, the intellectual lens is a bringer to bear of information requisite for necessary action. The retina is defined as 'sensitive', and 'capable of receiving impressions'. So the moral retina is a responsive mediation of such information to the brain so as to motivate right action. This would seem to be what Ruskin means when he speaks of architecture as a 'motivating power'. It is emotional, in the strict sense of first 'entertaining', that is, holding, us; and then moving us, towards 'the love that moves the sun and all the stars.'[23] If S. Matteo, Genoa, presents architecture as intellectual lens, the Orvieto Palazzo del Popolo of 1280 is surely retina, a tactile receptor for modes of human busyness: steps that invite the tread of feet, or children sitting; the roped-together windows placed where you want them, as Ruskin would say, low in the wall; the rostrum with its capacious cavities conveniently below.[24]

Comparing Ruskin to Viollet-le-Duc, Nikolaus Pevsner implicitly confined the latter to the role of quantity surveyor or tax-gatherer: his approach to Gothic, says Pevsner, is 'rational'. Ruskin's approach he defines, with equal pertinence, as 'emotional':[25] emotional, one might add, in the sense of supplying, not merely material provision for something, but 'motivating power' for something good. In this context, Viollet-le-Duc's drawing of the Colosseum, as though restored (not a contract he would have refused, perhaps) is illuminating.[26] Skimming over it in his bird's eye view, one gets a fair impression of the size and capacity of the thing. The intellectual lens is here the awning of the arena, its circular opening focusing the sun, Apollo, god of civilisation himself. He is here intelligible as the alter ego of the divine emperor whose head appears on the god's statue in his Roman temple. Delos, Apollo's sacred birthplace, protected from pollution by the dialogous and conquered Greeks, is now, under Roman compulsion, the human cattle market of the Mediterranean: one may reckon on as many as 10,000 slaves being auctioned there in a day, some for exhibition in this arena. The moral retina would be the great shaded cavity below, into which the undifferentiated crowd is herded, suborned into complicity with the festivals of murder — theologically, public sacrifices of human beings to the shades of divine emperors — which are the Roman substitute for theatrical entertainment.

Ruskin's reaction might be judged by that of his exact contemporary and fellow Oxonian and Hellenist, Arthur Hugh Clough:

> No one can cavil, I grant, at the size of the great Coliseum.
> Doubtless the notion of grand and capacious and massive amusement,
> This the old Romans had: but tell me, is this an idea?[27]

'Amusement': the Greek negative, 'amusia', or 'denial or desolation for want, of the Muses,' as Ruskin defines it: and not 'entertainment', which is quite a different thing. Milton's Belial, whose distinction it is to pretend that Pandemonium is really not so bad, is a gamesome devil; and hopes to see the good angels 'amus'd' by a hostile explosion of diabolic gunpowder. Amusement, Ruskin comments, has always been despairingly sought by generations 'whom any manner of thoughtfulness tormented'.[28] Entertainment, on the other hand, is the recreation of thought. We speak of 'entertaining' an idea. So, to speak unkindly of Viollet-le-Duc and kindly of Ruskin for a moment, one might say the former was 'rational' – interested in the engineering problems of erecting a given building, supposing someone else had thought of it, and would pay taxes for it; while the latter is 'emotional' – that is to say, interested in the motivating power that makes it possible to think of it and achieve it; and therefore also in every aspect of the cost of it, as sanctuary or charnel house.

However, Ruskin cannot have everything his own way. The quality of his architectural vision, and emotion, is innovative, disturbing, yet also necessarily rooted (some might even say, 'stranded') within his own age and his own sexuality. In his preface to *Sesame and Lilies*, he equates himself, as by implication does T. S. Eliot in his epigraph to *The Waste Land*, with Guido Guinicelli (*c*.1230-76), defined by Dante as hermaphrodite (*ermafrodito*).[29] The androgynous connotations are significant and enabling, in the case of both writers; and so, one might argue, is the 13th-century referent, and its Greek forerunner, Tiresias the Theban, symbol of the androgynous mind from Homer's *Odyssey* to Eliot's *The Waste Land*, and revered as such by writers as various as Coleridge and Virginia Woolf. Yet not everything can be structured from learned referents, or from the androgynous posture so familiar from bourgeois modernism.

And yet (to continue the contradiction), there is a degree of sanity in Ruskin's predilections, even if their constructive implications are less clear. Ruskin's favourite architectural lens and retina might be taken as the Palazzo Pubblico, Siena (1297-1344). The literally 'episcopal' tower – which 'overlooks' from its great height the town and landscape by actually rising above the cathedral itself – is the focusing lens gathering the results of its surveillance onto the concave retina and centre for receiving impressions which is now the town hall, no longer the cathedral.[30] Energising, yet also slightly alarming, from Ruskin's viewpoint, is the fact that this secular tower dwarfs the theological imperative that the cathedral stood for: in the preface to *The Crown of Wild Olive* and elsewhere he explores the ambiguities of civic virtue in the real world as motivating power, in place of aspiration for a heavenly crown. There is a no doubt admirable stubbornness in Ruskin's choice of the Siena archetype. In the 'War' lecture and elsewhere he foresaw no less than Nietzsche the actual type of regression that Europe was heading for in the 20th century: much closer to Roman habits of tyrant-idolatry and brute force passing itself off as an idea than to any brief balance of power as imaged in late-medieval Siena: the latter no true blueprint for a modern world, either; but inclining, when all is said, towards a prejudice in favour of the good as contrasted with the reductive mindlessness of totalitarian regimes.[31]

Sexually and socially, there remain oddities and discomforts, comical and sublime. Ruskin is anomalous genderwise in Victorian England: also, in terms of class in the Victorian age of transition. On the latter count, one may compare him with Enrico Scrovegno, sculptured in the niche he had to buy for himself: donor, not of an arena, but of the Arena Chapel in Padua, whose fresoes by Giotto became the subject of a seminal study by Ruskin. Daniel Waley calls him 'a typical second-generation figure in a successful family' – despised, as Ruskin would be, by the gilded youth of the true aristocracy, being financed into preferment as Ruskin was by his father, who in Ruskin's case bought him the status of 'gentleman commoner' at Christ Church. Scrovegno, the perennial arriviste, died in 1336, just before the completion of the Palazzo Pubblico at Siena.[32] He was, in other words, like Ruskin, the ambiguous product of a transitional age; and no argument for those notions of static hierarchy of which the arriviste Ruskin cannot quite rid himself.

If Ruskin is like Scrovegno, grasping at a niche, he also anticipates in the British context a figure like the left-wing dramatist David Hare, the son of a Scottish ship's purser (Ruskin's antecedents included a sea-captain and a ship's chandler), educated at that dizzy epitome of the Gothic Revival, Lancing College, and drawn, somehow, to achieve establishment status while simultaneously attacking the establishment, a trail surely blazed by Ruskin. Interviewed for the *Guardian* in November 1999, Hare tellingly chose to be photographed in front of a vernacular sample of 'Ruskinian' Gothic – with its two-tone brickwork and other constituents of duality and contradiction, including a crudely defined 'cross'. Sir David's motto supplied a caption: 'Self-hatred was my fuel for years': the untenable tenet of the British cultural anti-establishment, yearning for an impossible future and an imaginary past.[33] One might unkindly add the name of William Morris, anarchic socialism and all, to this uncomfortable gestalt. Insular, as well as imperial; provincial, though dominant; surprisingly innovative, yet paleologue: Ruskin, and his often unwilling influence on the 'gothic revival' is part of that Victorian pattern. A brutal half-truth from Richard Norman Shaw seems apposite: 'It was always supposed that "Gothic" was to develop, and there was any amount of tall talk as to what it was to do – but it didn't do anything. It was like a cut flower – pretty enough to look at – but fading away before your eyes ... so unlike the French ... their Architecture was alive – ours dead – a mighty difference – and arising of course from their having a School – and we have none.'[34]

Claiming, in 1874, a beneficial 'direct influence' on Street's Law Courts, Ruskin simultaneously lamented the architectural 'Frankenstein monsters' erupting all over England as a result of his 'indirect' influence with lesser architects and builders.[35] This is not the place to argue this perennially challenging point (I have suggested elsewhere that Ruskin's close personal involvement in architectural problems often had results that stand the test of time),[36] nor is this the place to raise the even greater question of Ruskin's surely massive array of influences on the problems of architectural materials, function, and environment. He is a 'poet in prose', as Christina Rossetti acknowledged, and must be granted the Shelleyan corollary of unacknowledged legislator to the world. It remains to suggest ways in which his status as Victorian Tiresias relates to his architectural vision and requires to be accommodated for the fuller understanding of his 'intellectual lens and moral retina'.

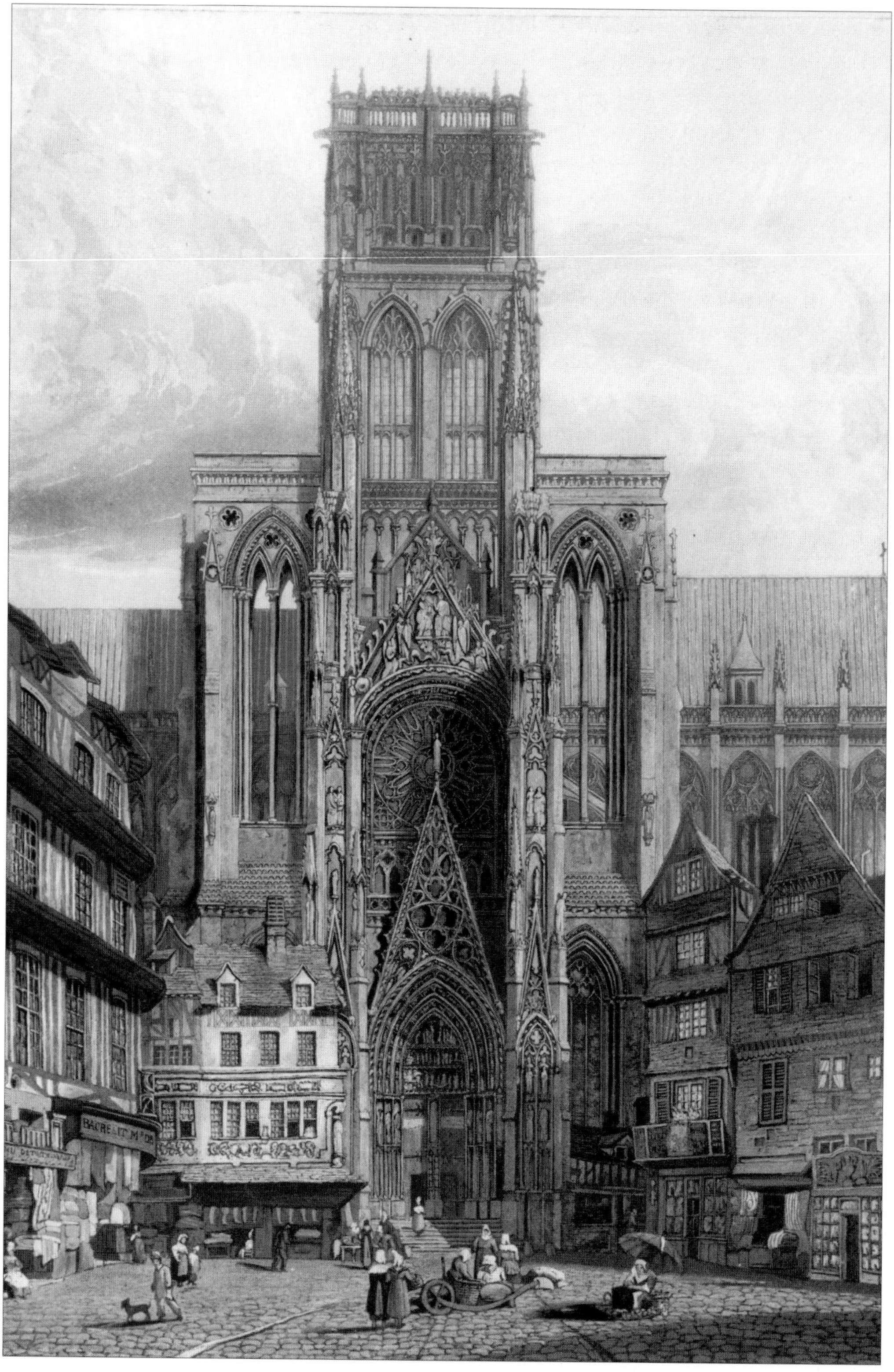

Charles Wild's view of 1831 of the south transept of Rouen Cathedral provides an opera-set view, the tourist's view of controlling capacity for purchase.[37] The façade is seen frontally, and annexed to the whole of its height: the square before it is disposed according to the canons of linear perspective; picturesque costume figures complete our sense of being in the stalls at Covent Garden or inspecting some folkloric revival. We are spectators whose lens is focused for us, with no intellectual demands, or requirements, and whose retina is pleased, before luncheon or that overdue interval drink, with a sufficiently delectable eyeful. Our only intervention would be to buy something: a souvenir programme, a bottle of calvados.

The minuteness of Ruskin's drawing of 1854, taken in the seam between the cliff of the south transept and the vernacular dwellings that abut it, involves a wide scale of values: the more particularised the details, the more complex and far-reaching the implied pattern. The search for this pattern begins in the geophysical, and its retributive nature depends on its being manifested as finite: which is to say, contained by a mystical infinite. This exquisite, idiosyncratic, not entirely fluid drawing – elusive blue-grey, coral, faint turquoise and grey-brown in colouring – is a highly-organised fragment of cliff in transition: tiny plants spring from its crevices; tattered advertisements (one offers a house for sale) cling to the shop walls that nudge in to the speleological mystery that appears without beginning or end, yet which Ruskin's little stain of water colour strives to ingest into a structural pattern of the ecological and economic universe that stretches far beyond

Opposite:
Charles Wild, south end of the transept of the Cathedral of Rouen, from *Twelve Select Examples of the Ecclesiastical Architecture of the Middle Ages, chiefly in France* (1831). Hand-coloured print (*British Library*).

Below:
John Ruskin, entrance to the south transept, Rouen Cathedral, 1854. Pencil and water colour (*Fitzwilliam Museum, University of Cambridge*).

J. C. Armytage, windows of the Fifth Order. Engraving (lower part of plate XVIII) from John Ruskin, 'The Sea-Stories', *The Stones of Venice* 2 (London 1874), opposite p. 266 (*Malcolm Hardman*).

Wild's proscenium. Ruskin's is a world of possiblities and apprehensions, never for a moment static as Wild's view is static. Yet it is also a world in some sense brought forcibly together, high and low, sacred and mundane, weeds, prophets, and advertisements. This is a wisdom from a feminine 'source within', that delights in what Margaret Atwood calls the wisdom of the 'seam', and what Ruskin, anticipating that idea, called the 'acicular' function of theoria. If one insists, this is related to eclecticism and the patchwork; but a suggestive eclectic, a patchwork that makes myth.[38]

Curiously enough, while Ruskin was making this drawing, his friend F. J. Furnivall was preparing to reprint the 'Nature of Gothic' chapter from *The Stones of Venice* for the illumination of the Working Men's College, with all that followed for Morris and many others. Ruskin, however, won't stay in the 19th century. He reminds one of those 'miraculous, seminal, intermediate beings' that fascinated Angela Carter, the myth-haunted novelist who died in 1992. His, too, was an imagination dislocated by the decay of Genesis: he, too, is 'pressed between the leaves of a book of silence'.[39] His best influences must surely be unpredictable.

An engraving by J. C. Armytage for the 1874 edition of *The Stones of Venice* looks almost as though it might be capable of being copied in a middle-class villa, or a suite of offices for the administration of a gas company. But a Ruskin drawing of the same subject (the Palazzo Priuli), is a momentary vision snatched in the seam of a dying world being reborn in unpredicatable ways. In the grave of imagination that is Armytage's engraving, the intellectual lens is lightless; and the moral retina unresponsive: but in Ruskin's water colour the sea from which the Venetians drew their understandings shakes its light into the windows – what in Armytage is a grave is in Ruskin a sepulchre of resurrection, the 'speleological apotheosis of Tiresias', to quote Angela Carter again, joyously responsive to the 'omnivorous inscrutability of the sea.'[40]

Very characteristic is his evocation of the speluncar apse of Murano in the second volume of *The Stones of Venice*.[41] It is more than a mere prologue to the often-quoted description of St Mark's that follows. For Ruskin, Murano is, literally, the line in the sand between the 'builders of [his own] day and the builders on that sand island long ago'. These latter 'did honour something out of themselves; they did believe in a

John Ruskin, Venetian balcony (Palazzo Priuli), brush drawing in grey wash and graphite (*British Museum*).

A Reappraisal of Ruskin's Architectural Vision

Plans of San Donato [SS Maria e Donato], Murano. Drawn by John Ruskin, engraved by R. Cuff. Plate 1, figs 2-6, from *The Stones of Venice* 2 (1874), opposite p. 14 (*Malcolm Hardman*).

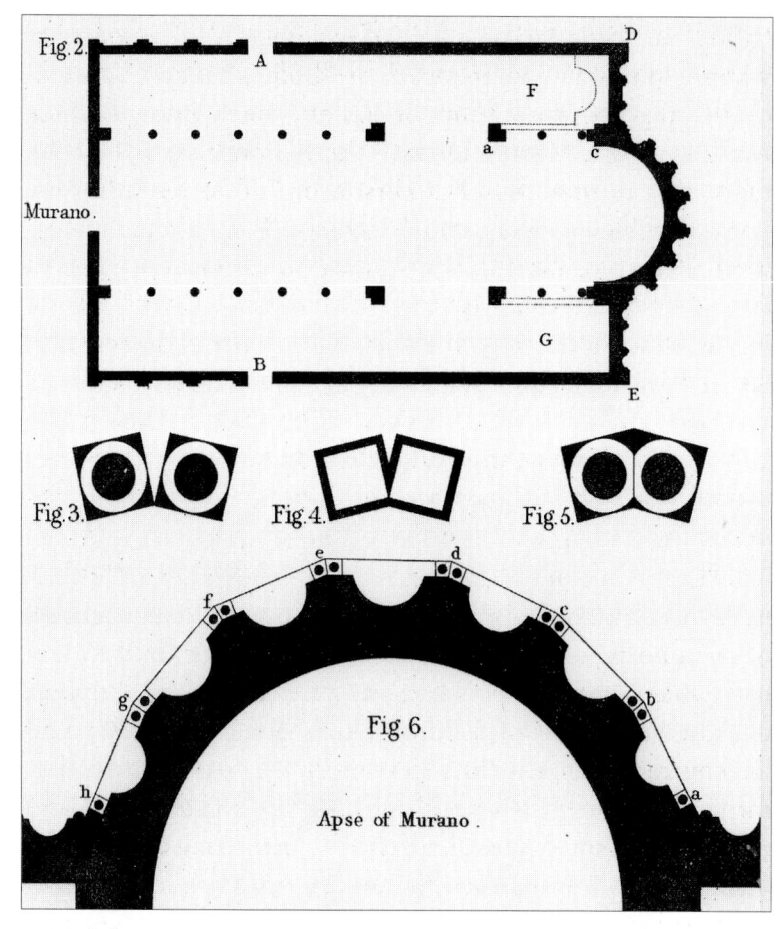

spiritual presence'. For better for worse, it is that line in the sand that Ruskin's intellectual lens and moral retina refuse to overlook.

In *The Stones of Venice*, our first glimpse of Murano is as a 'discordant feature' in the lagoon – the smoke that hovers above its glass furnaces spoils the tourist's reverie, but at least supplies 'the last signs left of human exertion' hereabouts: fittingly, we approach this remnant of vitality beyond the blank wall of a modern cemetery; and our quest is a Byzantine fabric whose Christian font was once a pagan sarcophagus. On arrival, we look in vain for the cafés of Venice proper: 'But there is some life in the scene more than is usual in Venice.' The 'Mother Church', however, is a little removed – beyond one of the main channels of the lagoon. Ruskin delights to emphasise that this royal building (literally, 'basilica', founded by Otho the Great) is also a people's church: in monkish

Latin, *'Sta Maria Plebania di Murano'*. Since the 12th century, when a piratical raid acquired the body of St Donatus of Cephalonia for this church, it has also been known as the basilica of Santi Maria e Donato: there is nothing that can be called real disapproval in Ruskin's record of this latter history.

Still visible – beyond much debased 'Renaissance upholstery' in stucco, and the tinsel of a now almost meaningless festival – is the 'Greek Madonna ... on a field of gold', vibrating as though floating free from her enshrining apse; yet defined by the Greek lettering that announces her to be 'Mother of God': a Christian variant of the oriental pagan cult of the Great Mother, Cybele. For Ruskin, part of her sanctity depends on her wearing 'simply the dress of the women of the time'.

Dating from the 7th, but rebuilt in the 9th and 12th centuries, the basilica is for Ruskin primarily of interest because of this apse, which he is sure must have been 'part of the original earliest church'. All is femality here. Myth would have it that the Virgin herself directed Otho to the 'triangular field ... covered with red lilies' on which he was to build her shrine: not merely within is concavity celebrated, but there are no less than thirteen speluncar recesses making up the outer east wall: and these are adorned with exquisite trefoils of shaped and etched marble, in five or six colours, repeating, five or six hundred times, but hardly ever of the same size, the mystic trefoil, perfect emblem of 'fulness with order', the very life-source itself. Here is not merely variety, but 'purposeful variation'; here is no mere symmetry, but a 'love of harmony' that delights in 'alternate proportions', and a triumphant 'unity' achieved by 'the avoidance of repetition'.

The 'whole edifice is ... simply a temple to the Virgin', Ruskin warns his Protestant readers. We approach her across a 12th-century pavement 'of Greek mosaic, waved like the sea', and excelling even St Mark's 'in the extraordinary play of colour obtained by the use of variegated marbles'. Ruskin has enjoyed his own 'extraordinary play' in drawing and defining the archivolt of the external apse: 'one zone', he calls it, 'of white, relieved on a purple ground', and enlivened by related fabric to produce a 'whole cord of colour', fastened together by a cross flanked by sun and moon, set within a

Archivolt in the Duomo of Murano. Drawn by John Ruskin, engraved by J. C. Armytage. Plate V from *The Stones of Venice* 2 (1874), opposite p. 45 (*Malcolm Hardman*).

circle within a triangle. Not merely a geographical term, and a technical term for certain organic markings in marble, the Greek-derived 'zone' (in Latin, *cestus*), is also, and chiefly, a 'female girdle': notably of Venus/Aphrodite in her role as Aglaia, or 'splendour of the sea'.

It need not truly disturb us, Ruskin pleads, to see Mary here confused with 'the Athena of the Acropolis, or the Syrian Queen of Heaven'. The difference that really matters lies 'between those who worship and those who worship not'. At some level, Ruskin seems to have the opening paragraph of Vitruvius's *De Architectura* in mind when he calls the non-worshippers 'calculating'. The word connotes closely with the Vitruvian term '*ratiocinatio*', which refers to architecture regarded in the abstract from the point of view of the 'calculation' of scale and cost: the metier of the quantity surveyor. Ruskin consecrates the worshippers as 'struggling': a pointer to the Vitruvian '*fabrica*', which defines architecture from the viewpoint of the 'builder', or more properly, the 'furnace workman', or 'forger', exerting himself to achieve architecture in very fact. For Ruskin, as for Guido Guinicelli, to be '*miglior fabbro*', in poetry or any other art, was the desirable accolade. In medieval parlance, such a workman shares the 'mystery' of the 'empyreal' or 'burning' forge of the divine craftsman himself, in terms of which the carpenter of Nazareth is also the Logos that gave the pattern for the making of the world. Of this mind, one may be sure, was the 'contradictory' Ruskin who refused with elaborate scorn the Gold Medal of the Royal Institute of British Architects in 1874, but expressed himself 'delighted' with some locks and sluices built of wood and iron on the River Weaver near Winnington: 'Such a lovely bit of "building!"'. Their architect went on to design the Manchester Ship Canal. One senses that Ruskin as aesthete would have shrunk from the latter enterprise. Ruskin the theorist, however, allows us to respect it.[42]

Shipping of all kinds, and the demands of seacraft were primary for Ruskin, as for Venice and Athens. Most especially, the sea was not merely the source of life and all myth, as it was for Homer, but also the groundwork of a 'massy commonsense'[43] in building, as all else. In his lecture, 'The Literary Influence of Academies' (1864), Matthew Arnold, ever vigilant in the cause of good taste, censured Ruskin for 'trying to make prose do more than it can perfectly do'.[44] The dénouement of this 'Murano' chapter of 1853 comes close to earning the impeachment, yet one would not wish it otherwise. Ruskin relates the labour of the Murano fisherman to the fabric of the miraculous floor of this Virgin's temple. Here is a pavement that is also both a sea and a net, and which he describes as 'one of the most precious monuments of Italy, showing thus early, and in those rude chequers which the bared knee of the Murano fisher wears in its daily bending, the beginning of the mighty spirit of Venetian colour, which was to be consummated in Titian'. Here, before Hopkins can have coined the terms, is Ruskin's art of 'inscape', and exploration of 'instress'. The 'Murano' chapter began by likening the whole of Venice to an 'outwearied ... human frame'. Here, with a compression of detail that requires some unpacking, we have the sign of its surviving vitality: a portrait for the outwearied frame. One may begin by noting that 'wears' is used in two senses simultaneously. A pedantic expansion might thus explain that 'those rude chequers which the bared knee of the [generic] Murano fisher wears [down over centuries] in its daily bending', are the same, yet never the same, as 'those rude chequers which the bared knee of the [individual] Murano fisher wears [the mark of] in its daily bending.' Human flesh itself becomes both sign and transmitter of a mystical writing, as supremely recorded by Titian, whose testimony to 'this clay that burns, this colour that changes', whether of gentleman or fisher, is always of the man. The Murano fisher's indented 'Flesh' is consecrated by patterns of 'Spirit', every day, as mystical as those made by the apostles kneeling into the web of nets (noticed by Ruskin earlier) to gather them, and heave them, so as to draw the miraculous draught of fishes at the bidding of the risen Christ.[45]

Through the female act of conception, the prayer and the work become one, and are proclaimed as one by the patterns of right building. Out at sea, the Murano fishers who knelt century after century before 'that lonely figure standing on the gold field' also 'conceived [her as receiving] their prayer at evening', kneeling into the net, 'where they only saw the blue clouds rising out of the burning sea': rising, that is, like the blue Virgin from her golden apse, not merely from the Murano glass furnaces, but also out of the 'empyreal' or 'burning' forge that is the heaven-reflexive sea of our imagination, the divine-in-human incarnation of all icons, and all life. Ruskin surely means all that, and more: for the word 'chequers' is in itself an important clue to the daedal art of lettering, and to the binary pattern of life itself (in terms of what would now be called 'the genetic code'), intuited by Ruskin when he ventured to correct Darwin's evolutionary calculations a little: species are connected, he thought, 'not in chains, but in chequers'.[46] Ruskin-Tiresias, the living binary, and one of our greatest deployers of metaphor, exerts his intellectual lens and moral retina not only to discriminate, but to relate, the patterns of life and environment across cultures and times, moving beyond mere detail towards an intenser regard for the universal in the particular.

Notes
[1] *Works*, 21, pp. 77, 79; 38, p. 188.
[2] Thomas Cole, *The Architect's Dream*, 1840, oil on canvas, 134.6cm. x

213.5cm., Toledo Museum of Art, Ohio. Compare *Paradise Lost* 1.670-792. For Cole as Anglo-American Romantic, see Malcolm Hardman, *Classic Soil* (London and Cranbury, NJ, 2003), pp.138-59.

[3] Jan van Eyck, *St Barbara*, 1437 brush drawing on panel, 32.2cm. x 18.6cm, Antwerp Royal Museum. Compare *Works*, 3, p. 129; 7, p. 230; 10, pp. 269, 370. Ruskin invariably associated Palladio with the anti-Gothic 'good taste' he despised. Mistaken or otherwise, his contempt was based on patient observation. Thus Palladio's Basilica at Vicenza 'unworthy and unadmirable' according to *The Stones of Venice* (*Works*, 11, p. 45), is nevertheless the subject of an elegant sketch by Ruskin. Stephen Wildman suggests a date of 1845. Black graphite pencil, charcoal, white, on grey paper, 22.8cm. x 16.5cm., Santa Barbara Museum of Art.

[4] *Works*, 10, p. 154.

[5] *Works*, 20, p. 388.

[6] *Works*, 15, pp. 345, 353-5; 22, p. 158.

[7] Alfred de Musset, *Poésies Complètes* (Maurice Allem, editor) (Paris, 1957), p. 454: *'L'ennuyeux parc de Versailles'*.

[8] Christopher Marlowe, *Tamburlaine the Great*, Part 2, Act 2, Scene 4. Earlier and later Ruskin agree in showing us a less dogmatic Goth than the 'central' persona of *The Seven Lamps* and *Stones of Venice*. Thus, April 1841 saw Ruskin in Rome, quoting Marlowe and revelling in the 'beauty of design' of the dome of St Peter's, while by 1864 ('Traffic') he judged 'whatever is good … in … India is just good … for the same reasons [as apply to] Europeans'. *Works*, 1, pp. 389-92; 18, p. 445.

[9] For discussion of Venetian 'presence of mind', see Malcolm Hardman, *Ruskin and Bradford* (Manchester, 1986), pp. 117, 226-8.

[10] John Ruskin, *The Campanile, Piazza San Marco*, water-colour, 16.3cm. x 12.6cm., British Museum.

[11] *Works*, 1, p. 5.

[12] Aristotle, *The Nicomachean Ethics*, (edited by J. S. Brewer) (Oxford, 1836), p. 228. Ruskin's copy with his drawings and MS marginalia (British Library).

[13] *Works*, 8, p. 20; 19, p. 313.

[14] J. S. Mill, diary entry 21 January 1854. For discussion see Malcolm Hardman, *Six Victorian Thinkers* (Manchester, 1991), pp. 45-6, 76, 92.

[15] *Works*, 19, p. 39.

[16] Hardman [note 9], pp. 136-7.

[17] *Works*, 29, pp. 82-97.

[18] See Alain de Lille, *Anticlaudianus* (edited by R. Bossuat) (Paris, 1955); J. P. Migne (editor), *Patrologiae Cursus Completus: Patrologia Latina*, 221 vols (Paris, 1844-64), vol. 210, col. 486-576. I am indebted to Peter Dronke for the transcription and elucidation of Alain de Lille, *Sermo de Sphaera Intelligibili*.

[19] *Works*, 9, p. 10; 19, p. 38. Compare Francis Bacon, *Meditationes Sacrae*, in James Spedding, Robert Leslie and Douglas Denon Heath (editors), *The Works of Francis Bacon*, 14 vols (London, 1857-74), vol. 7, pp. 240-2.

[20] For the historical background see Daniel Waley, *The Italian City-*

Republics (London, 1969), pp. 231-4. Compare *Works*, 19, p. 32.

[21] *Works*, 4, p. 36.

[22] *Works,* 19, p. 38.

[23] Dante, *Divina Commedia*, fin. *Works*, 19, p. 38; 'Eye, the', in *The National Encyclopaedia*, 14 vols. (London: 1895), vol. 5, pp. 396-401.

[24] Waley [note 20], pp.151-2, 155 and fig.

[25] Nikolaus Pevsner, *Ruskin and Viollet-le-Duc* (London, 1969), p. 42. Intriguingly, Ruskin decorated the endpaper of his copy of Viollet-le-Duc, *Dictionnnaire Raisonné de l'Architecture Française*, 9 vols (Paris, 1867-70), vol. 3, with a sketch of a neoclassical building in the Sansovino manner (information from Stephen Wildman).

[26] E. E. Viollet-le-Duc, *Vue restaurée du Colisée rempli de spectateurs* (1836), water-colour, 21.1cm. x 33.5cm., Ecole Nationale des Beaux-Arts. M. le Directeur regrets the impossibility of reproducing this image, which gives a strong sense of the construction of the cavity of the amphitheatre below the huge awning (*velarium*), the circular opening (*oculus*) of which throws a vivid light down onto a section of the audience (represented by blobs). A dimmer diffused light reaches the delicately suggested mess of the sanded floor (*arena*).

[27] Arthur Hugh Clough, *Amours de Voyage* 1.2, in *The Poems*, edited by A. L. P. Norrington (London, 1968), p. 178.

[28] *Works*, 29, pp. 161-2. Compare *Paradise Lost*, book 2, lines 210-25, book 6, lines 620-3.

[29] *Works*, 18, p. 48. T. S. Eliot, *Collected Poems 1909-1962* (London, 1962), p. 61. For '*ermafrodito*' and '*miglior fabbro*' (Guido's compliment to Arnaut Daniel), see Dante, *Purgatorio*, 26.82, 117.

[30] Waley [note 20], pp. 148-51, 217 and fig.

[31] Hardman [note 14], p. 189 and [note 9], pp. 149, 267-87.

[32] Waley [note 20], pp. 46-7 and fig; *Works*, 24, pp. 1-123.

[33] 'The Guardian Profile', in *Guardian Saturday Review*, 13 November 1999, pp. 6-7.

[34] Letter of 1910 from Richard Norman Shaw to the authors, quoted in Marjorie and C. H. B. Quennell, *A History of Everyday Things in England 1733 to 1851* (London, 1954), pp. 152-4.

[35] *Works*, 10, p. 459.

[36] Malcolm Hardman, 'Ruskin's "Massy Commonsense"', *British Journal of Aesthetics*, 16 (1976), pp. 137-43. The quoted phrase is Ruskin's description of the sea.

[37] Charles Wild, *South End of the Transept of the Cathedral of Rouen*, in *Twelve Select Examples of the Ecclesiastical Architecture of the Middle Ages, chiefly in France* (London, 1831), fol. 4.

[38] John Ruskin, *Entrance to the South Transept, Rouen Cathedral* (dated 18-23 May 185[4]) in Ruskin's MS. Pencil and water-colour, 48.2 cm. x 30.5 cm., Fitzwilliam Museum, Cambridge. Here as elsewhere, the camera fails to reproduce detail of plants, advertisements.

[39] Angela Carter, *The Passion of New Eve* (London, 1999), pp.180, 185.

[40] John Ruskin, *Venetian Balcony* [Palazzo Priuli], brush drawing in grey

wash and graphite, 11.9cm. x 18.6cm., British Museum. Compare *Works*, 10, pp. 310-11, plate XVIII and (for sea-cave and resurrection connotation) Martin Biddle, *The Tomb of Christ* (Stroud, 1999), p. 83, on Constantine's shrine for the Holy Sepulchre: 'The west wall was apsidal and covered by a conch'. Ray Haslam tells me the Armytage engraving was made from a daguerrotype, evidently taken at a different time of day from the sketch by Ruskin, who was naturally drawn to a telling effect of light. See also Carter [note 39], pp. 176, 186.

[41] *Works*, 10, pp. 36-68.

[42] *Works*, 34, p. 513. John Ruskin to Margaret Ruskin, Winnington Hall, 29 May 1868, in Van Akin Burd (editor), *The Winnington Letters* (London, 1969), pp. 630n, 633. The 'builder' was Edward Leader Williams, knighted in 1887 for his plans for the Manchester Ship Canal, and a devotee of Ruskin's architectural drawings.

[43] See note 36.

[44] Matthew Arnold, *Lectures and Essays in Criticism,* edited by R. H. Super (Ann Arbor, 1962), p. 251.

[45] *Works*, 10, pp. 36, 40, 64, 67. Compare *Works*, 19, pp. 5-7. On Turner and 'the miraculous draught', see Hardman [note 9], pp. 219-20. Brunelleschi (sometimes condemned by Ruskin along with Palladio) also most particularly desired that his model Christian temple, S. Spirito, would be 'visible to fishermen on the Arno' (L. H. Heydenreich, *Architecture in Italy 1400-1500* (New Haven and London, 1996), p. 17).

[46] *Works*, 19, p. 359.

7

Ruskin and Pugin

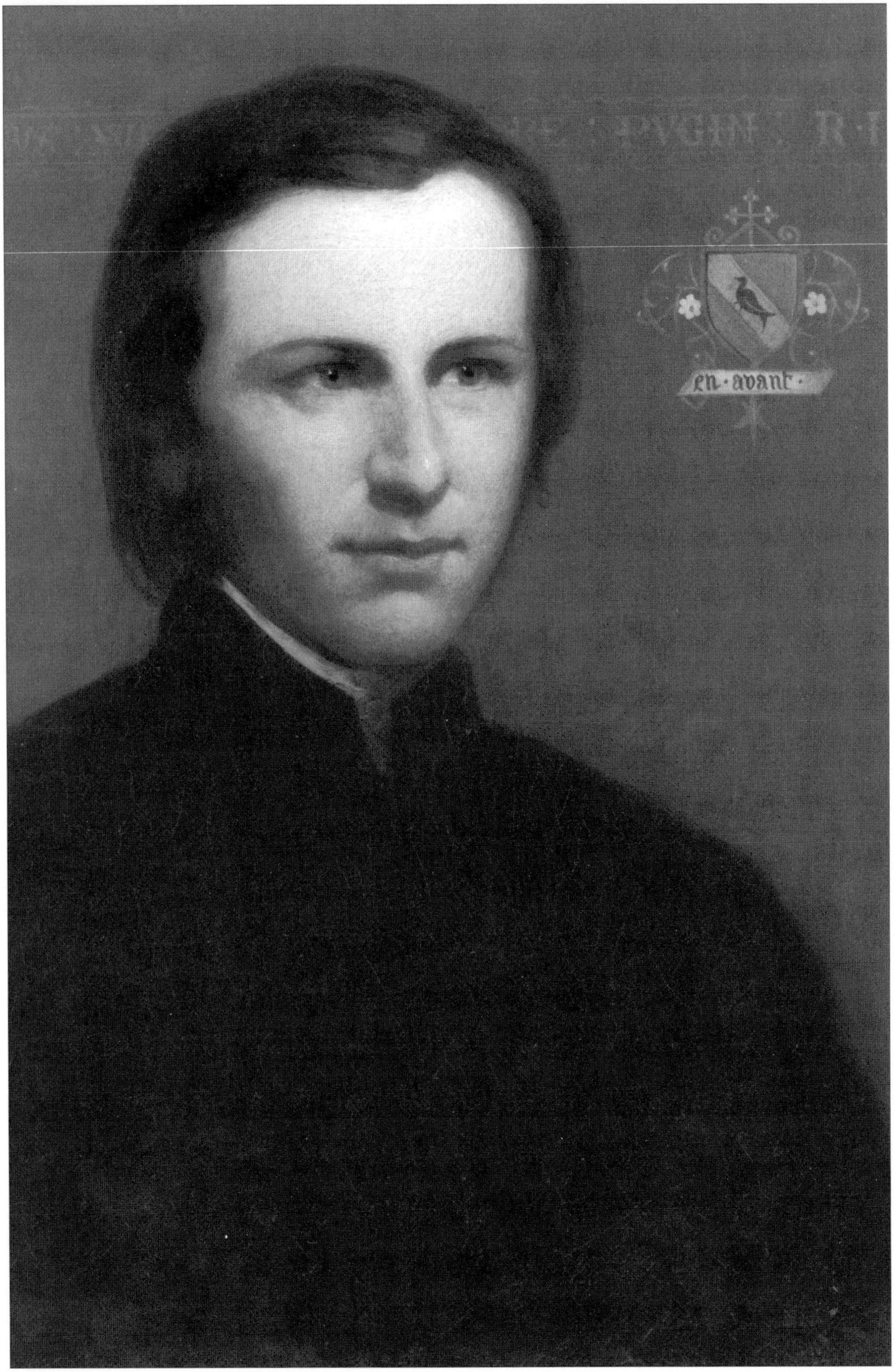
en · avant ·

Ruskin and Pugin

Rosemary Hill

IN FEBRUARY 1852 the painter Frank Howard gave a paper to the Liverpool Architectural Society entitled 'Stones of Venice and Principles of Art.' In it he accused Ruskin of first stealing Pugin's ideas and then attacking him. 'Am I too severe,' he asked 'in supposing that Mr Ruskin hoped, by his abuse of Mr Pugin as an architect, to throw his uninformed reader off the scent, and to conceal how much he had plagiarised from his victim?'[1]

Five years later the paper was published. *Building News*, reviewing it under the headline 'Ruskin Unmasked', agreed with Howard, regretting only that by 1857, with Pugin dead and Ruskin no longer 'the literary art lion of his day', it was something of 'a spent cannon-ball ... the momentum that impelled it ... gone.'[2] Such was not the case. Howard's accusations were to be repeated during Ruskin's lifetime and revived in the next century by those who came to retrieve Pugin's faded reputation: Nikolaus Pevsner, Kenneth Clark and others. To add to the evident unfairness of Ruskin's attacks on Pugin came further damning evidence that he had in fact read Pugin's *True Principles of Pointed or Christian Architecture*, a book of which he had denied knowledge.

Not until 1978 did Ruskin find a champion in Patrick Conner.[3] It was Conner who published Ruskin's notes on *True Principles*. Yet he did so in the course of an attempt to disprove the accusations of plagiarism or even substantial influence. On those points most often cited by Pugin's supposed defenders, the role of function and the nature of honesty in architecture, neither Pugin nor Ruskin was completely original. For Ruskin the most important precursor was Robert Willis, whom he knew and acknowledged as a source. Willis wrote in 1835 (before either of the others had published):

> The Romans attempted concealment, and hence introduced discordance between the decoration and the

Opposite:
A. W. N. Pugin, (1812–52) artist and date unknown. Pugin is shown as a romantic. The long hair swept away from the high forehead, pale face, dark clothes and the emphasis on the expression of the eyes are all typical of romantic portraiture, recalling similar images of Victor Hugo and Liszt (*by courtesy of the National Portrait Gallery, London*).

mechanism of the structure. The Gothic builders in later times more wisely adapted their decoration to the exact direction of the resisting forces required by the vaulted structure.[4]

Much else in Ruskin that might have come from Pugin derives, as Conner points out, from their mutual familiarity with the works of Humphry Repton and John Britton.

There the quarrel may be laid to rest. It is time instead to attempt a more constructive comparison between the two men whose influence so largely shaped the Victorian Gothic Revival. One consequence of efforts to set them up against each other has been to obscure the important common ground they shared and which Conner began to uncover. This chapter is written from a position of much greater familiarity with Pugin's work than Ruskin's. Since, however, Pugin has been seen as the injured party this may add weight to its argument that, while neither man incurred any intellectual debts he could not repay, the ideas of both grew from common roots into comparable forms. Though there could be no meeting of minds their intellectual paths crossed and recrossed at several points.

A. W. N. Pugin (1812–52) and John Ruskin were born within seven years of one another in houses not half a mile apart in Bloomsbury. For both the experience of childhood was unusually rich and formative. Each was the adored, unhoped for only child of older parents who nurtured their sons' talents with unusual care. Neither was sent away to school. Their imaginative characters grew naturally, unchecked by intellectual convention and unmodified by criticism. Nothing in the outside world was ever as real to either as his own ideas and they preserved into adult life a mixture of precocity and naïveté. Pugin shared exactly that quality of 'childlike audacity' ascribed to Ruskin.[5]

The two men also shared a profound religious sense articulated in the language of Low-Church Protestantism. The interminable sermons of Edward Irving, which Pugin was taken to hear by his mother, left their mark on his prose long after he had become a Roman Catholic. Ruskin remained, during Pugin's lifetime, a committed Evangelical and the cadences of the Bible, especially the books of prophecy,

John Ruskin by George Richmond, c.1843. Richmond was a celebrated portrayer of eminent Victorians, a status which Ruskin achieved, while Pugin remained an outsider (*by courtesy of the National Portrait Gallery, London*).

resound through *The Seven Lamps of Architecture* as they do through Pugin's *Contrasts*.

Ruskin's was the more comfortable and conventional upbringing. As another native of Bloomsbury, Anthony Trollope (born in 1817) recalled, the area could hardly be called 'fashionable' in the early 19th century, nor was it 'much affected by the nobility.'[6] Ruskin was only four when his father, the prospering sherry merchant John James, took the family to live at Herne Hill where his childhood was spent in the suburban pastoral recalled in *Praeterita*.

Meanwhile the Pugins remained in Bloomsbury clinging ever more perilously to the fringe of gentility. Pugin's father Auguste Charles (1769–1832) patched together a living from watercolour painting, illustration, print dealing and architectural draughtsmanship.[7] In the early 1820s he began to produce books of measured details from Gothic buildings. In

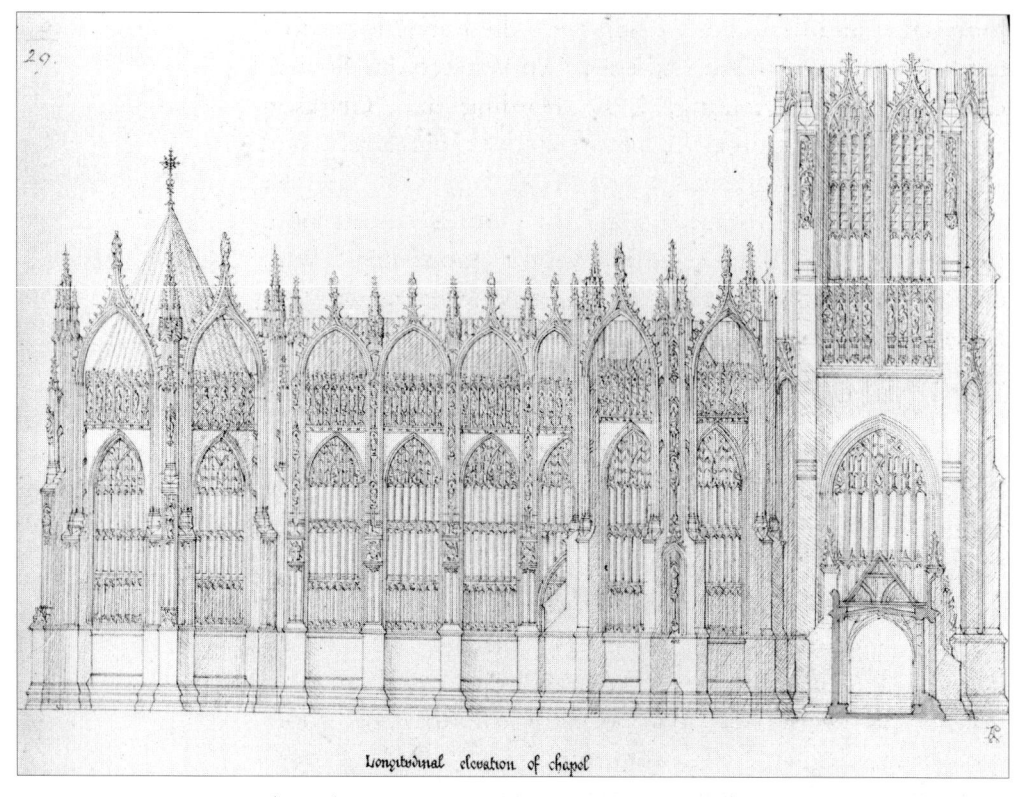

'Longitudinal section of chapel' by Pugin from the 'Ideal Scheme' 'St Marie's College' of 1834, pen coloured ink. The 'Ideal Schemes' that Pugin drew in his early 20s are anthologies of all he knew and liked in Gothic architecture. The elaborate arcading here derives from Rouen, a city that was a formative influence on both Pugin and Ruskin (*Victoria and Albert Museum*).

these he was assisted by pupils who came to study in the family home in Great Russell Street.

So Pugin grew up in late Georgian London in the bustling midst of the commercial art world. His father worked with John Britton and with Rudolph Ackermann. As a boy Pugin knew Ackermann's Repository in the Strand. He was soon frequenting the brokers' shops of Soho, the theatres and spectacular shows that were all the rage, including the Diorama in Regent's Park, which was housed in a building designed by his father. By the time Pugin was fourteen he was working with Auguste. The world of his childhood was stimulating and slightly shabby, socially *declassé* and morally raffish. Over its further edges hung the shadows of destitution and degradation that haunted families like the Pugins and the Trollopes.

It was all very different from the comfortable respectability of Herne Hill. Yet many names would have been familiar in both households, for the Ruskins were typical patrons of the art that the Pugins and their neighbours typically produced. Genteel but not rich, cultivated rather than educated,

John James and Margaret Ruskin were the public for whose tastes Ackermann, Britton and the Old Watercolour Society catered. Copley Fielding, J. D. Harding and Clarkson Stanfield were among the artists known personally and admired by both families.

When Ruskin recalled, with the condescension of a maturer taste, the 'simple company of connoisseurs ... who crowded into happy meeting, on the first Mondays in Mays of long ago, in the bright large room of the Old Water-colour Society; and discussed, with holiday gaiety, the unimposing merits of the favourites, from whose pencils we knew precisely what to expect', he evoked a scene in which A. C. Pugin was a familiar figure, only recently departed.[8] He exhibited with the Society from 1807 until 1831, the year before his death.[9]

It has surprised later critics that the 'minor artists' of this 'trade association' should have been taken so seriously by Ruskin in *Modern Painters*.[10] Their relevance to Pugin has been quite overlooked. Yet the watercolourists, or more specifically their aesthetic, were important in forming both Ruskin and Pugin's views of architecture.

The taste for watercolour had grown up with the picturesque. The works of the OWS were formed and informed in constant reference to the dicta of Uvedale Price and Richard Payne Knight, long since absorbed into polite taste. Since the end of the 18th century when the Continent was closed by war and architectural commissions were, for the same reason, scarce, it was the English school of topographical artists, especially the watercolourists, who gave the most prominent visual expression to the growing impact of romanticism on the Gothic Revival. This would remain the case until Pugin himself began to build.

Like the novels of Walter Scott, whose influence has also been underrated since his literary reputation declined, they marked forever the imaginations of that rising generation who would reform the Gothic Revival. In writing of Samuel Prout's influence on the depiction of architecture, Ruskin describes a sensibility that bears an obvious relationship to his own: 'decomposing composition ... intricate grouping ... breadth of inartificial and unexaggerated shadow'.[11]

'Veue du chasteau prise du jardin', by Pugin from the 'Ideal Scheme' *Le Chasteau*, 1833, pen and coloured ink. Pugin was half French and grew up both literally and aesthetically bi-lingual (*Victoria and Albert Museum*).

J. D. Harding, who taught Ruskin and published the admirable but scarcely innovatory *Principles and Practice of Art* in 1845, became obsessed with the belief that everything Ruskin wrote was merely a 'recook' of his own ideas.[12] It was not true, but there was truth in it.

As a young man Ruskin saw Rouen through Prout's eyes as 'one labyrinth of delight, its grey and fretted towers ... letting the sky like blue enamel through the foiled spaces of their crowns of Work ... meshed like gossamer with inextricable tracery'.[13] Pugin saw Rouen for himself as a child, on drawing expeditions with his father and the pupils. For him, like Ruskin, that city was a continual reference point. He was already too much the incipient architect to care for decay but he was attracted to exactly the same qualities of intricacy and elaboration. His 'Ideal Schemes' of the early 1830s are the graphic equivalent of Ruskin's words, taking off from the reality of the Palais de Justice into soaring flights of playful imagination.

Pugin copied views from J. D. Harding into his sketchbook and absorbed the principles of Repton from his father. Like Ruskin's his taste matured and was refined, yet he never left the picturesque entirely behind, he loved sequential views and in his churches sought what Payne Knight characterises as typical of Gothic: 'dim and discoloured light diffused through unequal varieties of space divided but not separated'.[14] All his life Pugin responded to light and weather in an almost programmatic way. In his troubled last years he wrote from Ramsgate to his friend John Hardman: 'I have been frantic all day but a ray of the setting sun striking on the chancel arch has restored tranquillity to my soul.'[15] Late sunlight slanting through a Gothic church: it is an image Pugin must have seen many times on the walls of that 'bright large room' on 'the first Mondays in Mays of long ago.'

In their early familiarity with the watercolourists lie the common roots of much that Ruskin was later accused of taking from Pugin. Their most important shared legacy, however, so all-pervading that it has escaped much comment, was the romantic sensibility. Like the watercolourists whose art aspired to represent the emotional mood as much as the physical appearance of a scene Pugin and Ruskin saw architecture as expressive, imbued with meaning.

That this should be a moral, religious meaning was inevitable given their temperament and upbringing. Indeed had they not seen architecture in this way they could never have exercised such influence on the mid-19th-century mind. As much as anything that either of them wrote about what buildings should look like, it was their conception of what architecture could be and mean that awoke the enthusiasm of George Gilbert Scott and his kind. They also provoked the same baffled irritation in those who could admit no connection between building and belief, from their contemporary, W. H. Leeds, arguably the first architectural critic of the modern kind, to the present day.

Despite the difference in their ages Ruskin and Pugin made their debut as architectural critics within a year. Pugin published *Contrasts*, his satirical attack on the modern city, in 1836. It was an instant, controversial success. More quietly in 1837 Ruskin, now an undergraduate at Oxford, produced a series of articles, 'The Poetry of Architecture', for J.C. Loudon's *Architectural Magazine*. Loudon, a publisher, architect and indefatigable author, was a typical figure in the world

Opposite: Rugby School Chapel by William Butterfield, 1870–2 and 1882. Butterfield was greatly influenced by Pugin at the beginning of his career and got to know him in the 1840s. By that time Butterfield was moving away from purely English 'Puginian' Gothic. In 1849 *The Stones of Venice* had an immediate, transforming effect on his work (*Rosemary Hill*).

of Pugin's early life, a world he was fast leaving behind but where he was not forgotten. Within a few pages of Ruskin's concluding article on 'The Cottage', readers could find W. H. Leeds, as 'Candidus', fulminating against 'Welby Pugin [who] has just broken out afresh ... with indiscriminate abuse of the whole profession.'[16]

In Ruskin's articles he did some fulminating of his own, anticipating Pugin in his mockery of 'pinnacles without height, windows without light, columns with nothing to sustain and buttresses with nothing to support'.[17] Ruskin was still close enough to his picturesque sources for Loudon to use one of his articles as an appendix in his new edition of Repton's works. However, there was much that was original and foreshadowed Ruskin's later writings. It is a useful moment to compare him with Pugin for it is a point at which their paths might seem to converge but in fact merely cross in opposite directions.

Pugin in 1837 was designing St Chad's, Birmingham, in a German brick style. It is sometimes cited as an instance of his pre-Ruskinian Ruskinism. Ruskin, in his articles, pondered the nature of national characteristics in building and praised brick for its 'cleanness and freshness of colour, admitting of little dampness or staining'. It suited what he called the 'simple blue' country, places where 'the matter-of-fact business-like activity' of 'working and money-making members of the community are perpetually succeeding and overpowering each other.'[18] All of this fits Birmingham aptly enough, but Pugin explained his choice in his own terms: 'I have adopted a foreign style of pointed architecture because it is both cheap and effective and likewise because it is totally different from any protestant erection.'[19]

St Chad's impresses, as Pugin hoped, by its 'size and grandeur of mass' and by the way it occupies its steeply sloping site.[20] In all of this it looks forward to the later 19th century. But Pugin's account of its style is neither convincing, nor convinced. His interest in brick developed no further. Though he was often obliged to use it for economy he always regarded it as second best. Less than a year after the consecration of St Chad's he was warmly endorsing the *Ecclesiologist's* sarcasm at the expense of Ambrose Poynter's

St Paul's, Cambridge, a 'CHEAP CHURCH OF THE 19TH CENTURY' built in 'very red brick indeed.'[21] By 1842 Pugin could not remember having ever thought differently of 'brick work applied to churches'. 'I utterly detest it in this country' he wrote, '& have only used it from extreme necessity.'[22]

On the question of national style Pugin also changed his

Details of narthex. This was a later addition to Rugby School Chapel. It is possible that Butterfield took the form of these windows from Pugin's 'Ideal Scheme' 'St Margaret's Chapel' having seen it in an exhibition after Pugin's death. If not it is a remarkable coincidence.

mind. He, like Ruskin, had made annual trips abroad with his parents and knew France and the Netherlands well. Germany he had discovered by himself more recently. In his 'Ideal Schemes' of the early 1830s he used Flemish and French elements in ways that now seem uncannily prescient of High Victorian buildings, of Butterfield at his most extreme. A striking instance is the narthex of Rugby School chapel: its windows are the same convex triangles within straight sided triangles that light the undercroft of Pugin's St Margaret's chapel. It is a strange device, the huge scale at eye level dramatic and disturbing.[23]

'North Elevation' by Pugin from the 'Ideal Scheme', 'St Margaret's Chapel', 1833, pen and coloured ink. In this scheme the elements are predominantly English. Like Ruskin, Pugin in his youth preferred Gothic in its most intricate and densely detailed forms (*Victoria and Albert Museum*).

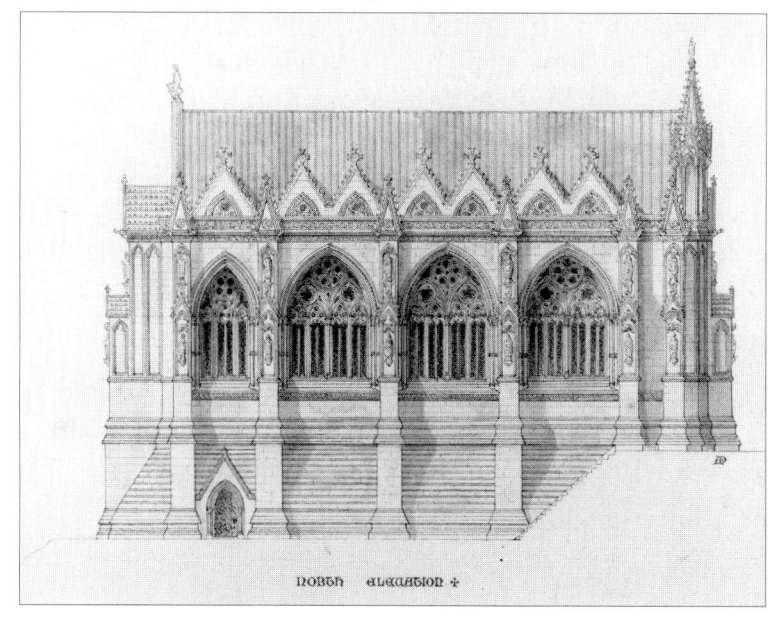

232   Ruskin and Pugin

'East End' from 'St Margaret's Chapel'. The dramatic windows set into the batter of the undercroft look forward to High Victorian 'muscularity' as advocated by Ruskin (*Victoria and Albert Museum*).

In a more moderate form the influence of German Gothic appeared in Pugin's built architecture not only at St Chad's but also at St Mary's, Derby, of 1838 and St Alban's, Macclesfield, 1839. The Convent of the Sisters of Mercy at Bermondsey (1839) was in the Flemish style. In 1840, however, the experiments with Continental Gothic were abandoned. He decided to purge his work of foreign influence. After St Alban's there are no references to Continental Gothic in his buildings for several years. On his frequent foreign tours he filled his sketchbooks with only such details as could make use of without 'violating ... our own peculiar style of English Christian architecture'. In 1841, in *True Principles* he confessed that he 'once stood on the very edge of a precipice in this respect', until Dr Rock, Lord Shrewsbury's chaplain, recalled him to the surer ground of a pure, native style.[24]

So it was in English Gothic that Pugin worked between 1840 and 1845, in the busiest years of his architectural career. This was the period that brought him international fame. It saw the publication of *True Principles* and, in 1843, *An Apology for the Revival of Christian Architecture in England*, as well as two articles from the *Dublin Review* combined as *The Present State of Ecclesiastical Architecture in England*, and more than a hundred major architectural commissions. Meanwhile Ruskin, after the failure of Loudon's magazine and a disillusioning visit to Walter Scott's Abbotsford, began work on *Modern Painters*. He continued of course to think about architecture but published nothing. It would therefore seem to many, when *The Seven Lamps of Architecture* appeared in 1849, that he was a debutant in a field so dominated by Pugin that a debt to him must be inevitable.

It is difficult, if important, to summarise Pugin's own development during these intervening years. It is difficult because Pugin was both changeable and dogmatic. With no formal training in architecture there was more than the usual degree of trial and error in his early work and, had he lived as long as Butterfield, we might regard all the buildings we have by him as 'early work'. In addition to which he was learning all the time about the Middle Ages.

Pugin experimented and changed his mind but, unlike Ruskin who delighted in contradiction and used it as an intellectual method, Pugin would never admit to it. John Henry Newman, who was as unfair sometimes to Pugin as Ruskin was, nevertheless had a point when he complained that:

> Mr Pugin ... is disentombing what has been hidden for centuries amid corruptions; and, as, first one thing, then another is brought to light, he, like a true lover of the art, modifies his first views, yet he speaks as confidently and dogmatically about what is right and what is wrong, as if he had gained the truth from the purest and stillest founts of continuous tradition.[25]

Having nailed so many colours so firmly to the mast before he was thirty Pugin inevitably found himself at times compromised, unable to manoeuvre without impugning the absolute truth of his earlier statements. He then either indulged in retrospective rationalisation or just contradicted himself without comment.

Between 1842 and 1845 his ideas underwent a change. In fact hardly had he found his perfect model, the English 14th-century parish church, before he began to move beyond it. His attitude to revivalism altered, he came to accept the need for a modern interpretation of Gothic and to prefer, if not always to practice, a plainer style. His ideas, in fact, developed, independently, along the same lines as Ruskin's and took him back, at some points, to his earlier position. He gave up his commitment to English Gothic, making several excursions in the direction Ruskin would point in the 1850s. Pugin was not alone in this, but it is an aspect of his career so far unexplored. He built little after 1845 so his later ideas were never realised on any great scale, yet there is a case to be made for an incipient 'High Victorian' Pugin.

In 1843 when Pugin published *The Present State* and *An Apology*, nobody who reviewed the books seems to have noticed that they represented a flat contradiction. *The Present State* comprised the two *Dublin Review* articles written in 1841 and 1842. In them Pugin foreswore invention in architecture: 'The only hope of reviving the perfect style is by strictly adhering to ancient authorities;...We seek for authority not originality' he wrote.[26] By 1843 he had changed his mind. Gothic he now thought should change, should grow 'so it may be modified to suit actual necessities'.[27] As his patron the Earl of Shrewsbury summarised it: 'Pugin calculates that ... had the old men gone on to our times, they would have been constantly incorporating new discoveries with their style'.[28]

Another new idea which suddenly appeared in the *Apology* and which was to be central also to Ruskin's 'Lamp of Beauty', was that of 'natural architecture'. The use of nature as a model was axiomatic to the watercolourists but to Pugin, who had been taught to make measured drawings and to copy casts, it was new. In *True Principles* he had used examples of medieval textiles, metalwork and other antiquities. Now, however, he suggested there was a better model for art than art itself.

Details of a school (later a convent) by Pugin for Ambrose Phillipps, Whitwick, Leicestershire, 1842. Pugin's work in Leicestershire and Ireland taught him to appreciate the qualities of stone and the skills of local masons. Here a modest building is given 'nobility' in the way Ruskin later recommended by the use of 'massy stones' laid in the 'rude and irregular' manner of vernacular architecture (*Rosemary Hill*).

'A pointed building is a natural building' he wrote.[29] He urged architects to look at timber barns and gates and 'the mere essentials of good masonry' for models. 'The rubble stones and flinty beach furnish stores as rich for the natural architect as the limestone quarry or granite rock'.[30] He several times promised a treatise on natural architecture but it never appeared. What Pugin had already learned, however, about the qualities of stone was apparent in buildings like the little school at Whitwick in Leicestershire of 1842. It is a perfect illustration of Ruskin's argument in the 'Lamp of Power':

> The smaller the building, the more necessary it is that its masonry should be bold ... For if a building be under the mark of average magnitude, it is not in our power to increase its apparent size (too easily measurable) by any proportionate diminution in the scale of its masonry. But it may be often in our power to give it a certain nobility by building it of massy stones or, at all event, introducing such into its make.[31]

In 1845, when St Giles, Cheadle, was nearly finished, Pugin's ideas developed further. Considering designs for a pro-Cathedral in Liverpool he was now critical to some extent of 'the old men' as he called the medieval builders and in retreat from the dense elaboration of St Giles:

> my impression is that something even grander than most of the old things can be produced by simplicity combined with gigantic proportions. I think the old buildings are for the most part too much cut up by detail which

236   Ruskin and Pugin

perishes in a few years & destroys the idea of permanency. I think all sort of Lace work in stone is bad in principle & lofty windows and pillars, huge projecting buttresses grand severe lines are the true thing.[32]

Pugin was moving towards the same view of 'permanence' as Ruskin, leaving behind the canopied niches and clustered pinnacles of *True Principles*. Both men were maturing. Ruskin also began to find the 'foiled spaces' and 'inextricable tracery' of Rouen too elaborate,[33] the tower of St Ouen little better than 'the burnt sugar ornaments of elaborate confectionery'.[34]

By August 1845 Pugin's view of the relative merits of past and present had completely reversed. In the *Builder* he published an open letter to J. R. Herbert about the National School of Design at Somerset House. In it he was optimistic about the capabilities of modern art. The School should, Pugin thought, revive only the 'spirit' of the medieval architects and painters. It should also be 'a true expression of our period' which might then see art 'carried to a far higher degree of perfection than they ever attained during the middle ages.'[35] Once again he emphasised the importance of nature: 'Any garden and field can supply beautiful models for the sculptor ... The first productions of Christian art are the closest approximations to nature.'[36]

Pugin's 'work on vegetable and floral ornament', mentioned in the letter to Herbert as being in preparation, did not appear for four years. When *Floriated Ornament* was at last published Pugin was more explicit about the newness of his views and the usefulness of natural principles in 'removing the reproach of mere servile imitation' from Gothic architecture.[37]

Perhaps the fact that he had found a way of developing and varying his designs without bending his principles too far was one reason for his relative equanimity when, in 1846, the *Ecclesiologist* suddenly attacked him. In 'The Artistic Merit of Mr Pugin' the paper accused him of having run out of steam. 'The rocks upon which artistically he has split, are quickness and versatility. Having already attained ... a certain high degree of excellence ... he fell back upon that excellence and reproduced himself when he should have

Wilburton Manor, Cambridgeshire, 1848, copy of a 19th-century photograph. Built for the Pell family, High Anglicans sympathetic to Pugin, the design was the fruit of his only visit to Italy. It is remarkable for its use of Venetian tracery just a year before the publication of *The Stones of Venice* (*Rosemary Hill*).

Opposite:
St Marie's, Rugby, 1999 showing part of A. W. N. Pugin's church of 1847. The church was split in two in 1864 and a new nave and chancel, by E. W. Pugin, sandwiched between the halves. The tower and spire by B. Wheelan were added in 1872 obscuring the original design (*Rosemary Hill*).

been advancing.'[38] Pugin's published reply was moderate. In private he merely commented to John Bloxam that 'it quite surprised me. The publication must have changed hands.'[39]

By the time the review appeared Pugin had in fact moved far beyond the English 14th-century models that were becoming, it was true, clichés in the hands of many imitators. In 1847 he decided to visit Italy for the first time: 'the test act of a Goth's faith' as he described it.[40] 'Pugin is here abusing everything of course,' Bishop Gillis noted in Rome.[41] Elsewhere, however, Pugin found much to praise. Assisi thrilled him in a way Ruskin would have understood:

> rising in ... simple majesty from its rocky base adapting itself to every irregularity of surface & growing up as it were a part of its foundation sequential arches thrown across clefts mighty buttresses rising from promontories all crowned with lofty towers it forms the most gratious & imposing mass of building I have ever beheld.[42]

The architectural fruit of the visit, however, was interesting rather than successful. This was Wilburton Manor, Cambridgeshire, built the following year with square-headed windows and Venetian tracery. On the garden front only a buttress against the long, sheer wall plane marks the division between house and offices. The windows of the latter have mullions but no tracery. As the building of Wilburton does not seem to have been supervised by Pugin, its faults should not be entirely laid at his door, but the essential features of the design are his.[43] What is significant is its unique status in his work as an essay in the Venetian and an attempt to introduce his ideas about mass and severity of line to domestic architecture.

Left:
St Marie's, Rugby, 1847, photograph of c.1860. This church with its saddle-backed tower and tough buttresses continuous with the wall plane anticipates the architecture of the later 1850s and '60s. It shows Pugin becoming less 'Puginian' and more 'Ruskinian' as he returned to Continental models.

Pugin's other High Victorian experiment was made at around the same time. This was St Marie's, Rugby, of 1847. Pugin showed a view of it at the Royal Academy in 1849 which the *Ecclesiologist* found 'pretty', commenting that 'Mr Pugin has had the laudable courage to put a saddlebacked head to the tower.'[44] Indeed he had gone once more so far towards the precipice. The church has since been so drastically altered that the effect has been obscured. However, a photograph of about 1860 shows what a successful composition it was. The tower in particular, and the end buttresses continuous with the wall planes, look forward to the 1850s.

In 1849 Pugin published *Floriated Ornament* and Ruskin *The Seven Lamps of Architecture*. Several people claimed to have influenced Ruskin. J. D. Harding inevitably was one. The

Ecclesiologist also pronounced itself flattered by the imitation in some places of its own views and in a long review made no reference to Pugin. W. H. Leeds dipped his pen ready for an attack on the 'frothy, vapouring cant' of another opinionated young hothead.[45]

Pugin said nothing about *The Seven Lamps* in public or, apparently, in any of his surviving private letters. Yet with Ruskin's return to architectural criticism the affinities between them were certain to become apparent and since they could never have agreed they were bound to collide. In January 1850 the liberal Catholic magazine, the *Rambler*, published an article on town churches. It was part of a debate that quickly spread across the fence to the *Ecclesiologist*, prompting G. E. Street's famous article on the proper characteristics of a town church.[46] John Moore Capes, the *Rambler's* editor, was a friendly antagonist of Pugin whose attempt to revive Gothic architecture he regarded as 'an utter waste of toil and talent.' Capes argued for a style of church building that would grasp 'the great facts of the time' as, he said, Gothic had in its own day.[47]

This latest article was illustrated with a design by Matthew Hadfield. It may reflect the direct influence of Ruskin. He is not mentioned, yet *Seven Lamps* certainly had just such a rapid effect on Butterfield and Beresford Hope's plans for All Saints, Margaret Street. If Hadfield had not read Ruskin then his town church merely emphasises the extent to which 'Ruskinism' was the pushing of an open door. The proposed style was German, 'the Rhine churches which have afforded the principles upon which the present design is founded [being] particularly suited to the habits and feelings of many of our countrymen.'[48] Its circular aisle windows are punched through the wall plane, 'as if the surface had been completed first and the windows cut out of it'.[49]

Whether Pugin saw any irony in this enthusiastic discovery of ideas he had himself explored, rejected and rediscovered over thirteen years is doubtful. His reply, *Some Remarks on the Articles which have Recently Appeared in the Rambler*, makes no direct allusion to his own early work. He rejects the idea of a church occupying the whole of its site and has some satirical fun with the bull's eye windows, which 'forcibly recall the cosmoramic walk in a popular tea-garden' and the interior which Pugin finds 'very like the Hungerford Market, only not quite so handsome.'[50] The *Ecclesiologist* regretted that he had nothing to say on the controversial question of 'constructional polychrome', and indeed it is a striking omission.[51] Although Pugin once commented to his pupil Hardman Powell that the Italians' 'fine marbles did away with much need for architectural decoration on walls' he never seems to have considered following their example.[52]

The truth seems to be that Pugin was uncertain of his own mind about the question of decoration, but this was something he could not admit. He had turned against wall painting, as his letter of 1845 and his own church, St Augustine's, Ramsgate, with its sheer ashlar interior, demonstrated. Characteristically he now claimed never to have liked it and put the blame for the interior of St Giles, Cheadle squarely and somewhat unfairly on his patron the Earl of Shrewsbury.

In 1841 Pugin had been actively campaigning for wall paintings: 'a stained window in a white church is a mere spot' he wrote in the *Dublin Review*, where he enthusiastically described his plans for the interior of St Barnabas, Nottingham.[53] Only the year before the *Remarks*, in *Floriated Ornament*, he had published patterns 'principally intended for stencilling'.[54] In fact the designs may have dated from 1845, when he first mentioned the work on 'vegetable ornament', while the text incorporated his more recent ideas. Indeed, as the *Ecclesiologist* pointed out, the illustrations were not at all what the text led the reader to expect.[55] In *Remarks* the issue is fudged.

Perhaps the *Rambler* made Pugin, not given by nature to retrospection, review his own progress for the *Remarks* turns into an apologia for the career of which, in his private letters, he now often spoke in terms of bitterness and failure. It was this part of the pamphlet that most provoked Ruskin in the violent attack he now made on Pugin in the first volume of *The Stones of Venice*, published the same year, 1850. Ruskin, no more than Pugin, could bear to see the things he loved in the hands of the profane. The anti-Catholicism of 'Romanist Modern Art' is imbued with the same violent hatred with which Pugin treated the iconoclasts of the Reformation. Not all Ruskin's points were unfair. Not all Pugin's difficulties could be blamed on lack of money or lack of sympathy. Yet had there been less in common between them Ruskin might not have recoiled with such violence.

Their tastes, formed by the same influences in the same galleries were similar in more than architecture. Ruskin was in Venice during the Royal Academy exhibition of 1849 at which Pugin showed his view of St Marie's, Rugby, and Millais exhibited his first Pre-Raphaelite painting, *Isabella*. 'That's going to be the man,' Pugin said when he saw it, 'He has got the Medieval spirit in him.'[56]

How little Ruskin knew of Pugin's character is revealed by a letter of 1851 to W. H. Harrison, who was Ruskin's publisher and another figure from the literary world of his, and Pugin's, early lives. Harrison had been to stay with Pugin at Ramsgate: 'What sort of place has he,' asked Ruskin, 'I cannot imagine him living by the sea ... The sea has such a harsh-practical body of rebuke - and massy commonsense about it - I cannot conceive anything more adverse to Gothic pinnacles than its wild rough-level unity.'[57]

Pugin's love of the sea was even greater than Ruskin's and life-long. He was an experienced sailor, a more practical man than Ruskin would ever be and heartier, less highly strung in person than in print, as Gilbert Scott discovered.[58] What Pugin thought of Ruskin, if anything, is not known. He seems not to have mentioned him in his correspondence, though it is reported that when he was told of the attack on him in *The Stones of Venice* 'he merely said: "Let the fellow build something himself" and then turned back to his work.'[59] If so it was an acute riposte.

To Pugin in the last years of his life the rejection of his ideas by his fellow Catholics was far more painful than Ruskin's criticism could be. He was in despair at what he saw as the failure of the Catholic Gothic Revival and at war with the Oratorians. He still hoped for a reunion with the English Church. *The Stones of Venice* would not have touched him very deeply.

Nevertheless, Frank Howard, speaking to the Liverpool Architectural Society, believed that Pugin was preparing an answer to Ruskin. Perhaps he had been, but by the time the Society met it was too late. In February 1852 Pugin collapsed into insanity. Seven months later he was dead. Ruskin outlived him by nearly half a century, by which time his mind too had given way and the overlapping waves of the Gothic Revival had brought a returning admiration for Pugin.

This chapter is a revised and slightly expanded version of an article published in the British Art Journal, *2 no. 3 (Spring/Summer 2001), pp. 39-45.*

Acknowledgments: I am grateful to Sir David Hughes for showing me material relating to Wilburton Manor; Christopher Wilson for much help in identifying medieval sources in Pugin's 'Ideal Schemes' and Andrew Saint and Gavin Stamp for valuable conversations. I am particularly indebted to Lucy Thackray of Rugby for the loan of material in her possession.

Notes
[1] Reported in *Building News*, 20 November, 1857, pp. 1214-15.
[2] Ibid., p. 1214.
[3] Patrick R. M. Conner, 'Pugin and Ruskin', *Journal of the Warburg and Courtauld Institutes,* 41 (1978), pp 344-50.
[4] Robert Willis, *Remarks on the Architecture of the Middle Ages especially of Italy* (Cambridge, 1835), pp. 17-18.
[5] M. Hardman, 'Ruskin's Massy Commonsense', *British Journal of Aesthetics,* 16 no. 2 (Spring 1976), p. 169.
[6] Quoted by Victoria Glendinning in *Trollope* (London, 1992), p. 4.
[7] For a fuller account of A. C. Pugin's career, see Rosemary Hill, 'A. C. Pugin,' *Burlington Magazine,* 1114 (January 1996), pp. 11-20.
[8] *Works,* 14, pp. 389-90.
[9] *The Royal Watercolour Society, The First Fifty Years 1805-1855, An Antique Collectors' Club Research Project* (Woodbridge, 1992), pp. 217-18, gives a list of the works he exhibited.
[10] Tim Hilton, *John Ruskin, The Early Years* (London 1985, paperback edition, 2000), pp. 34, 64.
[11] *Works,* 12, p. 313.
[12] Quoted in Hilton [note 10], p. 283 n. 5.
[13] *Works,* 12, p. 311.
[14] Richard Payne Knight, *An Analytical Enquiry into the Principles of Taste* (London, 1805), p. 174.
[15] Correspondence with John Hardman in a private collection, on microfilm in the House of Lords Record Office, Hist. Coll. 304/716.

[16] *Architectural Magazine and Journal,* 5 (May 1838), p. 221.
[17] *Works,* 1, p. 8.
[18] Ibid., p. 141.
[19] Ms letter n.d., *c.*1837, Birmingham Diocesan Archives, published in Margaret Belcher (editor), *The Collected Letters of A. W. N. Pugin* (Oxford, 2001), p. 77 (hereafter Pugin Letters).
[20] Ibid.
[21] Quoted by Pugin in *The Present State of Christian Architecture in England* (London, 1843), p. 90. First published in the *Dublin Review* (February 1842).
[22] Pugin Letters, p. 373.
[23] It is possible that Butterfield may have known Pugin's 'Ideal Scheme' if it was among the drawings exhibited by Edward Pugin after his father's death. Butterfield knew Pugin personally and was much influenced by him in his earliest work.
[24] Pugin, *The True Principles of Pointed or Christian Architecture* (London, 1841), pp. 66-7.
[25] John Henry Newman to Ambrose Phillipps, 15 June 1848 in Stephen Dessain (editor), *The Letters and Diaries of John Henry Newman,* vol. 12 (London, 1962), p. 221.
[26] *The Present State,* p. 113.
[27] *Apology,* p. 38.
[28] John Talbot, 16th Earl of Shrewsbury to Daniel Rock, 21 December 1844, letter in Southwark Archdiocesan Archives, uncatalogued.
[29] *Apology,* p. 15.
[30] Ibid., p. 21.
[31] *Works,* 8, 113.
[32] Ms letter, n.d., *c.*1845, Liverpool Diocesan Archives, RCLV/63.
[33] *Works,* 12, p. 311.
[34] Ibid., 8, p. 65.
[35] *Builder,* 3, 1845, p. 367.
[36] Ibid.
[37] Pugin, *Floriated Ornament* (London, 1849), introduction (pages unnumbered).
[38] *Ecclesiologist,* 5 (1846), p. 11.
[39] Letter to John Bloxam, Magdalen College, Oxford, MCO/528/65.
[40] Alexandra Wedgwood (editor), 'Pugin in his Home, A Memoir by J. H. Powell', *Architectural History,* 31 (1988), p. 188.
[41] Ms letter in Scottish Catholic Record Office, Edinburgh, ED2/10/12.
[42] Note in a volume of sketches now in the Metropolitan Museum, New York, vol. 3, fol. 52v.
[43] Phoebe Stanton leaves the question of Wilburton's attribution to Pugin open in her monograph *Pugin* (London, 1971), p. 166 but his monogram on the date stone proves that the design, if not the execution, was his.
[44] *Ecclesiologist,* 9 (1849), p. 370.
[45] W. H. Leeds, *Ruskin's Doctrine Concerning the Orders, an appendix to*

Rudimentary Architecture, (2nd edition, London, 1851). Edition of 1906, p. 94.

46 Published in the *Ecclesiologist,* 11 (1850), pp. 227-33.

47 *Rambler,* 4 (August 1849), pp. 234-5.

48 Ibid., 5 (January 1850), p. 16.

49 *Works,* 8, p. 183.

50 *Some Remarks on the Articles which have Recently Appeared in the* Rambler (London, 1850), pp. 3-4.

51 'Mr Pugin and the Rambler', *Ecclesiologist,* 10 (1850), p. 398.

52 'Pugin in his Home …' [note 40], p. 189.

53 *Present State*, pp. 30, 64 and plates between pp. 62-3.

54 *Floriated Ornament*, introduction.

55 'Pugin's Floriated Ornament', *Ecclesiologist,* 10 (1850), p. 325.

56 'Pugin in his Home … ' [note 40], p. 182.

57 Quoted in Hardman [note 5].

58 Sir George Gilbert Scott, *Personal and Professional Recollections*, edited by Gavin Stamp (Stamford, 1995), p. 89. Scott found Pugin 'tremendously jolly' with 'almost too much bonhomie to accord with my romantic expectations.'

59 Quoted in Michael Trappes-Lomax, *Pugin, a Mediaeval Victorian* (London, 1933), p. 58.

8

G. F. Bodley and the response to Ruskin in Ecclesiastical Architecture in the 1850s

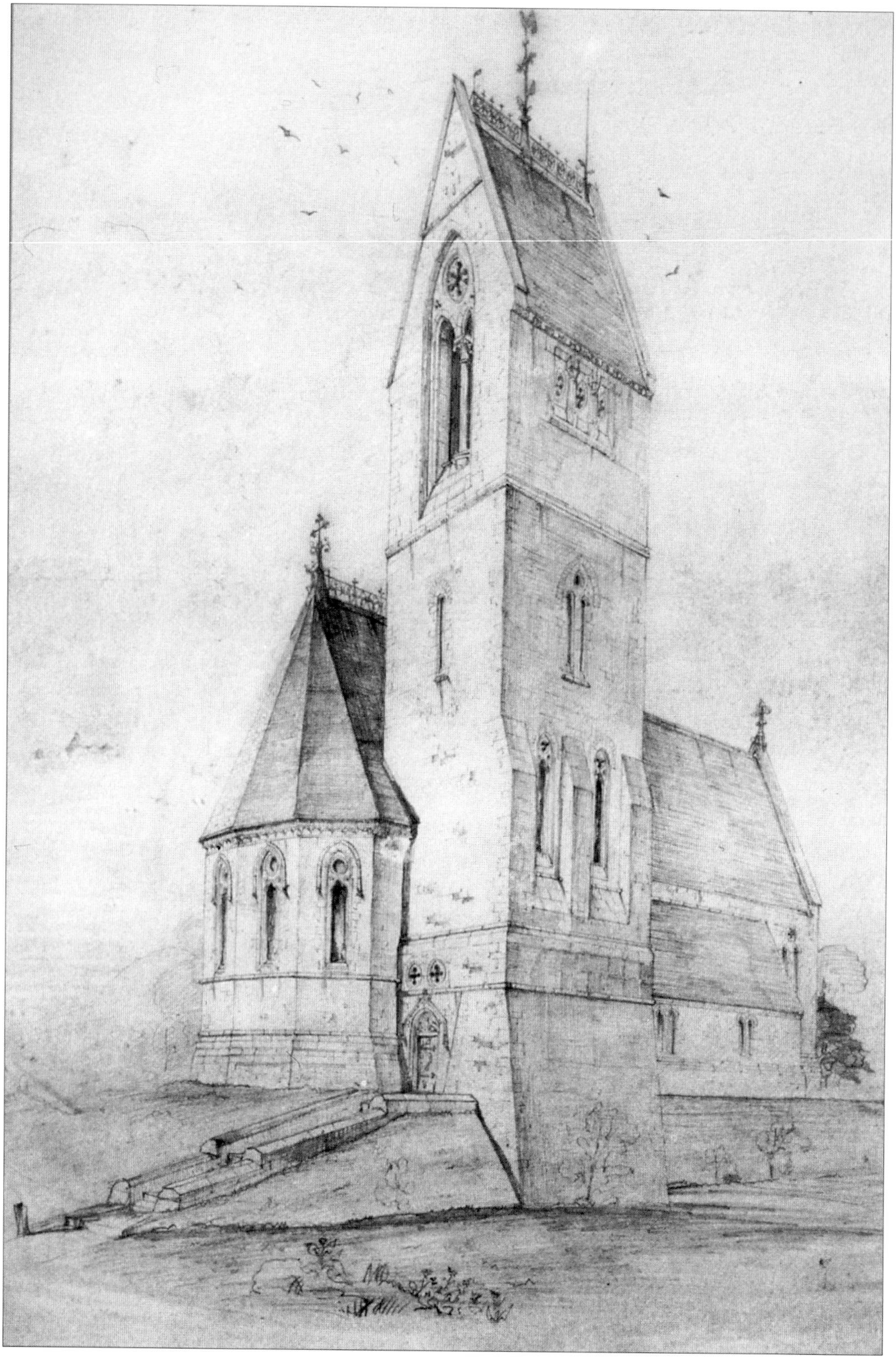

G. F. Bodley and the response to Ruskin in Ecclesiastical Architecture in the 1850s

Michael Hall

IN MAY 1883, the 19-year-old Ninian Comper took up a pupillage with the architects Bodley and Garner at 14 South Square, Gray's Inn, London. After his second day in the office, he wrote to his mother, 'Circumstances have brought me a special privilege. The pupils' room is quite full enough, for it is small and so I have taken up my abode at a little desk alongside of Mr Bodley, in his private room ... Mr Bodley has been talking to me a good deal to-day; he was at work upon some carving of stones and iron into crowns and flowers for Magdalen College. One time I saw him smile over his work and then he said "I wonder what Mr. Ruskin thinks of this, or if he ever looks at it" – so that led to some talk about him ...There are many things you would enjoy hearing - but in a letter it takes more time than I have'.[1]

If only Comper had had more time to write his letter, it might have been possible to suggest more certainly what Ruskin meant to Bodley, who was then, with his partner, Thomas Garner, at work on St Swithun's Quadrangle at Magdalen College. He would have known that Ruskin had just resumed lecturing at Oxford as Slade Professor. Yet Comper's anecdote reveals more than the fact that Bodley never forgot Ruskin's teachings. Why did he smile? Surely it was in part an ironic reflection about what Ruskin would have made of an architect preparing working drawings for sculpture and ironwork, rather than entrusting them to the creative instincts of a craftsman. That suggests a certain detachment from Ruskin's attitudes to craft and to architecture, which needs to be balanced against Bodley's undoubted admiration. But the irony may go deeper than that. Although by the early 1880s the influence of Ruskin on Bodley's architecture had evidently waned, it may always have been equivocal: although the buildings Bodley designed

Design by G. F. Bodley for All Saints, Selsley, probably drawn in late 1858 or early 1859. It was then planned to build the tower on the north-east corner; its intended position was changed twice (*Paul Barker/Country Life Picture Library*).

during his first decade in practice, from 1852 to 1862, embody what is now meant by 'Ruskinian' architecture, the meaning of his churches is, I would argue, in important ways fundamentally un-Ruskinian.

The records of Bodley's life are so scant that almost no other direct comments by him on Ruskin or his books survive, apart from the occasional reference in his published lectures to 'Mr Ruskin, to whose teaching we owe so much in the whole field of art'.[2] Ruskin never mentions Bodley, and so it seems unlikely that they were acquainted, nor is there any evidence that Ruskin was conscious of any of his buildings, but they certainly met. Bodley, like G. E. Street, William Burges, Benjamin Woodward and Philip Webb, was a member of the Hogarth Society, a short-lived club founded in 1858 for private exhibitions and convivial entertainments which drew in many pre-Raphaelite painters as well as Ruskin, until he resigned, following, it was said, the introduction of a billiard table.[3]

Both Ruskin and Bodley spoke at a meeting of the Ecclesiological Society in March 1861 to discuss ways of bringing to public attention the destructive restoration of French cathedrals and their sculpture. Bodley's detailed and incisive 'communication' on the subject, published in the *Ecclesiologist*, defers at several points to Ruskin's authority and reveals how well Bodley had absorbed the lessons not only of *The Seven Lamps of Architecture* but also of the chapter 'The Nature of Gothic' in the second volume of *The Stones of Venice*: 'Mere copyism, which is the avowed aim of these restorations, is not a healthy employment for men', Bodley stated. 'No really great and thorough work can be done except by those who take interest and pleasure in it. Mere reproduction will be done without love, for bread alone.' His conclusion, that 'protection, not imitative reproduction is what is wanted' is one of the earliest uses of the word 'protection' in this context.[4] The foundation of the Society for the Protection of Ancient Buildings was still sixteen years away, but it is possible that Bodley's rhetoric was sharpened by his friendship with William Morris, with whom he was then embarking on the first of several professional collaborations; the writings of Ruskin to which Bodley alludes had

had a decisive impact on Morris when he read them as an undergraduate in the mid-1850s, not long before he and Bodley became acquainted.

Bodley's own introduction to Ruskin's writings probably occurred during his pupillage in the office of George Gilbert Scott between 1845 and about 1850.[5] He joined the firm shortly after it had completed St Giles, Camberwell, opened in 1844. Here Scott had direct contact with Ruskin, who, with his old school friend Edmund Oldfield, a founder of the Arundel Society, had made designs for the stained glass of the east end, executed by Ward & Nixon. This was an ambitious project incorporating some 69 subjects and 64 additional figures; a pamphlet by Oldfield elucidates their scheme, praised by the *Ecclesiologist* for its 'adoption of the symbolical theory'.[6] The windows depict scenes from the Old and New Testaments in typological pairings, which tell the narrative of the unfolding of divine revelation from the birth of Christ to the Second Coming, culminating in scenes from the Apocalypse, with, in the topmost cinquefoil, Christ on the throne of judgment, with the seven lamps burning in front of him.[7]

Scott encountered Ruskin again in Venice in 1851, when Ruskin was hard at work on *The Stones of Venice*. North Italian inspiration derived from this foreign tour was to be evident in Scott's rebuilding of the Camden Chapel in Camberwell, begun in 1854, in the decoration of which Ruskin took a close interest. The now-demolished chapel's polychrome Romanesque apse, derived from S. Fermo Maggiore in Verona, was perhaps the most Ruskinian design Scott ever produced.[8] Whatever Ruskin's feelings about Scott as a restorer of old buildings, he had considerable admiration for him as a designer of new ones, and for example in 1872 consulted him about the design of St Margaret's Well at Carshalton, 'beautified and endowed' by Ruskin in memory of his mother.[9] But he never spoke as warmly of Scott as he did of G. E. Street, who joined Scott's office as an assistant in 1844 and started in independent practice in 1849. Ruskin knew and liked Street and in February 1859 introduced a talk by him on recent photographs of Venetian architecture at a meeting of the Architectural Photographic Association: 'Mr.

The nave of St Paul, Herne Hill, London, a church of 1843–5 by George Alexander, rebuilt by G. E. Street after a fire. Street's work, completed in 1858, includes the nave arcades. His use of bands of Devonshire marble below the capitals (carved by Thomas Earp) probably prompted Ruskin's public praise in 1859 of Street's use of constructional colour (*Michael Kerney*).

Street', he said, 'whose own designs were pure beyond anything he had ever seen in modern architecture, in exquisite propriety of colour and in fineness of line, would not, he felt confident, recommend to the meeting an imitation of the luxury of Venetian architecture; but he was equally sure that he would enter into the beauty of their colouring, which was principally derived from their great study, the sea'.[10]

Street, whose creative and critical engagement with Ruskin's teachings probably went deeper than any other architect's, had a lasting influence on Bodley, a friend as well as a former colleague.[11] Where Bodley's work appears to look to Ruskin - for example in his use of carved ornament - it is always possible that his interest is mediated through the older architect. For example, the lush but tight foliate forms of the carved capitals in the nave arcade of St Michael, Brighton, designed by Bodley in 1858, can be related to the Gothic exemplars illustrated by Ruskin in *The Stones of Venice*, but this detail, like many other aspects of the church, also reveals the influence of Street's All Saints, Boyne Hill, Berkshire, designed in 1854-5.[12] Of particular importance to Bodley were Ruskin's ideas about architectural colour, the aspect of Street's work which Ruskin had singled out for special praise at the meeting of the Architectural Photographic Association referred to above. On that occasion, Ruskin praised Street's restoration of St Paul, Herne Hill, which had been completed that year: 'this restoration', he said, 'was remarkable for a piece of colouring admirably introduced', which he doubted 'could be excelled by any of the colours in ancient art'.[13] He was referring, it seems, to Street's striking use of bands of Devonshire marble in the nave arcade. Ruskin believed that, like the Venetian architects they both admired, Street's colour harmonies were inspired by the natural forms of sea and sky.

This makes explicit a belief, which soon passed into common currency, that the use of constructional polychromy in buildings alluded metaphorically to the natural world.[14] In a

The chancel of All Saints, Boyne Hill, Berkshire, designed by G. E. Street in 1854–5. The banded ornament of the chancel walls may relate to Ruskin's recommendation in *The Stones of Venice* that the courses of a wall should be built in different colours to suggest 'the natural courses of rocks and beds of the earth itself'. The church building thus symbolically portrays the natural world, as created by God: at this date, geological study was thought to be revealing facts about divine purposes (*Paul Barker/ Country Life Picture Library*).

G. F. Bodley and the response to Ruskin in Ecclesiastical Architecture passage from the section devoted to the 'wall veil and the shaft' in the first volume of *The Stones of Venice*, Ruskin states:

> it is perfectly natural that the different kinds of stone used in [a wall's] successive courses should be of different colours; and there are many associations and analogies which metaphysically justify the introduction of horizontal bands of colour, or of light and shade. They are, in the first place, a kind of expression of the growth or age of the wall, like the rings in the wood of a tree ... they are valuable in their suggestion of the natural courses of rocks and beds of the earth itself.[15]

G. F. Bodley's St Michael, Brighton, photographed shortly after it was opened in 1862. The banding of the walls and voussoirs has an immediate model in Street's All Saint's, Boyne Hill; in both cases, an analogy with geological forms may be intended (*Brighton Central Library*).

It is hard to believe that Street did not have this passage in mind when three years later he embarked on the design of All Saints, Boyne Hill, where the banding of the chancel walls in brick, stone and tile strongly suggests geological strata.[16]

Street and Bodley must have discussed constructional colour in the early 1850s. Bodley's first completed building, the school at St Paul's Training College in Cheltenham, was designed in 1852 and opened in 1854. Resembling in many ways Street's contemporary designs for Cuddesdon College, it is innovatory in its use of coloured materials, consisting of alternating bands of red and white stone in the voussoirs of some of the windows and coloured tiles in the lunettes. This is among the first, if not the very first, secular High Victorian building to make use of constructional polychromy.[17] Bodley's churches of the 1850s all employ constructional colour to some degree, and although his use of the geological metaphor is never so insistently prominent as Street's, it was there, in, for example, the bold brick banding of the walls and voussoirs in St Michael, Brighton, another detail that looks back to All Saints, Boyne Hill.[18]

Geology was of course not only Ruskin's most sustained intellectual passion, it was also central to the way science, art and religion came together in a highly charged form in the 1850s. David Brownlee's close analysis of the changing philosophy of the Ecclesiological Society in the late 1840s has shown how A. J. Beresford Hope and the historian E. A. Freeman introduced into architectural thinking ideas of development derived from Newman's understanding of development of doctrine.[19] According to Freeman and Hope, architecture must be developed into a modern style, an idea that appealed to men brought up on Liberal historical ideas of human progress. It was Freeman, Hope and Benjamin Webb who suggested that development could be achieved by encouraging architects to range more widely in their sources, both in time and space, and that new attitude is one reason why architects were so receptive to Ruskin's books. Moreover, if architecture was to be progressive, it was argued, it should draw on not just new materials and technology but also scientific ways of looking at the world.

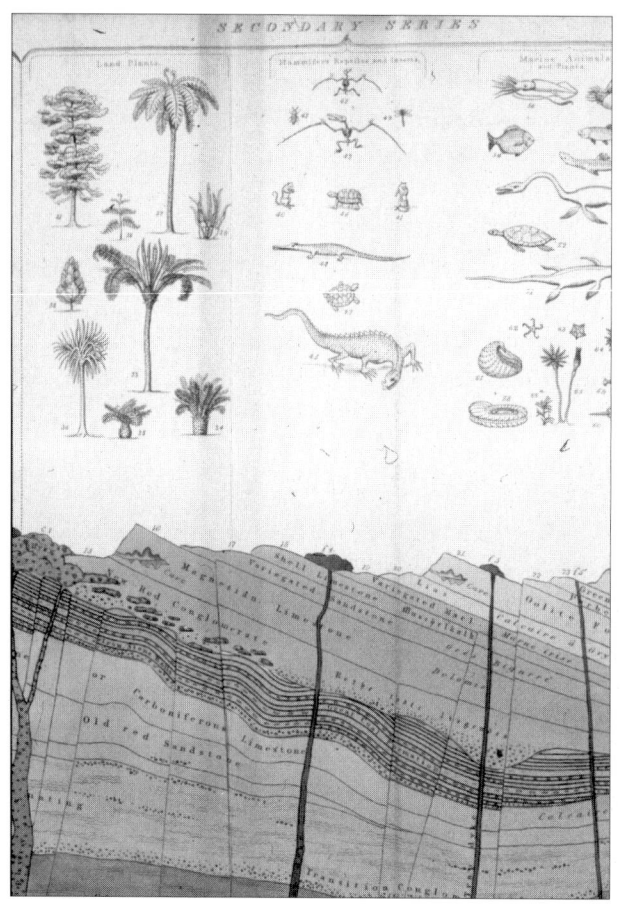

That is where, I would argue, that geology came in: it was a science of particular interest to architects and was itself explicitly based on notions of development, as it showed how the rocks embodied the history of the earth, and how the fossil record demonstrated the successive creations of plants and animals of increasing complexity. These were ideas that, arguably, were present in the metaphorical implications of constructional polychromy, as well as in the use of naturalistic ornament derived from plant forms, which is such a distinctive feature of churches in the 1850s.

The scientist most responsible for casting geological discoveries in forms acceptable for orthodox opinion was the distinguished professor of geology at Oxford, William Buckland, who had taught Ruskin and knew him well. Buckland was liked by theological commentators because he based his approach to palaeontology on the argument from design - the old belief that the existence of God could logically be deduced from the evidence of design in the universe. He demonstrated, for example, that an apparent monster such as the megatherium, an extinct giant South American ground sloth, was perfectly adapted to its environment, and not a freak of nature, as had been assumed when the bones were first discovered.[20] It thus reinforced the argument from design, and took its place in God's unfolding plan for creation, which had culminated in man. That plan is depicted with a geological section in Buckland's most influential book, *Geology and Mineralogy Considered with Reference to Natural Theology*, first published in 1836, which went through several editions up to 1869. It juxtaposes the geological record with the development of species, then thought of as individual acts of divine creation, not yet linked by evolution. Such schemes were paralleled in the contemporary understanding of architectural history: writing in the *Builder* in 1859, James Parker suggested that Buckland had shown a 'connection in the very grammar of the two sciences' and went on to compare 'the primary, secondary and tertiary, preceded by the igneous, to the first, second and third Pointed, preceded by the Norman, on which the others rested, if indeed it could not be said from which they were developed'.[21]

Ruskin, although an enthusiastic geologist, was notably uninterested in fossils: he was concerned to use geological knowledge to understand the world as he saw it, not to construct histories that were implicit rivals for a biblical understanding of creation. Ruskin had been brought up in the Evangelical belief that creation was a hypostasis of God – an independent aspect of the deity which opened up direct access to him.[22] This was an idea he never abandoned, and in part as a result, ideas about development had little interest for him; moreover he was not a Liberal and distrusted ideas of progress. Ruskin mentions the megatherium in the chapter on the Lamp of Truth in *The Seven Lamps of Architecture*, taking, I suspect, his lead from Buckland, who several times compares animal anatomy with Gothic architecture, but Ruskin turns the analogy to the ends of his anti-progressive philosophy – a human architect constructing a megatherium would have used a wide variety of materials designed to suit its particular needs, suggests Ruskin, but God used the same bone as he had used for all other animals, on 'the great principle to which all creation bears witness, that order and system are nobler things than power'.[23] In other words, the megatherium is an anti-progressive demonstration that architects should not seek new materials, such as iron.

Ruskin's best-known remark about geology may have helped give rise to a misunderstanding about the attitudes of architects and their patrons. In May 1851 Ruskin wrote to Henry Acland, Professor of Clinical Medicine at Oxford and chief promoter of the Oxford Museum:

Opposite:
the idea of 'development' which so preoccupied architects in the 1850s was an unRuskinian notion which related in part to the use geologists made of the term, when seeking to explain the appearance of fossils of ascending degrees of complexity in geological strata. 'Development' is visually embodied in the chart opposite, from William Buckland's *Geology and Mineralogy Considered with Reference to Natural Theology* (1836), a book which interpreted geology as the unfolding of a divine plan.

G. F. Bodley's All Saints, Selsley, Gloucestershire, from the south. This view shows how the church sits on a high ridge overlooking Stroud, a major industrial centre at the time the church was opened, in 1862. It also reveals the radical simplification of architectural forms which Ruskin promoted in 'The Lamp of Power'. The sculpture of the Resurrection above Marling's tomb is visible on the south wall of the chancel (*Paul Barker*/Country Life Picture Library).

> You speak of the Flimsiness of your own faith. Mine, which was never strong, is being beaten into mere gold leaf, and flutters in weak rags from the letter of its old forms; but the only letters it can hold by at all are the old Evangelical formulae. If only the Geologists would let me alone, I could do very well, but those dreadful Hammers! I hear the clink of them at the end of every cadence of the Bible verses – and on the other side, these unhappy, blinking Puseyisms; men trying to do right and losing their very Humanity.[24]

This letter is often quoted by historians studying the Victorians' supposed loss of faith, so it should be said at once that Ruskin never lost his. He attempted, as he suggests, to steer a path between rationalism and Puseyism, the sacerdotal, sacramental beliefs of the Oxford Movement. This was because Ruskin's Evangelical upbringing left him with not just a faith founded on study of the Bible but also an intellectual outlook based upon it: he believed not only that his study of nature was analogous to biblical study in that it revealed facts about divine purposes but also that art was there to embody those facts in the form of imagery or metaphors drawn from the natural world. His lifelong hostility to the Oxford Movement, to which he alludes in this letter, is a sign of strength of faith not weakness: there is little sense of frailty of belief in his polemical essay *Notes on the Construction of Sheepfolds*, published separately in 1851 after it had outgrown its original place as an appendix to the first volume of *The Stones of Venice*. It is an attack on Roman Catholicism, on Pugin's influence and on High Church beliefs about the nature of the Church and the authority of the priesthood: 'Three centuries since Luther', he thunders, 'three hundred years of Protestant knowledge - and the Papacy not yet overthrown! Christ's truth still restrained, in narrow dawn, to the white cliffs of England and white crests of the Alps'.[25] Note how easily Ruskin colours his polemic with geological metaphor. Although by the late 1850s he was repudiating many of his earlier statements of Protestant enthusiasm, it is notable that when he reprinted *Notes on the Construction of Sheepfolds* in 1875 he made almost no changes.

The architects and patrons of the churches designed in a style we think of as Ruskinian were certainly aware that they did not necessarily share his religious beliefs. The reviews of his books in the *Ecclesiologist* show that they found it relatively easy to fillet them for architectural suggestions and overlook what they saw as his ideological bigotry – as the anonymous reviewer of volume one of *The Stones of Venice* remarks, 'we may adopt, almost without reserve, Mr Ruskin's principles of criticism without in the least degree sharing his hatred of Catholicity'.[26] Away from High Church circles, it may be, as it has often been argued, that Ruskin made the Gothic Revival acceptable for patrons suspicious of its papal or Puseyite associations. That may explain why the most purely Ruskinian of all Bodley's buildings was designed for a man of unequivocally Protestant principles. That building is All Saints, Selsley, Gloucestershire, where Bodley fulfilled in a single building all the precepts laid down by Ruskin in *The Seven Lamps of Architecture*.[27]

In 1858 John Gibson, formerly a fellow of Jesus College, Cambridge, was instituted to the college living of King's

Stanley, to the south of Stroud. He found that there was a long-standing plan, initiated by his predecessor, for creating a new district with its own church for the hamlet on Selsley Beacon, a high ridge overlooking the industrial town. Many of the inhabitants worked for the local landowner, Sir Samuel Stephens Marling, a wealthy millowner, at the gates of whose country house, Stanley Park, the church was to be built. Marling had joined his family textile firm in 1832, and in 1844 had transferred its flourishing business to Ebley Mill, visible in the valley below his house; he kept a firm grip on the enterprise until his death in 1883, at the age of 73. His tomb, on the south side of the chancel of All Saints, below a beautiful relief sculpture of the Resurrection carved by Joshua Wall, is part of Bodley's original design; Marling clearly intended this church to be his monument.

The 1850s and 1860s were a prosperous age for Gloucestershire textile manufacturers, following the introduction of power looms in the 1840s, and Marling was one of the wealthiest.[28] When considering his career, enriched by the proceeds of industrialisation, it is hard not to recall 'Traffic', the second section of Ruskin's *The Crown of Wild Olive*, which has its origins in a lecture given in 1864 as advice to the citizens of Bradford, who were about to embark on building a new exchange. His lesson was that there could be no worthwhile discussion about modern architecture without first addressing the purposes of the society which that architecture served. In a celebrated peroration, he invited his audience to reflect on the goal to which contemporary society aspired, by imagining a bank of land, overlooking the town, on which stands:

> a beautiful mansion, with two wings; and stables, and coach-houses; a moderately-sized park; a large garden and hot-houses; and pleasant carriage drives through the shrubberies. In this mansion are to live the favoured votaries of the Goddess [of Getting-On]; the English gentleman, with his gracious wife, and his beautiful family; he always able to have the boudoir and the jewels for the wife, and the beautiful ball dresses for the daughters, and hunters for the sons, and a shooting in the Highlands for himself. At the bottom of the bank, is to be the mill;

not less than a quarter of a mile long, with one steam engine at each end, and two in the middle, and a chimney three hundred feet high. In this mill are to be in constant employment from eight hundred to a thousand workers, who never drink, never strike, always go to church on Sunday, and always express themselves in respectful language.[29]

Marling's death, caused by heart failure while he was sorting through the family's jewellery in his counting-house in Ebley Mill, would seem to make him an embodiment of the targets of Ruskin's social criticism, but his patronage of Selsley church suggests how alive he would have been not just to the social message of *The Crown of Wild Olive*, but also to the precepts of *The Seven Lamps of Architecture*. The choice of Bodley was almost certainly a result of John Gibson's knowledge of his work for the Tractarian clergy associated with Thomas Keble at Bisley, on the far side of Stroud. Although Marling presumably knew of these connections, he cannot have approved of them, for, as he wrote to Gibson, he would not countenance in a church for which he was responsible any feature, such as chancel screens, which were 'a distinguishing feature of High Church & Ritualistic teaching with which, as you will know, I have no sympathy'.[30] Yet such views do not seem to have clouded his relationship with Bodley, since Marling's letters suggest that he liked and admired him.

After Bodley had prepared the original designs for All Saints, which were complete by the beginning of 1859, it was clear that he would exceed the modest budget of £1,860; the cheapest estimate was for £2,343.[31] At that point Marling intervened and offered to make the difference up out of his own pocket; we know from his account books that the final cost of the building was £3,785, suggesting that he contributed nearly £2,000.[32] He had also given the site and provided the endowment. According to Samuel Lloyd, chairman of the building committee:

> Mr Marling ... wishing to have a handsomer structure (as it was to be on his own grounds and near his residence) ... promised the additional funds for a Tower - Granite

Columns – and the other most expensive parts, which while they are great additions to the work are not exactly essential.³³

In other words, Marling was complying with the first lamp, the Lamp of Sacrifice. This was Ruskin's stand against meanness in architecture, a stand based on his reading of Leviticus and of the second book of Samuel: 'Neither will I offer unto the Lord my God of that which doth cost me nothing'. It is, writes Ruskin, 'the opposite of the prevalent feeling of modern times, which desires to produce the largest results at the least cost'.³⁴

Marling was not content simply to pay for the design; he took an active interest in it, and here we come to the second lamp, the Lamp of Power. It is well known that Marling is said to have insisted that the form of All Saints' saddle-back tower should be modelled on that of the church at Marling in the Tyrol. The source for this story is the memoirs of his grandson, Colonel Sir Percival Marling, which were published in 1931.³⁵ Anyone who has visited All Saints will know that Sir Percival, who was born in the year before it was consecrated, visited the church at Marling for himself, and commissioned the watercolour of it which still hangs in All Saints. Historians have not surprisingly doubted this story, if only because the form of the saddle-back tower, which Bodley used for the first time here, was repeated in several other churches, both in projects and in built form, and was clearly influenced by Butterfield's handling of the same motif.³⁶

Yet, like many family stories, there may be a kernel of truth here. Although the idea for the

A watercolour of the church at Marling in the Tyrol, commissioned from A. W. Rimington in 1905 by Marling's grandson to demonstrate his belief that his grandfather had asked Bodley to model All Saints on the church. There are indeed analogies in both form and setting.

All Saints, Selsley, from the south-west. The ground falls steeply away towards Stroud and the Severn Valley, making the tower a prominent landmark. (*Paul Barker*/Country Life *Picture Library*).

tower was presumably Bodley's, Marling was clearly involved in discussions about its position. In the earliest recorded version of the design, as described in the *Ecclesiologist* in 1859 and depicted by Bodley in a rare and powerful drawing which also hangs in the church, the tower was on the north side of the chancel, where its lowest storey formed a vestry.[37] North is the side facing out towards Stroud. Yet by the time

Below: detail of a watercolour by Ruskin of the church at Courmayeur in the Val d'Aosta, as reproduced in *Works* 5, p. xxvii. It demonstrates Ruskin's beliefs about the interdependency of architecture and landscape, to which Bodley and Marling were so sensitive at Selsley.

the contract drawings were signed, in March 1860, Bodley had moved the tower to the opposite corner, the south-west, where its lowest storey forms the porch. There is no explanation in the records for this change, which may have been prompted by a desire to save money by conflating the tower with a previously separate porch, but it probably also relates to Butterfield's use of the same idea, most notably in his St John, Hammersmith, completed in 1859. The change would have made the tower much less prominent in views of the church from Stroud. Yet as built the tower could hardly be bolder, for it ended up on the church's north-west corner, where it is visible for miles around. This change seems to have been made in the course of construction or very shortly before the building was begun, for in his personal ledger Marling notes an undated payment of £12 10s as an addition to the contract price, 'for placing the tower on north instead of south side of church'.[38]

We do not know what prompted the change, but the result can be interpreted in Ruskinian terms. Ruskin's interest in architecture was first aroused by the use of buildings in landscape painting, which provides the theme for his undergraduate essays published in a series of articles in the *Architectural Magazine* in 1837-8 and republished as a book, *The Poetry of Architecture*, in 1893. It was the discussion of J. M. W. Turner's depiction of architecture in *Modern Painters* which caused Ruskin to break off from that work to compose *The Seven Lamps of Architecture*, and in a sense his understanding of buildings always had a pictorial bias, in that he was drawn most strongly to the elements in buildings which appeal to painters: colour, line and ornament and the way that architecture sits in the landscape. With that last element he begins his chapter 'The Lamp of Power', where he writes 'It does not need much to humiliate a mountain. A hut will sometimes do it', yet 'when to the actual impression of no mean comparative size, is added the sense of the toil of manly hand and thought, a sublimity is reached, which nothing but gross error in arrangement of its parts can destroy.'[39] In other words, architecture acts upon a landscape just as much as the setting acts upon a building, and it is this sense of the balance between the two which gives a meaning to Ruskin's watercolours of church towers in the Alps, such as his depiction of Courmayeur in the Val d'Aosta.[40] This is of course something he had learned from Turner, and it is an effect he recalls in his *Lectures on Architecture and Painting*, delivered in 1853:

> There are probably few in the room who have not been in some parts of South Switzerland, and who do not remember the beautiful effect of the grey mountain churches, many of them hardly changed since the tenth and eleventh centuries, whose pointed towers stand up through the green level of the vines, or crown the jutting rocks that border the valley.[41]

It is words like these which suggest a link between an obscure church in the Tyrol and All Saints on its high ridge above the Severn valley, just as much as the coincidence of the name of Marling.

For the Lamp of Power, sublimity is not found simply in a building's relationship with its setting; it is an inherent and desirable quality in architectural forms. Ruskin urged on architects simplicity of outline and sheerness of surfaces. It was a message that struck home powerfully in the 1850s, particularly in the town-church ideal we associate with Street or James Brooks, where an aesthetic of the sublime was combined with a self-conscious primitivism analogous to the Pre-Raphaelite movement to give churches a newly powerful presence in urban settings. This is a quality which All Saints' tower unforgettably possesses, and we should not forget that in the 1860s this church looked out over an industrial landscape, of which the most prominent feature was Marling's Ebley Mill, given in 1862-5 a new wing with a campanile-like staircase tower by Bodley himself. Indeed, the way that the two towers, of church and factory, face each other across the valley may have had significance to Marling, as a way of emphasising the congruence of religion and commerce in his life. Bodley's interest in tower design was lifelong, and there can be no doubt that he studied carefully the account of towers in volume one of *The Stones of Venice*, to which Ruskin attached his famous illustration contrasting the campanile of St Mark's in Venice with one of the gatehouse towers of William Playfair's New College in

Edinburgh, completed in 1850.[42] 'There must be no light-headedness in your noble tower', he writes: 'impregnable foundation, wrathful crest, with the vizor down, and the dark vigilance seen through the clefts of it'.[43]

Throughout his life Bodley was eager to persuade his clients of the merits of towers. In 1861, for example, he prepared alternative designs for All Saints, Cambridge, one with a tower and one with a spire. Unfortunately, the tower design does not survive, for to Bodley's dismay the building committee was wedded to the idea of a spire. On 13 May 1861 he wrote to the incumbent: 'The fellows of Jesus College liked the sketch for the gabled Tower & I cannot but feel that it wd in *reality* be *better* liked than the spire. The vertical lines of the Tower wd have more vertical tendency & I think [be] more *Teaching* than such a spire as it wd be in our power to build.'[44] The use of the word 'teaching' is significant; it surely derives from a belief in the moral force of architectural forms, and who could have taught Bodley that? To a degree which is often underestimated, Bodley maintained High Victorian or Ruskinian design principles to the end of his life, long after he had abandoned the stylistic approaches of the 1850s and moved towards a more abstract, less metaphorical approach to architectural design and symbolism. It was for example in his maintenance of the sense of the wall plane – what Ruskin called the wall veil – which he punctuates but never breaks up with window openings, buttresses or ornament, that Bodley demonstrates most clearly his life-long adherence to the Lamp of Power.

In style, All Saints, Selsley, looks principally to early-13th-century French churches, of the sort we know Bodley studied closely, for Robert Johnson refers to his assistance in preparing the illustrations for his book *Specimens of Early French Architecture*, published in 1864.[45] Even more, All Saints owes a great deal to Butterfield's example: not only St John, Hammersmith, but also St Matthias, Stoke Newington, completed in 1853. All Saints, Selsley, is in some ways a homage to Butterfield. The lychgate even reproduces, with only minor modifications, one of the older architect's published designs, from the Ecclesiological Society's *Instrumenta Ecclesiastica*, and on a working drawing for the

Opposite:
the interior of All Saints, Selsley, looking east. From the use of natural materials to the opportunities given to young craftsmen in sculpture and stained glass, the church embodies all of Ruskin's Lamps. However, the restrained use of constructional polychromy is in part Bodley's response to a new lighter aesthetic embodied in the stained glass by Morris, Marshall, Faulkner and Co. – an aesthetic change that only a year later led him to a radical change of stylistic direction (*Paul Barker/Country Life Picture Library*).

chancel pavement, made of Godwin's tiles, Bodley has noted 'tiles to be yellow glazed ones like those used by Mr Butterfield as to colour'.[46] Such a tribute brings us naturally to Ruskin's Lamp of Obedience, and its discussion of architectural style. Ruskin states that, 'the architecture of a nation is great only when it is as universal and as established as its language; and when provincial differences of style are nothing more than so many dialects'.[47] That is something with which Bodley, Street and Butterfield would have agreed, and helps explain why the ecclesiastical architecture of the 1850s has a sense of common purpose it was not to recapture for 20 years.

At the conclusion of the first edition of *The Seven Lamps of Architecture*, published in 1849, Ruskin famously presents a list of four acceptable styles – Pisan Romanesque, early Italian Gothic of the western republics, Venetian Gothic and the English 'earliest decorated'.[48] More important to an understanding of All Saints is Ruskin's revision of this proposal in the preface to the second edition, published in 1855, in which he states, 'I have now no doubt that the only style proper for modern Northern work, is the Northern Gothic of the thirteenth century, both English and French.'[49] That of course is the style that Bodley chooses for All Saints, but we have to beware of seeing this simply in terms of Ruskinian influence. Street's interest in 'early French' Gothic architecture was compelling, and it is possible that Ruskin's changing position about the preferred models for contemporary design was influenced by what was being built rather than the other way about.

It is not hard to see how the interior of All Saints embodies three of the last four of the lamps. In terms of materials and construction, the Lamp of Truth is obeyed: natural stone, marble and granite predominate. What is interesting is Bodley's individual aesthetic: budgetary constraints cannot alone explain the reticent way he uses constructional polychromy in the interior, in contrast with Butterfield or Street, just as the touches of colour on the exterior are highly restrained. This is a matter of the architect's individual personality.

Bodley's use of stylised natural ornament recalls the precepts of the Lamp of Beauty, but for Bodley, as for Ruskin, natural form was the guide for abstract as well as representational forms: as he wrote many years later, 'Nature, our great guide, never stops in her refinement. We cannot gauge the infinite delicacy of nature, nor her redundance of life and its variety. Now it is in refinement for architectural work, that this expression of life is chiefly shown'. Architecture's characteristics, he continues, 'should be those of nature, in the spirit, though not in the letter'.[50] It is the form of his mouldings, a life-long priority for Bodley, that gives the surfaces of his buildings the lively, tactile and hard-edged qualities that no photograph can convey.

Obeying the precepts of the Lamp of Life, Bodley gave splendid opportunities to his young craftsmen. His sculptor was a local man, Joshua Wall, who was then only 27; a sketchbook by Wall reveals him to have been an inventive designer, but his capitals of the nave arcade also suggest knowledge of Ruskin's illustrations for *The Stones of Venice*, interpreted with outstanding freshness and originality.[51] However, even Wall's remarkable contribution is overwhelmed by the most famous element of All Saints's interior, the stained glass by Morris, Marshall, Faulkner and Co, which is among their earliest commissions, and especially important as a complete scheme executed at one time. It was entirely paid for by Marling.[52]

At the time Selsey was being built, Bodley urged the Ecclesiological Society to persuade architects 'to secure the services of painters like Holman Hunt, Rossetti, and other such men.'[53] This recalls Ruskin's attempts to secure Millais's help with the decoration of the chancel of the Camden Chapel in Camberwell. Nothing came of that, or of Ruskin and Acland's attempts to get Rossetti to contribute to the decoration of the Oxford Museum. Pre-Raphaelite involvement in architectural decoration came to fruition with Bodley's collaborations with Morris, although stained glass rather than mural painting was to be their principal medium.

Capitals in All Saints, Selsley, carved by Joshua Wall, who had been born in Selsley. They demonstrate his knowledge of French 13th-century sculpture, but also suggest an appreciation of Ruskin's analysis of foliage forms in architectural ornament, as discussed in *The Stones of Venice* (Paul Barker/Country Life/Picture Library).

The climax of Morris's work at Selsley is the west wall's rose window depicting the seven days of Creation, designed by Morris and Philip Webb, which is the major clue to how this church embodies the most misunderstood of all the seven lamps of architecture. The Lamp of Memory has two aspects: the second, and better known, is Ruskin's analysis of the way the effects of time manifest themselves on a building to form a historical record. This is the basis of his stand against restoration, which seeks to expunge those effects. But the first aspect of the Lamp of Memory is the way a building commemoratively embodies the time when it was built. What does All Saints commemorate? It is here, I would suggest, that Ruskin and Bodley most significantly part company.

If the arguments about the metaphorical nature of constructional polychromy are accepted, that it drew on the theological implications of geological science, one can see that such meanings are immeasurably enhanced by the depiction of the days of Creation. This is not biblical literalism, but an embodiment of the way it was thought that science, by its revelation of a progressive development of the species through the long history of the earth, was demonstrating God's unfolding plan for creation. That was not a belief that interested Ruskin. His discussion of buildings as commemorations of the age in which they were built illuminatingly discusses domestic and then civic buildings, but makes no mention of ecclesiastical ones, perhaps because the contemporary meaning of churches was so fraught with controversy. In the 1850s and 1860s, architects drew on a belief that science and art could work together in the interests of religion while developing architecture in new, progressive ways. That was an enterprise that fell to pieces with remarkable speed in the 1860s, following the publication in 1859 of *The Origin of Species* and in 1860 of *Essays and Reviews*, the attempt by Broad-Church writers to apply the conclusions of modern biblical scholarship to contemporary Anglicanism, with results that outraged High Church opinion. The relationship between science, scientific biblical criticism and religious belief was made yet more fragile by the appearance in 1862 of the first part of *The Pentateuch and Book of Joshua Critically*

The days of Creation as depicted in the west window at All Saints, Selsley, by Morris, Marshall, Faulkner and Co. This spectacular window forcibly reiterates the themes of so much ecclesiastical design in the 1850s and early 1860s: by drawing on the natural world as a souce of ornament, architects were demonstrating a progressive belief that science was revealing the story of Creation – a belief that went further than Ruskin was prepared to go (*Paul Barker*/Country Life *Picture Library*).

Examined by J. W. Colenso, Bishop of Natal, which openly questioned the historical veracity of the first five books of the Bible.[54] We know the architecture of the 1850s and early 1860s was rejected on aesthetic grounds, because it had come to seem coarse, but it was also rejected by many because it seemed too Protestant and even secular, as science and religion went their separate ways.

In 1875 Marling discussed with Gibson the choice of artist for the stained glass windows Marling wished to contribute to Gibson's own church at King's Stanley, then being restored by Bodley. Gibson wanted Hardman, who was eventually chosen, Bodley had suggested Burlison and Grylls, but Marling wanted Morris again. Gibson wrote to him as follows: in stained glass:

> you must follow the old models, you must have good colour and drawing & ecclesiastical treatment of subject. – At Selsley, you obtained one thing of these, ie well chosen colour, and in the rose window in the w. wall very masterly and original treatment due to a pictorial subject but I cannot say I think the rest of the work fulfils any

conditions but that of colour. Still the work is very interesting, tho' somewhat secular in sentiment.[55]

Bodley never used Morris again, and turned his back on the Ruskinian vision of the independent creativity of the craftsman. In the future, the personalities of the craftsmen he chose were subsumed into the architect's controlling vision. That is one reason why Comper observed him smiling over his drawing board. But there may have been more to it than that. By the 1870s, Bodley's interests had turned towards a new aesthetic, based on a concept of churches as sacramental spaces standing outside time, not shaped by earthly history, ideas that would have had no interest for Ruskin.[56] Constructional polychromy, coloured marbles, narrative schemes in stained glass or mural painting and carved ornament derived from the natural world – all the elements we now think of as 'Ruskinian' - disappear abruptly from Bodley's architecture in the mid-1860s in an aesthetic and ideological reaction that was both dynamic and creative, and not the sheepish retreat into genteel historicism portrayed by most historians of the Gothic Revival.[57]

The failure of what we might call the High Victorian enterprise in architecture would not have surprised Ruskin, who always knew the storm cloud was close to breaking; the spiritual son of Carlyle, he was, like Carlyle, fundamentally a pessimist. 'I could smile when I hear the hopeful exultation of many, at the new reach of worldly science, and vigour of worldly effort; as if were again at the beginning of days', he wrote at the conclusion of 'The Lamp of Obedience'. 'There is thunder on the horizon as well as dawn. The sun was risen upon the earth when Lot entered into Zoar.'[58] Yet what makes the architecture of the 1850s and 1860s so compelling is its buoyant, youthful optimism, based on a belief that by reinventing Gothic for the modern age it had indeed returned to the beginning of days. It was an optimism that was never to be recaptured, because the circumstances that brought it about, a union of art, science and religious belief, have never recurred. That, I would suggest, is what we see when we look into the Lamp of Memory that still burns on Selsley Beacon.

I am most grateful to Michael Kerney for his advice and for help with the illustrations.

Notes

1 J. Ninian Comper to his mother, 22 May, 1883; Comper papers (private collection). I am grateful to the Rev. Anthony Symondson SJ for permission to see and quote from this letter.

2 G. F. Bodley, 'On Some Principles and Characteristics of Ancient Architecture, and their Application to the Modern Practice of the Art', *Builder,* 48 (1885), pp. 294-7, at p. 296.

3 Deborah Cherry, 'The Hogarth Club: 1858-61', *Burlington Magazine,* 122 (1980), pp. 238-42.

4 G. F. Bodley, 'Church Restoration in France: A Communication', *Ecclesiologist,* 22 (1861), pp. 70-8. For Ruskin's contribution to the meeting, see 'On the Destructive Character of Modern French Restoration', *Builder* 19 (1861), p.423, and Michael W. Brooks, *John Ruskin and Victorian Architecture* (London, 1987), pp. 270-2. I am grateful to Chris Miele for pointing out to me the significance of Bodley's use of the word 'protection'.

5 The best outline of Bodley's career is David Verey, 'George Frederick Bodley, Climax of the Gothic Revival', in Jane Fawcett (editor), *Seven Victorian Architects* (London, 1976).

6 *Ecclesiologist,* 4 (1845), p. 89.

7 [Anonymous], *A Description of the Painted Window in the Chancel of St Giles' Church, Camberwell* (London, n.d.). There is a copy of this rare pamphlet in the Southwark Local Studies Library, London.

8 Illustrated in *Builder,* 12 (1854), p. 363. For a discussion of this project, see Brooks, op. cit. [note 4], pp. 56-60.

9 Tim Hilton, *John Ruskin: the Later Years* (London and New Haven, 2000), pp. 220-1. For Scott's involvement, see *Works,* 38, p. 347.

10 *Works,* 16, pp. 462-3.

11 On Ruskin and Street, see Brooks, op. cit. [note 4], pp. 156-65, and Dale Dishon, 'Three Men in a Gondola: Ruskin, Webb and Street', in Christopher Webster and John Elliott (editors), *'A Church as It Should Be; The Cambridge Camden Society and Its Influence* (Stamford, 2000).

12 The carver of the capitals at St Michael, Brighton (built 1861-2) is unknown, although David Beevers, *St Michael and All Angels Church, Brighton: A History and Guide* (Brighton, 1993), p. 5, plausibly suggests Thomas Earp, who carried out similar work at Bodley's St John the Baptist, France Lynch, designed in 1854 and built in 1856-7 (Earp's work there was completed in 1859). Earp was also responsible for the carving at Street's All Saints, Boyne Hill, and he supplied the pulpit for Bodley's All Saints, Selsley, opened in 1862. However, the notes of expenditure on St Michael kept by the Rev. Charles Beanlands, who commissioned it (East Sussex Record Office, PAR 275/9/1/1), do not mention Earp. It is possible that either the main contractor, John Fabian of Brighton, or Field of Westminster, responsible for what Beanlands refers to as 'marble work',

supplied a carver. On Bodley's use of Ruskin as a source for ornament, see Shirley Ann Ferguson, 'The Victorian and Medieval Sources for the Early Churches of George Frederick Bodley' (unpublished MA Report, Courtauld Institute, University of London, 1979).

13 *Works,* 16, p. 463.

14 For a more detailed analysis of this point, see Michael Hall, 'What do Victorian Churches Mean?: Symbolism and Sacramentalism in Anglican Church Architecture' in *Journal of the Society of Architectural Historians,* 59 (2000), pp. 78-95.

15 *Works,* 9, p. 347.

16 Michael Hall, op. cit. [note 14]. I am indebted to Michael Kerney for this suggestion.

17 This was pointed out to me by Paul Joyce. Bodley's design for the school was exhibited at the Royal Academy in 1854 [no. 1155] and illustrated in the *Civil Engineer and Architect's Journal,* 21 (1858), opposite p. 317.

18 Although Street's church is plainly the principal model for St Michael's, it is interesting that the *Ecclesiologist*'s critic detected the influence of Butterfield's All Saints, Margaret Street on Bodley's original design (subsequently revised), which seems to have proposed more constructional polychromy than was eventually executed: see *Ecclesiologist,* 20 (1859), p. 67.

19 David B. Brownlee, 'The First High Victorians: British Architectural Theory in the 1840s', *Architectura,* 15 (1985), pp. 33-46.

20 On Buckland, see Nicolaas A. Rupke, *The Great Chain of History: William Buckland and the English School of Geology (1814-1848)* (Oxford, 1983).

21 *Builder,* 16 (1859), p. 781.

22 See Michael Wheeler, *Ruskin's God* (Oxford, 1999), p. 12. I have relied greatly on this account of Ruskin's religious beliefs.

23 *Works,* 8, p. 72.

24 Ruskin to Henry Acland, 24 May 1851, quoted in *Works,* 36, p. 115.

25 *Works,* 12, p. 557.

26 *Ecclesiologist,* 12 (1851), p. 276.

27 For a penetrating account of the impact of aspects of *The Seven Lamps of Architecture* on ecclesiastical architecture in the 1850s, including All Saints, Selsley, see Edward N. Kaufman, '"The Weight and Vigour of their Masses": Mid-Victorian Country Churches and "The Lamp of Power"', in John Dixon Hunt and Faith M. Holland (editors), *The Ruskin Polygon: Essays on the Imagination of John Ruskin* (Manchester, 1982). He argues, as I do, that architects followed Ruskin's belief that architecture should metaphorically embody ideas about the natural world, but implies, as I would not, that architects shared Ruskin's pessimism and his lack of interest in contemporary scientific understanding of geology. He also does not consider the question of the difference between Ruskin's religious views and those of such architects as Bodley and Street and many of their clients.

28 On Marling's career, see Esther Moir, 'Marling & Evans, King's Stanley

and Ebley Mills, Gloucestershire', *Textile History,* 2 (1971), pp. 28-56.
29 *Works,* 18, p. 453.
30 S. S. Marling to John Gibson, 11 October, 1874, parish records of St George, King's Stanley (Gloucestershire Record Office), P190/CW4/3.
31 Records of the Incorporated Church Building Society (Lambeth Palace Library), file 5572, application for grant.
32 Marling papers (Gloucestershire Record Office), D873/F9, S. S. Marling's personal ledger, fol. 279.
33 Samuel Lloyd to the committee of the Incorporated Church Building Society, 8 May 1860, loc. cit. [note 31].
34 *Works,* 8, p. 31.
35 Colonel Sir Percival Marling, *Rifleman and Hussar* (London, 1931).
36 Bodley had also proposed using a saddle-back form of tower in 1856, in his third-prize-winning design for the Crimea Memorial Church in Constantinople: see *Ecclesiologist,* 18 (1857), p. 106.
37 *Ecclesiologist,* 20 (1859), pp. 68-9.
38 Marling papers, [note 32].
39 *Works,* 8, p. 104.
40 Reproduced in *Works,* 12, plate 6.
41 Ibid., p. 41.
42 Reproduced in *Works,* 9, opposite p. 248.
43 Ibid., p. 246.
44 G. F. Bodley to the Rev. W. C. Sharpe, 13 May 1861, All Saints, Cambridge, parish papers (Cambridgeshire Record Office), P20/6/4.
45 Robert J. Johnson, *Specimens of Early French Architecture, Selected Chiefly from the Churches of the Isle de France, and Illustrated in Geometrical Drawings and Perspective Views* (Newcastle upon Tyne, 1864).
46 Marling papers [note 32], D873/R2, drawings for All Saints, Selsley: 'Design for chancel pavement September 1861'. Butterfield's lychgate design was published in *Instrumenta Ecclesiastica,* edited by the *Ecclesiological late Cambridge Camden Society* (London, 1844-7), plate LXV 'Stone Lichgate'. Butterfield himself executed the design at St Saviour, Coalpit Heath, Gloucestershire (1844-5).
47 *Works,* 8, p. 252.
48 Ibid., p. 258.
49 Ibid., p. 12. The best recent discussion of the interest taken by architects in early French Gothic architecture at this period is Gavin Stamp, 'Le revival Gothique Haut Victorien et l'architecture Normande', in Martin Kay Meade, Werner Szambien and Simona Talenti, *L'Architecture Normande en Europe: Identités et Echanges* (Marseilles, 2000), pp. 132-40, where the crossing tower of the 13th-century parish church at Verson, Calvados, is identified as a source for Selsley's tower.
50 G. F. Bodley, [note 2], p. 294.
51 Wall, who died in 1869, aged 34, lived in Selsley and had his workshop in John Street, Stroud. The sketchbook, which is in the Stroud Museum, contains drawings relating to his major commissions; the sculpture at St Laurence, Stroud (rebuilt 1866-8 to designs by Willson and Willcox of Bath), which he both designed and carved. As well as a remarkable series

of foliate capitals, his work there includes two small sculptured roundels above the chancel arcades, a Ruskinian motif.

52 Marling papers [note 32], fol. 310. For a complete description of the scheme, see A. C. Sewter, *The Stained Glass of William Morris and his Circle* (2 vols., New Haven and London, 1974-5), vol. 1, pp. 171-3.

53 G. F. Bodley, [note 4], p. 77.

54 For Ruskin's response to the Colenso controversy, see Wheeler, op. cit. [note 22], pp. 183-4.

55 Gibson to Marling, 22 May 1875, [note 30].

56 Michael Hall, [note 14].

57 On the social and architectural context for this transformation, see Michael Hall, 'The Rise of Refinement: G. F. Bodley's All Saints, Cambridge, and the Return to English Models in Gothic Architecture of the 1860s', *Architectural History,* 36 (1993), pp. 103-26.

58 *Works,* 8, p. 266.

9

'Theoria' in Practice:
E.W. Godwin,
Ruskin and Art-Architecture

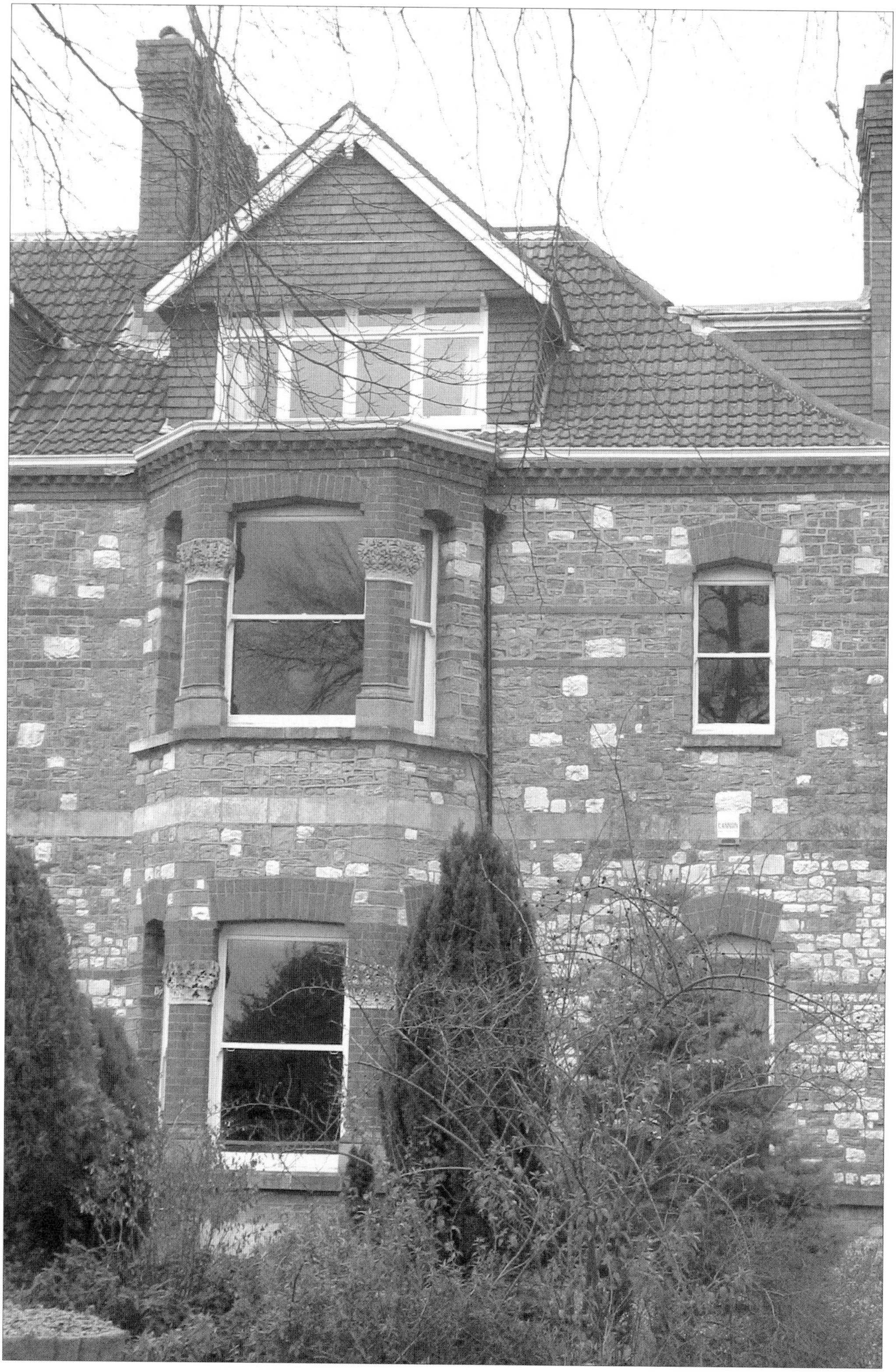

'Theoria' in Practice: E. W. Godwin, Ruskin and Art-Architecture

Aileen Reid

> Remember that the most beautiful things in the world are also the most useless; peacocks and lilies for instance – John Ruskin.[1]

> The utterances of the architects have had ... but one and the same end in view ... the bettering of the people ... it is ... certain that one of the great civilising influences of the age is in our hands. I see the promise of a future that will be bright enough to show that their labour was not in vain – E. W. Godwin.[2]

IN NOVEMBER 1877 John Ruskin gave a lecture in Oxford in which he characterised his work as a writer between 1845 and 1875 as dividing neatly into halves: the first was devoted to 'art-work' (most famously *Modern Painters*, *The Seven Lamps of Architecture* and *The Stones of Venice*), the second to what he calls 'reprobation' – his writings on social and political issues, which began, according to this interpretation, with the writing of *Unto this Last*. With *Unto this Last*, 'art-work' was given up.[3]

A year, almost to the day, after Ruskin made these assertions the architect E.W. Godwin stood up in front of an audience of young architects in Manchester and described his own architectural career over the previous 25 years in similar, pleasingly simple terms.[4] After outlining his early career Godwin described how in 1858, aged 25, he 'began to read Ruskin', and what the impact of this epiphanic experience had been on his work – in particular on his design for Northampton Town Hall, his most important early building. Then in 1864, he related, after a few other smaller projects similarly full of Ruskinian qualities, came another town hall design – Congleton in Cheshire - and '*The Stones of Venice* already had been dropped'. Much as Ruskin 'gave up' 'artwork', Godwin 'dropped' Ruskin.

These two seductively simple self-analyses have proved

Opposite:
10 Rockleaze, Bristol, 1860-2. Godwin's use of varied materials – brick and rubble of varying textures and sizes – is the ultimate architectural expression in his work of that quality that Ruskin admired in mountains of 'utmost possible stability ... attained with materials of imperfect or variable character' (*Works*, 9, p. 88) (*Aileen Reid*).

highly attractive to subsequent writers on and biographers of Ruskin and Godwin. Ruskin's simple dichotomy of 'Ruskin the writer on art' being supplanted by 'Ruskin the writer on social issues', for all its apparent truth, has, however, already been demonstrated to be a gross over-simplification (in that – to oversimplify – Ruskin wrote on social issues before 1860, and did not entirely abandon art after 1860).[5] By contrast, Godwin's binary opposition of discrete Ruskinian and post-Ruskinian phases in his own career still provides the broad template for most subsequent analyses of his work.

According to this conventional narrative, Godwin read Ruskin at a time when he was a young architect in thrall to the Gothic Revival's programme to generate a distinctively and authentically new architecture for the modern age by divining a set of 'principles' from the best medieval buildings and applying them in a 19th-century context. Ruskin's writings on architecture – first *The Seven Lamps of Architecture* then *The Stones of Venice* – furnished Godwin with a rich new set of architectural forms which inspired him to design a number of characteristically 'Ruskinian' buildings, chief among which is Northampton Town Hall – replete with constructional colour, decorative carving and 'Venetian' features. But Godwin wearied of this mode of architectural expression, abandoned first Ruskin and then, after a few years, the pursuit of a new architecture via the Gothic Revival altogether. Thereafter he pursued a totally different path that led to the Aesthetic or freestyle architecture of the late 1870s, a mode that reached its apotheosis in his first designs for studio-houses in Chelsea for the painters James McNeill Whistler and Frank Miles – designs deemed by the planning authorities as too *outré* to be built. Thereafter Godwin all but gave up architecture and devoted himself to furniture and theatre design.

The aim of this chapter is not a simple debunking of this conventional discourse of Godwin's career, and the view implicit in it that the impact that Ruskin had was both superficial and short-lived. To ignore these superficial Ruskinian qualities in Godwin's work is to ignore an important aspect of that impact, just as, in attempting to divine the more subtle and theoretical influence that Ruskin's writings had on architects in the 1850s and 1860s, it is possible to forget that the most lasting and widespread influence was also the most obvious – it was the illustrations in Ruskin's books that were the easiest to apply architecturally: for every architect who bathed in the light of the Lamp of Sacrifice or took up the cudgel of Savageness, there were ten others who took a fancy to Ruskin's illustration of S. Pietro in Pistoia in *The Stones of Venice* and sought to emulate its pretty coloured stonework in buildings of his own.[6] Ruskin, himself, bitterly bemoaned this.[7] Godwin was certainly part of that tendency, so it is worth looking in some detail at those of his buildings, especially Northampton Town Hall, that openly declare their Ruskinian allegiance.

However, the aim is also to show that to focus only on superficial 'Ruskinian' qualities – plate tracery, Venetian capitals and so on – and to accept Godwin's own estimate of the limited extent of Ruskin's influence, is to underestimate not only the range of ways that Godwin responded to his reading of Ruskin during the late 1850s and early 1860s, but also his continuing engagement with those ideas long after their superficial impact ceased to be manifest in his architectural designs.

This continuing engagement is especially startling because it occurs at a time when a Ruskinian/Aesthetic rift apparently opened up, epitomised in the 1878 trial *Whistler* v. *Ruskin* (in which Godwin's close friend and client Whistler sued Godwin's old muse Ruskin for defamation for his published criticism of one of his paintings, *A Nocturne in Black and Gold: The Falling Rocket*). Because Godwin is traditionally seen by this date as a confirmed supporter of Whistler's position – philosophically as well as personally - (Max Beerbohm described him as 'the greatest aesthete of them all'),[8] any residual trace of Ruskinian sensibility comes as a surprise. But it was there and it ran deep.

Although by the time he died in 1886 Godwin had become the acme of metropolitan sophistication, with friends and clients in the social, artistic and theatrical elites, his background was both modest and provincial, a fact which may help explain why he did not read *The Seven Lamps* until nearly ten years after it was published.[9] Born in 1833,

Design for an unidentified house, early 1850s. This is a rare example of a Godwin design made before he read Ruskin. Slight as it is, its restraint in the use of buttresses, unfussy roofline, unbroken wall surfaces and simple pairs and triplets of ogee-headed and flat-headed windows suggest the influence of William White and G. E. Street – Godwin later claimed to have been greatly struck by an illustration of Street's Cuddesdon College, Oxon, which he saw in the *Illustrated London News* in 1853 (*RIBA Library Drawings Collection, RAN 7/L/15*).

Godwin trained with William Armstrong (died 1858), one of Bristol's three City Surveyors. By the time he completed his articles with Armstrong in 1852 or 1853, he had come under the influence of Robert Willis,[10] had also published a number of antiquarian articles, and had co-written a book, *The Antiquities of Bristol*.[11] This aspired to be the first in a series which, as well as fulfilling their antiquarian brief, would offer 'some remarks [on] the revival of Gothic Architecture in the Neighbourhood'.[12] Godwin was not yet seventeen, and this aspiration to be a critic of contemporary architecture suggests both that his antiquarian work was an adjunct of the architectural, and that he was not afraid to express his own strong opinions, both crucial to his future engagement with Ruskin's writings.[13]

The evidence for Godwin's architectural manner before he read Ruskin is rather limited. Among his surviving drawings there is a design for a small house,[14] in a manner suggestive of the Tudor Gothic of the 1840s. It is infused with a touch of Puginian 'practical utility' and perhaps a hint of the young George Edmund Street's design for Cuddesdon College, Oxfordshire, which Godwin had admired after it had been published in the *Illustrated London News* in April 1853.[15]

By 1856, one small school and a minor church restoration

were the sum total of his executed work,[16] so that year Godwin went to help his engineer brother Joseph (1823-82) in Londonderry with the competition designs for a railway bridge – a most unlikely project for a nascent Ruskinian. They did not win but Godwin secured a commission to design a small church, St Baithen in St Johnstown, Co. Donegal, his only complete surviving building from the period before his encounter with Ruskin's writings. Godwin himself described it as looking 'perfectly new and somewhat like cast iron' when he revisited it in 1875.[17] The roof pitches are sheer and the tracery aetiolated, an unusual mixture of idiosyncratic, Geometrical forms and Early English uncusped circles. Is this Godwin's interpretation of 'development', the attempt by the early Gothic Revivalists to determine the best phase of Gothic architecture and 'develop' a new, avowedly 19th-century style of architecture from this starting point?[18] Certainly, Godwin was an enthusiast for the work of one of the chief 'developers', George Gilbert Scott, and wrote him a congratulatory letter at this time.[19]

Godwin claimed in his 1878 Manchester lecture that he read Ruskin after he returned to Bristol from Ireland (i.e.

St Baithen, St Johnstown, Co. Donegal, 1856-7. The design of the church, with the separate chancel, short transepts and bellcote, suggests the Gothic of A. W. N. Pugin transmitted through the blood-line of early Scott and Street. One unusual feature at St Baithen is the foliage carving to one of the tracery spandrels of the west window, suggesting that Godwin might have read his Ruskin while the church was being built (*The Conway Library, Courtauld Institute of Art: photograph c.1970*).

1858).[20] Certainly the content of his letter to Scott of December 1856, with its congratulation of Scott for his defence of 'our English modification of Xtian art' does not suggest someone who has just read *The Stones of Venice* or even *The Seven Lamps*. Another letter, just three months later in the *Builder* under the headline 'Gothic v Classic', seems at first broadly in keeping with Scott's 'developmental' line on revived Gothic: 'I believe ... that a style will *grow upon* the hitherto but little understood *principles* of the Medieval style ... conformable to the progress of invention.'[21] But what is so striking is the impassioned language of the letter, the ideas of deference to Nature, and Godwin's almost numinous veneration for the Gothic, about 'fixing' roofs with 'due regard to the elements' and reading 'more diligently that volume of Nature'.[22] There is much more in this vein, much talk of 'accumulation of sin', and the exercise 'of a deeper sympathy with all the glorious creations of the Great Good'. One can see how reference to 'the just and humble veneration for the works of God upon earth'[23] appealed to Godwin when he later came to read Ruskin.

Godwin might not have read his Ruskin by this time, but this indicates one reason why *The Seven Lamps* and *The Stones of Venice* would satisfy a need in him that had so far not been met by his reading of Willis, or even Gilbert Scott. Godwin clearly had a romantic, quasi-religious response to Nature and to Gothic architecture that transcended his antiquarian interest. Hints of this emerge from his occasional diaries.[24] In the summer of 1852 Godwin had set off with his fellow architectural pupil James Hine (1829/30-1914) on an antiquarian holiday in Cornwall. After measuring various churches, he finally arrived at Land's End where he found:

> the sound of the breakers below, with at intervals the screech of the wild sea gull ... could not but impress one as an awful evidence of the supreme power and majesty of the Earth [and] ... the joyful hope of ... that eternity of which the outstretched ocean is but a flat and temporal image.[25]

This is startling stuff when one is accustomed to the

Opposite:
Ruskin used fig. 18 in *The Stones of Venice* to illustrate his theory, expounded in 'The Nature of Gothic', that tracery 'began in the use of penetrations through the stonework ... cut into forms which looked like stars when seen from within, and leaves when seen from without'. He says of these 'foils' that 'the pleasure received from them [is] the same as that which we feel in the triple, quadruple, or other radiated leaves of vegetation, joined with the perception of a severely geometrical order and symmetry'.

image of Godwin as the louche bohemian who ran off with another man's wife and produced a couple of love children. But that was fifteen years after he wrote these words. As well as a passionate admirer of medieval architecture, Godwin was a product of that very 'Evangelical Bristolian' background he later gently mocked,[26] and, as such, was primed to respond both to the romance in Ruskin and to what George Meredith called Ruskin's 'monstrous assumption of wisdom' and 'preposterous priestly attitude'.[27]

And when Godwin did read Ruskin the effect on his architectural designs was immediate. At first, it is just what he called his 'fit for plate tracery' that we notice – the design of the south aisle windows at St Paul de Leon, Staverton, Devon, is clearly taken from figure 18 in the 'Nature of Gothic' in *The Stones of Venice*. These also featured in Godwin's designs for Western College, Plymouth in 1858 and in a perspective he produced for an unbuilt competition design for St Philip and St Jacob's schools competition in Bristol in 1860. A sympathetic client with bigger coffers for carving, constructional colour and towers was what

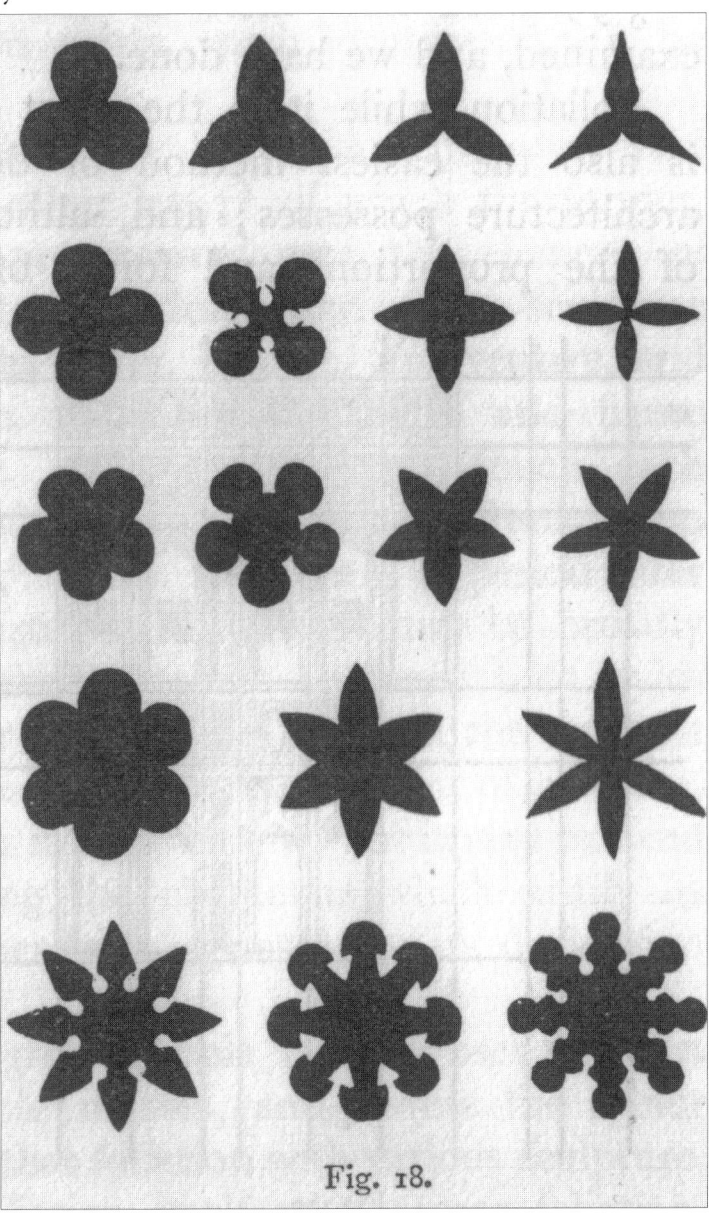

Fig. 18.

St Philip & St Jacob's School, Bristol: perspective for a competition design, 1860. This design has the full armoury of Ruskinian features – tower, parti-coloured voussoirs, carved capitals and archivolts – that Godwin was to deploy to greatest effect at Northampton Town Hall. It also demonstrated a fatal flaw in the Ruskinian manner in its most full-blown guise – it was very expensive. The budget for the schools was £2,000 and, although Godwin did get the commission, all his fancy touches, including the tower, were omitted (*Haslam & Whiteway, London*).

Godwin needed – and this he found when he won the competition to design a new town hall at Northampton in 1861.

With Northampton Town Hall, Godwin 'began his career, truly and practically'.[28] Town halls were a growing market – more than 400 were built during Godwin's architectural career.[29] It was a building type that was to prove particularly attractive to him and he entered more than 25 competitions for them.[30] Northampton is typical of the towns that built them in the 1850s and 1860s in that its reformed corporation, still with relatively limited powers, wanted a new town hall not principally for increased office accommodation, but, in the words of one of its members, as 'an ornament to the town'.[31] The Ruskinian programme was ideally suited to the expression of civic pride.

Godwin described Northampton Town Hall as 'entirely founded on *The Stones of Venice*'[32] and this applies even to the plan – in that the plan so little affects the impact of the building. Planning was not a concern to Ruskin and he very rarely offered a plan or even described the organisation of a building. Although it is the more abstract or philosophical 'Nature of Gothic' in the second volume of *The Stones of Venice* that has attracted most attention – partly because of its role as a key text of the Arts and Crafts movement[33] – it seems that it was the practical considerations of good construction and fitting ornament in volume 1 that had greatest impact on architects at the time.[34] And in that volume, Ruskin, in his concentration on wall-base, wall-veil and so on, and their ornamentation, barely penetrates beyond the front of the building. Northampton Town Hall reflects this attitude to design in that so much of the architectural focus is on the main front. Even within the building the planning is really only geared to producing a series of boxes for display – circulation is almost cut off: the main staircase is pitifully cramped, tucked in between the courtroom and the cavernous vestibule.

Northampton Town Hall, main front to St Giles' Square, 1860-5. This is Godwin's fullest exposition of the qualities Ruskin most admired, from the nebulous 'breadth of surface' and emphasis on 'mass' rather than 'line', through the varying of the widths of the arches and the colours of stone between courses, to the tympana carvings. These represent local historical events – a statement of the town's antiquity and national significance, and a fulfilment of Ruskin's words about the 'memorial' function of carving (*Aileen Reid*).

'Theoria' in Practice: E.W. Godwin, Ruskin and Art-Architecture

Northampton Town Hall, first-floor windows of the council chamber, with statue of Richard I carved by Richard Boulton and capitals, spandrels and archivolts by Edwin White. The animals among the capitals illustrate Aesop's fable, 'The Cock and the Jewel', on the left. Godwin, mindful of all Ruskin had to say about the role of the workman, took White to Chartres to show him the 'delicate carving of the north and south portals' (*Aileen Reid*).

In saying that the design was 'founded on *The Stones of Venice*' Godwin did not mean that he literally reproduced any Venetian building. The main façade is symmetrical, with semi-basement and two storeys of seven bays and a central tower. Its antecedent is, of course, the Oxford Museum (1854), although the French, rather than Venetian, character of the window jambs, the general design of the windows and the open vestibule suggest, variously, Scott's first Gothic design for the Foreign Office (1856), his Hamburg Town Hall design (1854), and Waterhouse's design for Manchester Assize Courts (1859). Godwin was well versed in what the leading Gothic men were doing - and how they were responding to Ruskin.

There was one feature of the main front of which Godwin was particularly proud 'because Mr Ruskin was in a measure responsible for it'.[35] He made the outside arches of the arcades on both floors slightly narrower than the others, which he believed gave it an increased appearance of strength – the *appearance* of strength being as important as real

Northampton Town Hall, vestibule tympana and triangular relief carvings. While the triangular relief carvings on the main front of the Town Hall are almost directly copied from the illustrations of Murano in *The Stones of Venice*, those in the vestibule are a more evolved response to Ruskin's words about geometrical decoration and 'surface Gothic'. Like the carver of the pinnacle of the Scaligeri tombs in Verona (figure 20 in *The Stones of Venice*), Edwin White fitted his carving to the triangular form without sacrificing the naturalism of the treatment of the leaf (*Aileen Reid*).

strength, according to Ruskin. This reflects the 'exquisite delicacies of change' that Ruskin admired in the west front at Pisa Cathedral.[36]

But there was also posterity – Memory – to consider. Ruskin had asserted in *The Seven Lamps* that 'multitudinous sculptural decorations afford means of expressing either symbolically or literally, all that need be known of national feeling or achievement.'[37] And the sculptural programme at Northampton certainly sought to do this for local feeling. The front is an essay in what Ruskin called the 'highest forms' of the 'proper material of ornament' – foliage, birds, man and other mammals.[38] Man as the highest in this hierarchy is represented in eight large figures of kings and queens at first-floor level, and in relief carvings in the seven tympana

Northampton Town Hall: capital from the back wall of the vestibule, carved by Edwin White. White, who 'had read Ruskin', took account of his words about balancing naturalism and conventionalism in his leaf carving: the carving also 'respects' the architectural form of the capital. Ruskin further asserted that colour should come from the uncarved portion – the shaft – to contrast with the whiteness of the stone of the richly carved capital (*Aileen Reid*).

of the ground-floor level and six within the vestibule, which depict scenes of national and Northampton history. Further scenes of local industry and other activities are woven into the foliage of the ground-floor capitals while characters and animals from Aesop's fables disport themselves on those at first floor. This memorial programme extended to the interior, where painted decoration in an appropriately medieval 'outline' style was introduced in the council chamber and in the great hall – fictive stonework, figures of Winter and Summer over the council chamber fireplaces, and Alfred the Great, symbolising Northampton's ancient origins, and Moses, symbolising the law-giving function of the building. As Ruskin succinctly put it, no one from Egyptian to medieval Christian, 'when in their right senses, ever think[s] of doing without paint'.[39]

Of course, Godwin, in common with many of his contemporaries, was not above making some almost direct quotations from *The Stones*: the

Below right: peacock finial from one of the council chamber fireplaces. This archetypal symbol of Aestheticism was not inspired by Godwin's enthusiasm for Japan, but is an example of a near-direct quotation from plate 8 of *The Stones of Venice*, which shows sculpture on the front of the Palazzo Gritti-Badoer (*Aileen Reid*).

peacock finial in the council chamber from plate 8, the main archivolt design from plate 5 and the course of triangular carved reliefs just below the first-floor stringcourse from the illustrations of Murano in plates 24, 25 and 26, for example. There are many others.[40]

But not all the triangular decorations are such a direct quotation from the Murano plates. Godwin was ever wary of copyism, and in the vestibule there is another band of triangular reliefs but this time they are filled with conventionalised but still naturalistic leaves of various kinds, which fill the shape in the prescribed 'Surface Gothic' manner, described and illustrated in the 'Nature of Gothic'.[41]

One way in which Godwin explicitly emphasised the Town Hall's Ruskinian credentials was the manner in which the carved ornament was produced. He had read what Ruskin had to say about the potential of the workman – his belief that 'there is many a village mason who, set to carve a series of Scripture or other histories, would find many a strange and noble fancy in his head'.[42] Godwin's village mason was a man named Edwin White who had produced capitals and other carving for him in churches all over Wiltshire, Somerset and Cornwall, and would carry on working for him into the late 1860s at Castle Ashby and Dromore.[43] At Northampton, White carved all the foliage and animal carving in the capitals and spandrels inside and out of the building. Godwin was not the only architect of the 1850s and 1860s to hear this call but it was his relationship with White that perhaps took Ruskin's words most to heart. As he later explained:

> I remember taking a carver over to Chartres for one day only … it was extraordinary how, in the few hours spent in merely looking at the treatment, without making a single sketch, he managed to extract sufficient of the spirit of the old workers to produce a very creditable series of foliage decorations.[44]

This, the importance of hand-work and the freedom of the workman was, according to Ruskin, the key part of his writing on architecture. He later claimed it was the neglect of this aspect, and of his warnings about restoration practice, by the architectural profession that made him decline the Gold Medal of the RIBA in 1874 and give up writing about architecture. But the sculptural ornament may have been one reason why Ruskin was moved, according to Godwin, to write him 'one or two very complimentary letters about [Northampton Town Hall]'[45] and to name Godwin as one of the few modern Goths of whom he could approve – along with Scott, Street, Butterfield, Waterhouse and Woodward. This was elevated company indeed.[46]

Northampton is the most completely and obviously Ruskinian of Godwin's buildings, but there are a number of others that demonstrate, in their diversity, the dynamic nature of Ruskin's writing on architecture and the range of ways in which it was possible to apply what he said. In 1858 Godwin had got a rather unpromising commission to design new showrooms and offices to front the works of Perry Brothers, a long-established firm of coachbuilders in Bristol.[47] There was no call for plate-traceried windows here. The coaches had to be seen – from the street on the ground floor, and be well-lit by large expanses of windows on the first and second floors.[48] For all the oft-quoted Ruskinian mantra that architecture was nothing more than the association of sculpture and painting in noble masses,[49] this is surely Godwin's response to the admonition in 'The Lamp of Power': 'Let therefore, the architect who has not large resources, choose his point of attack first, and if he chooses size let him abandon decoration'.[50] Or again from 'The Lamp of Power' the 'sublimity of arcades' at the Doge's Palace.[51]

The carriage-works contrast greatly with nos 10 & 11 Rockleaze, on Durdham Down in Bristol, a pair of semi-detached houses Godwin designed in 1860. They are a striking pair, especially as they were built for a speculative builder. Godwin mentions neither Perry's nor Rockleaze in his 1878 lecture – by 1878 they were perhaps just too shockingly 'Savage' – and, it must be said, dated – to show to his student audience. Especially Rockleaze, with its picturesque asymmetry, the window of No 11 thrust into the corner, the contrast of rubble walling and rubbed red-brick dressings, the naturalistically carved capitals and sloping wall-base.

Opposite: former offices and showroom of Perry's carriage-works, 104 Stokes Croft, Bristol, 1858-9. When built, the ground-floor arcades were open to the street. As at Northampton the outside arches are narrower, but here the fact is emphasised as only the outer arches have pointed arches. Despite the absence of carved decoration, this is just as 'Ruskinian' as Northampton Town Hall: the mix of rubble and ashlar masonry emphasises Ruskinian qualities of 'savageness' and 'power' appropriate to the building. The building was gutted by fire in 1992 (*Aileen Reid*).

Left: 10 & 11 Rockleaze, Bristol, 1860-2. Their striking design is all the more surprising as they were designed for a speculative builder, and form a notable contrast with the other houses on the street. Here Godwin interprets most literally Ruskin's suggestion that 'When the materials of which this [wall] veil is built are very loose, or of shapes which do not fit well together, it sometimes becomes necessary … to introduce courses of more solid material' (*Works*, 9, pp. 80-1) (*Aileen Reid*).

Rather it was another speculatively built pair of houses – St Martin's Villas, in Billing Road in Northampton, designed in 1863 – that Godwin described in his lecture as 'the "Stones of Venice" all over again.' Although the pair do have the prescribed Ruskinian 'natural' colouring and 'breadth of surface', as well as the carved lunettes over the doors depicting St Martin distributing alms and St Martin and the beggar, they seem, to use a Ruskinian way of looking at them, less expressive of savage wolfish life, than Rockleaze. Perry's, Rockleaze and St Martin's Villas demonstrate just how dynamic the Ruskinian programme was: they are all very different from each other, yet all equally 'Ruskinian'.

What St Martin's Villas look like, in fact, is the acceptable face of Ruskinism to the Godwin of 1878. He continued his account of his career with his design for Congleton Town Hall, with which design he said, 'The "Stones of Venice" already had been dropped'.[52] This is self-evidently untrue, as we shall see, but there were two principal reasons why Godwin, speaking to his student audience in Manchester on

26 November 1878, should have constructed a narrative of his career in which the influence of Ruskin on it was subject to tight limits both in nature and duration. One was that Ruskin was no longer fashionable. He had moved from being the 'Apostle whose sayings it was blasphemy to contradict' that had first attracted Godwin in 1857, to 'a fogey with a niche in the Temple of Orthodoxy' by 1878.[53]

The other reason, though related, was more personal to Godwin. That evening in Manchester he was fresh off the train from London where he had been in court to see his friend, the artist Whistler, humiliated – and subsequently financially ruined – by the award of only a farthing's damages in his suit against Ruskin.[54] Ruskin had famously called Whistler a 'coxcomb' for demanding 200 guineas for flinging a pot of paint in the public's face. The issue was whether Whistler's paintings had value because they embodied ideas – 'a lifetime's experience' – rather than 'finish' or craft. The trial is seen as a 'watershed' in the history of the Aesthetic movement,[55] as the pitting of one school of thought about art – Realist in a philosophical sense, concerned with the labour of craft, narrative in representation and morality – represented by Ruskin, against another – Idealist in a philosophical sense, unconcerned with craft, or with narrative or moral content, 'art for art's sake', 'Aesthetic' – represented by Whistler. Godwin by 1878 was decidedly seen as belonging to the Whistlerian tendency. Yet how had this happened in 15 years? After all, Godwin had sought successfully to identify himself as a Ruskinian architect in the early 1860s. Northampton Town Hall is his manifesto of that commitment.

The truth is that the opposition embodied in the *Whistler v. Ruskin* trial is, if not a false one, then not as absolute as has been accepted. And further that Godwin's position is more nuanced than it is generally presented, or than he sought to suggest, in his 1878 lecture. One key lies in Godwin's evolving attitude to the 'style question'.

What did Godwin mean when he said that 'the "Stones of Venice" already had been dropped with Congleton Town Hall'? Congleton is a recognisable cousin of Northampton – a symmetrical front with tower, some structural polychromy,

Opposite: St Martin's Villas, Billing Road, Northampton (1863-5): a much more 'refined' design than Rockleaze. There is a smoother, more regular finish, a reduction in decorative detail and variety of 'apertures' and an emphasis on the horizontal in the combination of imposts and stringcourses. Godwin offered it as an example of Ruskin's influence upon him, perhaps mindful of his assertion that 'it matters little, so that the surface be wide, bold and unbroken, whether it be of brick or of jasper' (*Works*, 8, p.109), and the contrast with Rockleaze demonstrates the range of possible architectural responses to Ruskin, even within a single architect's work (*Aileen Reid*).

East Retford Town Hall, Nottinghamshire: perspective for a competition design, 1864. Although Godwin claimed to have 'given up' *The Stones of Venice* by this time (presumably because it is more obviously French in inspiration than his Northampton Town Hall design), East Retford still has a clutch of obviously Ruskinian features – Florentine tower, memorial and foliage carving and structural polychromy (all but lifted from Ruskin's plate 13 – of S. Pietro, Pistoia – illustrating 'Wall-veil decoration') (*Victoria and Albert Museum*).

and a modicum of carving. Perhaps what he meant was that it is more emphatically French in inspiration than Northampton Town Hall – yet had not Ruskin himself already recommended the French Gothic of Notre Dame as 'the noblest of all'?[56] In 1864 Godwin unsuccessfully entered the competition for the town hall at East Retford in Nottinghamshire and we have another variation on the theme, this time with a more Florentine tower. And so this clearly Ruskinian manner of Godwin's went on right into the early 1870s in a succession of mainly public building designs – Bristol Assize Courts, Leicester Town Hall (both unexecuted), and Plymouth Guildhall (which was built) – with towers, 'memorial' and foliage carving, breadth of surface, some structural polychromy, and a robust French-inflected Gothic.

In his domestic practice, the story is more varied. At Castle Ashby, for example, where he built lodges and various other small works for the Marquess of Northampton in 1868-74, the carving and polychromy are still evident, though hints of 'pestilent' Classicism were creeping in. More obviously Ruskinian, in that, as at Northampton, ornamental painting and sculpture are an essential part of the architectural conception, was Dromore Castle, in Co. Limerick for the Earl of Limerick, 1866-73.[57] Equally, although obvious Ruskinian or even Gothic features are largely erased in his 'domestic revival' manner of the late 1860s and early 1870s (for example, his unbuilt design for a house for his cousin Percy Waite, or Beauvale in Nottinghamshire for Earl Cowper), this is hardly at odds with much of what Ruskin wrote. The Gothic was, after all, neither essentially an architecture of pointed-arched windows, nor an ecclesiastical manner. Its universal applicability was part of its appeal, part of what made it suitable to the modern age.

Despite Godwin's keenness to suggest that Ruskin's influence was limited to the period, approximately, 1858-64, there is almost nothing in his architectural designs that conflicts with Ruskin's key messages until the mid-1870s. If one reads his architectural journalism, however, a more complex story emerges. Godwin began his writing career as an antiquary, producing carefully researched papers influenced by his reading of John Britton, Pugin senior and, especially, Robert Willis, in local and national archaeological periodicals. From the early 1860s he found a new outlet for his ideas in the local press, especially the *Western Daily Press* in Bristol, and, later, in the mid- to late-1860s in the national architectural journals, notably the *Building News*, the *Architect* and, from the mid-1870s, the *British Architect*.

In the *Western Daily Press* in the early 1860s he published papers he had delivered in his role as Secretary of the Bristol Society of Architects. In one he took the opportunity to give his views on current architectural practice, and the dangers of architects falling into certain design 'grooves'. One of these was the expected 'scientific' groove – the men who, like his old master Armstrong, are 'great on girders [and] delight in drains'.[58] Another, less expectedly, given his own antiquarian pedigree, was the 'archaeological groove', the main danger of which was that the architects might become 'mere collectors and transcribers of the designs of those who have gone before us'. In mounting his attack on the archaeological groove, Godwin revealed not just that he feared archaeology that might lead to 'copyism' but a concern that the Gothic Revival was necessarily flawed because of its 'archaeological underpinnings': 'Constantly looking back, with no faith in ourselves, no trust in the present, and no hope in the future, we cannot wonder if our power has declined, we cannot be astonished if our works possess no attractions for others.' What we see here is an anxiety resurfacing that Ruskin had to some extent quelled.

Godwin's aspiration, which he shared with many architects of his generation, to develop a new style out of the Gothic by divining either 'principles' or manipulating forms, predated Ruskin and outlived the obvious impact of him. The anxiety was that it was only the *principles* of Gothic which would yield a new and living style, yet these were elusive; the more accessible *forms*, on the other hand, would be forever mired in the past, incapable of revivification. Ruskin, however, was not really interested in the creation of a new style, either by collective 'development' or by some more individual 'originality': 'We want no new style of architecture ... But we want *some* style ... it does not matter one marble splinter whether we have an old or new architecture'.[59]

This was reassuring stuff for young architects in the 1850s who were struggling with the rather nebulous abstract concept of 'development'. Ruskin made it safe to be an archaeologist – for him, the fusion of archaeological and artistic elements was enough, when coupled with the moral attributes promoted especially in the 'Nature of Gothic' in *The Stones of Venice*, and in the Lamps of Obedience, Sacrifice and Truth.

Already in 1864, the year of his Congleton Town Hall design, Godwin was beginning to have doubts. Ruskin had said that the Gothic was enough – this was what Godwin, and many of his contemporaries came to reject. But hand-in-hand with this disenchantment with the Revival, inherent in his dismissal of the 'archaeological groove', comes a wave of anxiety about quite a different side-effect of reading Ruskin, in Godwin's warnings about what he calls the 'artistic groove'. When he described the 'artistic groove' as being home to those with a 'fever for chamfering and notching', 'worshippers of the Holy Zebra' and an over-enthusiasm for stripes of vari-coloured brick, we know to what he was alluding. This was the beginning of a constant theme in his architectural writing – the anxiety that seeking of a new architecture from within the architecture of the past – 'a restless wandering to and fro from the ends of the earth'[60] – is a doomed exercise.

For all the anxieties expressed in his writing in the 1860s, Godwin was sustained as a Goth for a long time by his antipathy to Classicism. It only took an attack by Classicists to bring out the knee-jerk Goth in Godwin; in 1873, he was still describing himself as 'a Gothic Architect of nearly 20 years standing'[61] and a year later as 'a Goth like me'.[62] Even in 1878 he said of Sir Gilbert Scott, 'we who are nearly all of us more or less his pupils.'[63]

This positioning of himself as a Gothicist coloured Godwin's initial response to the Queen Anne movement.[64] Six months later he was showing clear anxiety about the death knell being sounded for the Gothic Revival by commentators such as T. Roger Smith, who suggested 'Renaissance is more nearly in harmony with [modern pan-European taste] than Gothic', and it is telling that it was Ruskin that Godwin turned to in seeking ammunition:

> Would it not be well, then, for some to think a little more of that true architecture (the Gothic) of Europe, which they seem so ready to cast stones at, and ask themselves the question whether they understand it or not. ... There was a time when architecture was traditionary ... In such times we hear of no architect marked and set

White House, 35 Tite Street, London, for the artist, James McNeill Whistler: main elevation of the first design, 1877. Although Ruskin would no doubt have spurned this design for its 'haughty severity' and touches of 'debased Classicism', it none the less shows the extent to which Godwin's conception of architecture was still Ruskinian in a broader sense. All Ruskin's aphorisms about architecture may have been predicated on the assumption that he meant *Gothic* architecture, but much of what he wrote – the emphasis on architectural composition (features, decoration and colour) rather than planning, the focus on the façade or 'wall-veil' – underpins the art-architecture of Godwin in the late 1870s, just as much as his earlier Gothic Revival modes (*Victoria and Albert Museum, E.540-1963*).

apart by name and specially honoured as the designer of this or that building. Directly however, that a distinct age of copyism arose ... then began the era of sham architecture, the fatal separation of building and architect.[65]

These are Ruskinian mantras trotted out and used as a comforter.

By 1875, however, Godwin had come to an accommodation with the Queen Anneites and was writing of the 'success that has attended what has very improperly been called the Queen Anne Revival'[66] in the hands of 'Messrs Shaw, Bodley and Stevenson'. He seems finally to have severed his allegiance to Ruskin in the same article when he says that 'the enemy is not any given style, but ornament itself' and recommends architects adhere to a 'Spartan regime' for a season.

It was a regime that he, himself, famously adhered to. The architectural designs by which he is best remembered – the first designs for studio-houses for Whistler (1877-8) and Frank Miles (1878), both in Tite Street, Chelsea – are charac-

Studio-house, 44 Tite Street, London, for the artist Frank Miles: main elevation of the first design, 1878. In its lack of decoration, this design, like that for the White House, appears almost wilfully anti-Ruskinian, yet, once again, the focus on façade, on compositional display, on form, would not have happened if Godwin had never read Ruskin. As at the White House, a major feature is a balcony (which the *Building News* described as being of 'archaic appearance'). This is enlivened by memorial carving – although not of a type Ruskin would have admired, perhaps. All in all, this shows the concept of 'breadth of surface' carried to its logical conclusion (*Victoria and Albert Museum*, E.556-1963).

terised by their almost abstract play of solid and void – inspired, it has plausibly been mooted, by his Aesthete's enthusiasm for Japan[67] and a lack of ornamentation which it has been suggested was 'proto-Modernist' in intent.[68] These two designs represent, perhaps, the extreme point of Godwin's retreat from the Gothic Revival; a retreat, too, from Ruskin, it would seem, in their 'haughty simplicity'.[69] And there was worse to come. Godwin threw in his lot with the Classicists and produced a series of designs which ranged in inspiration from the Greek (in the loosest sense)[70] to various shades of Renaissance.

The Aestheticism apparently inherent in this capitulation to a morally neutral, pragmatic eclecticism seems to be reflected in Godwin's wider work in his writings. In his art criticism, especially, which appeared in the architectural press

Dublin Museum of Science and Art, perspective for the competition, 1883. Godwin had so far abandoned his Ruskinian allegiance to produce a Classical design, complete with this Schinkelesque perspective drawing. None of Godwin's Classical designs, such as this and his 1878 competition design for the Brompton Oratory (illustrated in the *British Architect*, 12 (1879), p. 6), is entirely convincing. He never relinquished Ruskin's elastic laws of composition, derived from Gothic architecture, which jarred with Classical forms, and produced an out-of-balance effect (more Speer than Schinkel) and oddities such as the dome and tower (*RIBA Library Drawings Collection, RAN 7/I/1*).

from the late 1860s, he seems to have forgotten Ruskin. He is concerned almost exclusively with formal characteristics of colour and composition, not with content or craft.[71] He is an especial enthusiast for Albert Moore[72] and, of course, Whistler: by 1881 he was barely concealing his criticism of Ruskin's attitude to Whistler.[73]

Moreover, from the late 1860s, Godwin spent an increasing amount of his time in the production of decorative designs – for furniture, textiles, wallpaper and so on.[74] These activities not only involved an even more direct severance between designer and creator than occurred in architecture, but he was, in pursuing them, also far more involved in the money-grubbing business of profit and loss, the enslaving environment of the factory.

This apparently anti-Ruskinian severance of designer from producer is also reflected in the way Godwin conducted his architectural practice throughout his career. From the late 1850s he entered into a series of short- and long-term collaboration agreements with other architects – James Hine, James Adams Clark, Henry Crisp, R. W. Edis and J. P. Seddon – in which it was more or less explicitly stated that Godwin would produce the designs – meaning devise the planning and design the elevations – but the partner would produce working drawings, engage contractors and superintend the works.[75] This smooth division was not always apparent in practice, but the intention was there, and it complies very closely with C. R. Cockerell's suggestion, made in the 1830s, that there should be 'the Art Architect to design, and the practical architect to carry out and superintend'.[76] Equally it contravenes Ruskin's stern words about the 'division of labour' being, in fact, 'a division of men',[77] his promotion of the notion of the painter grinding his own colours or the architect working in the mason's yard[78] and his denial that 'one man's thoughts can be, or ought to be, executed by another man's hands'.[79]

Thus Godwin and Ruskin appear to have reached, by the late 1870s, a position of polar opposites in the conception of architecture: Ruskin a morally absolute Realist position in which building as craft is key; Godwin an Aestheticised, morally neutral Idealist position in which design concept, not execution, is key.

While it is perfectly possible to argue these extreme positions, the truth is somewhat more complex and nuanced, for both Ruskin and Godwin, so that there is a surprising amount of common ground between them. Specifically, for Godwin, the influence on him of reading Ruskin not only consisted of rather more than a continuing enthusiasm for 'memorial' sculpture and structural polychromy, but also lasted much longer – right to the end of his life, in fact.

The most obvious manifestation of this is Godwin's ongoing enthusiasm for things medieval. Although this is not an exclusively Ruskinian phenomenon, there are two aspects that do seem to be specifically Ruskinian. Godwin continued to publish his drawings, measured plans and details of medieval buildings into the late 1870s, long after he designed the White House for Whistler. It is telling that he chose to publish them not in any archaeological or antiquarian journal, but in the architectural press. From this and from the content of his several series of advice columns aimed at students in the late 1870s and early 1880s, it is clear that, although he had abandoned the idea of the Gothic as the fountainhead from which would eventually burst a new architecture for the 19th century, he still saw it as a dynamic source of architectural ideas, not as something solely of antiquarian interest.

Southport Free Library and Art Gallery: preliminary design for the competition, 1876. Godwin had a frenzy of competition-entering in the late 1870s and it is striking – given that it was at this time he designed Frank Miles's and Whistler's houses – how often these designs are not just Gothic but Gothic of a robust early character. Godwin never really embraced what Ruskin called the 'pestilential' Perpendicular, although in the final version of this design (RIBA Drawings Collection RAN 7/M/2), he changed the triple lancets to a more fashionable later style of window (*Victoria and Albert Museum, E.242-1963*).

This belief that the Gothic was still a valid form of architectural expression, even if it could not generate the elusive 'new style', was also expressed in his own designs, where his tastes still bore an unmistakable Ruskinian imprint. Although Godwin had what *appear* to be kind words for Bodley's St Augustine, Pendlebury,[80] and he published a fanciful scheme for rebuilding St Philip, Stepney which suggests he has been looking at the designs for J. L. Pearson's St Augustine, Kilburn,[81] there was no Late Gothic Revival for him. His conception of revived Gothic did not really develop after 1870. He described Pearson's church as 'incongruous'.[82] Godwin's Gothic remained essentially Ruskinian[83] in the later 1870s and 1880s, characterised by that same 'breadth of surface' Ruskin so valued, and by a rejection of the 'pestilential' Perpendicular in favour of a more muscular, usually Early French or Middle Pointed style. These designs of the 1870s and 1880s are more freely treated than those from the early 1860s, but they are definitely robust rather than refined, right up to his last identifiable competition design, for the Nottingham municipal offices competition of 1883.[84] These Gothic designs are almost all failed competition designs; if Godwin had been a more successful competitor, our conception of him today might be rather different from what it is.[85] He never entirely recovered from his fit for plate tracery.

Neither was his way of organising his practice quite as contrary to Ruskinian dicta as at first sight might appear. Godwin's attempt to establish for himself a role as art-architect in contradistinction to the executive architect seems at absolute odds with Ruskin's admonitions about the recognition of the workman, and the need for the designer also to be the 'maker', but Ruskin was more of a pragmatist than the often-quoted sections of the 'Nature of Gothic' suggest.[86]

If what drew Godwin to Ruskin in the first place was his passion for the Gothic, one reason he felt able to respond to that attraction was, as already suggested, Ruskin's pious evangelising tone. That this should have survived in Godwin's approach to architecture after the mid-1870s, given his identification with Aestheticism, is perhaps surprising. But survive it did. Godwin's architectural journalism, in particular, continues to be laced with quotations from the Bible and, if not from Ruskin from his hero Carlyle,[87] puritanical exhortations to students to work hard and cultivate moderate habits.[88] Moreover, as Richard Hayes has pointed out, Godwin was publishing his various series of 'Scraps for Students' and 'Letters to Art Students' at just the time that Ruskin was publishing *Fors Clavigera*, his 'Letters to the Workmen and Labourers of Great Britain'.[89]

But what is most striking is how this moralising tone runs through so many of Godwin's architectural concerns in the later 1870s and 1880s, some of which might appear on the face of it archetypally Aesthetic and, consequently, incompatible with a surviving Ruskinian agenda. Yet they are absolutely rooted in Ruskin's writings. Some of these aspects are self-evidently Ruskinian – a continuing veneration for Nature, for example – expressed countless times in his writings, including, ironically, in a critique of Whistler's Peacock

Room.[90] Another theme is the opposition between the art-architect (himself) and the money-grubbing trade architect, more interested in the business and technical sides of architecture. This is not just a morally neutral opposition between what Godwin had called in the early 1860s 'the scientific groove' – drains and dilapidations men – and the artistic groove (Godwin); it is also by implication an opposition between architects with higher motives - love of art, bettering of society (Godwin again) – and those motivated by 'money-wealth':

> There are a smaller proportion [of architects] still clinging to art in some fashion, and through books, lectures, or periodical papers endeavour to keep the heavily laden pilgrim of art from sinking altogether into the slough of the mere trader and money maker.[91]

But even when Godwin was making an apparently anti-Ruskinian argument, for example, in urging architectural students to forswear ornament – 'these meaningless fritterings of arch and string-course and jamb'[92] – this exhortation is still couched in the Ruskinian/Evangelical language of praise and blame, good and evil.

This loading with moral value extends for Godwin, as it did for Ruskin, to the widest, and most abstract notion of beauty. Far from being the contentless, amoral abstraction of the Aesthete, Godwin asserted that:

> beauty has *not* been fully grasped and never will be ... a perfect work of art ... is impossible ... because it implies a perfect workman ... beauty and perfection are ideal and it is only in the endeavour to reach this ideal – in the act of moving ever and ever onwards – that a living art is possible. For the moment we assume the ideal to be reached – the moment we pause for self-gratulation that moment we die to Art.[93]

This recalls Ruskin's notion of 'exulting, reverent, and grateful'[94] 'Theoria', the word he used to distinguish an appreciation of beauty founded on moral impressions from 'Aesthesis', which he saw 'a mere operation of sense'[95]. This is precisely the distinction Godwin made when he castigated

> the mere sensuousness of eye and ear ... not troubling to separate the evil from the good; for there is evil side by side with the good in the best of thing ... Let us while reaping the pleasure, deny ourselves indulgence therein, that we may find time to discover the reason of the satisfaction which any special form of art gives to any special sense. ... So ... that lifting up of the soul and that standing aghast in admiration which certain architects tell us is their experience [of certain old churches] ... are not accidental, but have arisen in obedience to and sympathy with, the men who, building with stone instead of sounds, wrought out their architectural symphony in well apportioned rhythm and delightful harmony.[96]

There is no amoral Aestheticism here. This idea of a 'well apportioned rhythm and delightful harmony' provides another clue to Godwin's thinking about architecture in his later, apparently post-Ruskinian phase. In reading *The Stones of Venice* and *The Seven Lamps*, because everything is posited on the assumption that by 'architecture' Ruskin means 'Gothic architecture', it is easy to forget the extent to which he is offering a set of rules that have application far beyond the Gothic. The first volume of *The Stones* can be read simply as a treatise on constructional form – wall-base to cornice – and the ornamentation of all these parts. Ruskin himself wrote at the beginning of chapter 19 of the first volume: 'the reader has now some knowledge of every feature of all possible architecture'.[97] Of course, it is all predicated on the assumption that these elements are Gothic, but it was none the less capable of inculcating a way of looking at and designing buildings that transcended style. And this was its effect on Godwin. Some of these 'rules'– the Lamps of Truth and Beauty for example, much of the 'Nature of Gothic' – are self-evidently abstract.

For Godwin, however, it was not these abstract transcendental qualities in Ruskin that had most impact, but the essentially formalist aspects of his thinking and writing about architecture. The first volume of *The Stones of Venice*, as discussed in relation to the Northampton Town Hall, is an analysis of constructional and decorative characteristics that systematically rakes the front of the building from wall-base to cornice and roof, but which does not penetrate beyond that front. Ruskin had little interest in the planning of a building, and neither did Godwin, a lack of interest that was commented on by fellow architects[98] and by competition assessors, and probably explains why Godwin's competition premiums so rarely matured into commissions.[99] Among his many surviving architectural drawings, it is the beautifully wrought main-elevation drawings and perspectives that stand out. And it was usually these, rather than plans and sections, that he chose to publish in the architectural press – almost exclusively so after 1875. Godwin's Ruskinian concentration on the elevation is complemented by an equally Ruskinian emphasis on the elements that make up that elevation, and in their composition. This operates at a number of levels. At the broadest level Ruskin's formal distinction between such qualities as 'linear' and 'surface' Gothic in the 'Nature of Gothic'[100], between 'line' and 'mass', for example in the 'Lamp of Truth'[101] and 'delicacy' and 'majesty' in the 'Lamp of Power'[102] and the two kinds of 'Superimposition' – 'weight on lightness, and of lightness on weight' – in the first volume of *The Stones of Venice*[103] find their exact counterpart in much of what Godwin has to say about architecture in the late 1870s, for example in discussing 'light' and 'heavy' buildings, and, another Ruskinian conceit, 'Border' buildings, these being the perfect midpoint between light and heavy.[104] As late as 1884, Godwin was still employing a Ruskinian type of analysis in discussing Westminster Hall.[105]

But Ruskin's influence on Godwin's later conception of architecture is at its most profound, perversely, where Godwin is apparently at his least Ruskinian: in his analysis of the 'Queen Anne' Revival, and in his formula for developing a new style – which Ruskin asserted was 'not needed'.[106] The Queen Anne Revival, in that it employed certain Classical features, does not seem a prime candidate for reflecting a survival of Ruskinian influence. Yet Godwin's analysis of its essential qualities does reflect this in two ways. He asserted that its finest features are 'elements derived from the Gothic parentage, and not the Classic.'[107] This attempt to claim for the Queen Anne style a Gothic rather than Classic provenance is a clear attempt to sanitise it. Only a writer still wedded to the essential superiority of Gothic over Classic would attempt to do this. Secondly, it is also notable that Godwin chooses to characterise these 'finest features' as 'bricks of good colour, stout chimneys, full-grown dormers, absence of large sheets of plate glass' – not only are these features to be found just as well in Gothic as Classic buildings, but the anatomising of what constitutes the Queen Anne style is entirely based on the methodology of the first volume of *The Stones of Venice*.

Godwin employed this anatomising methodology on a number of occasions,[108] but it reaches its most fully developed form in '*Architectura vulgata*', an article he wrote in the *Architect* for July 1875. Here he recommended the Spartan regime that finds expression in the following couple of years in the White House and the first design for Frank Miles's house.[109] The article's argument is not complex – that a new architecture may be evolved from extracting the best elements of vernacular architecture from the Anglo-Saxon to the Renaissance and employing these elements unornamented. These ideas – the eclecticism, especially when it involves the 'debased' Renaissance, and the eschewing of ornament – may be antipathetic to Ruskin's message, but Godwin's methodology certainly is not: '*Architectura vulgata*' could not have been written if Godwin had not read *The Stones*. His statement of seven 'vulgate' conditions – for example, 'dormers and chimneys to be taller and larger than they now are' and 'the front door to be larger than it usually is' – are clearly derived from the rule-making methodology of *The Seven Lamps* and the first volume of *The Stones*. He also selects five styles – 'Saxon, Norman, Early Period, Later Pointed and Renaissance' – from each of which he selects the best that vernacular building had to offer. Again these are constructional forms – 'saddle back roof tower and the string course at the window cill level' of the Norman for example – which recall *The Stones of Venice* 1. But most striking of all is the way he couples these styles and their constructional elements with abstract qualities: the 'Picturesqueness' derived from the Saxon; the 'Steadiness' of the tower roofs and string-course' of the Norman, the 'Comfort and Homeliness of the Later Pointed' and so on. It is the 'Nature of Gothic' rewritten for the post-Gothic Revival age. When Godwin offered his seven vulgate conditions, he offered them as 'the basis for all future ordinary work'. '*Architectura vulgata*', in its messianic hubris, is pure Ruskin.

That Ruskinian influence should have survived in Godwin's architectural designs and architecture at a time when he is so much identified with the Aesthetic Movement is not as surprising as might at first appear. The dichotomy between Aestheticism and Ruskin, between Idealism and Empiricism, suggested by interpretations of the *Whistler v Ruskin* trial is not one that would have been universally accepted by contemporaries. For example, the Ur-Aesthete himself, Oscar Wilde, referred to 'that revival of culture and love of beauty which in great part owes its birth to Mr Ruskin, and which Mr Swinburne, and Mr Pater, and Mr Symonds, and Mr Morris, and many others are fostering and keeping alive, each in his own peculiar fashion'.[110] The quotations which opened this chapter show how it is possible with selective quotations to 'Aestheticise' Ruskin and to 'moralise' Godwin. This is not a sustainable position, yet Ruskin was certainly more 'Aestheticised' and Godwin more 'moralised' than is usually assumed.

This does not imply that Ruskin subscribed to a philosophy of 'art for art's sake', but it suggests that there was considerable common ground between Ruskin and the Aesthetes. That common ground, that which appealed to Godwin, lay partly in what Wilde calls Ruskin's 'love of beauty'. Ruskin is imbued with the numinousness of art and, by extension, architecture: 'an architect ... must tell us a fairy tale';[111] one of the two main Virtues of architecture is to conform to 'universal and divine canons of loveliness'.[112] It also lay in a love of and celebration of art, and a conception of architectural beauty defined by formal qualities – both abstract notions of 'mass' and 'surface', and constructional elements of wall and window, door and roof.

But equally, the putative 'Aesthete' Godwin, while he may have lost faith with Gothic in a way Ruskin did not, never abandoned the notion that there was, or should be, if not as in Ruskin a moral imperative, then at least a moral tone in architectural design and in the appreciation of architectural beauty. 'I plead here for Art – Greek, Hebrew, Christian, of whatsoever nation and whatsoever time; "not" as CARLYLE says, because of its effect, but because of itself; not because it is useful for spiritual pleasure, or even for moral culture, but because it is Art, and the highest in man.'[113]

This is the alternative Ruskinian tradition – the 'illegitimate' one, in that Ruskin would have abhorred the way it was manifested in Godwin's work. Yet while the Lamps of Life and Memory and the 'Nature of Gothic' certainly produced the Ruskinian tradition that is more generally recognised – William Morris, Philip Webb and their Arts and Crafts progeny – the Lamps of Beauty and Power, and the first volume of *The Stones of Venice* led just as surely to the work of E.W. Godwin in the 1870s and 1880s.

What Godwin read in Ruskin was a Gospel of Art couched in the language of Evangelical Anglicanism. Ruskin made it a moral duty to love art, to experience joy in art, and it was not a lesson Godwin forgot, even after he turned away from encrusted capitals and displays of constructional colour. Godwin retained a 'Theoretic' as opposed to an 'Aesthetic' approach to architecture, and in this, as in his formalist approach to architectural criticism and design, and continuing celebration of art, he remained a Ruskinian to the end.

Notes

[1] *Works*, 9, p. 72.
[2] 'Friends in Council No. 40: A Retrospect', *British Architect*, 16 (1881), p. 65.
[3] *Works*, 22, pp. 511-13.
[4] E.W. Godwin, 'On some buildings I have designed', *British Architect*, 10 (1878), pp. 210-12.
[5] This was most clearly demonstrated by Nick Shrimpton twenty years ago in '"Rust and Dust": Ruskin's pivotal work', in R. Hewison (editor), *New Approaches to Ruskin: Thirteen Essays* (London, Boston and Henley, 1981), p. 51.
[6] Plate 13 of *The Stones of Venice*, vol. 2 (*Works*, 9, facing p. 348, r).
[7] See for example the preface to the third edition of *The Stones of Venice* (1874): *Works*, 9, p. 11.

[8] Quoted by D. Harbron in *The Conscious Stone* (London, 1949), p. 115, and it has been referenced elsewhere as from Beerbohm's essay '1880' in the quarterly magazine, the *Yellow Book*. It does not, in fact, appear in '1880', from which Harbron also quotes (p. 151). I am grateful to Michael Hall for pointing this out to me.

[9] The only full-length biography of Godwin is Harbron's [note 8]; briefer but more reliable is Lionel Lambourne, 'Edward William Godwin (1833-1886): Aesthetic Polymath', in Susan Soros (editor), *E. W. Godwin: Aesthetic Movement Architect and Designer* (New Haven and London, 1999), pp. 19-43.

[10] E. W. Godwin reminisced about hearing Willis lecture to the Archaeological Institute in his obituary of Sir George Gilbert Scott: *British Architect*, 9 (1878), p. 155.

[11] For a more detailed discussion of Godwin's antiquarian reading and activities see Catherine Arbuthnott, 'E. W. Godwin as an Antiquary', in Soros [note 9], pp. 45-69.

[12] RIBA BAL GOE/3/5/1; the prospectus (a single folded sheet of paper) was issued from Brunswick Square, where Armstrong had his office.

[13] Given his prodigious output of antiquarian publications, it seems likely that Godwin, young though he was, was the leading force in the shaping of *The Antiquities of Bristol*.

[14] RIBA BAL Drawings Collection RAN 7/L/15, design for an unidentified house; it could be the house he was designing for himself in Colerne, Wilts, while he was working on the restoration there of the parish church in 1854-5 (V&A P&D E.226 E. W. Godwin notebook), as the spirelet on the chimney was copied from a house in the main street in Colerne on which he later published a short article: 'Notice of an Example of Domestic Architecture at Colerne, Wiltshire', *Archaeological Journal*, 18 (1861), pp. 125-7.

[15] 'the view of [Street's] design for Cuddesdon College, published in the *Illustrated News* of 28 April 1853 ... first attracted me, then a student, to this accomplished architect', quoted in D. Harbron, 'Edward Godwin', *Architectural Review*, 98 (1945), p. 48.

[16] For St John the Baptist, Colerne, see A. Reid, 'The Architectural Career of E. W. Godwin', in Soros [note 9], p. 132 and A. Reid, 'E. W. Godwin (1833-86): Towards an Art-Architecture', (unpublished PhD thesis, Courtauld Institute of Art, University of London, 1999), pp. 147-57.

[17] Godwin [note 4], p. 210.

[18] G. G. Scott, *A Plea for the Faithful Restoration of Our Ancient Churches* (London, 1850); G. G. Scott, 'The Architecture of the Future', chapter 12 in *Remarks on Secular and Domestic Architecture, Present and Future* (London, 1857), pp. 258-74; on the idea of development in the 1840s and 1850s see David B. Brownlee, 'The First High Victorians: British Architectural Theory in the 1840s', *Architectura*, 15 (1985), pp. 33-46.

[19] Letter 17 December 1856 from Godwin to Scott RIBA BAL ScGGS/4/4/2

20 Godwin's first commission back in England was the supply of drawings to James Hine for Western College, Plymouth, which is on the first page of what was presumably a new ledger (Archive of Art & Design, London AAD 4/9-1980).
21 '"Gothic and Classic"', *Builder*, 15 (1857), p. 176.
22 Ibid.
23 *Works*, 8, p. 102.
24 V&A P&D E.226-1963, E.W. Godwin notebook, 70.
25 Ibid., 34.
26 'Bristol Blunders', *Architect*, 15 (1876), 268.
27 Quoted in Nikolaus Pevsner, *Some Architectural Writers of the Nineteenth Century* (Oxford, 1972), p. 142.
28 Godwin [note 4], p. 210.
29 Colin Cunningham, *Victorian and Edwardian Town Halls* (London, 1981), *passim*.
30 For a catalogue of Godwin's competition entries Reid, 'E.W. Godwin (1833-86)...' [note 16], Appendix II.
31 Report of council business, *Northampton Mercury*, 5 January 1860.
32 Godwin [note 4], p. 210
33 For this strand of Ruskinian influence see M. Swenarton, *Artisans and Architects: The Ruskinian Tradition in Architectural Thought* (Basingstoke and London, 1989).
34 Stefan Muthesius demonstrated this in *The High Victorian Movement in Architecture 1850-70* (London, 1972), pp. 26-38.
35 Godwin [note 4], p. 211
36 *Works*, 8, p. 203.
37 Ibid., pp. 229-30.
38 *Works*, 9, pp. 265-6.
39 *Works*, 10, p. 110.
40 The plain, unchamfered shouldered windows at the semi-basement level are taken from plate 4 of *The Stones of Venice*; the mayor's balcony from fig. 25; the star tracery from fig. 18; the inlaid decoration in the fireplaces of the council chamber from plate 14; the design and decoration of the first-floor window archivolts from plate 13.
41 *Works*, 10, pp. 264-5.
42 Ibid., p. 129.
43 For White's work for Godwin see Reid, 'E.W. Godwin (1833-86)... [note 16], Appendix I.
44 E.W. Godwin, 'The Photographs of the Architectural Photographic Association for 1867', *Building News*, 14 (1867), pp. 147-8.
45 Godwin [note 4], p. 211; it seems curious that these letters do not survive among Godwin's papers in the V&A and the RIBA.
46 *Works*, 19, p. 23; Cook & Wedderburn indexed the 'Godwin' here as George Godwin but there is no reason why Ruskin should have meant George Godwin – it seems a mistake, the consequence of the extent to which E.W. Godwin's star had sunk by the early 20th century, when the

Library Edition was published.

47 'Account of Messrs Perry & Sons' in Godwin ledger Archive of Art and Design, London, AAD 4/9-1980, 9-10.

48 For a description of this building while it was still in use as a carriage showroom, see *The Ports of the Bristol Channel* (London, 1893), p. 194.

49 *Works*, 8, p. 11 – the introduction to the second edition of *The Seven Lamps of Architecture* of 1855, which, given that Godwin read the book in 1857 or 1858, might well have been the edition he read.

50 *Works*, 8, p. 105.

51 Ibid., p. 110.

52 Godwin [note 4], p. 211.

53 A. Cruse, *The Victorians and their Books* (London, 1935), quoted in N. Shrimpton, 'Ruskin and the Aesthetes', in D. Birch (editor), *Ruskin and the Dawn of the Modern* (Oxford, 1999), p. 141.

54 For the trial see L. Merrill, *A Pot of Paint: Aesthetics on Trial in 'Whistler v Ruskin'* (Washington and London, 1992); Merrill (pp. 346-7 n. 51) demonstrates, from the notes that Godwin took (notebook now in Dept of Prints, Drawings, Paintings and Photographs, V&A, London: E.248-1963), that it is probable that Godwin was present at both days of the trial.

55 For example, Lionel Lambourne, *The Aesthetic Movement* (London, 1996), p. 91.

56 *Works*, 8, p. 13.

57 See A. Reid, 'Dromore Castle, Co. Limerick: Archaeology and the Sister Arts of E.W. Godwin', *Architectural History*, 30 (1987), pp. 113-42.

58 'Mr E.W. Godwin on Architecture and Somerset Churches', *Western Daily Press*, 8 June 1864, p. 3.

59 *Works*, 8, p. 253.

60 E.W. Godwin, 'The Architectural Exhibition, 1867', *Building News*, 13 (1867), p. 337.

61 Copy of letter to Wm Clarke, Hon. Sec., Building Committee for New Unitarian Church [Nottingham], 1 September 1873 (Godwin letterbook 2, Archive of Art and Design, London, AAD 4/23-1988, 83-5).

62 'What I Noted in Passing Through Manchester and Liverpool', *Building News*, 27 (1874), p. 55.

63 *British Architect*, 9 (1878), pp. 155-6.

64 'The works of Mr R. Norman Shaw, A.R.A.', *Building News*, 25 (1873), pp. 449-50.

65 E.W. Godwin, 'The New European Style', *Building News*, 26 (1874), p. 269.

66 '*Architectura vulgata*', *Architect*, 14 (1875), pp. 16-17.

67 M. Girouard, *Sweetness and Light: The Queen Anne Movement 1860-1900* (London and New Haven, 1977), p. 180.

68 For example: 'his chief claim to the attention of architects must be his influence as a founder of the Modern Movement' ('E.W. Godwin: His Life and Work', *Builder*, 176 (1949), p. 330), and the White House 'is a remarkable example of functionalism at a very early date' (Alf Bøe, *From*

Gothic Revival to Functional Form: A Study on Victorian Theories of Design [Oslo, 1957], p. 130); for a subtle appraisal of the way Godwin's work as both designer and architect has been interpreted as prefiguring Modernism, see J. Kinchin, 'Godwin and Modernism', in Soros [note 9], pp. 93-113.

[69] 'no architecture is so haughty as that which is simple', in the 'Nature of Gothic', *Works*, 10, pp. 243-4.

[70] By 1884 he was reassuring his client the art dealer J. M. McLean that there was 'No fear of Queen Anne. My affections are much more Greek' and produced another abstract ornament-free masterpiece for McLean's shop front in Haymarket: letter from E. W. Godwin to J. M. McLean, 4 June 1884, Archive of Art and Design, London, AAD 4/90-1988.

[71] 'The Exhibition of Works of the Old Masters', *Architect*, 17 (1877), pp. 19-20.

[72] *British Architect*, 13 (1880), pp. 231-2.

[73] *British Architect*, 15 (1881), pp. 98-9.

[74] These aspects of Godwin's work are discussed by Catherine Arbuthnott, Joanna Banham and Linda Parry, in Soros [note 9].

[75] See Reid in Soros [note 9], pp. 129-31, and Reid, E. W. Godwin (1833-86)...' [note 16], pp. 107-31 for the complexities of Godwin's architectural practice.

[76] Quoted in A. Saint, *The Image of the Architect* (New Haven and London, 1983), p. 61.

[77] *Works*, 10, p. 196.

[78] Ibid., p. 201.

[79] Ibid., p. 200.

[80] Godwin, 'What I Noted in Passing Through Manchester and Liverpool', *Building News*, 27 (1874), p. 55: 'it is at Pendlebury that lovers of modern ecclesiastical architecture will find their chief delight'... without in fact indicating whether he counts himself among their number. This impression of ambivalence is confirmed later in the same article when he describes St John the Baptist, Tue Brook, as 'another of Mr Bodley's characteristic works'.

[81] 'St Philip's Church, Stepney, Showing Alterations Designed by E. W. Godwin, FSA', *Architect*, 6 (1871), illustration.

[82] 'The Royal Academy', *Architect*, 7 (1872), p. 222.

[83] In 1869 his list of the best buildings of the years 1841-61 are all more or less 'Ruskinian': 'Architecture at the Royal Academy', *Architect*, 1 (1869), pp. 242-3.

[84] 'Preliminary design for a town hall', RIBA DC RAN 7/M/12 (1-5); Archive of Art and Design: letter, description of design and diary entries relating to the competition, AAD 4/249-1988, 4/252-1988 and 4/8-1980.

[85] In fact Godwin had a higher success-rate than the average competitor (see Reid, 'E. W. Godwin (1833-86)...' [note 16], pp. 84-99 for a discussion of Godwin's activities as an architectural competitor, and pp. 380-420 for a catalogue of his competition entries).

86 'On a large scale … it is indeed both possible and necessary that the thoughts of one man should be carried out by the labour of others', *Works*, 10, p. 200.

87 'The "Daily News" versus Art', *Architect*, 14 (1875), pp. 281-2; 'Sir George Gilbert Scott', *British Architect*, 9 (1878), pp. 155-6.

88 See, for example, 'To Our Student Readers [I]', *British Architect*, 14 (1880), pp. 48-9; 'Friends in Council No. 40: A Retrospect', *British Architect*, 16 (1881), pp. 655-7.

89 Richard W. Hayes 'An Aesthetic Education: The Architecture Criticism of E.W. Godwin', in Soros [note 9], pp. 115-25.

90 'Features like these [scale pattern or feather pattern] belong to no particular country, to no particular style, for they are the common property of the world wherever birds or fish are found', 'Notes on Mr Whistler's Peacock Room', *Architect*, 17 (1877), pp. 118-19.

91 'Scraps for Students I', *Architect*, 15 (1876), pp. 237-8.

92 'Frozen Music', *Architect*, 15 (1876), pp. 76-7.

93 ' The "Daily News" versus Art', [note 87].

94 '[T]he mere animal consciousness of the pleasantness I call Aesthesis; but the exulting, reverent, and grateful perception of it I call Theoria', *Works*, 4, p. 47; quoted in Shrimpton [note 53], p. 141.

95 *Works*, 4, p. 35.

96 As note 92.

97 *Works*, 9, p. 240.

98 For example, on the letters pages of the *Building News*, 23 (1872), pp. 210-11, under the heading 'Leicester', a correspondent identified only as 'H', writing in response to Godwin's article the previous week, the fifth in his series 'Modern Architects and their Works', *Building News*, 23 (1872), p. 187, criticised Godwin's neglect of 'ease, comfort, mere arrangement and convenience' in his designs and until 'this "art-architect" shall pay greater respect to arrangement internal fitness of things' he was unlikely to enjoy much success in architectural competitions.

99 See, for example, *Building News*'s description (23 (1872), p. 76) of the competition entries for Holloway's Sanatorium at St Ann's Heath, Surrey. Of Godwin's design '*Mens*', the journal's critic says bluntly: 'The plan shows that the designer has not studied the requirements of a lunatic asylum'.

100 *Works*, 10, pp. 264-5.

101 *Works*, 8, pp. 89ff.

102 Ibid., p. 100.

103 *Works*, 9, p. 241.

104 *Building World*, 1/9 (1877), pp. 402-4; *Building World* was a short-lived publication of which Godwin's friend J. P. Seddon was art editor.

105 *British Architect*, 22 (1884), pp. 302-3.

106 *Works*, 8, p. 253.

107 E.W. Godwin, 'The ex-Classic style called "Queen Anne"', *Building News*, 27 (1875), p. 441.

[108] See for example, 'Curiosities of Architecture, *Architect*, 14 (1875), pp. 30-31; 'Old English or Saxon Building', *Architect*, 14 (1875), pp. 70-1; 'Lintel Architecture', *Architect*, 16 (1876), p. 157 – I think this last also reflects Godwin's reading of Alexander 'Greek' Thomson's Haldane lectures which were published in the *Building News* in 1874. Godwin had written approvingly of Thomson's architectural designs; and 'Odds and Ends About Construction', *Architect*, 16 (1876), pp. 225-6, 248-9.

[109] As note 66.

[110] Oscar Wilde, 'The Grosvenor Gallery', *Dublin University Magazine*, 90 (1877), p. 126, quoted in Shrimpton [note 53], p. 141.

[111] *Works*, 16, p. 347.

[112] *Works*, 9, p. 62.

[113] 'The "Daily News" versus Art' [note 87].

10

John Dando Sedding and Sculpture in Architecture: The Fulfilment of a Ruskinian Ideal?

John Dando Sedding and Sculpture in Architecture.

John Dando Sedding and Sculpture in Architecture: The Fulfilment of a Ruskinian Ideal?

Paul Snell

> 'Always have pencil or chisel in your own hand' –
> Ruskin to Sedding, 1876.[1]

OFTEN QUOTED, but as yet unexplored, the grappling of pencil and chisel was the fundamental message in a letter from Ruskin to the young John Dando Sedding (1838-91). Sedding remains a neglected figure of late Victorian art and architecture, known as the designer of the church of Holy Trinity, Sloane Street (1888-91) and little else. Studies on Arts and Crafts architecture mention him, but concentrate on other 'more representative' figures such as Webb and Lethaby.[2] The chronological development of his career has a sketch-like quality, and remarkably the most detailed descriptions of the Sedding office remain the memorial papers presented by his pupils after his sudden death, virtually hagiographic essays, now over a century old.[3] Thus, not surprisingly, the relationship between Ruskin and Sedding has remained largely untold.

One of the few attempts to redress this imbalance has been by Michael Brooks in *John Ruskin and Victorian Architecture* (1989) where he described Sedding as 'one of Ruskin's warmest admirers'.[4] Brooks identified Sedding as one of a group of architects who re-evaluated Ruskin in the 1870s and 1880s, at a crucial juncture in Victorian architecture. The outcome, Brooks argues, was a 'New Ruskinism', a selective approach to Ruskin's many architectural ideals. According to Brooks, by the 1870s Sedding had spurned Ruskin's idea that the glory of architecture lay in sculpture and painting, and instead focused on the primacy of building.[5] Sedding found himself in a radical camp, a band of architects and artists who stressed the importance of the method and personnel involved in building, not just design.

Non-archaeological Gothic. Detail of parclose screen door, St John the Baptist, Axbridge, displaying the monogram of St John, surrounded by foliate tracery and local fauna (*Paul Snell*).

Significantly, from this small group the Arts and Crafts Movement would evolve.

However, Brooks analysed Sedding's literary output, not his executed works. Consequently, the extent of Ruskin's influence in the projects undertaken by Sedding in this period remains unclear. In particular, his approach to sculpture in architecture needs analysis, for confusingly, despite reassessment and 'New Ruskinism', many of these later works appear to concentrate on a sculptural treatment, expressed in masonry and furnishings. Therefore, combining the literary and the built, this chapter aims to elucidate themes in Sedding's career and late Victorian architecture, focusing upon sculpture in architecture to assess the extent to which Sedding's career was a fulfilment of Ruskinian ideals.

Of course, the building boom of the mid-Victorian period saw the use, if not over-use, of both pencils and chisels. Restraint was abandoned in favour of the enthusiastic use of sculptural decoration. This was especially the case in ecclesiastical buildings, where sculpture was used to communicate symbolic ideology and differentiate parts of a building. The costly work heralded the munificence of the patron and parish fund-raising. Appropriately, the Gothic was perceived as a style that encouraged sculpture to be incorporated into the fabric, enabling the opportunity for sculptural decoration all the way through the structure. Sculptural treatment could emphasise structural points or nodes, the capitals, mouldings and vaults; otherwise blank surfaces could be embellished in a myriad of forms; and highly-worked fittings and furnishings could complete schemes, the sculptural decoration of pews, pulpits, and screens demanding the architect's attention. Sculpture could be produced in a multitude of materials – stone, wood and metalwork - and so it could be employed throughout a structure, making a greater impact. This enabled architecture to be more eloquent in communicating morals, a principal role of architecture voiced by Ruskin in *The Seven Lamps of Architecture* and *The Stones of Venice*. Indeed, in the preface to the second edition of *The Seven Lamps* (1855), he bolstered the position of sculpture in architecture, arguing that the role of the architect was to become a sculptor, and that without sculptural treatment a building remained just that, a lowly building, not architecture:

> Little by little, it gradually became manifest to me that the sculpture and painting were, in fact, the all in all of the thing to be done; that these, which I had long been in the careless habit of thinking subordinate to the architecture, were in fact the entire masters of the architecture; and the architect who was not a sculptor or a painter, was nothing better than a frame-maker on a large scale ... The fact is that there are only two fine arts possible to the human race, sculpture and painting. What we call architecture is only the association of these in noble masses, or the placing of them in fit places. All architecture other than this is, in fact, mere building.[6]

Not surprisingly, sculpture, being so championed by Ruskin and others, featured prominently in architectural schemes, whether in new commissions or as additions to pre-existing buildings, though perhaps not as Ruskin prescribed. For example, statues re-populated the many restored medieval buildings, niches re-filled after centuries of absence owing to the politics of iconoclasm. Indeed, with such a demand, craftsmen began to come to national prominence, with certain architects employing particular masons throughout their careers, such as Street and Thomas Earp. Commercially successful decorative art firms were founded, such as Farmer and Brindley, and Harry Hems of Exeter. Of the many large sculptural schemes, the most significant was George Gilbert Scott's Albert Memorial, the mid-Victorian epitome of sculpture combined with architecture.

However, if the Gothic Revival encouraged sculpture, it was not without controversy. A concern to Ruskin was the very method of sculptural production. As Hanson discusses in chapter 4, Ruskin regarded the Gothic Revivalist's product as too 'pure'. By 1859, he was disillusioned with contemporary Gothic Revival sculpture, as outlined in his publication of *The Two Paths*. Ruskin mocked the architectural profession, characterising them in the preface as saying: 'learn to carve or paint organic form ourselves! How can such a thing be asked? We are above that. The carvers and painters are our servants — quite subordinate people. They ought to be glad if we leave room for the..'[7] In the lectures contained within *The Two Paths*, Ruskin called for the unity of the arts, rejecting the division of architecture and sculpture. He reiterated his advice that architects should become directly involved in the production of their buildings, that they should 'carve but few and simple parts of it'.[8] This would result in a reappraisal of the division of labour, raising craftsmen to fellow designers with a correspondence of power. The end-product would be a building that had 'soul', rather than yet another mere caricature of Gothic or Romanesque. But the message was rebuffed, and the failure of the Oxford Museum, the project with which he was most personally involved, exasperated Ruskin. Ironically, the closest attempt to create Ruskinian sculptural architecture, inspired by nature and medieval models of production, was abandoned. The Oxford Museum would remain an unfinished experiment, isolated from the working methods of mid-Victorian architects, just like its master's message.

Gradually Ruskin's disillusionment spread, and some contemporaries began to bemoan the subservient nature of sculpture to architecture. The *British Architect* in 1874 stated that sculpture was 'forsaken by her Sisters and rejected by the Utilitarian world ... faltering and fainting in the cruel isolation of Neglect'.[9] Architects were still failing to co-operate with the sculptor, it was argued, and, if they did, they continued to work with the mentality that sculpture was but 'common architectural ornament'. In such a context, voiced the *British Architect*, it was not surprising that there were so few able sculptors in England. This subservient nature was also witnessed in the heavy-handed nature of the 'restorations' executed in the period, which further incensed Ruskin. Destruction rather than preservation too often occurred, the subtleties of centuries of weathering upon the texture of walls and sculpture literally scraped away. Not surprisingly, William Morris's rallying cry of the Society for the Protection of Ancient Buildings (SPAB) was 'Anti-Scrape'. SPAB opposed the insensitive, blunt and brutal treatment of sculpture, and the imposition of anachronistic foreign forms. Consequently, many campaigns were waged against destructive 'restorers', such as Scott, ironically one of the few architects who had responded to Ruskin and worked closely with craftsmen.[10] However, the SPAB's efforts, commenced in the late 1870s, came too late for Ruskin. By then sculpture's champion had long changed his focus, abandoning discussion of aesthetics for political economy. Significantly, this revised message would help to inspire a new generation of architects, including the young John Dando Sedding.

Sedding and his elder brother, Edmund, entered the office of G. E. Street in 1858, exposing them to the full brilliance of the Gothic Revival. During this period, Street commanded one of the leading Gothic Revival architectural practices, his reputation made by his daring church designs. These, like St James the Less, Westminster, were characterised by exotic, Continental muscular forms and a bold use of sculpture, work inspired by a reading of Ruskin. Street's office attracted brilliance and facilitated contacts amongst many of the most prominent architects and designers of the next generation, notably Webb and Morris. Yet despite this stimulating environment, the tutelage supposedly was full of friction, no doubt because of Street's controlling approach to design.[11] By the early 1860s, the brothers had left the office to start their own practice in Cornwall. The new practice, however, gained few commissions, and they were employed mostly in restoration work. After the sudden death of Edmund, John Dando moved to Bristol in 1868, hoping to secure more lucrative contracts, but he struggled to attract patrons. His most significant work was the result of family contacts; for example the remarkable commission at Boscombe, Bournemouth (1871-3), of church, rectory and school.[12] No significant commission was secured in Bristol itself, and undoubtedly due to this paucity of patronage, Sedding moved to London, basing himself in Bloomsbury in 1874. Unfortunately, the move did not engender a sudden change of fortune, for his commissions remained restorations or minor decorative arts schemes. Sculptural additions were many, notably reredoses, usually executed by G. W. Seale, a sculptor employed by Sedding throughout his career and, despite a Metropolitan base, these projects were predominantly restricted to the West Country.

However, around 1876, during this fallow phase, Sedding met Ruskin.[13] Despite the brief nature of their surviving correspondence, it can be argued that this contact with Ruskin was a major inspiration to Sedding's subsequent development. An affinity to Ruskinian principles had begun long before this, Sedding copying the plates from *The Seven Lamps* at an early age.[14] Indeed, his earliest published paper, 'Notes on St Buryan Church' (1869),[15] emphasised this loyalty by focusing his readers first on a quote from Ruskin: 'The glory of a building is in its age, and in that deep sense of voicefulness, of stern watching, of mysterious sympathy, nay, even of approval or condemnation which we feel in walls that have long been washed by the waves of humanity'.[16] This concurred with the tenor of his text on this 'quiet, obscure Cornish village church' and its neighbours, St Sennen and Sancreed, modest apart from their magnificent screens. Sedding pronounced that they were 'in the shade, yet shining,' for the churches demonstrated the spirit that guided the efforts of the medieval workman, the screens' details being 'all carved from the carver's brain'.[17] Of course, the qualities so admired were those that had been championed in *The Stones of Venice*, especially in the pivotal chapter, 'The Nature of the Gothic', qualities that would be questioned and developed as Sedding's career evolved.

Subsequently, in his many papers published in the architectural press, Sedding would often refer to 'Our dear friend, Mr. Ruskin'.[18] and it was Ruskin's criteria of architectural analysis that he regularly employed, even when the subject of the paper was one which Ruskin himself would find contentious. For example, in his appraisal of 'The Architecture of the Perpendicular Period' (1881), he appraised later English Gothic, consciously using Ruskinian analysis. Sedding resorted to Ruskin's two 'media of imagination' used for expression in architecture, namely the disposition of lines, mouldings, and masses in agreeable proportions, and sculpture.[19] Of course, in so doing, he was attempting to promote the Perpendicular, an architecture that had aroused animosity from architects, theoreticians and religious thinkers, Ruskin included. Nevertheless, he resorted to Ruskinian concepts to prove that the whole art-power of medieval England was achieved in the Perpendicular period, and it was Ruskinian principles that he would continue to return to throughout his theoretical papers, ideas that he thought were an essential part of the young architect's training. So in 1883 he offered advice to his fellow architects on architectural education, and voiced: 'let him read his Ruskin'.[20] After all, according to Sedding, Ruskin had played a crucial role in the Gothic Revival, as can be understood by a reading of Sedding's later paper 'The Relations of the Handicrafts to Architecture' (1887). Here Ruskin was named 'the Voltaire' of the Gothic Revival, 'the writer who with his pen shook down the whole fabric of tradition by appealing to the individual's own sense of beauty', in his role in rejecting the decrepit handicrafts of the age. Thus, despite differences of stylistic taste, there was a continuing adherence to Ruskinian principles. It was Ruskin who had first appealed to Sedding's own sense of beauty, and it was he that was to inspire the younger architect throughout his career.

Significantly, Sedding, for most of his career, would concur with Ruskin that the glory of architecture lay in painting and sculpture, as can be understood by an evaluation of Sedding's oeuvre and surviving documentation. Indeed this was the focus of Ruskin's surviving letter to Sedding, dated 1876. The object of the letter appears to be the art of drawing with Sedding apparently submitting examples to Ruskin, perhaps for a while being tutored in this art.[21] However, this was but the starting point for a letter that would evaluate contemporary architecture, the practice of architects, and deal with the whole nature of production. Ruskin's advice to Sedding developed themes already mentioned in works previously, notably *The Two Paths*. The crucial passage was: 'Modern so-called architects are merely employers of workmen on commission – and if you would be a real architect, you must always have pencil or chisel in your own hand.'[22]

To Ruskin the pencil and chisel played different roles in the architect's practice. Sensitivity to the complexity and subtlety of architectural forms could only be developed from meticulous study. By study, Ruskin meant drawing, the control of the pencil. In the letter he encouraged Sedding to sketch, to use pen and sepia, to empower his studies with close attention to light, shade and texture. The conventional drawing style of the architect, linear and flat, was rejected as lifeless. Instead the architect should look to nature for inspiration, incorporating its elements in working drawings, and study past masters, such as Holbein. Of course Ruskin's drawings and watercolours concentrated on just this, the plates of his many publications still celebrated for the acuity of observation, the delicacy of colour, the subtlety of their shading. After 1876, Sedding's surviving drawings and sketchbooks reveal an increasing concentration on nature and light and shade, often employing watercolour to convey realism to his studies.[23] Significantly many of these studies concentrated on sculptural features, either analysing existing examples in the many study tours that Sedding undertook, or of course communicating the form of designs for patrons and workmen alike.

With the chisel, Ruskin argued that the architect's role should change, corresponding with a growing proximity to the components of architecture, the raw materials of building. Closer observation should be matched with a closer relationship with the materials; the architect must choose and manipulate these himself. The 'modern' architect was depicted as dictatorial, removed from the practical work both geographically and socially. The ambitious professional architect was drawn to London, enabling easy access to a wealth of clients, the institutions and associations discussing the latest architectural developments, and the journals that could further reputations in their reviews of current buildings and debates.[24] This 19th-century architect was far removed from the concept of his medieval forebears, the wandering mason, designing on site, the team-worker, and expert in both fashions and mechanical work. Protected by his reputation and office, the 'modern' architect was no longer a craftsman or artist, challenged by the laborious nature of his task. The sacrificial 'truth' of work had been rejected for professional exams, institutional membership and a West End office. These 'modern' developments, rather than ennobling the architect and his work, had only led to the detriment of both profession and product. Ruskin's remedy was skilled manual work, a close collaboration between architect and workmen on site, symbolised by the architect grasping the chisel, and best expressed by sculpture integrated in the design.

It is unknown if the correspondence continued after 1876. No other letters appear to survive, and, of course, these were the years when Ruskin's correspondence was temporarily halted, owing to his nervous breakdown. Nevertheless, Ruskin's teaching, brief though it was, would make a significant impact on Sedding's understanding of architecture. In 1881, after a five-year gap, Sedding reiterated Ruskin's advice twice in published papers. First, in an article published in the *Transactions of the St Paul's Ecclesiological Society*, he outlined Ruskin's teaching:

> The gist of his teaching is that architects should be more than mere proportionalists, more than mere numerators and denominators, who can show that one is to two as three is to six, that they should be carvers and painters who watch the external forms of Nature, who can tell facts about Nature, bring out sympathy, share in the feelings of all living creatures, tell tales to amuse men, and to raise the human spirit's aspirations.[25]

Certainly, the letter's message had been understood, but that was not all. In the paper, Sedding sought the origins of the epistle's instructions, locating this in Ruskin's lecture called 'Influence of the Imagination in Architecture'. He directed his readers to it, stressing that he thought Ruskin had never written 'more truthfully or helpfully'. His allegiance had been asserted.[26] More significantly, the centrality of the letter is proven in the succinct leading article in the *British Architect*, entitled 'Architecture Old and New'.[27] Here Sedding actually began his article referring to the letter, directly quoting the crucial pencil and chisel section. Although strangely vague as to the date of the letter, he carefully analysed the message and its implications for his readers:

> Mr Ruskin is not without his disciples among the architects of the present day; but to the majority of us, such words are the words of a visionary who holds up an impossible standard of perfection, not knowing the requirements and conditions of the age in which we live.

> Yet I venture to think the theory that underlies Mr Ruskin's ruling in this matter is unassailable, whether practical or not ... The 'real' architect of a building is something different to the distant dictator who uses the agency of post and telegram to communicate his wishes, who draws the plans, writes the specification, and looks in occasionally at the works in progress. He must be his own clerk of works, his own carver, his own decorator; he must be the familiar spirit of the structure as it rises from the ground.

Sedding's argument was clear; despite its inherent difficulties, Ruskin's concept of the craft-architect was the only solution to the malaise of late-Victorian art and architecture. The shams and affectations of the many revivals of the period, spin-offs of 'the whirligig of fashion', as he described contemporary architecture, could be replaced with homogeneous productions, individual in character. The 'real' architect would produce 'real' buildings, with a sense of actuality, because 'building and site would be more intimately allied in the architect's brain'.[28] Subsequently, this same letter would be quoted and referred to in his pupils' eulogies, preserved for posterity, surely suggesting the centrality of its teaching not only to Sedding but also his many pupils.

Ruskin's message had been comprehended and endorsed, but the gist of Ruskin's teaching was not merely reiterated in papers. Rather, the themes of the craft-architect and the return to handicrafts, would dominate the work of Sedding for the rest of his career, resonating in his late oeuvre and, significantly, developed to the full in the last products to emerge from the Sedding office. For in the 1880s fortune's wheel shifted and with his appointment as Diocesan Architect for Bath and Wells suddenly commissions flooded into the practice with at least thirty in Somerset.[29] In addition, at long last he gained the rich, ambitious patrons who enabled him to realise his design ethos through a number of costly and complex schemes.

Furthermore, it was in the 1880s that a cohort of like-minded artists and architects grouped together to form art guilds, the most significant being the Art Workers' Guild, of which Sedding was the second Master in 1886-7. Here was the opportunity to share ideas, to inspire others and, significantly, to collaborate with other artists of the first rank. Thus the late works are many, and very often magnificent, due to a munificence of funding and inspired collaboration. Central to many of these schemes is a play of sculpture in architecture as a means to attain expression, and a focus upon this can engender an understanding of the relationship of Sedding to Ruskin, and his shifting ideas on later Victorian art and architecture. Five projects in particular, all ecclesiastical, illustrate this relationship, namely All Saints, Holbeton, Devon; St John the Baptist, Axbridge, Somerset; Holy Redeemer, Clerkenwell; Holy Trinity, Sloane Street, Chelsea; and St Peter and St Paul, Ermington, Devon. As surviving documentation for these particular schemes is limited, it is best to explore them in conjunction with contemporary papers by Sedding.

The first significant sculptural commission for consideration is that at All Saints, Holbeton, a restoration commission paid for by the lord of the manor, H. B. Mildmay of Flete. Richard Norman Shaw's work on this house is well known, and it was probably through the recommendation of his friend Shaw that Sedding gained this lucrative commission.[30] The church, nestling into the hill above this small Devon village, is largely a simple late-medieval building, constructed in rough granite. It can be regarded as typical of the West Country church. The exterior is plain without sculptural decoration or elaboration, long and low, apart from its western tower and spire. Conversely, the interior is extremely rich, with highly worked woodwork and furnishings throughout. In 1884, however, this was not the case, for only fragments of the late-medieval furnishings survived. Sedding's restoration, inspired by local medieval models, transformed the building by 1889 into one of the richest compositions of its date, and, it could be argued, created one of the most convincing contemporary reconstructions of a late-medieval church.

On entering the church one is immediately struck by the sheer mass of woodcarving. Every surface is alive with detail – a medieval manuscript in carved form. In such a restless interior the imagination could run riot, conjuring up insect

African or Indian? An elephant hiding in decorative carpentry. Detail of a pew back rail, All Saints, Holbeton, Devon (*Paul Snell*).

forms creeping out of spurts of vegetative growth. The pew ends, all individually carved and featuring a menagerie of creatures, would demand more attention were it not for the darkened interior and the attention-grabbing screen, stretching across both choir and aisles. The remnants of the early-Tudor screen, the product of an itinerant gang of 16th-century Flemish carpenters according to Sedding, with its mixture of foreign and local characteristics, were the starting points for the reconstruction, a design that bristles with detail.[31] The detail of the carving is outstanding, the pierced work immensely delicate, and it takes a keen eye to discern where the medieval stops and the Victorian begins. A detailed contemporary description is lacking, but Sedding's appraisal of the late-medieval screen of St Levan church, Cornwall, perhaps best describes the qualities attained in the work:

> The very beads of the mouldings, such as modern man would run in a machine and have done with them, are twisted and enriched, the stiles themselves are covered in snakes and cordage, intersecting with foliage in the true Celtic manner; long canopies, exquisitely carved, adorn the heads of the panels, the panels are enriched with shields, monograms, the instruments of the Passion and other devices, and at the bases are birds, beasts and portraits of men and women.[32]

More waits in the sanctuary. The choir stalls are replete with imagery; green men hide amidst the panoply of feral

Simple realism and incredible detail – a swan as an elbow rest, on the chancel stalls, Holbeton, executed by Sedding's Italian craftsmen (*Paul Snell*).

An artist in his way – the south porch door, Holbeton. Attention to detail resulting from the architect holding both pencil and chisel (*Geoff Brandwood*).

forms, ranging from squid to squirrels; birds nest in tracery niches, distractions aplenty from divine worship. Most notable are the pew ends, embellished with the evangelists and their books, a swan and even a monkey eating a banana. Here the simple realism and attention to detail is incredible, with the individual filaments of the swan's feathers, or gospel words picked out. Enrichment above echoes the stalls below, with the wagon roof busy with bosses brazen with gold, devils accompanying the angel choir, and completed by the exquisite marble altar frontal, framed with beaten silver floral forms. The diversity of the bestial and botanical gathered here could well be a response to Darwinism, and the obsession with nature of many contemporaries. The myriad of forms could be interpreted as mustering together to glorify the divine Creator. They could also be understood as a demonstration of the detailed natural history knowledge of their earthly creators, stimulated by readings of Darwin and Wallace.[33]

Returning again outside, the simple, almost rude, country church jars with the finesse of the interior. Perhaps to prepare the visitor for this, probably in 1886, Sedding deliberately designed the doors to mediate between the external simplicity and internal complexity.[34] The silvery, weather-worn doors act as precursors, picking up themes encountered within. The south porch door has Renaissance details, its criss-cross of timbers embellished with metal work, repetitive roundels of the sacred monogram, contrasted to the miniscule, animated angel orchestra, each individually designed. The west door is simpler, with a deeply cut, arched band depicting a hedgerow scene, hounds chasing a fox, pheasant and rabbits. Indeed, surprisingly, it is the doors that offer us the best explanation for the delights of the interior, for it appears that they were the first-recorded instance of Sedding as craft-architect, taking up Ruskin's chisel. Thus it is reported: '"You must write on my gravestone", he said shortly before his death, "He made the doors at Holbeton, and was an artist in his way."'[35] Surely, it can be surmised, that if the doors are the direct product of Sedding, so too is much of the interior woodwork. This theory would help justify the astronomic cost and slow progress of the restoration: the attention to detail was the result of the architect directly supervising the work, even to the extent that he himself undertook the manual work.[36] Such a move was remarkable in the context of late-Victorian architecture, but accords with Sedding's contemporary argument, that architects and their pupils should become familiar with the insides of workshops, 'possibly to turn architect-builders themselves'.[37] The professional architect in Sedding, it could be argued, began to be eschewed at Holbeton *and* the Ruskinian ideal began to be realised. But was this but one instance, a solitary swallow merely suggesting a summer?

Similar themes were pursued with work undertaken at St John the Baptist, Axbridge. The church, a glorious late-medieval building, renowned for its Jacobean nave ceiling, was in an appalling state in the late 1870s when Sedding began to restore it.[38] The costs were high, the fund-raising slow, and so urgent work making the building weather-tight took precedence in a restoration campaign that stretched over 12 years. In 1886 the fittings of the chancel finally began to be executed,[39] and with these Sedding again picked up on Ruskinian themes. Here the stalls are far less elaborate than those at Holbeton, characterised by horizontal linen folds and well-worked pew ends, enlivened with poppy heads. The work takes on a more solid nature, balanced perhaps by the mouldings of the masonry, the delicate late-Perpendicular roofs and the fine window tracery.

Massive in construction, yet graced with delicacy - general view of the parclose screens, St John the Baptist, Axbridge, completed c.1888 (Paul Snell).

This contrast of predominant solidity with occasional detail is best seen in the parclose screens, massive in their construction yet graced with delicacy of detail. And it is the screens that most suggest Sedding looking to Ruskin, sourcing nature in his attempt to produce an architecture that was modern, not a mere archaeological copy. Ruskin had, of course, bemoaned the 'dead' design emanating from the schools and museums, the tedious, repetitive products of 'South Kensington', and Sedding echoed him. In his paper 'Design' presented in 1888, contemporaneous to the work at Axbridge, he developed this further:

> We can do splendidly what we set ourselves to do – namely to mimic old masterpieces. The question is what next? Shall we continue to hunt old trails, and die, not leaving the world richer than we found it? Or shall we for art and honour's sake boldly adventure something – drop this wearisome translation of old styles and translate nature instead?[40]

The Axbridge screens can be interpreted as just such an adventurous attempt, transposing natural forms directly into architecture, dispensing with an architectural vocabulary overused and abused, and the quality of the carving suggests close personal supervision by Sedding himself, or perhaps the architect again personally creating the work.[41]

These screens are Gothic in spirit; Perpendicular tracery is retained as the skeleton of the work, but the other forms employed are original. Birds nest in pinnacle peaks, their plump, feathered forms featuring as finial crockets, and curved pendants fill the tracery panels, sinuous and voluptuous, almost Art Nouveau. Most impressive are the aisle doors, their deep-sunk panels arched with wandering briars, cusped with thorns, over-laid and entwined so as to create an organic tracery, delicate in comparison to the heavy pegged oak. This contrast is continued in the cornice: deep undercutting and the many layers of frieze-work are dispensed with; instead inter-twined letters puzzle the eye, interspersed with lozenges decorated with vernacular animal and plant life. Bats, hedgehogs and frogs inhabit the frieze, and where the cornice meets the stone mouldings of the piers, leaves and fronds curl around the stone, together expressing the organic growth emanating from the work. Thus, the Axbridge screens appear to fulfill Sedding's animated advice to the designer, to take:

> a stroll in the embroidered garden, a dip into an old herbal, a few carefully-drawn cribs from Curtis's *Botanical Magazine*, or even – for lack of something better– Sutton's last *Illustrated Catalogue*, is wholesome exercise, and will do more to revive the original instincts of a true designer than a month of sixpenny days at a stuffy museum.[42]

CHURCH OF THE HOLY REDEEMER ✠ CLERKENWELL

Archaeological Gothic had begun to be dispensed with; the screens are no product of a stuffy museum study, but develop themes seen at Holbeton, conforming to Ruskin's demand that a new school of English architecture would incorporate into the fabric sculpture that was inspired by the 'birds and flowers which are singing and budding in the fields around them'.[43]

Contemporary with Axbridge were the better-known commissions for the churches of the Holy Redeemer, Clerkenwell and Holy Trinity, Sloane Street. For these two churches Sedding had vastly different budgets, but he employed similar principles, for both concentrated on the development of new architectural models and forms, using collaborative design and production. Again, this is best understood by a study of the sculpture incorporated into the designs. At Clerkenwell, Sedding's budget was extremely restricted; a large, functional building was demanded on a difficult site.[44] The design solution was a church based on a combination of Renaissance and Wrenian precedent, with, perhaps, Romanesque elements employed.[45] The Wren influence is obvious, and must have been to Sedding, Clerkenwell being in close proximity to some of Wren's most accomplished churches, classical compositions he admired for their 'expressive planning and construction'.[46] The Romanesque is less so, due to over-zealous redecoration and the incomplete nature of the scheme; the lively polychromatic treatment of the walls and columns, with marble bands animating the otherwise ordered space, inspired by Tuscan Romanesque churches, has now been whitewashed. The murals intended for the altar wall appear never to have been executed.[47] Consequently, Wilson's later, multi-tiered, Romanesque campanile now seems incongruous in relation to the interior.

This hypothesis is borne out by a study of the capitals, in what appears to be a Renaissance arcade and the ciborium. Designed conceptually by Sedding, they were executed by Frederick W. Pomeroy, one of the leading exponents of the 'New Sculpture'. Keen to raise the profile of sculpture, and the recognition of the sculptor, Pomeroy too denounced the state of modern sculpture. In his 1891 lecture at the Art Workers' Guild on the relationship of sculpture and architecture, he stated:

Opposite: unfulfilled opulence – Holy Trinity, Clerkenwell, Gerald Horsley's drawing of the projected interior decoration. Worship would have been inspired by a wealth of sculpture and painting, accelerating in complexity around the ciborium (Builder 52 (1887), pp. 672-3).

in the future it is in the highest degree desirable that he, the architect, should endeavour to carefully select his sculptor and give him a fairly free hand in carrying out his work, for there is a chilly monotony that runs through modern foliage ornament.⁴⁸

Of course, it could be argued that Pomeroy was preaching to the converted. Significantly, the work at Clerkenwell predates this: the perceived monotony of the modern was rejected at the chucrh of Holy Redeemer in 1888. Pomeroy's capitals, individually treated, symbolise the recognition of the individual artist. The generator of the design is the architect, but the sculptor is the author of the finished product. These capitals, accompanying the banding, enliven the scheme, fulfilling Sedding's observation that 'In all living art the workman's capital is not merely in rules and principles, but in himself'.⁴⁹ As a result, the Clerkenwell interior could be read as a re-interpretation or translation of Romanesque models, perhaps even a 19th-century attempt to recreate Ruskin's beloved basilica at Torcello. It fulfils Ruskin's demand for variety, as explored in his close analysis of the Torcello capitals, in *The Stones of Venice*, and expressed in his belief that: 'change or variety is as much a necessity to the human heart and brain in buildings as books; that there is no merit, though there is some occasional use, in monotony'.⁵⁰

At Clerkenwell, Sedding, with Pomeroy, had proved that an Anglican church did not have to replicate medieval Gothic models. This was its obvious achievement, but what was also significant was the further consideration of the artistic process, questioning the role of sculpture and architecture. Sculpture here was an integral part of the building, not an afterthought, and thus reconsidered the relation between designer and sculptor, playing an essential role, endowing the building with both cohesive order and variety. Consequently, it rejected the 'fatal notion that art is a thing to be applied'.[51] that sculpture, for example, was a commodity or adjunct to architecture, a concern voiced by both Sedding and Ruskin. Rather it allowed a building to be the product of personalities, not one controlling mind, fulfilling Sedding's vision of 'design *by* living men *for* living men'.[52] Sedding and Pomeroy's angelic choir, inhabiting the ciborium and nave capitals, could be understood as a celebration of both the Eucharist and collaborative architecture.

The working relationship of Sedding and Pomeroy was further cemented at Holy Trinity, Sloane Street. Unlike Clerkenwell, Holy Trinity, owing to the lavish patronage of the Earl of Cadogan and the parishioners, was planned to be a celebration of *sculptors* in architecture.[53] Pomeroy was joined by his rivals in the execution of the building that would become known as the 'Cathedral of the Arts and Crafts Movement'.[54] The plans were astonishing, as borne out in the highly finished drawings published in contemporary architectural periodicals, drawings that delighted in the sculptural treatment.[55] The church would incorporate work by some of the most celebrated sculptors of the period, many of whom had been involved in architectural sculpture previously, but never before had so many worked together on one project.[56] The building was to be crowded with sculpture, a complex iconographical scheme stretching across all parts of the fabric. Of course, the furnishings would be splendid with Alfred Gilbert working the pulpit panels, Harry Bates the altar frontal, Pomeroy the screen and stall figures, and Sedding himself, with Henry Longden, working the chancel gates. But the sculptural embellishment was not to stop there, for the nave spandrels were to be carved by Armstead and the

Opposite:
Holy Redeemer, Clerkenwell. Pairs of capitals mirror each other along the nave, populated with an angelic orchestra, or angels bearing symbols of the Passion, culminating in the compostion of the ciborium (*Paul Snell*).

nave piers populated with the Apostles, executed by Hamo Thornycroft and with accompanying murals by Burne-Jones. Had the scheme been completed as intended, the interior would have been the *tour de force* of late Victorian sculpture, the pantheon of the 'New Sculpture'. Instead, the work, unfinished at Sedding's death, was subject to later additions and rationalising, such as Wilson's screens to the Lady Chapel and Eden's altogther less sensitive whitewashing of the interior. The end product is rightly celebrated for the outstanding quality of individual elements, but perhaps, owing to the incomplete architectural sculpture and painting, failed to create a unified interior.

Holy Trinity, Sloane Street could be seen as the culmination of collaborative architecture, the fulfilment of a Ruskinian ideal, and it is with this church that studies of Sedding usually end.

However, other late projects, developments on the periphery and largely unknown, also demand analysis. These schemes suggest that Sedding continued to question the role of sculpture in architecture, especially the significance of its production. Returning to the West Country, the restoration of St Peter and St Paul, Ermington, Devon (1889), again under the patronage of H. B. Mildmay of Flete, allowed a further exploration of collaborative architecture. The emphasis was on a vernacular sculpture, produced by members of the parish. Near Holbeton, this large medieval church was fortunate in the provision of sufficient funds from Mildmay to allow a thorough, yet sensitive restoration, that included work on the church roofs, patching up the walls, re-glazing all the windows, reseating throughout, and re-hanging the bells.[57] The church was also fortunate in its leadership, for the Rev. E. Pinwill would make a significant contribution to the refurnishing of the church, but not of a pecuniary nature. Pinwill had a large family of seven daughters, and they, with Sedding, would be personally involved in the church restoration which attempted to recreate a medieval church in spirit as well as style.

An apparent quality of medieval work, according to Sedding, was that architecture was the product of a locality. The papers he read to various art guilds and architectural societies stressed the inclusive nature of building in previous periods.[58] Developing his argument against the concept of the applied arts, medieval sculpture, whether in wood or stone, was described as 'decorative masonry' and 'decorative carpentry', and was celebrated for this.[59] Perhaps the work was less refined, but the building took on a coherency, and crucially reflected the locality. Here was a vernacular architecture, which expressed Ruskinian 'Sacrifice' and 'Truth'. In his paper entitled 'The Handicrafts in Old Days' (1890), Sedding analysed examples of medieval craft (not surprisingly many of them being of West Country derivation), appraising their sculptural qualities. One comment is particularly salient:

> Work of this class, found even in an obscure little church, bears out my remark, both as to the unstinted labour of old days and its all-round excellence, and it supports my assertion that the work is of local origin. It is not only local, it is parochial.[60]

At Ermington, the work conformed to these criteria. The church, like Holbeton, is most memorable for its woodwork. Unlike Holbeton, its 'decorative carpentry' was the product

Opposite: a celebration of sculptors in architecture - Holy Trinity, Sloane Street. Horsley's drawing reveals Sedding's intention to create an iconographically complex interior that also celebrated collaborative architecture. Unfortunately, only the chancel bays would receive part of this intended treatment (Builder, 55 (1888), pp. 253-4).

not just of Sedding and his workmen, but also the Pinwills. The chancel stalls and restored screen are obviously Sedding's, indeed they bear remarkable similarity to the contemporary work at nearby Holy Trinity, Salcombe (1889). However, the heavily-worked pulpit was the first of many pieces designed and produced by the Pinwill sisters. Tutored by Sedding's craftsmen, as a remarkable photo shows, with this piece they embarked upon a career in woodcarving that was to stretch well into the 20th century.[61] Their pulpit is crowded with detail: its restless quality betrays a lack of restraint and the obvious naivety of its designers and makers. Significantly, the architectural features and line, as found elsewhere in the Sedding oeuvre, do not contain the details, they intrude, overlap and distract. Craft here takes precedence, rather than architecture, and the result being more is less. Yet, as Sedding stressed, 'There is hope in honest error: none of the icy perfections of the mere stylist', and the work engages the viewer for its originality, especially the portraits of the three sisters, repeated at the base of the three panels.[62] This is a very personal work, a work peculiar to its location. Indeed, it is all the more remarkable for being the product of young females, and the authorship being so obvious in this context. This was the beginning of a vast body of work, the sisters being employed in projects across the West Country, notably in other Sedding restorations and refurbishments, and commissions for E. H. Sedding, John Dando's nephew, following in his uncle's footsteps.[63] One of the few contemporary instances of women being directly involved in the practical, manual work within architecture, rather than the decoration of a church through embroidery or painting, the work at Ermington was indeed a remarkable development.[64] With parallel work at St Mary, Langridge, near Bath, Sedding can be said to have pioneered 'parochial sculpture' in architecture.[65]

Thus, with sculpture in architecture, in its many forms, Sedding had been given the opportunity to reconsider some of the rudiments of architecture, and reassess Ruskin's concepts of architecture. Obviously, by the time of his death, his work laid a great emphasis on the role of sculpture in architecture. This can be seen in the buildings themselves, as well as his many theoretical papers delivered during the 1880s. Consequently, the role of sculpture in architecture was heightened in Sedding's work, with a greater realism and

Parochial architecture? The Ermington pulpit, purportedly with portraits of three of the Pinwill sisters, Violet, Mary and Rashleigh (*Paul Snell*).

growing variety in sculpture, in both form and materials. Sculpture could be employed throughout a building, in wood as well as stone; indeed, this 'decorative carpentry' increased the opportunity for expression, creating more complex interiors, texts rich with a symbolic vocabulary. Alternative styles, employed and developed in the late work, furthered the creative force of the work and the individuality of commissions. Late Gothic, Renaissance and Romanesque forms had been sourced and utilised, from which evolved the 'Free Gothic', a style that emerged, it could be suggested, largely from experiments in sculpture.

Furthermore, these developments arose from the attempt to fulfill the role of the craft-architect. The architect had been repositioned within the work, changing his role in the design and completion of a commission. Not surprisingly, it was the role of sculptor that was seen as most appropriate, as the work involved refinement befitting the architect's education in its close attention to originality and detail. The craft-architect could now be glorified in design and execution, to use Sedding's phrase, the artist becoming 'priest of form'.[66] Potentially, in this role of both designer and creator, the 'priest of form' could become even more dictatorial. However, in Sedding's later work, perhaps due to the scale of his ambitious decorative and iconographic schemes, instead this led to a developing dialogue between sculptors and architect, whether in the close partnership of Pomeroy and Sedding at Clerkenwell, or a whole team of sculptors at Holy Trinity. Indeed, perhaps even more radical, was an emerging vernacular architecture, a method of production that celebrated local craft and personality, even encouraging design by living women for living women (!),[67] a remarkable development for the age.

Sedding's sudden demise in 1891 at the relatively young age of 52 meant that many of these ideas, still in fledgling form, failed to reach fruition. Certainly, a new school of craft-architects had been set up. The Sedding office has often been called the 'nursery of the Arts and Crafts Movement', yet the many pupils and associates of the Sedding office would tread a different path to their master. The practice continued under Henry Wilson, but gradually its emphasis and expertise would change. Wilson is celebrated more for his metalwork and a concentration on sculpture itself, rather than sculpture in architecture.[68] With changing fashions, the work of the other pupils, such as Ernest Gimson and Ernest Barnsley, was characterised by a simpler use of materials, and the complexity of Sedding's work, the integral use of decorative carpentry and masonry, remained un-replicated. Perhaps, though, this was also due to the contradictory nature of much of Sedding's practice and theory, populated as it was with constantly shifting, evolving ideas, arising from a restless energy explicit in interiors such as Holbeton.

Indeed, just at the very point in his career when Sedding was overseeing work that celebrates the unity of the arts, the collaboration of sculptors and architect, he returned to reconsider the relationship of sculpture and architecture. In his 1889 paper entitled 'Expression in Architecture', he questioned the need for sculptural additions to the fabric of architecture, directly challenging Ruskin's earlier concept of architecture:[69]

> Take away the sculpture, and some accidental grace were gone, but the building in all its transcendent beauty would remain as single and specious as a statue ... Take away the sculpture and its air of sublimity would remain in the sheer weight and vigour of its masses and in the colossal scale of its architectural forms.[70]

Sheer weight and vigour of its masses – the lychgate at Ermington: bold, simple forms looking towards Lutyens? (*Paul Snell*).

This sense of weight, mass and scale was expressed in the pared down form of the lychgates at Holbeton and Ermington, works from the end of his career (*c.*1889).[71] Their bulky, grey granite forms, bereft of detail are loosely essays in a Classical vocabulary, their stout columns and rounded arches relieved only by curved brackets. Here is architecture as sculpture, statuesque in its elementary forms, an architecture of absence. The sober portals seem remote from the busy interiors of their respective churches. It could be argued that function dictated their forms. Being gates, they demanded simple treatment. However, this does not explain the choice of a Classical vocabulary deliberately used, and the effort and expense of the works. A better explanation is the contradictory nature of Sedding. Despite the fact that he had worked closely with sculptors, even on occasion a sculptor himself, at the very end of his career he questioned the need for sculpture in architecture. And, if this was the case with sculpture and architecture, it would also be the case with his concepts of design and production as a whole. Sedding would constantly expound theories on art and design, but would never produce one comprehensive and cohesive theory.

Ironically, in this contradictory nature, Sedding was close to Ruskin, for Ruskin too had both created and then rejected architectural theory and models in his long career. Moreover, if Sedding's work was not the fulfilment of a Ruskinian architectural ideal, then it was the closest late-Victorian realisation of it, and his attempts to integrate sculpture and architecture best express his proximity to 'Our dear friend Mr Ruskin'.

Notes

[1] *Works,* 37, p. 199. The original letter is in the Ruskin Library, Lancaster, manuscripts collection, L28.
[2] For example, Peter Davey, *Architecture of the Arts and Crafts Movement* (London, 1996), p. 6. Margaret Richardson's excellent survey of the Sedding office in *Architects of the Arts and Crafts Movement* (London, 1983) is a most useful starting point to a study of Sedding and his many pupils.
[3] These include: Henry Wilson, 'Concerning John D. Sedding, his Work and his Influence', *Builder,* 61 (1891), pp. 423-4; Henry Wilson, *A*

Memorial to the Late J. D. Sedding, being Illustrations from Some of his Works, compiled by the Architectural Association, with a Short Sketch of his Life by H. Wilson (London, 1892); J. P. Cooper, assisted by H. Wilson and C. Whall, *The Work of John D. Sedding* (unprovenanced (London?), 1897). See also W. R. Lethaby's obituary in the *Builder*, 61 (1891), pp. 270-1. Cooper's account of the life of Sedding was republished in Alastair Service, *Edwardian Architecture and its Origins* (London, 1975), pp. 258-79, a testament to the lack of Sedding studies to that date.

4 Michael Brooks, *John Ruskin and Victorian Architecture* (London, 1989), p. 257.

5 Ibid., p. 258.

6 *Works*, 8, pp. 10-11. The addition to the text in the second edition is significant, no doubt stimulated by his stress on craft and sculpture in *The Stones*, researched and published subsequently. Perhaps also this was a reaction to the Gothic Revival, by then in full swing.

7 *Works*, 16, pp. 251-2.

8 Ibid., p. 372.

9 *British Architect*, 1 (1874), p. 241.

10 See chapter 4 for Brian Hanson's review of Scott's attempt to educate the craftsman with the Architectural Museum project in the 1850s.

11 Andrew Saint, *Richard Norman Shaw* (New Haven and London, 1976), p. 15 states 'there was physical weakness in John too, belied by his antics in the office, from which he had to be restrained for fear of Street's wrath.' Later Saint (p. 187) describes the more relaxed nature of Sedding's office.

12 Sedding's wife, Rose Tinling, daughter of the Dean of Gloucester, was connected to various West Country gentry families.

13 As Lethaby [note 3] tells us.

14 Ibid.

15 Published in *Transactions of the Exeter Diocesan Architectural Society*, 8 (1869), p. 210.

16 *Works*, 8, pp. 233-4. Sedding misquotes this slightly. It should read: 'For, indeed, the greatest glory of a building is not its stone, nor in its gold. Its glory is in its Age, and in that deep sense of voicefulness, of stern watching, of mysterious sympathy, nay, even of approval or condemnation which we feel in walls that have long been washed by the passing waves of humanity.' Sedding also began his 1886 paper 'Religion in Art' with a quote from Ruskin: 'All great Art is praise' (quoted in *Arts and Handicrafts* (London, 1893) p. 25).

17 Sedding appears to quote extensively from Ruskin in this paper, yet, apart from the first quote, does not name his sources.

18 'About Modern Design', *Builder*, 44 (1883), p. 325.

19 *Transactions of the St Paul's Ecclesiological Society*, 1 (1881), p. 36.

20 'About Modern Design' [note 18], p. 327.

21 Lethaby [note 3], p. 271 writes: 'Personal contact with the great teacher [Ruskin] followed, and, for a time, he drew definitely under his guidance. The drift of his teaching was that however useful a diagram might be, a drawing did not fulfil its purpose until it suggested the light and shade of

the surroundings accurately in balance and gradation – "represented texture"'.

22 *Works*, 37, p. 199.

23 Two surviving sketchbooks survive at the RIBA, dated 1872-9 and 1876-81, and one at the Royal College of Arts, Wilson Archive, dated 1886.

24 Many contemporaries commented on this development, which was aided, of course, by the expansion of the railways. This included many provincial architects, envious of the success of their London-based counterparts. Consequently, national styles were developed and vernacular forms replaced.

25 Sedding [note 19], p. 40.

26 Ibid. Sedding directing his readers to the lecture in *The Two Paths* (*Works*, 16, pp. 346-74) stated: 'I do not think that he [Ruskin] ever wrote more truthfully or helpfully than in the lecture ... to which I can but refer you'.

27 *British Architect*, 15 (1881), p. 299.

28 Ibid.

29 From research in the Somerset Archive and Record Service and Lambeth Palace Library (ICBS files), the majority date from after 1880, when he became Diocesan Architect.

30 As is suggested by A. Saint [note 11], p. 455. Saint notes the proximity of many Sedding/Shaw buildings, and Holbeton could be an example of Sedding gaining work through his friend Shaw. However, it is difficult to ascertain this as Sedding had worked on a number of commissions in the area before this date.

31 The screen is briefly described in Sedding's paper 'On the Relations of Architecture and the Handicrafts' (1887), *Builder*, 52 (1887), p. 692. A preliminary drawing is illustrated in Wilson [note 3], plate 20.

32 'The Handicrafts in Old Days' (1890), in *Arts and Handicrafts* [note 16], p. 69. Sedding worked on the church between 1879 and 1889 (Cornwall Record Office, P122/2/3-5).

33 Indeed Sedding would refer to Darwin in 'About Modern Design', *Builder*, 44 (1883), p. 325, when commenting on the eclecticism of Victorian architecture: 'Darwin's experiment with six and three quarter ounces of pond mud, which were found to contain seeds of 537 distinct species ... was a mere trifle compared to the varieties of Victorian architecture'.

34 Work on one of the doors at Holbeton is briefly referred to in the Royal College of Art sketchbook, folio dated 20 August 1886. This sketches the basic dimensions of the south aisle door, not the porch and west doors.

35 According to Cooper [note 3]. Interestingly, on Sedding's grave at West Wickham, Kent, the epitaph fails to mention the Holbeton work.

36 Information on Holbeton is limited, owing largely to the munificence of Mildmay's private funding. Little documentation survives in the county record office, and no grant was sought of the ICBS. The only ref-

erence in the sketchbooks is on one folio in the Royal College of Art volume. Interpretation relies on Cooper and Wilson [note 3]. The cost of the restoration is supposed to have been £25,000, an astronomical sum that needs clarifying. Mildmay, as a partner of Barings' Bank, could no doubt have afforded this, especially as he paid for further church restorations in the vicinity.

[37] 'On the Relations of Architecture and the Handicrafts', *Builder*, 52 (1887), p. 694.

[38] As surviving contemporary photographs show, (Somerset Archive and Record Service, D/P/ax, 6/2/6). The restoration was undertaken in sections, and Sedding was responsible for all parts.

[39] As attested by references in the Sedding sketchbook now at Royal College of Art, folio dated 23 August 1886, and the restoration accounts dated (1888) (Somerset Archive and Record Service, D/P/ax 8/2/1).

[40] 'Design' (1888), in William Morris (editor), *Arts and Crafts Essays* (London, 1893), p. 409-10. Sedding's subject in this paper was ostensibly needlework, but the advice contained was deliberately wide-ranging.

[41] The authorship of the screens remains uncertain, as is the cost. The restoration work was contracted to Trask of Norton-sub-Hamdon, Somerset, who was frequently employed by Sedding, and was responsible for the carving of some of the finer church furnishings, e.g. Salcombe (1889). However, the screens are the highest quality, suggesting close supervision, if not execution by Sedding and his office. The restoration committee minutes are now inaccessible, due to their fragile state (Somerset Archive and Record Service, D/P/6/2/5, and D/P/8/2/1). The screen bears remarkable similarity to the later work of Henry Wilson at Norton-sub-Hamdon (*c*.1904).

[42] 'Design' [note 40], pp. 412-13.

[43] *Works*, 8, p. 12.

[44] Again, the surviving documentation on Clerkenwell is extremely limited, partly owing to the failure to gain an ICBS grant because of a late application from the incumbent, and a loss of material in the London Metropolitan Archives.

[45] In 1877, Sedding reportedly announced: 'for a city church he was convinced the most appropriate style was to be found in the Renaissance', in 'The Revival of the Later Styles of Gothic Architecture', *Architect*, 17 (1877), p. 361.

[46] Sedding cites examples such as St Stephen's, Walbrook and appraised them thus: 'Wren's noble series of City churches afford us quite an intellectual treat in this respect' in 'On Expression in Architecture', *Builder*, 57 (1889), p. 364. Of course, here Sedding and Ruskin would disagree strongly.

[47] Gerald Horsley's illustration of the intended scheme was published in the *Builder*, 52 (1887), pp. 672-3.

[48] F. Pomeroy, paper read to the Architectural Association, reported in the *Builder*, 60 (1891), pp. 86-8.

[49] From 'The Revival of the Later Styles of English Gothic', [note 45], p. 357.

50 *Works,* 10, p. 207. Interestingly, the pulpits of many of Sedding's late churches, such as Holy Trinity, Sloane Street and All Saints, Falmouth, echo the form of the celebrated one at Torcello. Was this the inspiration for the work?

51 'The Handicrafts in Old Days' (1890) [note 32], p. 78.

52 'Design' [note 40], p. 410.

53 The most detailed description and history of the work at Holy Trinity, Sloane Street is Peyton Skipworth's *Holy Trinity, Sloane Street* (London, 2002).

54 John Betjeman (editor), *Collins Guide to English Parish Churches* (London, 1958), p. 255.

55 The drawings of various sections of the church, again magnificently worked by Gerald Horsley, were published in the *Builder,* 55 (1888), pp. 253-4; 57 (1889), p. 260; 58 (1890), p. 11. The documentation on Holy Trinity again is scant. Owing to the munificence of the Earl and congregation, no grants were applied for, and few papers have survived in the London Metropolitan Archives.

56 See S. Beattie, *The New Sculpture* (New Haven and London, 1983) for a detailed exposition of the relationship of architecture and sculpture in the work of Thornycroft, Pomeroy and Bates. Some of these sculptors had worked with Sedding previously, such as Harry Bates and Onslow Ford on the Great Screen at Winchester (1885-7).

57 The most detailed description of the Ermington restoration is E. H. Sedding's review in *Transactions of the Exeter Diocesan Architectural Society,* 3rd ser., 1 (1894), pp. 57-6.

58 For example 'On the Relations of Architecture and the Handicrafts' in *Builder,* 52 (1887), p. 692 where he states: 'the vast majority of our parish churches were both designed and built by schools of workmen. To me they represent peasants' art. They are local not only in regard to conformity of certain types, but local in the thought and character expressed in them. They are of the soil, and made by children of the soil ... What little I know of art I have mostly got at the feet of the humble, but immortal peasant craftsmen of olden times'.

59 "The Handicrafts in Old Days" (1890) [note 32], pp. 67-8.

60 Ibid., p. 70 .

61 Plymouth and West Devon Record Office, Pinwill archive, 116/36. Published information on the Pinwills remains scant, despite the extensive scope of their work. Brief mention can be found in *Violet Pinwill: A Devon Artist: A Memoir Compiled by Members of her Family* (Plymouth, n.d.).

62 'Design' [note 40], p. 412. Here Sedding parallels Ruskin's advice. The Pinwill pulpit is not 'pure', rather it is created with toil, a 'naturalist' architecture, to use Ruskin's terms.

63 Thus the Pinwills would provide work for local church refurnishing and restorations, including Salcombe and St Mary's, Launceston for J. D. Sedding, whilst for E. H. Sedding they would execute carving at St Mary, Highweek, Newton Abbot (1904-8) and Lantlegos-by-Fowey (*c.*1903), both outstanding schemes, amongst others. For a fuller list, see Bridget

Cherry and Nikolaus Pevsner, *The Buildings of England: Devon* (London, 1989).

64 Other examples of Victorian feminine architectural adventures include the church designed by Sarah Losh at Wreay in Cumbria, from 1835 onwards, but Miss Losh did not undertake any of the carving herself, preferring her gardener to do this. The Great Screen at Winchester would have two small sculptures executed by a Miss Grant, a minor contribution in a scheme that would number at least 56 figurative sculptures.

65 In 1883, Sedding was employed to supervise a restoration of the remaining features. The work was only finished in 1892, supervised by E. H. Sedding. One remarkable feature is the nave pews, carved by the vicar and parishioners. Rough in texture, and bold in their floral detailing, the work is unlike the polished finesse of the pew ends found elsewhere in Sedding's oeuvre. Financial concerns cannot explain the parochial effort. See Somerset Archive and Record Service, D/P/langr 8/4/1 and D/D/CF (1892). This also appears to be the case at St Leonard, Bursledon, Hants. There the pulpit, completed in 1892, had various panels carved by the parishioners (Hampshire Record Office, 130M33/PW220).

66 An extraordinary claim in 'Religion and Art' (1886) in *Arts and Handicrafts* [note 32], p. 29.

67 'Design' [note 40], p. 410.

68 Wilson's oeuvre remains, like Sedding's, much admired but relatively little explored. The most accessible account of his work is J. Browning, 'Arts and Crafts Loyalist', *Country Life*, 166 (September 1974), pp. 700-2.

69 Published in the *Builder*, 57 (1889), pp. 363-5. It is largely upon this paper that Michael Brooks suggests that Sedding rejected Ruskin's concept of architecture. Sedding does clearly state: 'It is a mistake to suppose that a building is bound to be adorned with sculpture to have imaginative expression', (p. 364), but the late date should be noted. Prior to this, the other published papers and oeuvre of Sedding to the Ruskinian line, especially as until the mid-1880s Sedding's chief focus in architecture was sculptural embellishments and additions.

70 'On Expression ...' [note 69], p. 365. Note the Ruskinian reference in this quote, from 'The Lamp of Power' (*Works*, 8, p. 134): 'it is certain, that the relative majesty of buildings depends more on the weight and vigour of their masses, than on any other attribute of their design'. Even when directly challenging Ruskin's idea of the role of sculpture in architecture, Sedding relied on Ruskin. He sourced alternative ideas within Ruskin's corpus, and then employed Ruskinian terms.

71 According to Cooper [note 3], p. 269, work was finished at Ermington in 1889. Faculty papers at the Plymouth and West Devon Record Office are dated August-September 1889, concerning work inside the church. Drawings for the parclose screens of the church are dated 1889-90 (RIBA, RAN 71/9/4). The lychgate therefore must date from this period, if not later, and the similarity of this work to the two gates at Holbeton, would suggest a very close date of execution.

11

Ruskin Today: Building the Ruskin Library, Lancaster

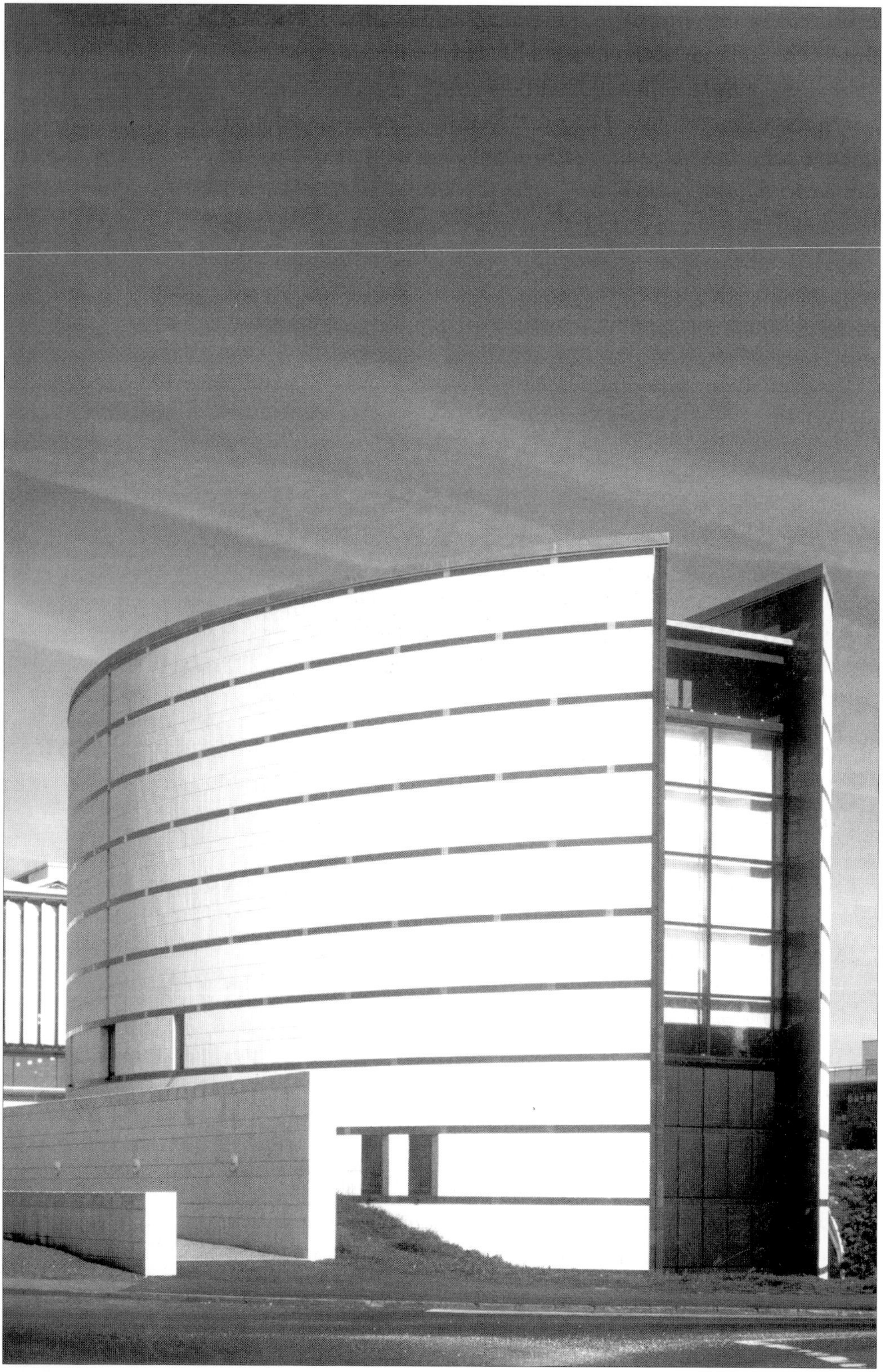

Ruskin Today: Building the Ruskin Library, Lancaster

Richard MacCormac

The Ruskin Library at Lancaster University contains the largest collection anywhere of material created by, about or once in the ownership of John Ruskin. It includes drawings and watercolours made by him, diaries and personal correspondence as well as material by contemporaries and associates such as Millais, Burne-Jones, Holman Hunt and Kate Greenaway. It was largely formed by John Howard Whitehouse (1873-1955), M.P. and educationist, who purchased much of the contents of Brantwood at a sale in 1931. It was held at Whitehouse's Bembridge School on the Isle of Wight until plans were made in the 1990s to house it in a purpose-built archive and reading room at Lancaster University. In 1993 MacCormac Jamieson Prichard were selected as the architects. Building commenced in September 1995 and was completed in December the following year at a cost of £4.5million. The Ruskin Library won the Independent on Sunday *Building of the Year Award, RFAC/BSkyB Building of the Year, University Winner 1998, and Millenium Products status awarded by the Design Council 1999. Here Sir Richard MacCormac reflects on the challenge involved and some of the ideas about the building which emerged before, during and since construction.*

HOW DOES a late-20th-century architect design a building to house a huge and varied body of material that belonged to one of the greatest artistic thinkers of the previous century? The collection includes manuscripts, drawings, paintings, daguerreotypes and books owned or produced by Ruskin himself, as well as complementary material from other sources.

I was no stranger to Ruskin, having read some of his writings and even given a paper about him in Australia. In fact 'The Lamp of Memory' essay in *The Seven Lamps* had made a powerful impression upon me with the idea that architecture should be able to tell stories. But this very notion presents a difficult challenge for the 'modern architect' (to use an ambiguous term of rather uncertain meaning). I come from

Opposite:
the Ruskin Library as seen from the west (*Richard Bryant Arcaid.co.uk*)

The library seen from within the University campus (*Paul Barker*).

a tradition which was still touched by the ideology of the Modern Movement, and part of that was clearly to shed allusiveness, mystery, history and metaphor. Thereby it was purporting to be an architecture of certainty which embodied technology and, in some way or other, expressed purpose. The Bauhaus was thus the architectural counterpart to the Logical Positivist circle of Vienna in the late 1920s.

I had to think carefully about how architecture could escape that reductive state and discussed the problem at length with my client at Lancaster University, Professor Michael Wheeler. He himself had written an interesting essay about 'The Lamp of Memory' in which he focused upon words like 'monument', 'story', 'history', and 'memory' and Ruskin's sense that architecture should be 'historical'. I came to feel that architecture could delve deeply into our collective memory. That then made me wonder whether there weren't ways of rendering the architecture of today 'historical'. By this I do not mean, for example, the kind of commonplace importation of Venetian Gothic into Victorian pub porches in Dulwich which caused Ruskin so much despair. Rather than a matter of historical style, it is a question of making architecture metaphorical and rich in allusion.

In what follows I propose to explore such issues principally in relation to the Ruskin Library but, before that, other earlier projects are discussed which set the scene. These were designed without Ruskin consciously in mind but allowed me to develop architecture for today which goes beyond mere technology and function.

Antecedents of the Ruskin Library

The library for King's College, Cambridge, in fact, was never built but the contents to be housed within it were in some ways comparable to the Ruskin project. The building, designed in 1987, was to accommodate a large and very important archive of manuscripts and books as well as a conventional undergraduate and postgraduate library where the material would have certain shelf-life. Our proposal was to contain the archive in a massive stone half circle – a kind of tiered burial chamber – which would keep cool through its sheer mass and was not accessible to readers. It was very monumental and later caused me to reflect that this word comes from the Latin *monere* – to remind – and the proposed building was to be a great storehouse for remembered information written down. By contrast, in the centre, there was to be a three-storey library in timber, with alcoved readers' spaces where the transitory information would be accessible and which we thought of as a kind of rookery. The library itself was to be above ground while the space beneath was intimately related to the adjoining garden. There was thus an upper and a lower world – a quasi-crypt with a church-like space above - which had a certain historical resonance about them. The architecture was firmly of the late-20th century but was aimed at expressing something of the content of the building and its temporal character.

Another building which explores the notion of underworld and overworld came out of the King's Library scheme

An early sketch of the Ruskin Library by Richard MacCormac (MacCormac Jamieson Prichard).

and was completed for St John's College, Oxford in 1994 with student rooms over public rooms. The big public rooms are 'Soanian' caverns with gardens on top of them. The architecture is made up of opposites of the kind that only have significance when considered together: above and below, dark and bright, heavy and light, equivalent to the opposites in nature, night and day, male and female which have meaning through their relationship, not on their own.

The immediate ancestor of the Ruskin Library is a little chapel for Fitzwilliam College, Cambridge, completed in 1992. Here the under and over concept is developed very carefully in terms of a small crypt with a chapel space above. It may have something to do with Gaudí's Güell Chapel with its dark crypt and (unfinished) bright place of worship above. I was also interested to develop the idea of a building inside another building (a characteristic of the King's College project), - in this case the inner construction is an ark suspended between the upper and lower world. The metaphor of the ship appealed to me greatly, being, as it is, deeply ingrained in human consciousness and religious imagery. The word 'nave' ,of course, comes from the Latin for a ship and all cathedrals are in a sense ships. Then there is a further idea which was to find its way into the Ruskin building – the notion of using light to separate spaces from each other, in this case the

Night view from the connecting causeway (*Peter Durant Arcblue.com*).

peripheral circulation from the place of worship. As in other works I was trying to produce a building that was new in a creative sense, which could not be pinned down stylistically but would be, in some ways, deeply familiar to the visitor and user. This was also precisely what was in my mind when it came to designing the Ruskin Library.

The Ruskin Library

Lancaster University is sited on a pronounced ridge. The Ruskin Library is sited near the entrance to the University, on the edge of the escarpment overlooking Morecambe Bay. I had in mind the idea of having the building sitting out on its own, isolated, but with a strong individual presence which seems appropriate to Ruskin. It was to be linked back to the University by a causeway above the ground, floating over the grass – an island, joined back to the mainland like Venice.

The allusion to Venice was fundamental to the scheme, but Ruskin would probably not have liked the reference to the causeway. Throughout the evolution of the project we were always trying to capture metaphors. Such things cannot be forced – one considers the characteristics of an architectural proposition, realises what it might mean and then decides whether or how to articulate the idea.

We realised we were constructing a building organised like a church with the archive as choir and the reading room as sanctuary. We began to consider what this structure would look like and how its space would be organised. It would be entered across a causeway and then, inside, one would find a big cabinet coming up through the floor which would in some way allude to Ruskin's love of Venetian Gothic – though at that stage we did not know quite how. The

The glass floor, the 'lagoon' through which the island/cabinet emerges (*Peter Durant Arcblue.com*).

metaphors now became more complex. Not only was the building a Venice-like island, but within there could be an island within an island, the surrounding floor an allusion to the lagoon and hence made of glass. As people came into the building they could look down through glass into an inaccessible underworld lit green like the sea.

Another metaphor evolved around the word 'keep' – both noun and verb. This was to be a building for 'keeping' things secure. So the outer circular structure and the inner rectangular structure are both 'keeps'. At this time there was an exhibition at the Tate by the American sculptor, Richard Serra. His big iron objects in the middle of the Duveen Gallery had the extraordinary effect of forcibly displacing the visitor from the centre of a classical space. This was exactly the way the Ruskin Library was developing in our minds; the archive displaces you from where you would normally expect to be. The collection thus acquires importance from the fact that it takes over your space and so forces you physically to go round it. I enjoyed the idea of thinking of the 'corpus' of Ruskin's work in the centre and this 'body' as, in a sense, Ruskin himself: you therefore have to go around him – I think he would have liked that.

In envisaging the archive I began to imagine it as an enormous cabinet – a three-storey high cabinet. It was then difficult not to think of William Burges's ambiguous pieces of furniture which are both buildings and furniture. Our quite elaborate cabinet involved an oak structure, fitted with blockwork and surfaced with polished red Venetian plaster panels coloured with red marble dust.

In the linear plan of the building, entrance, archive, reading room, the offices were sited on either side with exhibition galleries linked by a bridge through the archive from one gallery to another at first floor level. With the archive in the middle you pass down each side to reach the sanctuary-cum-reading room overlooking Morecambe Bay.

As the design evolved we were finding more and more words to describe the archive – 'cathedral treasure chest', 'great cabinet', 'reliquary' and 'ark' – and were reminded of Ruskin's reference in *The Stones of Venice* to St Mark's as 'a vast illuminated missal'.[1] I had the idea of working with the

First floor plan of the Ruskin Library showing the archive 'cabinet' at the centre of the building (*MacCormac Jamieson Prichard*).

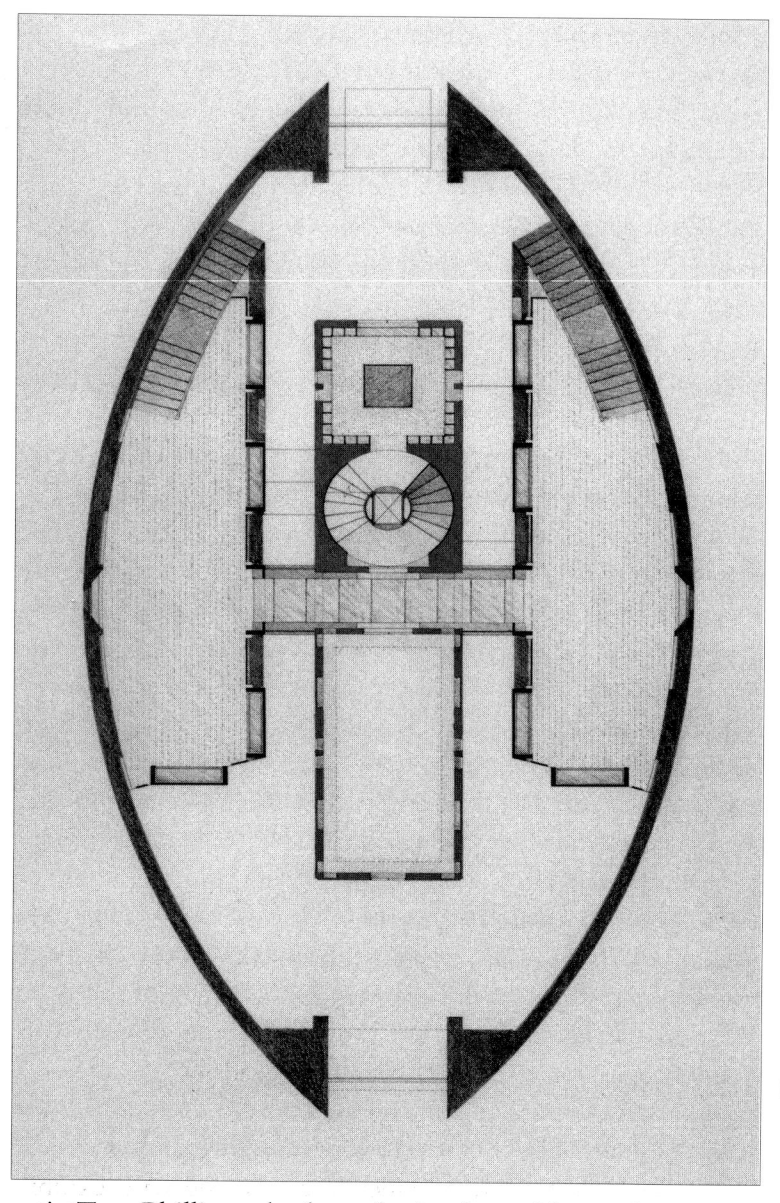

artist Tom Phillips, who has a fascination with words, to cover the archive with Ruskin aphorisms but this was, regrettably, beyond our budget, which did not cover the work of artists.

Lighting remained of the greatest importance to us. Daylight filters down through the whole three-storeys, separating the archive structure from the galleries on each side, just as it separates the centre of the Fitzwilliam Chapel from the periphery.

The metaphor of the inner and outer keep actually found

a physical interpretation in the environmental control of the building. It occurred to us that the very heavy outer structure and the heavy inner structure with lots of air between might lead to the first passively tempered archive in the U.K. – which in fact it has done. Apart from a small unit in the reading room, there is no air-conditioning as the relationships between mass and volume 'keep' the air at the right temperature and humidity for 'keeping' the archive.

In the external construction of the library the bands of green are perhaps un-Venetian but the vivid colour is to be found in Ruskin's watercolours of Italian architecture. As you go inside there is a vast image of the north-west portal of St Mark's taken from a 200mm high daguerreotype made by Ruskin. An artist with whom I often collaborate, Alex Beleschenko, scanned it into his computer – Ruskin would not have liked this – expanded it to 4 metres height and had the image made up in glass with platinum etched into it so that it is a very mysterious thing which is barely decipherable. I like to think of this as a Proustian metaphor for the fragility of memory.

Detail of the magnified daguerrotype of the north-west portal of St Mark's, Venice (*Richard Bryant, Arcaid.co.uk*).

The reading room furniture was designed with a local craftsman in an approximately Ruskinian way (actually made by Jeremy Hall of Peter Hall and Son).

In terms of materials there is a conscious blend of very modern and very antique – high-tech glass and metal in parts, elsewhere lime rendering and a translucent lime wash. There is also much concrete – not stone – and Ruskin would not have approved of that!

Note
[1] *Works*, 10, p. 112.

Notes on Contributors

Gothic Survival or Gothic Revival? Chris Brooks, 1996 (*Candida-Lycett-Green*).

Chris Brooks (1949-2002) made a major contribution to our understanding of the Victorian world. The son of a master printer, his family moved to Devon where he lived for most of his life. He began his career at the University of Exeter in 1974 and rose to become the Professor of Victorian Culture. His approach to the imaginative world of the Victorians was driven by a belief that it could only be understood by being seen as a whole. His published works (and brilliant lectures) put this into practice. His first book, *Signs for the Times: Symbolic Realism in the Mid-Victorian World* (1984) explored symbolism and notions of the 'real', re-assessing much of the work of Dickens, Carlyle, Ruskin, the Pre-Raphaelites, Pugin and Butterfield. Likewise, *The Victorian Church: Architecture and Society* (1995, co-edited with Andrew Saint) took the subject well beyond matters of style and provenance into the tougher world of politics and economics. It was this combination of detailed knowledge and imaginative sweep that marked him out intellectually. His great work of synthesis, *The Gothic Revival* (1999), dug into the layers of meaning behind this remarkable phenomenon and ranged widely in time from the rebuilding of Oriel College to Monty Python. His ability to read broad significance from minute detail led to the major reappraisal of one of the great Victorian icons in *The Albert Memorial: The Prince Consort National Memorial, its History, Contexts and Conservation* (2000). This built on an interest in 19th-century commemorative culture that had first borne fruits in his history of the Victorian and Edwardian cemetery – *Mortal Remains* (1988). He was active in many areas – in conservation (as chairman of the Victorian Society from 1993 to 2001), in the study of medieval glass, in the University where he inspired his students, in local cricket and local pubs – he was something of a Renaissance man whose loss is keenly felt by friends and the world of scholarship alike (*Martin Cherry*).

Geoff Brandwood is chairman of the Victorian Society, having succeeded Chris Brooks in 2001, and was previously chairman of its Activities Committee. He has written extensively on church architecture, especially of the Victorian and Edwardian periods. Publications include various studies of church and secular architecture in Leicestershire, churches entries for the Buckinghamshire and Leicestershire 'Pevsners', and the monograph *Temple Moore: An Architect of the Late Gothic Revival* (1997). Apart from continuing research on the late Gothic Revival, he is co-authoring a book on British historic pub interiors and is active in promoting their preservation and knowledge about them through the Campaign for Real Ale.

Michael W. Brooks teaches English at West Chester, Pennsylvania, U.S.A., and works in architectural research and historic preservation in New Jersey and Pennsylvania. He is the author of *John Ruskin and Victorian Architecture* (1987) and *Subway City: Riding the Trains, Reading New York* (1997). He is currently active in efforts to preserve Philadelphia's historic Laurel Hill Cemetery and is writing on the representations of the built landscape in recent American literature.

Gill Chitty is principal consultant with Hawkshead Archaeology & Conservation. Having worked with the Greater London Council's Historic Buildings Division and with English Heritage as an inspector of ancient monuments, she has been an independent consultant since 1993 specialising in research for conservation and the historic environment. Recent publications include *Managing Historic Sites and Buildings: Preservation and Presentation* (co-edited with David Baker, 1999) and *Heritage Under Pressure* (co-authored with David Baker, 2002); also articles on Ruskin in *Ruskin and Environment: the Storm-Cloud of the Nineteenth Century* (1996), and in *Oxoniensia* (2000). Her doctoral research at Lancaster University was on John Ruskin and the historic environment. She is a Fellow of the Society of Antiquaries of London, a member of the Institute of Field Archaeologists, and of the Institute of Historic Building Conservation.

Rebecca Daniels is working towards a doctorate in art history at the University of Oxford. She lectures in art and architectural history at Delaware and St Lawrence Universities on their London programmes and was formerly the events organiser at the Victorian Society where she devised the conference 'Ruskin and Architecture' (March 2000). She is currently bursary secretary of the Regional Furniture Society. Recent publications include 'Walter Sickert and Urban Realism: Ordinary Life and Tragedy in Camden Town', *British Art Journal*, (Spring 2002) and 'Press Art: the Late Oeuvre of Walter Richard Sickert', *Apollo* (October 2002).

Michael Hall is completing a book on Bodley and Garner. Among his recent articles is 'What do Victorian Churches Mean? Symbolism and Sacramentalism in Anglican Church Architecture, 1850-1870', in the *Journal of the Society of Architectural Historians*, 59:1 (2000). His most recent book is a history of *Waddesdon Manor* (2002); he has also edited a volume of essays, *Gothic Architecture and Its Meanings 1530-1830* (2002). He is the deputy editor of *Country Life*: he is also a trustee of the Victorian Society and the chairman of its Activities Committee.

Brian Hanson is an architectural historian who has also been deeply involved in contemporary architectural and urban practice. He has written on various aspects of 19th- and 20th-century architecture and urban design, and has taught in the U.K., the U.S.A., Europe and the Middle East. For more than a decade he advised the Prince of Wales on architectural and planning matters, and edited the Prince's influential *A Vision of Britain* (1989). From

1994 to 1998 Dr Hanson was Director of the Urban Design Task Force, which *The Times* called 'one of the Prince's most effective initiatives'. He is currently researching the significance of new scientific concepts for architectural and urban theory, and is writing an 'intellectual biography' of the architect Christopher Alexander, entitled *Theory and Design in the 'Gene Age'*.

Malcolm Hardman is Reader in English and Comparative Literary Studies at Warwick University, and Adjunct Reader in Ruskin Studies at the University of Lancaster. He is also a member of the Ruskin Society. Publications include *Ruskin and Bradford: An Experiment in Victorian Cultural History* (1986); *Six Victorian Thinkers* (1991); *A Kingdom in Two Parishes: Religious Writers and Monarchy 1521-1689* (1998); and *Classic Soil* (2003), on early Victorian Lancashire (for which a sequel on the 1890s is in preparation). He has also contributed to *The Yearbook of English Studies, The British Journal of Aesthetics, Textual Practice*, to other collections, and to reference works on George Eliot and 19th-century thinkers. His work has received subvention from the British Academy, the Twenty-Seven Foundation, and the Leverhulme Trust. His first degree, at Trinity College, Cambridge, was in classics, and he plans to combine two of his interests with a work on Victorian Hellenist Poets.

Rosemary Hill is a writer and historian currently working on a biography of A. C. and A. W. N. Pugin. Her publications in this area include: 'A.C. Pugin', *Burlington Magazine*, 1114 (1996), pp. 11-19; 'Reformation to Millenium: Pugin's *Contrasts* in the History of English Thought', *Journal of the Society of Architectural Historians*, 58 (March 1999), pp. 26-41 and 'Catholics, Romantics and Late Georgian Gothic' in *Gothic Architecture and Its Meanings 1530-1830*, edited by Michael Hall (2002). She is a trustee of the Victorian Society, an editorial advisor to the Crafts Council of England and Wales and a regular contributor to the *Times Literary Supplement* and the *London Review of Books*.

Peter Howell has been a member of the Victorian Society Main Committee since 1968, and was the Society's Chairman from 1987 until 1993. He taught Classics at Bedford and Royal Holloway Colleges in the University of London between 1964 and 1999. His architectural publications include the chapter 'Architecture 1800-1914' in volume 7 of the *The History of the University of Oxford* (2000). He also wrote (with Elizabeth Beazley) the *Companion Guide to North Wales* (1975) and *South Wales* (1977), and (with Ian

Sutton) edited *The Faber Guide to Victorian Churches* (1989). He is now working on a history of the triumphal arch from Roman times to the present day.

Richard MacCormac is chairman of MacCormac Jamieson Prichard, founded in 1972. He has lectured widely and published articles on urban design and architectural theory. He served two terms as a member of the Royal Fine Art Commission and was an English Heritage commissioner 1995-8. He was President of the RIBA 1991-3 and was awarded a CBE in 1994. Apart from the Ruskin Library, notable award-winning building projects include: Cable & Wireless College, Coventry; Garden Quadrangle, St John's College, Oxford; Bowra Building, Wadham College, Oxford; Burrell's Field, Trinity College, Cambridge; the Wellcome Wing at the Science Museum; and Southwark station, Jubilee Line Extension. Current projects include Building One in Paternoster Square adjacent to St Paul's Cathedral and the redevelopment of Broadcasting House for the BBC at Portland Place. Exhibition design includes 'Ruskin, Turner and the Pre-Raphaelites' at Tate Britain (2000) and 'Surrealism – Desire Unbound' at Tate Modern.

Aileen Reid was educated at Edinburgh University and the Courtauld Institute of Art, London University, from which she received her PhD for a thesis on the architecture of E. W. Godwin. She has contributed to numerous books, exhibition catalogues and journals, and has written mostly on late-19th and early-20th-century architectural and design subjects. These include the extended essay on Godwin's architectural career in *E. W. Godwin: Aesthetic Movement Architect and Designer*, edited by S. W. Soros (1999), and *Brentham: A History of the Pioneer Garden Suburb* (2000). She has previously worked at the National Gallery of Scotland and Dulwich Picture Gallery, and currently divides her working life between the *Sunday Telegraph*, where she is assistant literary editor, and the Emery Walker Trust, for whom she curates the collection at 7 Hammersmith Terrace in west London, the former home of Sir Emery Walker (1851-1933), typographer, antiquary and intimate of William Morris.

Paul Snell is researching for a PhD in art history at Manchester University, concentrating on the office of J. D. Sedding to facilitate a new understanding of the development of Free Gothic and the Arts and Crafts Movement. Having studied at the School of Modern History at Oxford University, he completed an M.A. at the Courtauld Institute. His research focused upon the early career of G. F. Bodley and his so-called High Victorian phase (1852-65). He then taught history in Thornbury, South Gloucestershire, for a number of years before embarking on his current research project. His chapter on Sedding's sculpture in architecture was first presented as a paper to the Henry Moore Foundation conference on Sculpture in Architecture (2002).

Geoffrey Tyack was educated at St John's College, Oxford and received his doctorate from the University of London. He is Director of the Stanford University Centre in Oxford, a Fellow of Kellogg College, Oxford and a Fellow of the Society of Antiquaries. He is the author of *Sir James Pennethorne and the Making of Victorian London* (1992), *Warwickshire Country Houses* (1994), and *Oxford: An Architectural Guide* (1998). He has lectured widely on English architectural and urban history in both Britain and the United States, and is currently writing a book on the modern architecture of St John's College, Oxford.

Index

★ indicates an illustration or a reference within an illustration caption. In the latter case there may also be a reference within the main text of the page

Abbeville (Picardy): 102, 113
Abbotsford (Roxburghs): 97, 117 n. 29, 234
Ackerman, Rudolph: 226
Acland, Henry Wentworth: 58, 61-2★, 63, 64, 65, 66, 69, 71, 74, 76, 77, 78-9, 80, 81, 127, 141, 146, 257, 269
Acland, Sarah: 63, 79
Adam brothers: 138
Aestheticism/Aesthetic movement: 280, 281, 295, 301, 303, 305, 306, 307, 310
Albert, Prince Consort: 146-7
Alexander, Christopher: 161 n.126
Alexander, George: 252★
Allen, Charles Bruce: 142
Allingham, William: 61
Amiens Cathedral: 16, 200
Antwerp Cathedral: 130
Apology for the Revival of Christian Architecture (Pugin) 234, 235
Architectural Association: 148
Architectural Magazine: 28, 29★, 30★, 93, 98, 229, 234, 264
Architectural Museum: 135-6★, 141-8, 151, 152
Architectural Review: 160 n.107, 251-2, 253
Aristotle: 191, 198, 201, 202, 203
Armstead, Henry Hugh: 341
Armstrong, William: 282, 298, 312 n.12
Armytage, J. C.: 210★, 211, 214★
Arnold, Matthew: 103, 215
Art Nouveau: 18
Arts and Crafts movement: 16-17, 19, 89, 96, 113-15★, 151★, 152, 184, 185-6, 287, 311, 322, 346
Art Workers' Guild: 16, 330-1, 339-40
Arundel Society: 251

Ashbee, Charles Robert: 16, 113
Athenaeum: 42
Atwood, Margaret: 210
Axbridge (Som), St John the Baptist: 320-1★, 336-9★

Bacon, Nathaniel: 171
Banham, Reyner: 17-18
Barcelona, Güell Chapel: 360
Barnsley, Ernest: 347
Barry, Sir Charles: 59, 83 n. 20, 144, 172
Barry, Edward Middleton: 64, 65★
Bartholmew, Alfred: 135
Bates, Harry: 341
Bauhaus: 130, 185, 358
Bauhütte(n): 122-3★, 129ff★, 185
Beleschenko, Alex: 365★
Beerbohm, Sir Max: 281
Birmingham: 105
 – King's Heath, Highbury: 104★
 – St Chad's Cathedral: 230, 233
Blow, Detmar: 113-14★
Bloxam, Matthew Holbeche: 33
Bodley and Garner: 249
Bodley, George Frederick: 13-14, 60, 80, 248ff★, 300, 304
Boulton, Richard: 288★
Bournemouth, Boscombe, St Clement: 325
Boyne Hill (Berks), All Saints: 252, 253★ 255, 273 n. 12
Brandon, J. Raphael and J. Arthur: 33, 53 n. 16
Brantwood (Cumbria): 112-13★, 117 n.16
Brighton, St Michael and All Angels: 252, 254★, 255
Bristol, 10-11 Rockleaze: 278-9★, 293★, 295★
 – Assize Courts competition: 297
 – Perry Brothers' offices: 292-3★
 – St Philip & St Jacob's schools: 285-6★
Bristol Society of Architects: 298
Britton, John: 33, 224, 226, 227, 297
Brontë, Charlotte: 30

Brooks, James: 265
Brown, Denise Scott: 18
Brownlee, David: 255
Brunelleschi, Filippo: 219 n. 45
Buckland, William: 256-7★
Budapest, Parliament Buildings: 172
Burges, William: 131, 183★, 184, 250, 363
Burke, Edmund: 39, 40, 126, 127,
    153 n.13
Burlison and Grylls: 271
Burlison, John: 133
Burne-Jones, Sir Edward Coley: 185★,
    342, 357
Bursledon (Hants), St Leonard: 353 n.65
Butterfield, William: 71, 101, 230-1★,
    232★, 234, 240, 262, 264, 266,
    267, 268, 275 n.46, 285, 292

Cadogan, George, 5th Earl of: 341
Cambridge, All Saints: 266
    – Fitzwilliam College, chapel:
        360-1, 364
    – King's College Library: 359
    – St Paul: 231
Cambridge Camden Society: 32, 176
Canterbury (N.Z.), Council Chamber:
    172-3★
Capes, John Moore: 240
Cardiff Castle: 183★
Carlyle, Jane: 67
Carlyle, Thomas: 40, 68, 99, 127, 129,
    139-40, 145, 149, 153 n.15,
    157 nn.61-2, 68; 272, 305, 311
Carshalton (London), St Margaret's Well:
    251
Castle Ashby House (Northants): 291,
    297
Century Guild: 16
Chamberlain, John Henry: 104★, 105,
    118 n. 55
Chamberlain, Joseph: 104, 118 n. 55
Chartism: 36, 37, 167★
Cheadle (Staffs), St Giles: 236, 241
Cheltenham, St Paul's Training College:
    255
Christian Art and Symbolism (Tyrwhitt): 71
Civil War, English: 170-1, 172
Clark, James Adams: 302

Clark, Kenneth, Lord: 223
Clayton, John Richard: 156 n.51
Clough, Arthur Hugh: 204
Clutton, Henry: 159 n.96
Cobham, Richard, Viscount Temple:171★
Cockerell, Charles Robert: 147, 303
Codd, Frederick: 147
Cole, Thomas: 192
Colenso, Bishop John William: 270-1
Cologne Cathedral: 122-3★, 129ff★
Communist Manifesto (Marx & Engels):
    177
Comper, Sir John Ninian: 249, 272
Compton, Charles, 3rd Marquess of
    Northampton: 297
Congleton (Cheshire), Town Hall:
    279, 294, 299
Coniston Old Hall (Cumbria): 29★
Conner, Patrick: 223-4
Constable, John: 124★
Constantinople, Crimea Memorial
    Church (Bodley's design):
    275 n. 36
Constructional polychromy: *see*
    Structural polychromy
Contrasts (Pugin): 59, 94, 225, 229
Cork Cathedral: 131
    – Queen's College: 59
    – Town Hall: 59, 67
Cottage Plans and Common Sense
    (Unwin): 114
Cottingham, Lewis Nockalls: 158 n.72
Courmayeur (Val d'Aosta): 263★, 265
Cowper, Francis Thomas de Grey,
    7th Earl: 297
Crisp, Henry: 302
Cronkhill (Salop): 117 n.30
Crown of Wild Olive, The: 184, 206, 260,
    261
Cuddesdon College (Oxon): 255, 282★
Cuff, R.: 212★
Cuypers, Petrus: 185

Dante Alighieri: 191, 201-2, 205, 233
Darwin, Charles/Darwinism: 216, 335
Deane, Kearns: 59
Deane, Sir Thomas; Deane, Thomas
    Newenham: 59, 67, 76

Deane and Woodward: 59-61, 64-7, 77, 82 n. 4, 135★
de Grey, Earl: 158 n.96
de Lille, Alain: 201, 203
de Musset, Alfred: 195
Derby, St Mary (Pugin): 233
'Deteriorative Power of Conventional Art over Nations' (lecture): 147, 152
'Development' in 1840s/1850s architecture: 207, 255-8★, 270, 283, 298
Devey, George: 98
Dippenhall (Surrey), houses: 114-15
Dromore Castle (Co. Limerick): 291, 297
Dublin, Museum of Science & Art competition: 302★
— Trinity College Museum Building: 58★, 59-61★, 67
Dublin Review (Pugin articles): 234, 235, 241

Earp, Thomas: 252★, 273 n. 12, 323
Eastlake, Sir Charles Locke: 39, 84 n. 78, 105
East Retford (Notts), Town Hall: 296★
Ebley Mill (near Stroud, Gloucs): 260, 261, 265
Ecclesiological Society: 250, 255, 266, 269
Ecclesiologist: 39, 41, 42, 136, 137, 158 n.84, 230, 237-8, 239, 240, 241, 250, 251, 255, 259, 263, 273 n. 18
Edinburgh: 46, 100★, 101-2
— New College: 265-6
Eliot, George: 27, 30
Eliot, Thomas. Stearns: 205
Engels, Friedrich: 177, 179
Ermington (Devon), St Peter and St Paul: 342-5★, 347★, 348
Essays and Reviews (Wilson ed.): 270

Fabian, John: 273 n.12
Fairbairn, William: 77
Falkner, Harold: 114-15, 119 n.83
Farmer and Brindley: 323
Ferrara Cathedral: 32★, 33★
Fergusson, James: 32, 53 n.16, 76, 144

Ferrey, Benjamin: 158 n.75
Field of Westminster: 273 n.12
Fielding, Copley: 227
Florence, S. Miniato: 202
Floriated Ornament (Pugin): 130, 237, 239
Fors Clavigera: 109, 110★, 114, 115, 117 nn.16, 29; 153 n.1, 184, 305
France Lynch (Gloucs), St John the Baptist: 273 n.12
Freeman, Edward Augustus: 32, 43, 53 n.16, 255
'Freemasons of the Church': 135
Fuller and Jones: 172
Furniss, Frank: 184-5
Furnivall, Frederick James: 67, 210

Garbett, Edward Lacy: 144
Garden City movement: 17, 89, 107, 108, 114, 115-17★
Garner, Thomas: 249
Gaskell, Elizabeth: 30
Gaudí, Antoní: 360
Geddes, Patrick: 17
Geerts brothers: 154 n.30
Genoa: 199
— S. Matteo: 200★, 202, 203
Geology, influence on architecture: 253-8★, 270
Gibbs, James: 171★
Gibson, John: 259-60, 261, 271
Gilbert, Alfred: 341
Gilchrist, Alexander: 57, 80
Gimson, Ernest: 96, 113-14★, 115, 119 n.83, 347
Gimson, Sydney: 114
Giotto: 206
Glastonbury (Som), Abbot's Kitchen: 67
Godwin, Edward William: 14, 149, 278ff★
Godwin, George: 144, 147, 313 n.46
Godwin, Joseph: 283
Godwin (of Lugwardine) tiles: 267
Goethe, Johann Wolfgang von: 129, 133, 139, 154 n.27
Gordon, Osborne: 107
Gothic novels: 172-3
Gothic Revival
— in Austria: 131
— in Belgium: 154 n.30, 185

– 'development' in: 207, 255-8★, 283, 298
– in England, foreign influence on: 15, 102, 104-5, 177, 240, 251ff, 279ff
– in Germany: 129ff, 185
– in Netherlands: 185
– in Oxford and Cambridge, early: 164-5★, 174
– meanings of: 167ff
– origins of: 167ff
– politics of: 164-87
Grant, Miss M. L.: 353 n.64
Great Exhibition (1851): 179
Greenaway, Kate: 357
Grossteste, Bishop Robert: 202
Güell Chapel, Barcelona: 360
Guild of Handicrafts: 16
Guild of St George: 105
Guinicelli, Guido: 205, 214
Gwilt, Joseph: 126

Haddon Hall (Derbys): 93★
Hadfield, Matthew: 240
Hall, Jeremy: 365
Hall, Peter Hall & Son: 365
Hamburg, Nikolaikirche: 130★, 132ff
– Rathaus/Town Hall: 71, 288
Hampden House (Bucks): 170★, 172
Hampden, John: 170★, 172
Harding, J. D.: 227, 228, 239
Hardman, John: 59, 156 n.51, 229, 270
Hardwick, Philip: 63, 64, 146
Hardwick, Philip Charles: 64
Hare, Sir David: 206-7
Harrison, William Henry: 242
Heideloff, Carl Alexander: 155 n.32
Hems, Harry: 323
Herbert, John Rogers: 237
Hine, James: 284, 302
Hogarth Society: 250
Holbeton (Devon), All Saints: 331-5★, 348
Holloway Sanatorium (Surrey), competition: 316 n.99
Holy Cross Abbey (Co. Tipperary): 58
Homer: 205
Hope, A. J. B. Beresford: 136, 147, 240, 255
Hopkins, Gerard Manley: 215
Horsley, Gerald: 339-40★, 342-3★
Hotman, François: 170
Howard, Charles, 11th Duke of Norfolk: 172
Howard, Frank: 223, 242
Hunt, William Holman: 269, 357

'Influence of the Imagination in Architecture' (lecture): 329
Instrumenta Ecclesiastica (Ecclesiological Society): 266
Izenour, Steven: 18

Jackson, Sir Thomas Graham: 151, 155 n.41
Japanese influence in the arts: 290★, 301
Johnson, Robert: 266
Jordanes: 168

Keble, Thomas: 261
King's Stanley (Gloucs): 259-60
Knight, Richard Payne: 227, 229

Laing, J. J.: 146
Lancaster University, Ruskin Library: 12, 19-20, 356-65★
Langridge (Somerset), St Mary Magdalene: 345
Lassus, Jean-Baptiste: 177
La Touche, Rose: 81, 150
Laurence, Samuel: 190-1★
Lectures on Architecture and Painting: 45, 46-7, 265
Leicester Town Hall competition: 297
Leeds, William Henry: 229, 230, 240
Le Keux, J. H.: 69★, 73★, 83 n.35
Lemere, Bedford: 78
Letchworth (Herts), Garden City: 115
Lethaby, William Richard: 113, 321
Lewis, George Robert: 155 n.31
Libeskind, Daniel: 12
Lille, Adam de: 201, 203
Limerick, William Hale John Pery, 3rd Earl of: 297
Linton, William James: 112
Linz Cathedral: 131★

Liverpool, pro-Cathedral: 236
— St John the Baptist, Tue Brook: 315 n.80
Lloyd, Samuel: 261
London, Albert Memorial: 184, 323
— All Saints, Margaret Street: 240, 273 n.18
— Architectural Museum: 135-6★, 141-8, 151, 152
— Brompton Oratory: 302★
— Camden Chapel, Camberwell: 251, 269
— Convent of Sisters of Mercy, Bermondsey: 233
— Government Offices/Foreign Office competition: 19, 70, 288
— Hampstead Garden Suburb: 115★
— Holy Redeemer, Clerkenwell: 338★ 339-41★, 346
— Holy Trinity, Sloane St: 321, 339 341-3★, 346
— National School of Design, Somerset House: 237
— Royal Courts of Justice (Law courts): 150★, 151, 199, 207
— Palace of Westminster: 172★, 173, 174
— Red House, Bexleyheath: 107
— St Augustine, Kilburn: 304
— St Giles, Camberwell: 155 n.83, 251
— St James the Less, Westminster: 325
— St John, Hammersmith: 264, 266
— St Margaret's Chapel: 232-3★
— St Margaret's Well, Carshalton: 251
— St Matthias, Stoke Newington: 266
— St Paul, Herne Hill: 252★, 253
— St Philip, Stepney: 304
— no. 44 Tite Street: 300-1★, 309
— Travellers' Club: 59
— Waterlow Court, Hampstead: 115★
— Westminster Hall: 308
— White House, 35 Tite Street: 300-1★, 303, 309
Longden, Henry: 341
Losh, Sarah: 353 n.64
Loudoun, John Claudius: 28, 92-3, 98, 229-30, 234
Lucas Brothers: 67, 74

Lupton, Geoffrey: 119 n.83

Macclesfield (Ches), St Alban: 233
MacCormac Jamieson Prichard: 357
Mackmurdo, Arthur: 16, 113
Maidment, Brian: 26
Manchester Assize Courts: 288
— Town Hall: 131
Marinetti, Filippo: 115-16
Marling, Colonel Sir Percival: 262★
Marling, Sir Samuel Stephens: 258★, 260-5★, 271
Marling (Tyrol), church: 262★
Marx, Karl: 177, 179, 183
Maurice, Frederick Denison: 140, 141
Meredith, George: 285
Mildmay, Hugh Bingham: 331, 343
Miles, Frank: 280, 300-1★
Mill, John Stuart: 199
Millais, Sir John Everitt: 71, 82 n.12, 101, 125, 143, 242, 357
Milton, John: 204-5
Modern Painters: 27, 29-30, 31, 32, 37, 45, 49, 124★, 149, 156 n.46, 191, 193, 202-3, 227, 234, 264, 279
Moore, Albert: 302
Morris (Marshall, Faulkner) & Co.: 16, 266★, 269-70, 271-2★
Morris, William: 16, 17, 18, 21 n.12, 26, 44, 96, 107, 113, 152, 185★, 186, 207, 210, 250-1, 310, 311, 324, 325
Mountfort, Benjamin: 172-3★
Mumford, Lewis: 17
Munro, Alexander: 72★, 79★, 80
Murano, SS Maria e Donato: 211-16★, 289★, 291
Musset, Alfred de: 195
Muthesius, Hermann: 115
'Mystery of Life and its Arts' (lecture): 80
Nash, John: 117 n.30
Nature and the natural world protrayed in architecture: 253-5★
'Nature of Gothic': see *The Stones of Venice*
New Earswick, York: 115, 116-17★
Newman, John Henry: 119 n.83
Northampton, Charles Compton, 3rd Marquess of: 297

Northampton, St Martin's Villas: 294-5*
- Town Hall: frontispiece, 19, 279, 280, 281ff*, 307
Notes on the Construction of Sheepfolds: 259
Nottingham, municipal offices competition: 305
- St Barnabas: 241

Oakham Castle (Rutland): 100-1*
O'Dwyer, Frederick: 57, 66, 67, 70, 76, 77, 81 nn.4, 16, 19; 83 n.35, 85 n.87, 141
Oldfield, Edmund: 155 n.83, 251
Old Watercolour Society: 227
Opening of the Crystal Palace, The: 44, 46, 76-7
Origin of Species, The (Darwin): 270
Orvieto, Palazzo del Popolo: 203
O'Shea, James and John: 61, 73-5*, 76, 80, 81, 82 n.3, 183*
Ottawa, Parliament Buildings: 172
Oxford, Ashmolean Museum: 62-3
- Balliol College Chapel: 71
- Christ Church: 164-5*
- Magdalen College: 249
- New College: 42
- North, houses in: 110-11*
- St John's College: 359-60
- Union Debating Hall: 71, 151
- University Museum: 13, 15, 56ff*, 135*, 141, 146, 149, 152, 183*, 184, 257, 269, 288, 324
Oxford Architectural Society: *see* Oxford Society for Promoting ...
Oxford Society for Promoting the Study of Gothic Architecture: 32, 33-4, 62, 76, 78, 138

Padua, Arena Chapel: 206
Paley, Frederick. Apthorp: 32-3
Palgrave, Francis Turner: 80
Palladio, Andrea: 64, 217 n.3, 219 n.45
Parker, Barry: 116-17*
Parker, James: 257
Parker, John Henry: 32, 53 n. 16, 62
Pater, Walter: 310
Patmore, Coventry: 26, 41, 43
Pendelbury (Lancs), St Augustine: 304

Perpendicular style: 304*, 326-7
Pery, William Hale John Charles, 3rd Earl of Limerick: 297
Pevsner, Sir Nikolaus: 17-18, 20, 124, 204, 223
Philadephia (U.S.A): 184-5
Phillipps, Ambrose: 236
Phillips, John: 63, 73
Phillips, Tom: 363-4
Pick, Frank: 21 n. 12
Pinwill, Edmund: 343
Pinwill sisters: 343, 344-5*
Pisa Cathedral: 289
Pistoia, S. Pietro: 281, 296*
Plaw, John: 97
Playfair, William: 265
Plymouth, Guildhall: 97
- Western College: 285
Poetry of Architecture, The: 28-9, 30*, 48*, 49*, 50*, 92, 93-4, 95*, 113, 198, 264
Pollen, John Hungerford: 69, 80
Pomeroy, Frederick William: 339-41, 346
Poole, George Ayliffe: 53 n.16
Powell, John Hardman: 241
Poynter, Ambrose: 30-1
Praeterita: 91, 117n.29
Pre-Raphaelites: 65, 125, 250, 269
Present State of Ecclesiastical Architecture (Pugin): 234, 235
Price, Uvedale: 227
Prince Consort: 146-7
Prout, Samuel: 89*, 227, 228
Pugin, Auguste Charles: 225, 227, 297
Pugin, Augustus Welby Northmore: 13, 32, 39, 59, 62, 94, 117 nn.30-31; 126, 130, 156 n.45, 172, 176, 178, 222-45*, 283*
Pusey, Philip: 63
Puseyism/Tractarians: 39, 258, 259

Quatremère de Quincy, A. C.: 126
Queen Anne Movement: 299, 300, 308-9

Rambler: 158 n.84, 240, 241
Ramsgate, St Augustine: 241
Regional Planning Association (U.S.A.): 17

Reichensperger, August: 129, 185
Repton, Humphry: 92, 97-8, 224, 228, 230
Richmond, George (portrait of Ruskin): 10-11★, 225★
Richmond, Thomas: 119 n.74
Rickman, Thomas: 33
Rimington, A. W.: 262★
Rock, Daniel: 233
Roe, Mr, of Lambeth: 61
Rogers, Ernesto: 18
Rome, Colosseum: 204
    – St Peter: 217 n.8
Rossetti, Christina: 207
Rossetti, Dante Gabriel: 57, 61, 65, 68-9, 71, 76, 79-80, 143, 269
Rossetti, William Michael: 69, 80
Rouen: 24-5★, 31, 226★, 228, 237
    – Cathedral: 71, 208-9★
    – St Lo: 36★
    – St Ouen: 237
Royal Institute of British Architects: 25, 44, 63, 123, 198, 199, 201-2, 203, 215, 292
Rugby, St Marie: 238-9★, 242
    School Chapel: 230-1★, 232★
Ruskin, Effie (wife of John): 101
RUSKIN, JOHN
Ruskin's writings are indexed by their titles, e.g. *The Stones of Venice* under S
– architectural profession, views on: 25, 106-7, 112-13, 123-5, 152, 198, 202, 323-4, 327, 328
– architectural styles, favoured: 15, 177, 267-8
– architecture *v.* building: 14-15
– artisans, ideas about: 16, 81, 106-7 123ff, 184, 249, 272, 291, 303, 305, 323-4, 327, 329-30
    – Brantwood: 112-13★, 117 n.16
– brickler, as, at Oxford Museum: 78-9
– building planning: 308
– Carlyle, influence of Ruskin: 139-41, 149, 151, 272, 305
– Classical/Hellenist sensibilities: 191ff, 311
– colour, interest in: 104-5, 252-5★, 328
– cottages, love of: 16, 91, 94-7, 108, 113
– craftsmen, ideas about: see 'Artisans ...' above
– drawings by: 24-5★, 29★, 30★, 32★, 33-5★, 36★, 48★, 49★, 50★, 70★, 77★, 88-9★, 92★, 93★, 95★, 100-1★, 112-13★, 197-8★, 209★, 211★, 212★, 214★, 219 n.42, 263★, 281, 296★
– foreign Gothic, promotion of/interest in: 15-16 102, 104-5★, 177, 235, 240, 251ff, 267-8, 325
– garden cities, influence on: 17, 89, 107, 108, 114, 115-16★
– geology, interest in: 256-8
– German working practices, interest in: 123ff
– Goethe, admiration of: 129, 149-50, 154 n.27
– houses, influence on: 13, 88ff★
– 'Kata Phusin' (pseudonym): 28, 198
– landscape/environment, buildings in: 16, 47ff, 89ff
– marriage: 36, 61, 63, 101, 141
– motto: 'To-Day': 11
– muscular architecture, advocate of: 233★, 325
– ornament, interest in: 15, 17, 18-19
– Perpendicular architecture, comment on: 304★
– political views: 38, 40, 126-7, 140, 165ff, 191, 199-200, 202, 203, 279
– portraits/picture of: 10-11★, 62★, 190-1★, 225
– Prout, Samuel, influence on Ruskin: 89★, 95
– religious inclinations: 13, 39, 40, 224-5, 258-9, 270, 273 n.27, 306, 311
– reputation/influence in C19: 13ff, 25ff, 115, 223-4, 225★
– reputation/influence in C20: 17-20, 25ff, 115-16, 118 n.61, 223-4
– reputation/influence in C21: 12,

Index 379

19-20, 25ff, 116
- restoration/conservation, comments: 25-6, 37-8, 40, 42-6, 52, 108, 165, 178, 184, 250, 251, 253, 291-2, 324
- RIBA Gold Medal, refusal of: 25, 215, 292
- 'Ruskinian'/'Ruskinism': 13ff, 26, 44, 61, 89, 104★, 114, 143, 147, 148-9, 154 n.18, 183★, 184-5, 207, 230, 240, 250, 251, 259, 264, 266, 272, 276 n.51, 279, 280, 281, 283, 285-6★, 291, 292, 294, 295, 297, 300★, 303, 305, 304, 306, 308, 311, 321, 327, 335, 342, 343
- sculpture, interest in: 15, 321ff
- sea, love of: 215, 242, 252
- Slade Professor/lectures at Oxford: 44, 107, 108, 191-2, 249
- social concerns/criticism: 15-16, 38, 40, 44, 99-100, 107ff, 150, 174-5, 182-4, 198, 203, 260, 279-80
- structural polychromy, influence on: 104-5, 254-5★, 272, 280, 285-8★, 295, 299, 307
- Stuart & Revett's *Antiquities of Athens*, subvention of: 191
- upbringing: 22, 89-92★, 224-9
- workmen, ideas about: *see* 'artisans ...' above
- *Whistler* v. *Ruskin* trial: 281, 295, 310

Ruskin, John James (father of John): 206, 225, 227
Ruskin, Margaret (mother of John): 227
Ruskin Library, Lancaster University: 12, 19-20, 356-65★
Ruskin To-Day programme: 11

St George's Guild: 149
St Johnstown (Co. Donegal), St Baithen: 283★
St Levan (Cornwall), St Levan: 333
Salcombe (Devon), Holy Trinity: 345, 351, n.41
Salisbury Cathedral: 24-5★
Sanmicheli, Michele: 64

Sansovino, Jacopo d'Antonio Tatti: 64
Schinkel, Karl Friedrich: 128-9, 130, 302★
Schmidt, Friedrich F. von: 131
Scott, Sir George Gilbert: 13, 26, 42, 43, 44, 64, 70-1, 128, 129, 130★, 133ff, 184, 229, 242, 251, 283, 284, 288, 292, 299, 323
Scott, Mackay Hugh Baillie: 114, 115★
Scott, Sir Walter: 97, 117 n.29, 174, 227, 234
Scott, William Bell: 79
Scrovegno, Enrico: 206
Seale, G.W.: 325
Sedding, Edmund: 325
Sedding Edmund Harold: 345, 353 n.65
Sedding, John Dando: 14, 106, 113, 320ff
Seddon, John Pollard: 302, 316 n.104
Seddon, Thomas: 142, 155 n.31, 161 n.121
Selsley (Gloucs), All Saints: 248-9★, 258★, 259-72★, 273 n.12
Serra, Richard: 363
Sesame and Lilies: 205
Seven Lamps of Architecture, The: 13, 14, 19, 24ff, 38, 40, 45, 59, 95, 98, 99, 101, 103, 123-4, 127, 139, 144, 145, 146, 149, 165, 166, 172, 175, 177, 179, 182, 195, 211, 225, 234, 240, 257, 259, 261, 264, 266★, 267-8, 279, 280, 281, 284, 289, 298, 307, 309, 322, 326, 357
- 'The Lamp of Beauty': 125, 175, 235, 268, 307, 311
- 'The Lamp of Life': 178, 268
- 'The Lamp of Memory': 19, 40, 44, 103-4, 178, 270, 272, 357, 358
- 'The Lamp of Obedience': 15, 38, 127, 176, 267, 272, 298
- 'The Lamp of Power': 236, 258★, 264, 265, 266, 293, 308, 311
- 'The Lamp of Sacrifice': 15, 38, 262, 281, 298
- 'The Lamp of Truth': 257, 268, 298, 307, 308
Severn, Arthur: 90★, 91★, 113★
Severn, Joan: 113★
Shaw, Richard Norman: 207, 300, 331

Shotover (Oxon), Gothic Temple: 168-9★, 171
Shrewsbury, John Talbot, 16th Earl of: 233, 235, 241
Siddal, Elizabeth: 61, 71
Siena: 15, 206
– Palazzo Pubblico: 205, 206
Skidmore, Francis: 76, 77, 78, 156 n.51
Smith, George: 35
Smith, T. Roger: 299
Soane, Sir John: 138
Society of Antiquaries: 44
Society for the Preservation of Ancient Buildings: 25-6, 44, 250, 324, 325
Southport (Lancs), Free Library: 304★
Speer, Albert: 302★
Stanfield, Clarkson: 227
Statz, Vincenz: 131★
Staverton (Devon), St Paul de Leon: 285
Steindl, Imre: 172
Stevenson, John James: 300
Stokes, William: 58
Stones of Venice, The: 13, 44, 45, 47, 59, 98, 99, 100, 101, 105, 106, 108, 113, 140, 144, 179-83, 193, 202, 210, 211, 212, 230★, 238, 241, 242, 251, 252, 253-4★, 259, 265, 269★, 279, 280, 281, 286★, 287, 294, 295, 296★, 307, 308, 309, 311, 322, 326, 340, 363
– 'The Nature of Gothic': 44, 106, 127, 144, 179-80, 183, 184, 186, 193, 210, 250, 285★, 287, 298, 305, 307, 308, 311, 325
Stowe (Bucks), Temple of Liberty: 171★
Strasbourg: 102
– Minster: 155 n.33, 160 n.104
Street, George Edmund: 13, 26, 44-5, 47, 59, 62, 80, 98, 99, 101, 106, 128, 135, 137, 138, 147, 148, 149, 150★, 151, 152, 198, 199, 240, 250, 251, 252★, 253★, 255, 265, 267, 273 n.12, 282★, 292, 323, 325
Structural polychromy: 104-5, 251-5★, 266★, 270, 272, 280, 285-8★, 295, 299, 303, 307

Swinburne, Algernon Charles: 310
Symonds, John Addington: 310

Tacitus: 149, 168, 180
Talbot, John, 16th Earl of Shrewsbury: 233, 235, 241
Temple, Richard, Viscount Cobham: 171★
Tennyson, Alfred, Lord: 30
Thornycroft, Hamo: 342
Tiresias of Thebes: 205, 211, 216
Torcello, Cathedral: 340
Town hall building in the U.K.: 286
Tractarians/Puseyism: 39, 258, 259
Trask, Charles, & Sons: 351 n.41
Trevelyan, Pauline, Lady: 67, 71, 79
Trevelyan, Sir Walter: 192
Trollope, Anthony: 225
True Principles ... (Pugin): 223, 233, 234, 235, 237
Tuckwell, William: 72
Turner, J. M. W.: 264, 265
Two Paths, The: 323-4, 327
Tyrrell, James: 168-9★, 171
Tyrwhitt, Richard St John: 71, 81

Ulverscroft (Leics), Gimson cottages: 113-14★
Underwood, Henry Jones: 62, 63
Unto this Last: 107, 114, 184, 279
Unwin, Raymond: 96, 114, 115, 116-17★

Van Eyck, Jan: 193, 194★, 195, 201
Venice: 15, 31, 36★, 45, 100
– Ca' d'Oro: 105
– Campanile, Piazza S. Marco: 197-8★
– Casa Visetti: 59, 60
– Ducal Palace: 146, 158 n.75
– Palazzo Dario: 59, 60
– Palazzo Gritti-Badoer: 290★
– Palazzo Priuli: 211★
– Ruskin Library, Lancaster, influence: 361-5
– St Mark: 15, 142, 158 n.75, 197-8★, 211, 213, 265, 363, 365★
Venturi, Robert: 18

Verona: 102
- S. Fermo Maggiore: 251
- Scaligeri tombs: 289★
Verstegen, Richard: 170
Vienna Secession: 185
- Town Hall: 131
Viollet-le-Duc, Eugène Emmanuel: 177, 204, 205
Vitruvius: 214
Voysey, Charles Francis Annesley: 114, 115

Wagner, Otto: 18
Waite, Percy: 297
Wall, Joshua: 260, 269★
Ward & Nixon: 251
Waterhouse, Alfred: 131, 288, 292
Webb, Benjamin: 53 n.36, 135, 136, 142, 255
Webb, John: 157 n.57
Webb, Philip: 238★
Wheeler, Michael: 358
Whewell, William: 53 n.15
Whistler, James McNeill: 280, 281, 295, 300★, 302, 303, 305-6
White, Edwin: 288★, 289★, 290★, 291
White, William: 282★
Whitehouse, John Howard: 357
Whitwick (Leics), school: 236★
Wilburton Manor (Cambs): 238★
Wild, Charles: 209, 210
Wilde, Oscar: 310
Williams, Edward L.: 219 n.42
Willis, Robert: 53 n.15, 223-4, 282, 284, 291
Wilson, Henry: 339, 342, 347, 351 n.41
Woodward, Benjamin: 13, 19, 56★, 57-8, 59, 61, 64-5, 67, 68, 69, 70, 71, 72-3, 74-6, 77, 79-80, 81, 85 n.87, 146, 250, 292
Woolner, Thomas: 69, 76, 80
Wordsworth, William: 29-30, 96, 117 n.15
Working Men's College: 141, 146, 210
Wright, Frank Lloyd: 17, 18
Wyatville, Sir Jeffry: 117 n.22

York, New Earswick: 115, 116-17★

Zwirner, Ernst Friedrich: 130★, 133